CHRISTIANITY IN IRELAND

In memoriam
Donal Kerr
(1927-2001)

Edited by Brendan Bradshaw and Dáire Keogh

Christianity
in Ireland

REVISITING THE STORY

the columba press

First published in 2002 by
the columba press
55A Spruce Avenue, Stillorgan Industrial Park, Blackrock, Co Dublin

Cover by Bill Bolger
The image from the Book of Kells is used by permission of The Board of
Trinity College Dublin.
Origination by The Columba Press
Printed in Ireland by Colour Books Ltd, Dublin.

ISBN 1 85607 350 5

Contents

Foreword

This collection originated in a colloquium on the religious history of Ireland, held under the auspices of the Fondazione Ambrosiana Paolo VI at Varese, Italy, in September 1999. The seminar was planned and directed by the distinguished Irish historian, Donal Kerr, Professor Emeritus of Ecclesiastical History at Maynooth, who was then based in Rome completing a biography of Jean Claude Colin, the founder of the Society of Mary of which he was a member. The proceedings were subsequently published according to custom in their original Italian versions (L. Vacarro and C.M. Pellizzi (eds), *Storia religiosa dell' Irlanda* (Milan 2001)). Dónal and the participants, acutely aware of the lack of a survey-history of the Irish church, decided on providing an English edition and additional contributions were duly commissioned. Unfortunately the project was incomplete when Donal died after a short illness on 10 May 2001, but the contributors to the present volume were unanimous in their determination to proceed with the project and to present the collection in his memory.

This volume is designed to provide the interested non-specialist as well as undergraduates with a means of informing themselves about the history of the church in Ireland from earliest times to the present. It does not fill the need for a comprehensive narrative of the odyssey of Christianity in Ireland. Rather it provides a series of sequences from which a sense of the full story can be obtained. These are presented by specialists in the area under discussion and are informed by the most recent scholarly research.

Our thanks are due to the publishers, Columba Press, and in particular to Seán O Boyle for his enthusiastic support for the project since its inception. We also take this opportunity to thank Luciano Vaccaro and Carlo Maria Pellizzi for their assistance. We must also express our gratitude to Katie Keogh for her help in preparing the text and to Ursula Ní Dhálaigh, a friend of Donal with long experience in preparing copy for publication, who read the entire manuscript to its enormous benefit. The generous financial support of St Patrick's College Drumcondra, Dublin and of the Irish Province of the Marist Fathers is gratefully acknowledged. Finally we express our thanks to the contributors for making it possible to honour in this way the memory of one who was not only an outstanding ecclesiastical historian but also, in the words of an obituarist, 'a citizen of the world and a saint of the church'.

The Golden Age

Principle monasteries and churches

N

Tory
Rathlin
Coleraine
Camus
Armoy
Raphoe
Derry
ULAID
NORTHERN
UÍ NÉILL
Connor
Bodoney
Antrim
Ardstraw
Bangor
Moville
Inishmurray
Donaghmore
Nendrum
Devenish
Tynan
Dromore
Clogher
Saul
Drumcliff
Armagh
Downpatrick
Killala
AIRGIALLA
Killevy
Achonry
Fenagh
Donaghmoyne
Kilmore
Louth
Linns
CONNACHT
Elphin
Granard
Fore
Monasterboice
Achagower
Mayo
Baslick
Kells
Slane
Inishbofin
Roscommon
Ardagh
Ardbraccan
Holmpatrick
Cong
Inchcleraun
SOUTHERN
Trim
Dunshaughlin
Tuam
UÍ NÉILL
Clonard
Swords
Annaghdown
Clonmacnoise
Durrow
Clondalkin
Finglas
Glasnevin
Roscam
Killashee
Tallaght
Inis Mór
Clonfert
Kilmacduagh
Kilcullen
Glendalough
Kilfenora
Terryglass
Seir Kieran
Moone
Inishcaltra
Killeshin
Sletty
Killaloe
Leighlin
Aghade
Inis Cathaig
Mungret
LAIGIN
Cashel
Derrynaflan
Ferns
Emly
Ardfert
Ardfinnan
Begerin
Taghmon
MUNSTER
Lismore
Inisfallen
Ardmore
Cork
Cloyne
Scelig Mhichíl
Ross Carbery

0   100 km

Irish Churchmen and Scholars in Europe

N

ATLANTIC
OCEAN

NORTH
SEA

Legend:
- Foundations of St Columbanus and his disciples
- Centres of Irish influence in the 10th–12th century
- Irish Benedictine 'Schottenklöster'

Bangor

St Davids

Glastonbury

Mecklenburg

Bremen

Cologne

Erfurt

Waulsort

Liège

Fulda

Péronne

Trier

Mainz

Nuremberg

Regensburg

Rouen

St Michel

Eichstätt

Vienna

Verdun

Metz

Reichenau

Melk

Annegray

Toul

Konztanz

Göttweig

Noirmoutier

Luxeuil

St Gall

Lure

Rheinau

Fontaine

BAY OF
BISCAY

PYRENEES

Bobbio

Lucca

ADRIATIC SEA

Rome

MEDITERRANEAN   SEA

Dioceses of Ireland

N

Raphoe

Derry

Connor

ARMAGH

Down

Clogher

Dromore

Killala

Armagh

Achonry

Kilmore

TUAM

Elphin

Ardagh
&
Clonmacnoise

Tuam

Meath

Wardenship of
Galway

Clonfert

Kilmacduagh

Kildare

Kilfenora

Dublin

DUBLIN

Killaloe

Ossory

Leighlin

Emly

Cashel

Limerick

CASHEL

Ferns

Cloyne

Lismore

Kerry

Waterford

Cork

Ross

0   100 km

CHAPTER ONE

Bishop Patrick and the earliest Christian mission to Ireland

Alfred P. Smyth

The beginnings of Irish Christianity are surrounded by all those unanswerable questions which relate to societies emerging from prehistory, having only recently come into contact with literate societies beyond their borders. Yet while we know little about the first Christians and missionaries on the island, Ireland is in an unusual situation in that we have two highly significant documents from the hand of an early fifth-century bishop, Patricius, a leading figure in the evangelisation of the Irish. These documents, the *Confessio* of Bishop Patrick, and his *Epistola* or *Letter* of protest addressed to the warlord Coroticus, take us closer to the mind of a great evangelist than anything that survives from either Augustine's mission to the English, or Colmcille's mission to the Scots and Picts. While Bede or Adomnán may be superior as historical writers on early England and Scotland when compared to the confused narration of Bishop Patrick, nevertheless in the case of Ireland it is the evangelist, Patrick himself, who addresses us with a burning faith across more than a millennium and a half from the late antique world of the fifth century. These precious writings of Patrick stand out as islands of literacy in a prehistoric seascape, where few other fixed historical points exist. The problems relating to their wider historical context and to our interpretation of Patrick's writings and his mission to the Irish are legion.

I

The study of the earliest Christian missions to Ireland has been surrounded by bitter academic controversy throughout the twentieth century, with scholars arguing for the existence of one, two, and even three separate Patricks. It is an historical debate beset with technical arguments relating to the date and precise provincial origins of Patrick's own Latin; how annalistic years were reckoned; philological arguments surrounding loan words borrowed into Old Irish via Roman Britain and Gaul; as well as the interpretation of seventh-century hagiographical texts which contain earlier traditions relating to St Patrick. In order to provide a balanced view of this academic debate in a very brief account, and one which must avoid excessive technical detail, it is wisest to begin with what we know and only then to venture into unknown areas. It might be imagined that the place to begin is 432 – the supposed year of arrival of St Patrick in Ireland. But not so. We ought to begin in 429 when, as recorded by Prosper of Aquitaine (c. 390-465) in his *Chronicon*, Bishop Germanus of Auxerre was sent to Britain by Pope Celestine to combat the Pelagian heresy, which was flourishing there. We are also given the crucial detail by Prosper that Celestine sent Germanus 'at the instigation of the deacon, Palladius'. It is possible but unlikely that Palladius was a Briton. He was clearly influential at the papal court, and viewed in an early fifth-century context that would suggest he was either a Gaul or Roman. When therefore Prosper tells us that this same deacon Palladius was ordained by Celestine in 431 and dispatched to take charge of those 'Irish believing in Christ', as historians we are permitted at least three observations. The first is that Ireland clearly already had a sufficient number of Christians to warrant sending them a bishop. And the Irish to whom Palladius was sent were inhabitants of Ireland proper rather than of the Goidelic colonies in western Britain. For Prosper notes in his *Liber contra Collatorem* (xxi) that 'whilst he [Celestine] strove to keep the Roman island Catholic, by ordaining a bishop for the Irish ... he also made the barbarous island Christian'. The second observation is that it was a highly unusual move for a pope of the late Roman Empire to send a mission across the borders of that crumbling empire to evangelise barbarians who had never known the *pax romana*. Lastly, it is a fair assumption – but no more than that – that Palladius's expedition to Ireland in 431 was in some way connected with the legation that Germanus led to Britain only two years before. Palladius, that influential papal adviser, was involved in both ventures, and a man who could advise and influence the pope on ways of controlling Pelagian beliefs in Britain would not himself have led an evangelising team to Ireland were that not also part of a wider strategy to contain the Pelagian problem. Perhaps there was already an incipient Pelagian problem in Ireland, or perhaps proper orthodox episcopal organisation of the Irish Christians was felt necessary to prevent Pelagianism spreading in that as yet uncontrolled Christian environment.

So far, the record of the earliest mission to Ireland would seem to have got off to an excellent beginning in terms of clear documentation. Bishop Palladius, like Augustine of Canterbury in later centuries, would seem to have been a safe pair of hands with which to entrust a Roman mission to a barbarian people. He was clearly a senior and respected churchman (albeit a deacon before his elevation) who was known and trusted at the papal court. The mission may have been part of a wider papal strategy to curtail the spread of Pelagianism throughout the British Isles, but however that may be, this mission to the Irish had direct papal backing – Palladius was consecrated by the pope – and was led by a man with strong Roman connections.

We know little or nothing, however, of the outcome of this venture. Irish annals are silent about the mission of Palladius; they do not provide a date for his death, but a note in the Book of Armagh (fol. 16r.a) and a mention in the Latin *Vita II* of St Patrick claim that Palladius was martyred at the hands of the Irish. Palladius is associated with three churches in Co Wicklow – Cell Fine, Tech na Románach and Domnach Airthe. According to Patrick's seventh-century biographer, Muirchú, the Irish rejected Palladius and he did not remain long among them. Palladius died, according to Muirchú, either among the Picts or among the Britons, while on his way back 'to him who sent him'. In Muirchú's eyes, however, Patrick was the saint who had to be given all credit for evangelising the Irish, so he was prejudiced against Palladius in spite of the claim that he had been 'sent' by the Roman pontiff. For Muirchú, Palladius was prevented by divine will from achieving his objective, and therefore Muirchú's views about the aborting of the Palladian mission or on the death of Palladius in Britain carry little weight.

Later Irish attempts to boost the power and prestige of the church of Armagh at the expense of what Palladius may have achieved in Ireland in the 430s need to be treated with caution. Armagh, claiming as it did to have been founded by Patrick, was rich enough by the seventh century to harness the services of writers such as Muirchú and Tírechán who were skilled hagiographical spin-doctors of their day. Claims that Palladius was either rejected or killed by the Irish or that he conveniently died on his return to Rome need to be read alongside the contemporary comment of Prosper that Celestine – through Palladius – 'made the barbarous island Christian'. While that phrase (*fecit barbaram christianam*) does not necessarily mean that Palladius personally evangelised the whole of Ireland, it does at least suggest that he established structures which made such an evangelisation possible. There is, on the other hand, nothing inherently improbable about missionaries abandoning their posts in the face of a hostile people. Bede's account of the team led by Augustine to England in the late sixth century can do little to hide the lack of resolution on the part of the Roman team – including, it must be said, on the part of Augustine himself who turned back for Rome while he was still only in Gaul on his way to England. Later, when the going got rough in Canterbury and elsewhere after the death of Augustine, the bishops Mellitus of London and Justus of Rochester fled to Gaul, while Laurentius, the successor of Augustine at Canterbury, also considered flight. The Roman mission to Northumbria, which was led by Paulinus and began in c. 627, was aborted as early as 632. Not all missionaries were of the stuff of which martyrs are made.

The Irish annals do not offer us a contemporary record of Irish affairs, however fragmentary, until after the middle of the sixth century. But we do possess two other contemporary accounts of an early Christian mission to the Irish in fifth-century documents from the pen of the leader of a Christian community – Bishop Patrick – writing to us in his *Confessio* and *Epistola*. The *Confessio* is neither a biography nor a confession of faith but an *apologia pro vita sua* somewhat similar to, but far less sophisticated than, the *Confessions* of St Augustine of Hippo. The *Confessio* of Patrick is a startling document. Here a man introduces himself to us who is not afraid of martyrdom at the hands of the heathen Irish, who has come close to death many times in the past and who may well end his life by dying for his faith. This Patrick is a bishop whose kinsfolk live in Britain (chapter 23). His father was the deacon Calpornius, son of the priest Potitus, who belonged to a town (unidentified) of *Bannavem Taburniae*. Patrick's father owned an estate near to *Bannavem Taburniae*, staffed by numerous workers. Patrick describes a Britain with its late Roman landed gentry still in place and with a leisured class of 'seniors' who were well versed in letters and in the study of the law. In chapter 10 of his *Letter* to Coroticus, Patrick tells us that his father was a *decurio* – a member of the municipal council – presumably in a town of significant size. In that same source he speaks of his own freeborn status and of the male and female slaves in his father's house – presumably also on that 'small estate' near *Bannavem Taburniae* mentioned in the *Confessio* (1). The point is crucial, because if this is Roman Britain that is actually being described, it cannot have been too long after the withdrawal of Roman legions from the province in 407 and might even date more appropriately from well before that time. The leisured and cultivated world of upper-class Roman citizens described by Patrick can only have flourished in the south and east of lowland Britain, and at no time was this class typical of the periphery in what is now Wales or Cumbria. Yet many scholars seem unable to locate Patrick's British origins anywhere other than in what later became the 'Celtic fringe' of Britain on the assumption that when Patrick was taken captive by Irish raiders he must have been living near the sea. A study of the slave trade in the later Viking Age in the ninth and tenth centuries shows that captives could be acquired anywhere inland in Britain or Ireland and that they could be sold on by their immediate captors to traders, middle-men or seafarers in any port. Patrick's origins ought never to have been tied to the western seaboard of Britain because he repeatedly describes a cultural setting for his family and for their society at large which reflects the villa culture of lowland Britain.

From the 350s onwards, not only was the western periphery of Britain in a lawless state but it was also experiencing a resurgence of native Celtic aristocratic culture which in turn was greatly encouraged by the colonisation of significant parts of what is now Cornwall, Wales and Argyll by Gaelic warlords from Ireland. Such turbulence is alien to the whole spirit of Patrick's

Confessio where the society of his early youth might just as easily have been located among the senatorial class of fourth-century Gaul, were it not that Patrick specifically alludes to his kinsfolk in Britain. So not only did Patrick most likely come from within the heartland of the Romanised area of Britain, but to have experienced that life he must have lived out his childhood in the late fourth century at the very latest. Bieler's guess at 385 for Patrick's birth is probably not far off the mark but even that may need to be revised backwards in time.

This Bishop Patrick who speaks to us from his *Confessio* knows nothing of Palladius and yet writes as though he is in charge of an Irish mission. He leads an infant church in spite of fierce opposition and open hostility on the part of some influential sections (at least) of the British clergy. He tells us of his rusticity, his lack of Latin learning – inevitable in a boy who idled at school and who spent six years after the age of sixteen in captivity as a slave to a barbarian master on an Irish hillside. Patrick was not only backward culturally and intellectually but his clerical peers rejected him for a sin that he had committed in his thoughtless youth. That sin, subsequently revealed to a synod of appointing clergy, almost cost Patrick his candidacy for episcopal ordination and his eligibility to lead the Irish mission. Patrick in his *Confessio* defends himself against clerical detractors who would appear to have accused him of being unsuitable on moral as well as intellectual grounds and also because of his supposed misuse of church funds and perhaps also because of matters of faith. Patrick vigorously refuted allegations of embezzlement and showed himself to be orthodox in faith. He admitted to an ill-spent youth and to his poor qualifications for the job of leading a Christian community.

In spite of the insecurity of Patrick's position, and in spite of glaring differences between even those self-confessed shortcomings of Patrick and the known high Roman papal credentials of Palladius, a number of historians since the early Middle Ages have suggested that Palladius and Patrick were one and the same person. What brought about such an apparently bizarre identification? The answer lies in the fact that early medieval Irish scholars were well aware of the entry in Prosper's *Chronicle* recording the sending of Palladius to the Irish by Pope Celestine in 431. Since little or no trace of Palladius could be found in the earliest Irish written records, and since Patrick towered above all other missionaries in written and oral traditions of the Irish church, it was an easy step to identify Patrick with the mysterious Palladius. So while Irish annalists copied Prosper's record of the sending of Palladius in 431, they invented that celebrated date of 432 for the arrival – not of Palladius – but of Patrick. In bringing Patrick to Ireland in 432, two things were accomplished at a stroke. Firstly, if Patrick were considered to be a different person from Palladius, then Patrick's arrival in 432 could be made to upstage anything that the elusive Palladius might be deemed to have accomplished. Secondly, if Patrick could be identified with Palladius, then he would acquire Roman credentials of a first class kind. Moreover, Patrick's church of Armagh, which by the seventh century was claiming jurisdiction over all the clergy of Ireland, was sending out a clear signal that Palladius, whoever he was, and with his excellent papal connections, had now been subsumed into the Armagh tradition.

Unfortunately the problematic story of Ireland's earliest evangelists does not end here, and things become more complicated as the fifth century wears on. According to Tírechán, another late seventh-century hagiographer (who was slightly later than Muirchú), Patrick died in 461, and so also do we find that same date for his death in the oldest Irish chronicle, which lies behind the text of the *Annals of Ulster*. But under the year 492 in those same annals, we find an alternative date for the death of Patrick – a date so far removed from 461 that one or other date must be either widely off the mark, or alternatively, we are dealing with two separate Patricks. It is this consideration that has encouraged some modern scholars to equate the first Patrick who died in 461 with Palladius and to identify the historical author of the *Confessio* with the Patrick who died in 492. Faint echoes of a similar historical debate are discernible in medieval Irish records, where the earlier Patrick who supposedly died in 461 is called *Sen Phátraic* or 'Old Patrick' while his younger namesake was regarded as Saint Patrick, national Apostle of Ireland. Such glosses betray Armagh's attempts to control disparities in the documentation in order to keep Armagh's 'real' patron in a position of primacy.

A very persistent early medieval Irish tradition about the historical Patrick relates to his founding of the church of Armagh, and to his death on 17 March. But an equally reliable and persistent tradition claims that he was buried at Saul in Co Down or in nearby Downpatrick. This has to be reliable, if only for its survival in the face of so much Armagh propaganda designed to glorify its position above all other Irish churches. No less a writer than the seventh-century Tírechán – himself a promoter of Armagh's interests – vouches for Saul as the place of Patrick's death. Why then was Patrick not buried in Armagh which he himself must have founded? Armagh is located close to Emain Macha and may well have shared in its fate when the power of the Ulstermen was broken by their Uí Néill rivals. As Patrick neared the end of his life the power of his royal protectors collapsed in the face of attacks from the Connachta, or ancestors of the Uí Néill. The Ulaid and their kings were forced to retreat eastward across the River Bann. Patrick, and some at least of his Armagh community, may have felt compelled to retreat with their protectors in the face of the expanding power of the as yet pagan Uí Néill kings of the north – ancestors of the Cenél nEogain and Cenél Conaill over-kings of Tara. This may also suggest yet again that Patrick the Briton, the author of the *Confessio*, carried out his mission in Ireland early in the first half of the fifth century rather than in the second half, for the fall of Emain Macha cannot have happened much later than 450 and may have happened long before.

Scholarly arguments over the chronological details of the life of Patrick, the author of the *Confessio* and *Letter* can distract from the evidence they present to us of a remarkable man of privileged birth and wayward youth who was dragged into captivity to a foreign and barbarous land. As an adolescent he discovered God in the misery of his lonely exile herding animals in forests and on a cold wet mountainside. Later he escaped to Gaul and finally returned to his family home in Roman Britain. Yet this man gave up his privileged life for a second time, voluntarily, in order to return and evangelise his earlier tormentors. He was a man of burning religious faith with an unshakeable conviction that however sinful, uneducated and wayward he had once been, he was now carrying out a divinely inspired mission to evangelise the people of Ireland. All this would sound like a hagiographical version of a secular heroic saga, were it not that Patrick himself relates the trials and tribulations of his spiritual journey in his own words – albeit in faltering Latin. We gather from his narrative that he was responsible for thousands of converts to Christianity, sometimes buying his way into the good offices of treacherous Celtic warlords. We gather too that he was responsible for establishing monastic communities for women as well as for men during his Irish mission. For monasticism had become not only acceptable but also popular in Gaul from the time of St Martin, Bishop of Tours from c. 371 to 403. But we also know from Patrick's writings that he was a bishop with orthodox Christian beliefs and that he founded what was primarily an episcopal church whose infant dioceses presumably coincided with the tribal territories or *tuatha* of the kings whom he converted.

Mention of St Martin of Tours reminds us that the cult of Martin was very strong at Armagh from at least as early as the seventh century, and some scholars believe that Patrick may himself have trained as a monk in the tradition of Martin's monastic rule during his stay in Gaul. He certainly visited Gaul, and it was to Gaul almost certainly that he made his escape from his Irish captivity. He reveals knowledge of Gaulish practices (*Letter* to Coroticus, 14), and he refers to his brethen in Gaul. In his *Confessio* he tells us:

> I would have been only too glad to head for Britain ... to see my homeland and family; and not only that, but to go on to Gaul to visit the brethren and to see the face of my Lord's holy men. (*Confessio*, 43).

Muirchú associates Patrick with Germanus of Auxerre (c. 380-448), but Muirchú shows us in that same passage that he was concerned with the role of Palladius, and how in Muirchú's view Patrick could not be consecrated bishop until the news of the death of Palladius had reached Auxerre. Muirchú would have been familiar with Prosper's record of Palladius's involvement in the sending of Germanus to Britain in 429. His tales associating Patrick with Germanus, therefore, might well have been prompted by genuine historical connections between Germanus and Palladius. On the other hand, Muirchú's statement that Patrick was consecrated bishop not by Germanus, as we might have expected him to claim, but by Amator, is remarkable. Amator had been bishop of Auxerre before Germanus died in 418, and if Patrick were to be associated with that bishop in whatever capacity it would suggest yet again a time early in the fifth century for Patrick's mission rather than in the late 400s. One of the *Dicta* or 'Sayings of Patrick' in the Book of Armagh runs:

> I had the fear of God as my guide for my journey through Gaul and Italy, and also on the islands of the Tyrrhenian Sea.

This is the earliest evidence (from the seventh century) associating Patrick with Italy or with what might have been a monastic training on one of the Tyrrhenian islands. Finally, it must be said that while the text of the *Confessio* and the related traditions outlined above point to an early fifth-century date for Bishop Patrick the Briton, there are other Irish traditions associating Patrick with a series of Irish rulers who flourished at the end of the fifth century. It is that set of associations which has prompted some Patrician scholars to prefer the 492 date for Patrick's death or to postulate the existence of two Patricks, the earlier one of whom might have been identical with Palladius. In all that discussion it is now clear to scholars that no credence can be given to Irish annalistic dates prior to the 550s, and too much weight has been given even in the more recent past to the dates (461 and 492) offered for the death of Patrick. Our major guide in all these debates must remain the *Confessio* and the *Epistola* to Coroticus.

II

A central problem in our understanding of early Celtic Christianity is to discover why a church which was set up under the episcopal organisation of Patrick and his helpers, Secundinus, Iserninus, Benignus and Auxilius, should re-emerge from the shadows of the mid-sixth century as a thorough-going monastic church ruled by abbots from key monastic *civitates*, bishops being retained for their sacerdotal and sacramental functions but seemingly shorn of real authority. What had happened in Ireland and Britain in the interval between the days of Patrick the Roman, on his father's estate near the elusive *Bannavem Taburniae*, and the arrival of new and domineering religious players such as Colmcille on Iona and Augustine at Canterbury in the closing years of the sixth century? This question is usually answered with the bland assumption that Irish episcopal organisation became tribalised and embraced monasticism that was much better suited to native social structures than the diocesan organisation of Rome. That explanation does not necessarily stand up to scrutiny. A diocesan mode might just as easily accommodate itself to tribal structures. The notion of a diocese has a strong built-in territorial dimension, which would have been well suited to warlords obsessed with ancestral tribal boundaries. We know for instance that Anglo-Saxon bishops quickly integrated into the ruling establishment of the warrior aristocracy and became part of the *witan*, those 'wise men' who advised the king in matters of peace and war. And the argument that because Ireland lacked townships it could not sustain Roman bishops trained to preside over late antique *civitates* only holds true up to a point. Augustine and his immediate successors presided over an agrarian society in Kent, their cathedral church perched in a ruinous Roman shanty town with Germanic wattle round huts thrown up in the middle of its ancient streets – hardly the sort of *caput* Augustine had been expecting to accommodate his metropolitan church.

It may be that Patrick's initial attempt at the evangelisation of the Irish was much more localised and took place considerably earlier than historians have recently been prepared to admit. If Patrick had indeed been brought up within Roman Britain when Roman government and the villa culture still flourished there in the fourth century, then that would allow time for the transformation of Christianity not only in Ireland but also in Britain by the middle of the sixth century. Whether or not Patrick's infant Irish church had to be re-founded or re-evangelised in the sixth century we may never know. What we do know is that Christianity well nigh died out in the Roman province of Britain where Patrick's father had earlier been a deacon and his grandfather a Christian priest.

It may well be that there was far less continuity between the world of Patrick and that of a great monastic founder such as Finian of Clonard than we have hitherto realised. And men like Finian may not all have been 'disciples' of their Welsh masters but rather spiritual pioneers in their own right as some of the sources suggest. We know very little of how the monasticism of the Egyptian Desert and of the 'islands in the Tyrrhenian Sea' was brought to Ireland, Wales and Brittany. And lastly, ought we to see the final and effective evangelisation of Ireland as having been accomplished neither by Palladius nor Patrick, whose labours may have been undone by the huge political upheavals that in Ireland accompanied the fall of Roman Britain? Perhaps we should look rather to the great monastic founders of the sixth century as missionaries who effectively built a new and different kind of church and who may well have evangelised the people of the *tuatha*. If that is true then Patrick as well as Palladius inhabited a late antique world that left little long-term influence on a church that was reconstructed on monastic principles in the early middle ages. That is not to minimise the extraordinary achievement of those courageous missionaries who dared to sail beyond the boundaries of Rome and 'make a barbarous island Christian'. For even if their fragile churches became seriously dislocated during those heroic migrations of Dál Riata, Déisí and Connachta which shook Ireland to its foundations in the fifth century, their names at least and the writings of Bishop Patrick survived among their followers to inspire the monastic rulers of a later age.

There are two documentary postscripts to the Patrick debate which have rarely been commented on by Patrician scholars. The neglect of these two early references to Patrick is all the more remarkable in that the first is considerably earlier than either Tírechán or Muirchú, and while the second is contemporary with those Armagh writers, it comes from a completely independent monastic milieu. Both references are found in impeccable historical sources. And yet, as ever in regard to Patrick, these interesting glimpses of the 'real' person present us with their own special problems. Cummian, in his celebrated *Letter* to Abbot Ségéne of Iona (written 632-3) admonishes his recipient to adopt the practice of the universal church and follow the Roman calculation for the holding of the Easter festival. Cummian refers in his *Letter* to an Easter cycle which 'St Patrick our father (*noster papa*) brought and made'. It is clear from the details that Patrick observed a calculation for Easter which was different from that of the Irish church in the age of Abbot Ségéne. But it is equally clear from Cummian's reference that by the early seventh century – well before Tírechán and Muirchú had started up their Armagh propaganda machine – Patrick's authority could be appealed to in matters of national ecclesiastical importance. The second early independent reference to Patrick is found in Adomnán's *Life* of Colmcille, where mention is made in the second preface to a British monk and holy man called Maucte, who was 'a disciple of the holy bishop Patrick' (*sancti Patricii episcopi discipulus*). Here again we have a reference to Patrick where he is clearly being viewed in the context of one, at least, of the founding fathers of Irish Christianity. Furthermore, this very important reference by Adomnán comes from that leader of the Columban church, then at the height of its power and influence and independent of the Armagh monastic confederation. But if *Maucteus* were indeed to be identified with Mochte, abbot of Louth who died in AD 535, then his spiritual master cannot have been that Patrick who wrote the *Confessio*. While the problems remain, the one constant feature in all this documentation is the central importance for early Irish writers in which the memory of Patrick, saint and Christian founder, was universally held.

CHAPTER TWO

The golden age of early Irish monasticism: Myth or historical reality?

Alfred P. Smyth

Recent decline in conventional religious practice has not unexpectedly led to a search for the more arcane traditions and practices of the early church that are perceived to contain special core truths lost or distorted in later Christian centuries. The early Irish church has proved a rich quarry for those engaged in this quest or for those seeking a supreme expression of indigenous Christian culture untrammelled by Rome or Byzantium. Since the Reformation, reformers have scrutinised records of early Irish Christianity attempting to locate evidence for an independent Celtic church operating in isolation from the dictates of Rome. Saint Colmcille in particular has been identified as a precursor of non-conformity in the British Isles.

In addition to specific ideological issues such as Roman supremacy, numerous other stereotypes regarding the early Irish church still pervade even the scholarly literature. References continue to be made to the *Age of Saints*, that supposedly heroic age of Holy Men who made up the first generation of monastic founders in Ireland and who spent their time performing an endless series of preposterous wonders – many of a highly questionable moral nature – which included striking people dead, cursing their enemies, and fixing dynastic succession on those who gave them material rewards. This notion of an *Age of Saints* was given added life by the writings of John Ryan, a Jesuit scholar with encyclopaedic knowledge of the hagiography of early Ireland, which in spite of his great learning was not always matched by a critical approach.[1] The notion of an *Age of Saints* was of course suggestive of a subsequent age of decline. For all heroic ages, whether spiritual or secular, reflect dissatisfaction with the realities of the present and a desire to reinvent the past in an idealised form.

Yet another and more pervasive myth about early Irish Christianity relates to its otherworldliness, characterised by a love of nature and of wild animals and an *ad hoc* monasticism, lived in a primeval wilderness and guided by a heroic asceticism with a conspicuous lack of bishops. What emerges is an image of a Dark Age hippy colony inhabited by gentle gurus doing their own Christian thing far removed from the stultifying influence of sub-Roman bishops and their dioceses. One can see how this vision has an appeal to a *fin de siècle* Christian outlook; similarly one can appreciate how tales of monks admitting foxes to become full members of their communities or refusing to allow oxen to drag heavy ploughs have a certain attraction for animal rights and environmental lobbyists in search of a Green Christianity.

In this essay I will attempt two things: firstly, to show briefly that the notion of an *Age of Saints* can have a very distorting effect on our understanding of early Irish Christianity, not least because of its concomitant idea of subsequent decline. Secondly, I will examine briefly the myth of otherworldliness surrounding environmentally friendly monks pursuing a proto-Franciscan gentleness of life in the wilderness. A good place to begin a difficult study such as this – where so much of our historical source material is either late or as yet inadequately studied – is with the monastic community on Iona.

I

Iona provides us with very early records including a set of contemporary annals which were recorded there, and a *Life* of Colmcille written by Abbot Adomnán in about the year 700.[2] Adomnán's *Life* in turn was based on an earlier *Life* written by Abbot Cuméne who died in 669. Not only was Adomnán a successor of Colmcille in the abbacy of Iona but he was also a kinsman. And the fact that the Iona monastic community constituted an eternal family living out its life in the geographical isolation of a tiny island in the Inner Hebrides, presents us with a unique case study of what was one of the foremost monasteries in the Celtic West. Adomnán's *Life* of Colmcille allows us share that writer's perceptions of a closed world inhabited by men following a way of life laid down by this remarkable Irishman, one of the most extraordinary Christian founders. By carefully analysing the images which Adomnán puts before us we find some of the myths surrounding early Irish Christianity evaporating while others stand up to scrutiny and are lent some substance at least in modified form.

The Colmcille described by Adomnán is not the classic super-saint of later Irish hagiography. Most of his miracles relate less to his magical powers and the performance of feats than to the efficacy of his prayers and his supposed gifts of prophecy and second sight. Magical tales do occur in this early *vita* but relatively speaking it is possible to penetrate the hagiography of Adomnán to reach something of the personality of the historical Colmcille: a holy man from the warrior aristocracy with towering presence, uncertain temper and phenomenal powers of leadership.

Colmcille was a member of the leading Uí Néill royal dynasty of Cenél Conaill. Had he not been a churchman he would have been eligible for the kingship of his own tribe and for the kingship of Tara. Indeed, not only was he a kingly person, it is quite clear from Adomnán's *Life* that Colmcille was a Holy Man for kings; many of his prophesying miracles, for instance, relate to outcomes of battles and to the fate of aristocratic warriors. However, he is not just a tribal saint. As well as being a powerful figure among his own people of the Cenél Conaill and elsewhere in Ireland, Colmcille is shown to have been on friendly terms with the king of the Picts, the Britons of Strathclyde and was kingmaker of aristocrats among the Scots of Dál Riata. Adomnán was also in close contact with Irish, Scottish and Pictish kings, and he enjoyed the personal friendship of Aldfrith, the Anglo-Saxon king of Northumbria. So while these churchmen were gurus living in a remote wilderness, they exerted a real and powerful influence over numerous neighbouring kingdoms. Not that we should see anything peculiarly Celtic about the fact that Colmcille was the confidant of kings, since this was a time in the history of the wider Christian world when holy men in the eastern Mediterranean were consulted by emperors and regarded as expert advisers on political and social matters.

Adomnán also shows us a Colmcille who engages in a very physical form of spiritual warfare – fighting demons off with pitchforks and entering the fray to rescue the souls of his dying friends from eternal hell-fire. In Adomnán's time, Colmcille's relics (clothing and books in his own hand) were displayed upon the altar of Iona or taken round the island to ward off drought and to intercede for other favours from heaven. Colmcille's tutelary role in defending his people was similar to that of the cult of St Demetrios of Thessalonica in the seventh century and we are reminded of how the relics of the Blessed Virgin Mary were displayed on the walls of Constantinople to save the city from Islamic conquest in 674-8. It is unwise therefore to see the peculiarly Celtic and arcane in a Celtic saint's cult which differs little from those of his contemporaries on the far side of the Mediterranean.

When we come to measure the 'otherworldliness' of Colmcille's spirituality, interesting points present themselves from Adomnán's narrative. It is certainly true that there is something decidedly tender in Colmcille's relationship with the animal world. A battle-scarred aristocrat he may have been, and a man of fiery temper who could call down vengeance on an enemy who plundered and slew the saint's friends, but Colmcille displayed a saintly tenderness towards animals that is indeed striking. He befriends an injured crane tossed by a storm onto the shores of Iona, and he encounters a heart-broken horse, downcast because he apparently knows that Colmcille's time in this world is coming to an end. But while Colmcille's kindness towards animals is marked it is also credible. Unlike Ciaran of Saiger, he does not admit foxes as monks into the monastery of Iona and farm animals as depicted in Adomnán's narrative are shown in a normal context, being put to use in conventional ways. As to the elusive Celtic organisation, while Colmcille's monks clearly do not follow the Rule of Benedict of Nursia, they follow a regular life nonetheless. Their days are taken up with chapel visits and prayers, proof-reading manuscripts in the scriptorium, going to the pastures, harvesting reeds, and working in the milking sheds. Colmcille is shown to us as a priest who says Mass, preaches, baptises and hears confessions. He is a hardliner on penance and deals with hardline sinners, one of whom had murdered his own brother and had slept with his mother. So much for a Celtic utopia on dis-tant Iona in the *Age of Saints!*

The question of the role of bishops in the early Irish church is a complex one deserving of further study. It is true that Colmcille ruled the monastery that he founded, and all its subject houses in the Hebrides and elsewhere in Scotland and Ireland, as a priest and monk. But some of his early successors on Iona, men such as Virgno (605-623), ruled as bishops as well as abbots. Iona's abbots were capable of showing surprising flexibility in regard to the administrative powers of a bishop when it came to organising their mission in Anglo-Saxon Northumbria. No doubt the abbot of Iona had to bow to Northumbrian English practice in sending bishops to rule the missionary church of Lindisfarne. We tend to forget, however, that the earliest Northumbrian church rulers – Aidan, Finán, Colmán, Cellach and Columbanus – were all consecrated bishops on *Iona* prior to their dispatch to Lindisfarne. And when Finán in turn consecrated Cedd, he summoned two other bishops to assist him. Similarly, when Vini consecrated Cedda, two other British bishops assisted in that consecration. It would appear therefore that while abbots might not themselves have been bishops and yet took precedence over bish-ops as leaders of a monastic community, bishops nevertheless retained a sig-nificant sacerdotal role within the early Irish church as the presence of Virgno on Iona or Cogitosus at Kildare would seem to indicate.

II

John Ryan's great book on *Irish Monasticism* did not bring the narrative of early Irish Christianity beyond the so-called *Age of Saints.* It is claimed, no doubt apocryphally, that the great Jesuit scholar felt his faith challenged by the study of laxity and degradation which supposedly characterised the later period. It would be more accurate to say that Ryan, in accepting the premise that there was an *Age of Saints,* found it difficult to set the subsequent devel-opment of Irish Christianity into a realistic historical context. I shall argue here for a more sober assessment of the age of the founding fathers of Irish monasticism and for a more balanced assessment of the later centuries, char-acterised as they were by lay abbacies, secularisation and unedifying violence and sexual licence. As ever, Iona will remain our chief guide.

Interestingly, all Iona's abbots, from Colmcille who died in 597 down to his biographer Adomnán who died in 704, were revered as *sancti* within their monastic community after their deaths and their saints' days were recorded in the Calendars. Similarly, Adomnán's two successors, Conamail (d. 710) and Dúnchad (d. 717) were also regarded as saints and their festival days are known. Fáelchú son of Dorbéne (717-24) and his successor Cilléne Fota (724-26) are the first abbots whose names we cannot identify in the Calendar of saints. On the other hand, Cilléne's successors – Cilléne Droichtech, Sléibíne, and Suibne (726-72) all have known saints' festivals, as has Bresal (772-801) if he can be identified with Bresal from Durrow at 18 May. Iona, therefore, was ruled from its foundation down to the Viking Age by a succession of abbots, the great majority of whom were regarded as *sancti* by their own brethren. It is also useful to bear in mind that all of these men, with the notable exception of Suibne II (767-72) and of Sléibíne (767-72), were kinsmen and collateral descendants of Colmcille, which suggests that nepotism within monastic houses either in Ireland or elsewhere in Christendom was not necessarily symptomatic of spiritual decline. It was rather a mirror image of how lay society was organised and led by a hereditary aristocracy which also controlled the landed wealth so necessary for the endowment of monasteries.

While it is important to establish that Iona continued to be ruled by holy men down to the beginning of the ninth century at least, it would be mistaken to consider Iona in this respect to be typical of Irish monastic life as a whole. In one sense it was typical in that, alongside Armagh, Iona was the most prestigious and probably the richest monastic community in the Celtic West. It was a place where kings from as far afield as Connacht, Fife or Northumbria retired to, and lavished their wealth upon. That wealth in turn was invested in luxury art works such as the shrine of Colmcille, the Iona and Durrow High Crosses in carved stone, or the remarkable Book of Durrow and the sumptuous Book of Kells. But if Iona's wealth and new-found political power had not led to a rapid falling off in standards, that may well have had much to do with the geographical isolation of the place as well as with the idealism of its saintly founder. Things did not fare quite so well for equally famous monasteries on the Irish mainland such as Armagh, Kildare or Clonmacnoise. And even Durrow – second only in importance to Iona itself within the Columban *parochia* – got sucked into the vortex of tribal violence and dynastic power struggles which came close to destroying Christianity in Ireland from the tenth century onwards.

One symptom of the change in Irish monasticism, which did make its appearance on Iona, was the introduction of a new title for the head of its community in the eighth century. It is then that we hear of the office of the *principatus* for the first time. The *principatus* or 'Royal Abbot' – for such he was – is a term which was symptomatic of the secularisation of the Irish mainland monasteries from the eighth century onwards, and the increasing involvement of the richer monasteries in the dynastic struggles of the warrior aristocracies. By the eighth century these richer monasteries had come to fill a vacuum in Irish economic and social life – a life that hitherto had been exclusively agrarian. The monks, living in organised communities and served by craftsmen and farm labourers, had inadvertently triggered the growth of monastic townships from the seventh century onwards. Monasticism rapidly came to exercise a monopoly over Irish urban development, with all the economic and political advantages that implied. Successful monasteries had attracted permanent settlements of craftsmen, agrarian tenants and serfs as well as merchants and scholars both young and old. Such novel and alarmingly successful communities must have excited the greed of the warrior aristocracy which, unlike their counterparts in Anglo-Saxon England and on the Continent, had no coinage to control and no traditional rights in the new markets which were the invention of the monks. Under such circumstances conflict and political manoeuvrings were inevitable, the incentive for all warlords being the control of rich monasteries from the inside. The obvious way to achieve that control was the intrusion of local dynasts into the abbacies of key monastic communities. It is in this context that the unexpected appearance of the office of the *principatus* should be viewed.

Jean-Michel Picard has reminded us that the term *princeps* was not an Irish invention, having a long ancestry in Old Testament studies and the term more particularly was applied to Gaulish bishops such as Germanus of Auxerre and Hilary of Poitiers.[3] Iona is as ever the barometer for cultural and political change in Irish monastic life, for although it was geographically removed from the Irish mainstream, its wealth of documentation allows us to map the changes. Iona's records refer to both the office of *principatus* as well as its holder or *princeps*. The first abbot specifically connected with the office of *principatus* was Dúnchad who we are told assumed his post in 707. Prince-Abbot or not, Dúnchad was later honoured as a saint of the Iona church with his festival day at 25 May. There are regular references to the *princeps* of Iona throughout the eighth century and it is very clear that this is a dignity bestowed on the abbot. For instance, we are told that when Abbot Fáelchú mac Dorbéni died in 724, Cillene Fota succeeded him in the *principatus,* and when Abbot Bresal died in 801 that it was in his thirty-first year as *princeps*. The vernacular equivalent of *princeps* (as we gather from the Würzburg Glosses) was *aircinnech*, a term explained in Cormac's glossary as *uasal cheand* or 'Noble Head' – a meaning which supports the idea of a 'Royal Abbot'. The female equivalent in the nunneries was the *ban-aircinnech* or *dominatrix*, who was undoubtedly a lady of royal kindred elected to represent the interests of the dominant dynasty in the region of the monastery.

The question now arises as to how long the title of *princeps* coincided with that of abbot, before the two offices may have become split between that of 'lay-abbot' or *aircinnech* of later centuries, and the spiritual leader proper. It is quite clear when we review the unedifying catalogue of Irish inter-monastic warfare of the eighth and ninth centuries that key positions within such monasteries had become secularised and were controlled in effect by local warlords who used rich monastic centres as pawns in their inter-tribal power struggles. It cannot be coincidence that the beginnings of monastic violence coincided with the adoption of princely titles by the heads of Irish monastic houses, and coincides also with clear evidence for the loss of celibacy among monastic leaders at Armagh and elsewhere. That loss of celibacy was related to the perpetuation of dynastic power within one ruling kindred in a monastery. So we read of the assassination of the Lócéne Menn, the abbot of Kildare, as early as 696, and of a massacre of the *familiae* of Suibne, an Armagh bishop, whose son and other kinsmen followed him in the abbacy and in the office of *oeconomus* or prior. Worse was to follow as the eighth century wore on. Monasteries went to war against each other and fought pitched battles as in the case of Clonmacnoise and Durrow in 764, while Colmcille's foundation at Durrow was again embroiled in 'a destructive battle' in 776. Great monastic houses such as Clonmacnoise, Armagh, Glendalough and Kildare were regularly attacked and burnt as the Christian establishment degenerated in a barbarous secular society over which it was unable to exercise moral control.

Does this mean, then, that I have taken up a stance with those revisionists who would have us believe that all churchmen were degenerate and that all monasteries were corrupt? By no means. I have already suggested that the evidence from Iona points to one great monastery which seems to have preserved its communal idealism and integrity among its abbots. It may be that, because Iona's leadership had been securely vested in the powerful royal dynasty of its saintly founder from the beginning, it was able to resist takeovers from rival warlords. Furthermore, when Iona's community was forced to flee to Kells on the Irish mainland in the face of the heathen Norse attack in the opening years of the ninth century, the monastery was still capable of providing volunteers who deliberately courted martyrdom at the hands of the Vikings in order to maintain a token community on Iona itself. One of that band, Blathmac, paid for his Christian idealism at the hands of the Norsemen who tortured him to death in 825 Walafrid Strabo, abbot of Reichenau in southern Germany, wrote up that account of Blathmac's martyrdom some fifteen years later.

Iona also offers evidence for the presence of a penitential community of anchorites located in an adjacent *dísert* or 'desert' site in the tradition of the

Egyptian fathers, and there is strong evidence to suggest that many mainland Irish monasteries maintained that tradition throughout the centuries of decline. There was a retreat for penitents at Muirbolc Mór on the island of Hinba, which was under the direction of Colmcille and not far from Iona in the sixth century. The famous letter of Cummian to Abbot Ségéne of Iona in 632 was also addressed to the *solitarius* or recluse, called Beccán, attached to Iona's community of anchorites. Adomnán speaks of a certain Finán who was a recluse at the Irish mainland Columban monastery of Durrow in his own time (c. 700). Kells, in the present Co Meath, also had its *dísert* community which as late as 1109 was ruled by its own *comarba*, a cleric called Óengus Ua Domnalláin, who was also 'the chief confessor (*prímh anamchara*) of the community of Colmcille'. The 'head of the Desert' (*Cenn in dísirt*) at Kells in 1133 was one Máel Maire Ua Robartaig.[4] St Lorcán Ua Tuathail (Laurence O'Toole) spent some time as an anchorite at the site of Kevin's Bed, in Teampall na Scellig at the *dísert* community at Glendalough (c. 1150). It was on that same remote and windswept shore of the Upper Lake that St Kevin, the founder of Glendalough, had spent his time as an anchorite more than half a millennium before.

Mention of *dísert* settlements reminds us that Irish monasticism from the outset had a built-in reformist and penitential dimension where the *miles Christi* (soldier of Christ) could pursue the spiritual warfare recommended by the early universal church. It is notable that Adomnán speaks of a *miles Christi*, one Virgno who lived out his life in the penitential community on Hinba. This term *miles Christi*, used many times by Adomnán, recurs in a specific way in sources of the late eighth and ninth centuries to indicate members of the Irish monastic reform movement known in the vernacular as *Céli Dé*. But the *Céli Dé* – literally 'members of the war-band of Christ' – although answering the specific challenge posed by a degenerate church in the eighth century, had in one sense never been absent from Celtic Christianity. And their founders, Fer-dá-Chrích, abbot of Dair-Inis, Dub-Littir of Finglas, Elair of Loch Cé, Máel Ruain of Tallaght, and Óengus the author of the famous *Martyrology* or *Félire Óengusso*, afford striking proof that in spite of decline and decadence, nepotism and violence, the Irish church was still capable of fostering a core group which believed in the ideals of the founding fathers. When Gothfrith, the pagan king of Norse Dublin, attacked Armagh in 921, 'he spared from destruction the prayer-houses with their communities of Céli Dé, and the houses of the sick, and also the monastery except for a few dwellings which were burnt through carelessness.' Even in the darkest days of the Viking onslaught a pagan Norseman was astute enough to treat the monastic core of the *civitas* of Armagh with respect. To have destroyed the Céli Dé community at Armagh would have been to deprive the township of its *raison d'être*, and it would have deprived Gothfrith of any opportunity for further raiding there. The glimpse that this record of the Armagh raid affords us shows too that, however much the office of *comarba Pátraic* (Heir of St Patrick) had become a family possession of the Cenél nEógain dynasty of the Northern Uí Néill, and however much the ecclesiastical leadership had been corrupted, an alternative core group of reformers had managed to maintain a community of discipline at the very heart of the monastery. The question of laxity and the survival of spiritual integrity in the early Irish church is a complex issue which requires a great deal of further study and an even-handed evaluation of a great wealth of historical evidence.

CHAPTER THREE

The contribution of Irish missionaries and scholars to medieval Christianity

Marie Therese Flanagan

From the sixth century onwards Irish Christians began to leave Ireland as *peregrini* to neighbouring Britain and mainland Europe. On the evidence of their own writings the Irish had a perception of themselves as living on an island at the outermost edge of the inhabited world: an Irish author, Cummian, writing about 632, described the Irish as 'almost at the end of the earth, and but a mere pimple on the face of the earth'.[1] The Irish perceived Christianity as having spread out to Ireland from the centre through the provinces, and finally to the far west in fulfilment of the biblical promise that the gospel had to be preached to all nations, a key inspiration for the best known missionary to Ireland, Patrick.[2] This geographical perspective of Ireland as located at the outermost limit of the earth generated an impulse to travel to that centre in which the great events that the Irish had read about had taken place, and where books and learning were thought to exist in a way that they did not in Ireland. It afforded one of the main motivations for the Irish *peregrini Christiani* who were leaving Ireland by the late sixth century.[3] Three key phases of Irish activity during the medieval period on the continent – and the focus here is on mainland Europe and not Britain – may be identified: the first in the pre-Carolingian period, the most important activity taking place in the seventh century; the second phase corresponding broadly to the era of Carolingian reform and renewal; and the third in the post-Carolingian period broadly spanning from the tenth to the twelfth centuries.

The impact of Irish *peregrini* on the Christian culture of medieval Europe has been assessed in very different ways and remains a subject of considerable controversy. In 1957 the Swiss scholar, Johannes Duft, described the pendulum of scholarly opinion on Irish influence abroad as oscillating between an over-optimistic *Iromanie* or 'Hiberno-mania' and, at the opposite end of the spectrum, a disparaging *Irophobie* or 'Hiberno-phobia'.[4] In not dissimilar vein, the Italian scholar, Edmondo Coccia, in 1967 assessed the Irish contribution to the culture of pre-Carolingian Europe as more of a myth than a miracle.[5] Coccia argued that the contribution of the Irish to European Christian culture had been greatly overestimated and that the notion of the Irish as outstanding scholars in an otherwise dark age was a myth. The debate about the Irish contribution to early medieval European culture prior to the 1960s centred primarily on the role played by Irish scholars who were believed to have enjoyed a unique and privileged access to classical learning and particularly to texts of the classical Latin poets, in the preservation and retransmission of classical literature to the continent,[6] but to focus on Irish knowledge or, as is now more accurately understood, paucity of knowledge of the classical heritage, is to do so at the expense of other more substantive areas in which the Irish did indeed make a material contribution to the formation of medieval Christianity. More recent scholarship has highlighted the Irish contribution to the shaping of a specifically medieval Christian culture and the development of what might be termed a new type of Christian mentality or scholarship.[7]

I

What was distinctive or original about the Irish contribution to medieval Christian spirituality and culture, and how far was it determined by the specific context in which Christianity had taken root and flourished in Ireland? Christianity had reached Ireland no later than about the year 400. Ireland was the first non-Romanised and non-literate society in western Europe to receive it. As St Patrick described the Irish, they were *barbarae gentes*.[8] Since the earliest missionaries to Ireland took the momentous decision that the Bible should be transmitted in Latin and not translated into the vernacular, of necessity Christianity had to be accompanied by the introduction of the Latin language. The conversion of Ireland, which was well under way by the fifth century, followed closely on an age, in western Christendom, of intensive production of Christian texts in the Latin language. The period between about 350 and 450 had witnessed the translation into Latin of the Bible, the creation of liturgical texts, the emergence of a Latin canon law, and the writing of monastic rules and hagiographical lives of saints in Latin. Ireland was the first country to be christianised in western Europe where the language of the Christian liturgy was not also the vernacular language and where, therefore, Latin had to be acquired as a second language if access to the Bible and Latin Christian scholarship was to be attained. The first two hundred years of the origins and history of Christianity and of the Latin language and scholarship in Ireland are irretrievable, since Latin texts written in Ireland only become available from the seventh century. When they do surface around 600, it is evident that Latin had not only been taught successfully by missionaries but had been successfully passed on to subsequent generations.[9] It is not tentative beginnings but confident attainment that is apparent in the earliest securely datable Hiberno-Latin texts.[10]

To be effectively Christian, that is to gain full access to the Bible and the other written texts of Christianity, the Irish had had to master Latin. This led them in the first instance to pursue an intensive study of the language in which those texts were written. As the Hiberno-Latin grammarian, known as the *Anonymus ad Cuimnanum* wrote, 'whoever desires Christian learning must not shun the craft of grammar without which nobody can be learned and wise'.[11] The study of the Latin language in Ireland began with existing grammars, such as that of the fourth-century Roman grammarian, Donatus. But Irish Christians were to progress to write their own textbooks because the available grammars, written as they had been for the use of native speakers, proved inadequate for those acquiring Latin as a second language.[12] The writing of new kinds of grammars by Irish authors, such as the seventh-century Virgilius Maro *grammaticus*[13] and Malsachanus,[14] or the previously mentioned anonymous work addressed to an Irishman, Cuimnanus, inaugurated a new development in western grammatical studies. Scholars in the ancient world had theorised about language and written grammars predominantly from the point of view of the native speaker. For the Irish it was necessary to adopt the standpoint of the foreign learner. The resulting transformation is reflected in the grammatical works that the Irish wrote – elementary descriptive grammars that sought to provide simultaneously an introduction to basic linguistic concepts and a more-or-less comprehensive account of Latin forms. Irish scholars were to make a positive contribution in the provision of elementary descriptive grammars, and indeed other basic teachers' handbooks and textbooks, and those texts were to prove their usefulness to other non-Latin speakers when taken abroad by Irish *peregrini*, most notably to the Germanic peoples of England and the non-Romanised or de-Romanised areas of mainland Europe, and were to prepare the ground for the revival of scholarship associated with the Carolingian Renaissance.

Since Irish was not a Romance language, and Latin had to be acquired as a second language, native Irish speakers tended to regard Latin primarily as a written or 'visible' language used for transmitting texts: they comprehended it by the eye rather than by the ear. This led them to develop new graphic conventions to facilitate visible access to the written word, practices that reflected the processes by which the Irish had acquired their knowledge of the Latin language. Irish scribes sought to achieve new standards of legibility, to improve the intelligibility of, or access to, information transmitted in the written medium. The Irish made a notable contribution to what has been termed the 'grammar of legibility'.[15] Irish scribes abandoned the *scriptio continua* of their exemplars and introduced spaces between words and new punctuation marks, in a graded series that indicated the pauses according to a hierarchy of importance, that is the number of pause marks increased according to the importance of the pause. The Irish deployed and popularised other techniques such as giving more visual emphasis to the beginning of a text, and to sections within a text, deploying such strategies as enlarged or decorated initials and the use of *diminuendo*. Punctuation, layout, decoration, construe marks linking grammatically related words, were combined to facilitate access to the written word, to enable Irish students to grasp the Latin language whose syntax and word order was quite different from their own. Another indication that Irish scribes, by comparison with contemporary scribes in other parts of Europe, perceived Latin forms primarily in graphic terms is the fact that they made more extensive use of abbreviations: one set of graphic symbols could readily be replaced by another set of purely graphic symbols. Such techniques in manuscript production, which are an indication of the care that Irish masters took over their teaching, are well advanced in the datable manuscripts produced at the end of the seventh century, such as the so-called Antiphonary of Bangor, a liturgical manuscript written at Bangor about 680-91 whence it was taken to the Columbanian foundation at Bobbio and is now in the Biblioteca Ambrosiana in Milan.[16] Concurrent with these visual developments in manuscript layout was a discernible shift in the conceptualisation of language in Hiberno-Latin grammatical commentaries from a primarily aural to an increasingly visual one with the use, alongside or instead of aural terms such as *vox* and *sonus*, of graphic terms such as *litteratura* and *superficies*.[17]

These practices of Irish scribes were developed in response to the needs of readers for whom Latin was a second language. The strategies developed to facilitate clarity and accessibility were of considerable benefit to the Irish readers for whom they were created, but they would also prove beneficial to others when exported to other non-Romanised or de-Romanised areas in continental Europe and at a time when, in any case, written Latin even in Romanised areas, was assuming peculiarly local forms. This is one explanation for the demonstrable influence of Irish practices in manuscripts subsequently produced on the continent. A letter from an Irish scribe, Colmán, to a fellow Irishman, Feradach, which is of seventh- or eighth-century date, affords a valuable insight into Irish methods of copying manuscripts.[18] Colmán announces to Feradach that he had acquired access to a more accurate copy of Sedulius's *Carmen Paschale*. His own copy was, as he described it, *depravata*, and he wanted to share with Feradach his sense of deep satisfaction at having found a more accurate version, and to send him a set of corrections that Feradach could write into his own manuscript should he wish to do so. Colmán offered a list of improved readings but, even more importantly, he explained his criteria for deciding on which was the better reading, exhibiting an impressive grasp of textual criticism. Intensive study of available texts may be identified as a distinctively Irish feature at this period. Irish scribes did not copy passively, however, and frequently recorded their personal response to the text in marginalia: respect for authority was tempered with an intellectual curiosity and an independence of judgement. Manuscripts then form a very important part of the evidence for Irish presence and activity on the continent.

The intensive effort made to study Latin in Ireland was focused on providing access to the Bible and scriptural understanding: it was undertaken in the service of Christianity. The scholarly contribution of the Irish in the pre-Carolingian period was characterised by a profound engagement with the biblical text and the production of biblical commentaries and exegetical scholarship. Overall, the production of scholastic biblical commentaries in the period between 500 and 800, or, put another way, between Cassiodorus and Bede, is meagre when compared with the period from the ninth century onwards. But in that early period the work of Irish scholars is significant disproportionately to the country's size or background. The eclectic nature of Irish biblical commentary material suggests that the Irish had little direct or continuous contact with the techniques of the late antique schools, so that what they did not learn directly from missionaries they had to glean from written texts. The Irish contribution to biblical exegesis in the early medieval West was first highlighted in 1954 by the German medievalist, Bernhard Bischoff, who went so far as to characterise Irish exegetical scholarship as a turning-point in the history of western biblical exegesis.[19] Until 1954 while many things had been claimed for medieval Irish scholarship, a legacy of biblical exegesis was not one. Bischoff listed over forty anonymous biblical commentaries which he believed were of Irish origin; a more recent tally by J. F. Kelly in 1990 has more than doubled that figure to one hundred and fourteen.[20] Prior to Bischoff's seminal article many of those works were virtually unknown and, in a single stroke, he may be said to have altered the perception of Irish scholarship in the pre-Carolingian period. Substantial *corpora* of anonymous exegetical and grammatical texts with Irish attributes have now been identified, and the painstaking task of editing these works has begun. Of course it is necessary to be aware of the danger of falling into a new trap of Hiberno-mania. Bischoff ascribed many anonymous exegetical works to Irish provenance on the basis of what he considered to be specific 'Irish symptoms'. A more general growth in studies of post-patristic exegesis has demonstrated that many of the features that Bischoff suggested as specifically Irish can indeed be found in other contexts and could now more properly be considered as 'pre-Carolingian' rather than distinctively Irish.[21] The precise nature of the differences between Irish and continental exegetical perspectives requires greater elucidation. The major task remains of comparing what are certainly Irish writings with other texts of the period in order to see what features, common in the Irish group, are noticeably rare or absent from the wider group. More generally, it is important to stress that the type of exegesis favoured by the Irish was not uniquely original: it was not Irish originality, but the vigour with which the Irish endeavoured to read and explicate the biblical text that is distinctive. It was their intensity of engagement with the Bible that contributed an important element to the early reputation of the Irish as scholars. The old notion that the Latin classics were brought to Ireland in the fifth century by scholars fleeing the Germanic invasions of Gaul and were preserved and retransmitted from Ireland back to the continent has been laid firmly to rest, but in its place there is a truer understanding of the, in many ways far more impressive, achievements of Irish scholarship in the pre-Carolingian period. The Irish scholarly contribution in the pre-Carolingian period can now more properly be recognised to lie in the provision of basic instructional and exegetical tools and commentary literature that enabled a deeper understanding of the Bible.

II

With the conversion of the Irish to Christianity largely completed by about 600, a number of Irishmen embarked on the path of *peregrinatio* to Britain and the continent. What motivated them to do so, and what was the distinctive nature of their impact on the societies to which they went in their exile? The tradition of *peregrinatio* was always explicitly founded on certain key scriptural passages, but for Irishmen it derived much of its force as a form of ascetic renunciation from the specific social and political structures of Irish society where the status and legal protection of the individual was intimately bound up with membership of a kindred group and local political community, and where, in secular law, expulsion from Ireland also operated as the ultimate sanction against a persistent offender who committed crimes of such a grave nature that they were considered to place him outside of society.[22] To choose *pereginatio* was voluntarily to relinquish status, a point asserted by Patrick in his *Confessio* and his tract on the crimes of Coroticus when he detailed the rank of his father and grandfather, and his renunciation of *patria et parentes* in the cause of his mission to Ireland.[23] Conversely, voluntary exile for Christ offered autonomy of action and freed the *peregrinus* from social and legal obligations to his family and local political community. Renunciation of the secular world was the central aim of any ascetic *peregrinatio*. While *peregrinatio* initially was practised within Ireland, in that a *peregrinus* voluntarily made himself a stranger by separating from his own kindred and political community, by no later than 700 the *peregrinus* had acquired a position of privilege in Irish society that transcended both legal disabilities and political boundaries. A contract in early Irish law required sureties to be given by both parties before it was valid, but detailed among the privileged or immune contracts that could be binding without a surety was a contract involving the participation of a *deorad Dé* or 'exile for Christ'.[24] The *peregrinus* renounced the world but the power which he attained in so doing as a representative of God and the saints prevented Irish society from renouncing him. A *peregrinus* acquired a legal status of immunity that was no longer circumscribed by political boundaries and therefore rendered nugatory an important element of his original ascetic impulse. The life of Columbanus written around 640 by the Bobbio monk, Jonas, distinguished between two grades of *peregrinatio*.[25] According to Jonas, Columbanus as a young man, still living in his native Leinster, had sought advice from a holy woman. She explained to him that fifteen years previously she had left home and settled in her *peregrinationis locus*, but, had she not been a woman, she would have crossed the sea and sought out a *potioris peregrinationis locus*. Columbanus' female adviser drew a distinction between internal exile within Ireland and external exile abroad. Initially, in pursuit of the lesser *peregrinatio*, Columbanus left Leinster for Bangor but eventually he was to opt for the *potior peregrinatio* and leave Ireland permanently for the continent. *Peregrinatio* was not, of course, a peculiarly Irish concept or practice – witness its inspiration for the Romano-Briton Patrick, – but it was to derive much of its force in an Irish context from the distinctive features of secular Irish society where honour and status were so intimately bound up with membership of a kindred group and local political community.

While the initial motivation for *peregrinatio* may have been ascetic renunciation, Irish *peregrini*, like Patrick, and possibly in direct imitation of him, were also to engage in evangelising activity: the concept of *peregrinatio* merged into that of mission. Owing to the vagaries of source survival and text transmission, the most detailed extant evidence for assessing the impact of the Irish as evangelists on mainland Europe comes from seventh- and eighth-century Gaul.[26] Gallic Christianity before the arrival of Irish *peregrini* in the late sixth century was still mainly urban in emphasis, and the rural population had hardly been reached by evangelisation.[27] The exposure of rural areas to Christianity, where such had actually been the case, was quite superficial. It was in that particular context that an influx of charismatic holy men inured to travel and risk and prepared to confront pagan rusticity in its rural habitat could make a difference. Irish holy men offered direct and sustained contact with powerfully motivated ascetics, monks and preachers who were actively prepared to demonstrate their beliefs and to reinforce the word which they preached by their actions. The impact of continuous presence and example and preaching are critical to the early stages of conversion. Without them the consolidation achieved in rural areas by Irish missionaries could not have occurred. Irish *peregrini* showed a capacity to make convinced converts out of loose adherents, to effect genuine conversion not only in rejecting the pagan past but in adhering to a life of duties towards God and charity towards one's neighbour. They helped to create conditions which made conversion rather than adhesion a genuinely persuasive option, something which Gallic urban-based Christianity had found difficult to achieve.

The arrival of Irish *peregrini* inaugurated a movement of spiritual renewal in Gaul which is manifest in a wave of new monastic foundations. Some two hundred and twenty monasteries existed in Gaul around AD 600 but some three hundred and twenty more were added during the seventh century under Irish influence,[28] the great majority located in northern Gaul which Pierre Riché has characterised as a barbarian zone.[29] More important than the increase in number, however, was the character of the new monastic foundations. As in Ireland, these new foundations were in rural areas and were not directly dependent for support on the local urban-based bishop but relied on the patronage of a rurally based newly emerging Frankish aristocracy and the direct labour of the monks. Reliance on manual work and economic self-sufficiency was well suited to the improvement of a developing rural economy. These monasteries provided stability and centres around which the Christian life of the countryside could be organised with the establishment of numerous small churches and chapels, shrines and *cellae* in outlying districts. Such monastic foundations played a crucial role in the re-christianisation of what had been frontier regions of the Roman empire, and also inaugurated the advance into those parts of Europe that had lain outside Rome's direct control.

The Irish approach to evangelisation did not take the form of closely organised or directed missions of the kind that St Augustine of Canterbury led to the Anglo-Saxons in 597. Arguably, however, Irish modes of evangelisation were more appropriate to the historic/geographic conditions of seventh-century Europe. Christianity had been introduced into Ireland without coercion or the imperialising political context of the Roman empire. Christianity necessarily had had to rely on the veracity of its witness and to seek an accommodation with Irish society. In Ireland for the first time in western Europe Christianity had encountered a non-Roman or barbarian society, an overwhelmingly rural society that had had no direct experience of the institutional or administrative structures of the Roman empire which were closely linked to urban centres and had been such a formative influence on the development of the Christian church. In Ireland the first Christians had had to accommodate themselves to an alien environment and to develop strategies for the establishment of church structures in those novel non-Romanised conditions. The adaptations made to local Irish conditions were also to provide suitable models of behaviour for Irish missionaries subsequently to deploy in England and on the continent. As the Venerable Bede expressed it,

'Gentiles learn best from Gentiles'.[30] Irish modes of evangelisation and their rurally based organisational structures were more suited to the contemporary outlook and the settlement patterns of most peoples north of the Alps who lived far from urban centres and who required not merely preaching but also appropriately adaptable models of behaviour. With the arrival of Irish *peregrini* in Frankia the transition from an attentuated late antique urban Christianity to a re-invigorated early medieval, rural based Christianity was effected.

It should be stressed that the spirituality of Irish *peregrini* differed not in its originality or innovative quality, but rather in its intensity and emphasis. In many respects it represented a return to the well-springs of ascetic Gallic Christianity. The ideals that the Irish sought to put into practice were those of Hilary of Poitiers, of Martin of Tours, and of Cassian.[31] They re-evoked the first age of monasticism in the west, and a return to the sources is generally typical of the first phase of a reform movement. Columbanus and his companions acted as catalysts for spiritual renewal in Gaul in the first half of the seventh century. But again one must be careful to guard against the enthusiasm of Hiberno-mania. The principal monastic founders and re-organisers of dioceses in Gaul following Columbanus were to be members of the Frankish aristocracy with whom he had forged links, a fact highlighted by Friedrich Prinz in the coining of the term *Iro-Fränkisch* or Hiberno-Frankish monasticism.[32] More generally, Columbanus made a unique contribution to the practices of the western church by his transmission to continental Europe of what his biographer, Jonas, termed the *medicamenta paenitentiae*, an Irish penitential regime of private expiatory penance that could be repeated as many times as was felt necessary, and which was to impact not only on monks and clergy but also on lay Christians.[33] While it is true that in Columbanus's own writings such themes as the perception of human life as a *peregrinatio* alienated from a heavenly *patria* are more prominent, though he does incidentally mention confession in his letter to Pope Gregory I, Jonas' life of Columbanus indicates that penitential discipline became a central feature of Columbanian monasticism in the generation after Columbanus's death.

Columbanus is the most famous of the Irish *peregrini* of the seventh century, though arguably he was atypical in having travelled so extensively, in having criticised popes so forcefully, preached to kings, founded such a large number of monasteries in different areas, and most importantly in having written a series of texts which survive to offer an insight into his religious inspiration. Columbanus was, as he described himself, a *rara avis*.[34] His *Instructiones*, monastic rules and penitentials represent the most coherent exposition of Irish spirituality to have come down to us from the formative period of early Irish monasticism.[35] It has too often been assumed, however, that Irish monasticism, and more specifically Columbanian monasticism, was radically different from that of St Benedict which was to become normative for western monasticism. But like Benedict, Columbanus preferred coenobites to hermits:

> Let the monk live in a commmunity under the discipline of one father and in company with many, so that from one he may learn lowliness, from another patience. For one may teach him silence and another meekness.[36]

Given the similar emphases in Columbanus and in Benedict, it is not surprising to find that the Benedictine rule itself was introduced into Gaul by immediate followers of Columbanus. It is first found about 625 in association with Bishop Donatus of Besançon, a former monk of Luxeuil, and soon afterwards there is evidence that Luxeuil itself was following a mixed rule drawn from both Columbanus and Benedict. It is not difficult to account for this development. Columbanus's *regula monachorum* and *regula coenobialis* are a set of sermons on the monastic life with few practical regulations. It was these latter that Benedict so well supplied. Benedict's rule perfectly complements Columbanus's in this regard, and it began its career in Gaul very much under Hiberno-Frankish auspices, though it might be an exaggeration to say as the English medievalist, Eric John, did that 'if it had not been for Columbanus and Luxeuil, I doubt if the *Regula Benedicti* would today be more than a literary curiosity'.[37] John's view of the importance of Columbanian houses in disseminating the Benedictine rule has been reinforced by Marilyn Dunn in her study of the *Regula magistri*, a monastic rule closely linked to Benedict's, which she argues was produced in Irish monastic circles on the continent and more recently has claimed was actually compiled at Bobbio.[38]

Not all continental foundations with an Irish origin were to retain continuous or significant links with Ireland and therefore Irish influence. The geographical location of the monastery of St Gallen in Switzerland, for example, owed its origins to the fact that the Irishman, Gallus, a follower of Columbanus, elected to withdraw into the wilderness of the Steinach valley rather than accompany Columbanus across the Alps into Italy.[39] Gallus established a hermitage that was visited by like-minded disciples during his lifetime and functioned as a place of pilgrimage after his death about AD 650. The medieval monastery of St Gallen, however, owed its institutional origin to an indigenous Alemannian, Otmar, who founded a monastery there in 719 which adopted the Benedictine rule in 747. The monastery of St Gallen derived its location from Gallus but little else. During the ninth, tenth, and eleventh centuries, however, Irish *peregrini* visited St Gallen in significant numbers and left manuscripts, *libri scottice scripti*, fifteen of which are still in the St Gallen library. Irish interest in St Gallen must have received stimulus from the translation of the relics of Gallus on the occasion of the building of a new church in the 830s. But Irish influence played little part in the institutional evolution of St Gallen and was a less than decisive influence in its intellectual formation.[40] By contrast, the church at Péronne in Picardy by the river Somme, associated with another Irish *peregrinus*, St Fursa, who was buried there c. 650, was to retain a continuous link with Ireland until its destruction by the Vikings in the 880s. So too did the monastery founded by Fursa's brother, Foilán, at Fosses in the diocese of Liège. Foilán was to be succeeded as abbot by his younger brother, Ultán who, in turn, was to be succeeded by another Irishman, Cellán (d. 706). The life of Fursa and the account of his visions written about 655, that is shortly after his death in 649, attests to the high reputation for holiness that not only he but also other Irishmen enjoyed. In both Péronne and Fosses, which were known in the ninth century as *monasteria Scottorum*, there is good evidence for continued staffing by prominent individuals from Ireland,[41] which is less apparent in the case of the Columbanian monasteries in Frankia or at Bobbio.[42] Any assessment of the Irish impact on the continent must allow for that distinction between monasteries which retained continuous Irish personnel and those that did not or did so only intermittently when, for example, Irish *peregrini* visited. Yet more shadowy traditions of Irish ascetics on the continent survive that are ill-supported by the scanty literary evidence, or obscured by later missionary ventures or are complete fabrications where, because of a generalised equation between 'Irish' and 'holy', saints about whose origins otherwise little was known were hibernicised such as St Frediano of Lucca and St Cataldo of Taranto or St Silao of Lucca who represents a twelfth-century fabrication *ab initio* of an Irish saint.[43]

It has also to be borne in mind that Irish monks might be found in continental monasteries that did not necessarily have an Irish origin. The presence of such Irishmen is known usually only through lists of names that have survived accidentally or through manuscripts written by Irish scribes. An Irish presence may also be attested through texts copied in an Irish manner or glosses in old Irish in manuscripts and, more indirectly, through theological works handled in ways that were particularly prevalent among the Irish. One reference to a solitary Irish name or one glossed manuscript has often been assumed to signify that a monastery was Irish, an example of what Johannes Duft termed Hiberno-mania. Continental monasteries, however, often welcomed individual Irishmen and their ideas. What is required is a comprehensive prosopography of the Irish attested on the continent, and their links with continental monasteries and with Ireland. Only then can a balanced appraisal of their contribution be made.

III

From the late eighth century onwards a change in the motivation for Irish travel abroad is discernible.[44] The nature of Irish *peregrinatio* changed from that of voluntary expatriation and evangelistic work to pilgrimage to shrines of special devotion, most notably Rome, but also those with Irish connections such as Luxeuil, Péronne, Bobbio and St Gallen, and, the object of the pious journey having been achieved, the pilgrims returned to Ireland. Another type of Irishman was drawn more specifically for reasons of scholarship by the intellectual climate associated with the Carolingian *renovatio*.[45] In the ninth century Irish are attested as scholars, teachers and students at Carolingian royal courts or in cathedral towns. John Scottus Eriugena is the most famous Irish scholar of the ninth century but, like Columbanus in the seventh century, Eriugena was a *rara avis*, a philosophic thinker and translator from the Greek. Despite or perhaps because of his brilliance, he made little impact on the contemporary intellectual climate. Appreciation of his scholarship and recovery of his thought began only in the twentieth century.[46] When read by his contemporaries he was little understood and hence open to suspicion of heresy. A more typical Irish scholarly representative of the Carolingian period was Eriugena's contemporary, Martin Hiberniensis (d. 875) whose activities as a teacher in the cathedral city of Laon is attested in no less than twenty-one manuscripts.[47] Ninth-century Irish scholars and teachers like Martin Hiberniensis profited enormously from the intellectual contacts and resources available to them on the continent. Their fields of study were widened considerably and their knowledge enhanced and perfected by continental resources. Notwithstanding some medieval Hiberno-scepticism, if not overt Hiberno-phobia, they continued to enjoy a reputation for scholarship, and their distinctively Irish trait, as in the pre-Carolingian period, can be identified as the intensity and commitment with which they availed of the scholarly opportunities afforded them.

That it was still possible in the ninth century for Irish Christian scholarship to make a substantial original contribution is evidenced by the dissemination of the early eighth-century canon law text known as the *Collectio canonum Hibernensis*.[48] The *Hibernensis* is a systematically organised compilation, that is to say classified by subject-matter, based on material drawn not only from the usual synodal proceedings and earlier canon-law collections, but also from the Bible and the church fathers. It was the most ambitious endeavour among early medieval canon law collections to codify Christian life and therefore one of the significant contributions of Irish scholarship to western Christianity. The *Hibernensis* was extensively diffused in France and central Europe in the later eighth and ninth centuries, and not later than the tenth century its Italian circulation had begun with vigour. It came to be preferred to the *Collectio Dionysia Hadriana*, the canon law text which was a product of the Carolingian reforming and 'Romanising' policy. The appeal of the *Hibernensis* was due in large part to its convenience and the acuity of the thematic rather than historical principle underlying its organisation but also to its extensive patristic allusions.

In the post-Carolingian tenth century the intellectual climate in Europe became less attractive to Irish scholars and emigration reverted to a more predominantly religious rather than scholastic motivation. Stray Irishmen are to be found in both tenth-century Germany and France but spread wide and thin and there is no clear dynamic for their activities such as is more readily discernible in the preceding centuries. The early eleventh century witnessed a sudden upsurge in Irish overseas pilgrimage as the Viking Age drew to a close and travel by sea became less perilous. Irish annals record pilgrimages of prominent individuals to Rome, including a number of Irish kings, and by the end of the eleventh century there is evidence for the existence of a community of Irish monks in Rome, *Sancta Trinitatis Scottorum*, whose names have been preserved written in an Irish hand that was inserted into a manuscript now in the Vatican Library.[49] Jerusalem was another important pilgrim destination and St Coloman, now honoured as patron of Austria, was one of a group from Ireland on their way to Jerusalem when he was martyred at Stockerau in 1012.[50] Related to this growth of pilgrimage was recourse to the practice of *inclusio* by a number of Irish individuals who attached themselves to continental churches. Such Irish *inclusi*, or walled-up recluses, are attested at Paderborn, Fulda, Köln, Mainz, and Regensburg (Ratisbon).[51] Noteworthy is the geographical convergence on Germany. In the second half of the eleventh century Irish activity on the continent found a focal point in southern Germany and more specifically at Regensburg on the Danube which became the head of a confederation of monastic foundations of Irish origin known to scholars as *Schottenklöster*.[52] The general context for that development was the political dominance of the German emperors but an additional factor attracting monks specifically to Regensburg appears to have been earlier Irish activity there during the eighth and ninth centuries. The monastic foundation c. 1090 of St James at Regensburg was to become the mother house of a filiation of twelve houses of Irish Benedictines that were to be financially supported and staffed by direct recruitment from Ireland. In 1112 Henry V issued an imperial privilege to the monastery of St James that certified the foundation as an independent monastery, which was followed by a series of papal privileges that placed the Irish monastery beyond the ecclesiastical control of all but the pope himself.[53] The *Schottenklöster* represent the final phase in the history of the medieval expansion of Irish Christianity but also the first phase of a movement of spiritual renewal within the Irish church which is traditionally known as 'the twelfth-century reform'.[54] The *Schotten-klöster* were to act as a conduit of reform influence and Europeanisation of the Irish church, particularly in the province of Munster, that was to feed into the reform and transformation of the twelfth-century Irish church.[55]

A continuous Irish presence in Germany between the tenth and the twelfth centuries, together with Irish scholarly and manuscript production, ensured that the Irish retained a reputation for holiness and learning in certain intellectual circles. Germany, however, encompassed the more conservative intellectual centres in medieval Europe. In other more progressive intellectual milieus the reputation of the Irish as saints and scholars was steadily undermined. Already in early twelfth-century England, and before English intervention in Ireland in the later twelfth century, a more sceptical view of the Irish as backward barbarians whose reputation as scholars was greatly inflated was being adumbrated by William of Malmesbury.[56] It was a view that was to be elaborated and publicised even more persuasively by the most notable European scholar of the mid-twelfth century, St Bernard of Clairvaux. Bernard wrote a biography of the Irish reforming bishop, Malachy,[57] whom he had known personally, in which Bernard depicted the Irish as a barbarous people in dire need of spiritual renewal. The chronological coincidence of the spread of the European church reform movement, traditionally known as the Gregorian reform, with the colonial intrusion of the Anglo-Normans and English into Ireland, who were to justify their intervention on grounds of ecclesiastical reform, ensured that the notion of Ireland as an *insula sanctorum* was to be permanently undermined.[58] In French, Norman and English intellectual circles the Irish reputation for holiness and for scholarship was relentlessly dismantled under the continual strain of incomplete colonial conquest throughout the remainder of the medieval period. In Germany, however, the Irish retained a more positive residual reputation, although the emphasis shifted to Ireland as an exotic otherworld location, a land of marvels and strange wonders.

Insofar then, as Irish 'saints and scholars' made a contribution to the formation of medieval Christianity, the high point of their influence may be located in the seventh century when the Irish proved to have the most to offer to European Christianity. The seventh century was indeed 'the period when Ireland mattered most in and to Europe'.[59]

CHAPTER FOUR

The Irish church in the Middle Ages

John A. Watt

For the Irish church, the Middle Ages were a period of great change, change to an extent perhaps undergone by few other churches in medieval Christendom. Change began early in the twelfth century and gathered pace through the first half of the century. It took the form of an ambitious attempt at fundamental reform. The second half of the century saw change of a different sort. Ireland lost its political independence with the assertion of lordship over the country by the kings of England, a dominion approved and validated by the papacy. Change accelerated in the thirteenth century when with extensive immigrant settlement, Ireland became an English colony. Thereby the Irish church underwent a radical process of anglicisation, introducing within it a duality of cultures, Irish and English. It became a church of two nations, often in confrontation. There were further changes in the fourteenth century when English governmental supremacy began to disintegrate bringing in its wake the need to find new relationships between the nations. The challenge of the Reformation was to follow.

I

What in the Irish church of the early twelfth century needed reform? Placed in the perspective of developments within the universal church as a whole, the Irish twelfth-century reform movement may be viewed as the particular experience of that general reform programme which historians have come to label 'Gregorian reform': a reform movement associated with the assertion of papal authority, with the development of uniform norms of canon law, with the renewal of clerical discipline, including the observance of celibacy, with the redrawing of the relationship between spiritual and temporal powers in the cause of the freedom of the clergy in their own ecclesiastical concerns. Each church in Christendom approached this programme in its own individual way since each began from a different starting point.

What we know of the starting point for reform in Ireland came first from outside the country. It comes to us from letters addressed to various correspondents in Ireland by two celebrated Italian archbishops of Canterbury, Lanfranc and St Anselm, formerly abbots of Bec in Normandy and both serious reformers. They had no firsthand knowledge of Ireland but had good informants. Before the death of Anselm (1109), six bishops-elect, four from Dublin, one each from Waterford and Limerick, sought consecration at Canterbury and had made professions of canonical obedience to its archbishops as their primate. The most significant of the letters in the reform context were those addressed to the most powerful of the provincial kings of Ireland, the kings of Munster, serious aspirants to the high kingship of Ireland itself. Lanfranc and Anselm identified specific evils: simony, maladministration of the sacraments and a highly defective law of marriage ('It is reported,' wrote Anselm, 'that men exchange their wives as freely and publicly as a man might change his horse.') Anselm was especially concerned with the number and quality of bishops in Ireland. Put briefly, his view was that there were far too many bishops with too little authority and without pastoral dynamism because they lacked a defined territorial area for which they held apostolic responsibility. 'Almost every single monastery had its own bishop,' Bernard of Clairvaux was to write some fifty years later, also on the authority of informants from Ireland itself.

There is information from within Ireland which helps the historian to identify what in the Irish church needed correction. A series of councils were held, especially in Munster, involving both lay rulers, and bishops and abbots, and presided over by papal legates. These councils tackled the ills detailed from Canterbury (this is not to argue that Irish churchmen needed to have them identified for them, but merely to record that the diagnoses agreed): simony, quality of the clergy, celibacy, control by laymen and matrimonial law. The establishment of a new diocesan structure was prominent on the conciliar agenda.

Such is the paucity of source material from within Ireland with which to chart the progress of reform in the first decades of the century that it is with some relief that the historian turns to the *Life of Malachy of Armagh*, written by Bernard of Clairvaux shortly after Malachy's death at Clairvaux in 1148. Not that Bernard's work is without considerable methodological difficulties. For the *Life of Malachy* is a supreme example of that particularly medieval genre of literature, hagiography. Pope Clement III found it very useful when deciding in 1190 to canonise Malachy but for the historian its long catalogues of the saint's miracles and his spiritual qualities make it rather less so. Nevertheless the request to write it having come from Ireland, some hard information about Malachy's career came with it. Two aspects of Malachy's apostolate, detailed by Bernard, command attention in the context of reform.

The first concerns his careful research in Scotland, England and France into the different types of religious life currently flourishing in these countries in this most progressive of ages in the evolution of monasticism. Malachy's explorations into this most important dimension of reform brought significant practical results. One was the introduction into Ireland of the rule for Augustinian canons as practised by the congregations of Arrouaise. The canons, with the flexibility and adaptability that the Rule allowed, were most appropriate for Irish conditions. The second, reflecting Malachy's own passion for Cistercian monasticism (Pope Innocent II refused to allow him to join the Clairvaux community) led likewise to the introduction of the Cistercian way of life into Ireland. The first house in Ireland, at Mellifont, soon to be a reforming centre, was established by Irish monks trained under the demanding eye of St Bernard, supported by more experienced French Cistercians. Both canons and monks so flourished in Ireland, attracting patrons and recruits very readily, that one may speak of the opening of a whole new chapter in the history of Irish monasticism.

The second aspect of Malachy's reforming work highlighted in Bernard's biography was the bringing to fruition, under strong papal guidance, of a territorially based diocesan structure, the essential framework for adequate pastoral ministry common to the ecclesiastical world outside Ireland. Reformers from the beginning of the century had acknowledged the need for this structure and the form it should take had been developed gradually in the reform councils of the earlier part of the century. Then in 1139 Malachy had been briefed to seek papal approval for a structure already agreed in Ireland. Innocent II responded encouragingly without accepting this proposal. Instead, appointing Malachy his legate, he instructed him to return home, summon a national council and seek its agreement to submitting a formal request for the granting of pallia. Perhaps the pope was uncertain as to how much support Malachy really commanded for the scheme he was advocating, but whatever the reason for delay, Malachy duly implemented his instruction and in 1148 again set off for Rome. He got no further than Clairvaux. There he died. Bernard expressed what he called his special friendship with Malachy by always wearing Malachy's vestments when he celebrated Mass and was buried in them, electing interment alongside the Irishman whose spirituality he so admired and celebrated in hagiography and homily.

So far as the new diocesan system was concerned, Pope Eugenius III dispatched his legate Cardinal John Paparo to Ireland and it was finally adopted at the council of Kells in 1152. It integrated the Hiberno-Norse dioceses into an Irish hierarchy, severing the link with Canterbury, affirmed the primacy of the traditional see of St Patrick at Armagh, and established four ecclesiastical provinces and thirty-eight dioceses. With some adjustments, which the architects of the system had anticipated, it has endured to our own day.

In a country as politically volatile as mid-twelfth century Ireland, the harmonious implementation of this new constitutional structure was a considerable success for the reformers. It has been hailed by some historians as nothing less than an ecclesiastical revolution, and so at least potentially it was. But there was still much to be done. It was one thing to organise a hierarchy. It was another to put in place an infrastructure to make it fully operational – parishes, officials, and chapters. That these would follow there was no reason to doubt. We may glimpse the implementation process in the Dublin episcopate of Laurence O'Toole (1162-80; canonised by Pope Honorius III in 1225). Further, that a warning against overestimating the success of the reformers (certainly one of the defects of Bernard's *Life of Malachy*), is needed, comes as the later Middle Ages have been more closely scrutinised. It has become clear that many of the ills against which twelfth-century churchmen struggled remained characteristic features of Gaelic Ireland: clerical marriage, hereditary control of monasteries and benefices, and anachronistic laws, including those concerning marriage. Nevertheless, the Irish church had opened itself to the changing world of twelfth-century Christendom. In the first half of the twelfth century, a wind of change had blown through the practice of both episcopal jurisdiction and the religious life. It was no small achievement.

II

In the second half of the century, however, the wind of change grew to gale force. Ireland quite suddenly lost its political independence and passed under foreign rule. It became part of the Angevin Empire – that conglomerate of territories stretching from the Pyrenees to the farthest point of northern England, ruled over by Henry II. The kings of England became lords of Ireland. How this change came about is not here my primary concern. The ecclesiastical consequences that attended it and followed from it are of immediate relevance.

Henry II was in Ireland from October 1171 to April 1172. During those six months he brought under his control those of his subjects from England and Wales who were engaged in repairing their fortunes by acquiring territory and power in Ireland, took oaths of fealty from most of the leading Irish rulers and sowed the seeds of a permanent English, royal administration in Ireland. He also gave close attention to the Irish episcopate. One of his first acts on landing in Ireland had been to hold an extended meeting with the papal legate, the Cistercian bishop of Lismore. Bishop Christian, a leading reformer, had been one of the men Malachy had left with St Bernard at Clairvaux to be trained as a Cistercian and had been a member of the first Irish Cistercian community. He had been abbot of Mellifont from 1142 to 1150, bishop of Lismore from 1151 and papal legate since 1152. Henry II required him to preside over a national council, summoned to Cashel in 1172. It was a council which promulgated decrees in the established reforming tradition. But it was much more. For each bishop (and a majority of them attended) acknowledged with a document under his seal Henry's lordship of Ireland. They then testified to Pope Alexander III that they had done this, informing him (so the Pope was later to say) how much in Ireland remained to be done in order to bring the Irish people to the full observance of divine law. In turn they were told by the Pope to cooperate with Henry II, to respect what pertained to his royal dignity and to excommunicate those who rejected the allegiances to which they had sworn. This council of Cashel marked a turning-point in the history of the medieval church in Ireland. Ireland's new ruler had been unhesitatingly accepted by the Irish bishops and emphatically endorsed by the papacy. This papal validation of the English lordship was to hold good throughout the Middle Ages. Indeed it was strengthened in 1213 when King John, in acknowledging to Pope Innocent III that he held England as a papal fief, acknowledged also that he held Ireland as a fief of the papacy.

The thirteenth century saw the steady growth of an English colony in Ireland. Historians have used that word 'colony' in different ways at different times. I use it here as referring to a body of immigrants settling in a new country which came to form a community which remained firmly connected, politically, institutionally, psychologically, with its parent state. Briefly speaking, a smaller England grew up across the Irish sea. Yet English settlement in Ireland was rather more than a simple dispossession of much of the indigenous ruling class and its replacement by a new, foreign aristocracy. This had been the essential nature of the Norman Conquest of England under William I. English settlement brought to Ireland considerable numbers of people of all levels of society. Not simply a new, variegated ruling class but peasants, cultivators of the fertile land, especially of eastern Ireland, merchants and artisans. Such settlement developed plantation boroughs, a village network, walled towns and new ports to exploit Ireland's considerable river systems for trading purposes.

These demographic, social and economic developments were accompanied by the exportation from England of its law and its characteristic institutions of government, central and local. 'All the laws and customs which are observed in the realm of England,' it was said in one typical decree, 'should be observed in Ireland.' The emergence of a colonial parliament, a replica on a smaller scale of that of England, best characterises both how closely the legal and governmental institutions of the Irish colony were modelled on those of England, and also how the colony had developed its self-identity as a community. But it was not an independent community nor did it seek to be. Over all, the English Crown exercised its control: making ministerial appointments, exercising appellate jurisdiction, receiving petitions, imposing taxation and auditing accounts. Above all, it exploited the wealth and resources of its colony to the full, particularly to finance its wars on the Continent, in Wales and in Scotland and to supply its armies with men, food and equipment. All this was a process of anglicisation; it evolved steadily throughout the thirteenth century and is generally considered to have reached its peak in the reign of Edward I (1272-1307).

It is important, at this point, to appreciate that the English conquest of Ireland was only partial, since the English monarchy failed to bring the whole of the country under its effective jurisdiction. The English colony constituted only a part of the country. The anglicisation process was limited in its extent. Significant areas of Ireland escaped radical anglicisation and their rulers retained the substance of their authority. Partial conquest had created what may be best described as a 'two-nations' situation, one Gaelic, the other English. It is the relationship of these two nations – of the Irish living within the colony with their English rulers and the Irish living outside the colony's effective limits with their English neighbours – which forms the central theme of Irish medieval history, and not least of the history of the medieval church in Ireland.

There was a major ecclesiastical dimension to the anglicisation process. The most obvious evidence of it is to be found in the composition of the episcopate. The proportion of English bishops in the Irish hierarchy increased in the course of the thirteenth century. When in 1215 twenty bishops from Ireland attended Pope Innocent III's Fourth Lateran Council, six, possibly seven, of them were English. By the end of the century, roughly half of the episcopate was English, mostly from immigrant families (or Anglo-Irish as some historians choose to call them). Their geographical spread provides a major indicator of the regions where English settlement was most firmly established: the whole of the Dublin province with dioceses from other provinces contiguous with it – three dioceses of the Armagh province and five of the Cashel province. Tuam, the ecclesiastical province of Connacht in the west of the country, with seven of the Armagh sees, remained preponderantly Gaelic.

Each of the English dioceses underwent swift and radical change. Gerald of Wales, chief reporter of Henry II's council of Cashel, recorded that it was the intention that for the future the Irish church was to be guided into accepting the practices and customs of the church in England. And so in colonial Ireland it came to be. English models were widely introduced: parishes established with the spread of subinfeudation and manorialisation; an ecclesiastical officialdom introduced as diocesan infrastructure with ecclesiastical courts exercising the same jurisdiction as those in England; cathedral chapters were organised and cathedrals and monasteries built in

English styles by English masons. Further, the bishop became a territorial lord, his see endowed with estates, sometimes of substantial size, and administered by another set of English-type officials.

In church as in state, the royal government in England had a role to play. Into Ireland, English lordship introduced its own interpretation of the relationship between church and the civil power. So far as the appointment of bishops was concerned, English practice (which had many parallels elsewhere in feudal Europe) was based on the principle that the bishop had a twofold official capacity – he was bishop and baron, a member of both spiritual and temporal aristocracies. As bishop he was to be chosen by election by the cathedral chapter and his election and person approved by the metropolitan of his province. But the chapter was not allowed to proceed to elect until the royal government (either in Dublin or in Westminster) had been informed of the vacancy and issued its licence for the election to go ahead. This allowed the government to put forward any preferred candidate it might have – a bishopric to reward faithful royal service, for example. The procedure also allowed the government an opportunity to disallow a bishop-elect (for political unreliability, for example) by refusing to restore the temporalities to him and thus depriving him of his official income. By and large the system worked reasonably well in colonial Ireland. The papacy was there to settle disputed elections but the curia was rarely called on in that context. No doubt consideration of the distance from Rome and the expense of travel and conducting legal proceedings were a powerful inducement to find a solution at home.

Edward I made various attempts to extend this procedure into Gaelic Ireland but without much success. In general these dioceses made their own appointments without interference from English officialdom. Here dynastic pressures were of more significance in the making of bishops. In both nations the way bishops were chosen ensured that normally a prelate of the appropriate nationality was appointed. Nevertheless, there was a constant risk of discrimination against the clergy of the other nation. A particularly glaring example of it came early in the thirteenth century when the English government was trying to force the pace of anglicisation. Shortly after the death of King John in 1216, and in the minority of Henry III, England was ruled by a Regency in which the most powerful member was William Marshal who, as Lord of Leinster, was also the leading aristocrat in Ireland. In 1217 he wrote to the Justiciar, the head of the English administration in Ireland:

> We order you in virtue of the faith by which you are bound to us that you shall not allow any Irishman to be elected or promoted in any cathedral church in our land of Ireland since when they are appointed our land of Ireland is thereby disturbed.

This letter he followed up with another in which he added:

> With the advice of Henry lord archbishop of Dublin along with your own, you will by every means obtain that our clergy and other honourable Englishmen necessary to us and our kingdom be elected and promoted to bishoprics and dignities as they become vacant.

Pope Honorius III, learning of this attempt to exclude Irishmen, vigorously denounced such discrimination (*acceptio personarum* he called it after St Paul, Rom 2:11) as against divine law: 'There is no respect of persons with God.'

There were to be counter-claims that the Irish discriminated against the English. Innocent IV in 1250, in response to a complaint of Henry III, condemned the alleged attempt of Irish clergy to debar any Englishmen from being admitted into a canonry in any of their cathedral chapters. There is no doubt that this sort of discrimination became a feature of Irish church life. Examples of it occur in every period of the Middle Ages. It was particularly pronounced in the fourteenth century and its adoption as official English government policy was to receive its most formal articulation in the Statutes of Kilkenny (1366).

III

On 5 June 1368, a splendid wedding took place at the door of Milan Cathedral. It was between Violante, daughter of Galeazzo Visconti, the Lord of Pavia, and Lionel, duke of Clarence, third son of King Edward III of England. It was not, however, a union destined to change the course of Lombard history. Five months later Lionel died, the result it was said of an excess of feasting and revelry. Lionel, however, had already made his mark in Ireland, a mark which was to give him a very particular niche of notoriety in its history. The duke was, in right of his first wife, also earl of Ulster. In September 1361 he arrived in Ireland not only in that capacity, but more importantly, as king's lieutenant, at once 'military chief of the colony, head of its civil administration and its supreme judge'. He was to hold that office until November 1366.

Many governors had left England for Ireland in the fourteenth century and departed without making much impression on a country which, with the weakening of English control, was steadily lapsing into a war-torn, bedraggled, localised society of many frontiers. A primary reason for the decline of the English colony was the increasing obsession of the English Crown with its claim to the throne of France and consequent involvement in what was to come to be called the Hundred Years War. Duke Lionel's spell of governorship, however, fell during a lull in the Anglo-French hostilities following that truce of mutual exhaustion, the Treaty of Brétigny in 1360. Money, resources and leadership could now be diverted to the troubles of the English in Ireland whose complaints of neglect by the metropolitan government had been increasing in volume and frequency as the century wore on. It cannot be said that Lionel's five-year term of office did very much to achieve his professed aim of delivering security and good order to the English colonists. But it is one of his attempts to do so which has made him notorious in Irish history.

The Statutes passed in the colonial parliament summoned to Kilkenny for February 1366 aimed at achieving security for the colonists now increasingly pressurised by the Irish dwelling both inside and outside the English regions. The Statutes of Kilkenny would command the historians' attention for the comprehensiveness with which the vulnerability of the colony was analysed and solutions proposed for its security. But what has made the Statutes notorious is what one English historian has recently called their 'oppressively defensive racism'. It was a 'racism' born of a situation where English conquest and colonisation had run out of steam. It was alleged by English officialdom that there was a danger of the colonial population being assimilated into Irish culture. Thus the so-called 'racist' legislation had two aspects: one which insisted that only the English language be used in the colony, with the Irish language prohibited, and that its inhabitants be held in every other way to adhere to the English way of life. A second forbade any intimate contact between English and Irish – notably, intermarriage, the most important single factor contributing to assimilation. Two of the statutes attempting to sever contact between English and Irish concerned the church. Clause 13 decreed that 'no Irishman of the nations of the Irish should be admitted into any cathedral or collegiate church by provision, collation or presentation of anyone nor to any benefice of holy church amongst the English'. Clause 14 ordered that 'no religious house which is situate among the English shall henceforth receive any Irishmen to their profession'.

Were the Statutes of Kilkenny rigorously enforced? Every historian of the Middle Ages knows well how often the legislation of medieval rulers represents aspiration rather than implementation. How far, then, were these ecclesiastical clauses of the Statutes effective in practice? These questions are not easy to answer because of that relative shortage of source material endemic in the study of Irish medieval history. That some English ecclesiastical institutions were determined to observe the Statutes of Kilkenny and keep out native Irishmen is very clear. Thus the Augustinian canons of Christ Church and St Thomas the Martyr in Dublin, as well as the chapter of St Patrick's Cathedral, had regulations forbidding membership of these communities to Irishmen. And no doubt their example was followed elsewhere. However, it is also clear that often in practice the full severity of the legislation was modified. Numerous examples are known where Irishmen were permitted to accept benefices among the English and allowed to join religious communities in the English areas. Such access was conditional on their being granted what in modern terminology would be called English citizenship. They were, so to say, naturalised, so in this way a type of licensing system enforced the Statutes of Kilkenny. This permissive device as practised in ecclesiastical circles had contemporary parallels in the practice of the English colonial towns, which allowed Irishmen controlled entry as freemen, despite municipal and guild legislation which forbade them entry. Such accommodations were constant – an element of that partial assimilation of the two nations which accompanied the suspicion and hostility between them. Nevertheless, it must not be forgotten that it was that hostility, and the institutionalised 'racism' which was both its cause and effect, which created the circumstances in which the pastoral ministry inevitably found itself shackled. A church which suffered discrimination was a damaged church.

When the sad story of such discrimination is reviewed and the unhappy evidence of deep antagonism between the Irish and English nations within the church assessed, it might readily be concluded that the history of the church in medieval Ireland is the progressive revelation of the unbridgeable nature of the division and a story of a permanent confrontation and mutual hatred between the two nations. Certainly there was confrontation and mistrust but that is not quite the whole story. The reality is more complex. The whole story must take into account the times when a harmonious *modus vivendi* was achieved, when the interaction of the nations was less than hostile. Both the negative and positive aspects of the interrelationships need attention. Let me select one major religious movement and try to show how both integration of the two cultures and the reality of discrimination actually worked. The major religious movement I select is the history of the mendicant friars.

IV

The introduction of the friars into Ireland was unquestionably one of the most fruitful of all the ways by which Ireland, in fulfilment of the aim of the original twelfth-century reformers, was opened to the full flood of the spiritual renewal which the universal church shared. Very broadly speaking the friars came to Ireland in two waves: Dominicans and Franciscans mostly in the thirteenth century; Carmelites and Augustinians in the later decades of the thirteenth century and especially in the first decades of the fourteenth. By around 1340 there were eighty-six houses of friars: thirty-three Franciscan, twenty-six Dominican, sixteen Carmelite and eleven Augustinian. In each of the Orders, the first friars came from England, they established themselves first in the colonial towns and each remained constitutionally linked to the parent English province, though in different degrees of dependence. But the really significant feature of this influx of apostolic men was how speedily they spread beyond the English colony into Gaelic Ireland and how together both nations were opened to that new approach to evangelisation characteristic of the first heroic age of the mendicant movement.

Within half a century of the Dominicans arriving in Dublin in 1224, twenty-three priories had been established. In at least six of them, Irish rulers and bishops were involved either as founders or patrons. Seven of the dioceses in the Gaelic areas chose Dominicans as their bishops in the thirteenth century. The studia of the Order outside Ireland were open to those qualified for higher study. There is nothing to suggest that ethnic divisions had become obstacles to progress. The evidence points to a successful transcendence of ethnic antagonism. As with the Dominicans, the popularity of the Franciscans in the colonial towns was immediate and widespread. And they, too, rapidly spread into Gaelic Ireland, with a number of houses established which owed little or nothing to the English colonists. Franciscans became bishops in both Gaelic and English sees. That these were houses of mixed composition is clear from the career of Thomas O'Quin who earned a reputation as a preacher especially in Connacht (where he would preach in Irish). Thomas had been a member of the Franciscan house in Drogheda, one of the most English towns in Ireland and had been its guardian or superior.

However, the integration between the nations, of which O'Quin's career is an example, was not to last. There appeared chronicle reports that at a general chapter of the Franciscans held at Cork in 1291, blood was spilt in a clash between Irish and English members of the province. The reports are not contemporary; they come from an external source and remain unsubstantiated in any Franciscan or Irish source. But whatever about the bloodshed (and the reports claim sixteen friars were killed in the clash), from the first decades of the fourteenth century trustworthy accounts of strife between English and Irish Franciscans survive. The chronicler John Clyn recorded that there was trouble throughout almost the whole Minorite community in Ireland, 'each one,' said Clyn, 'taking the side of his own nation while others were ambitious for promotion to prelacies and higher offices'.

The malaise within the Franciscans was brought to the notice both of Pope John XXII and of the Minister-General, Michael of Cesena. The Pope appointed judges-delegate to investigate the conduct of the Franciscan community and their work was supported by two *visitatores* appointed by the Minister-General. Their recommendations were promulgated in a general chapter held in Dublin in April 1324. Eight houses were named where it was claimed sufficient evidence had been provided to the judges-delegate (who were all English) that friars of the Irish nation had been acting in a way that 'constituted a danger both to the peace of the king and the general welfare of the whole community'. Some disciplinary measures against such friars were ordered. The main recommendation was that all communities should be mixed, composed of friars from both nations: 'for the greater peace and tranquillity of this country', the decree stated, 'we will and command that some English friars shall be members of communities in all places of pure Irishmen just as conversely Irish friars should be distributed among the English'. It is to be feared that either this decree was ignored or it was tried and found unworkable. The conclusion to be drawn from this whole episode must be that the first fine surge of Franciscan evangelisation in Ireland had come to grief through the acrimony of national distrust and enmity.

There was, however, to be a second part to the influence of the friars. For the fifteenth century saw a reform and renewal in all four Mendicant Orders, marked by new foundations as some ninety new houses were established in the late medieval period. A high proportion of these were in the Gaelic areas of Connacht and Ulster; nine of the ten new Dominican houses, for example, had Gaelic founders. Another part of the renewal was the adoption in Ireland of that reform affecting all four orders in Europe generally: the Observant movement. In Ireland, the Observance was particularly strong among the Augustinian friars and from the Gaelic areas it spread to such major colonial towns as Dublin and Drogheda.

It was, however, the Franciscans who made the biggest impact: in the number of new foundations, in the considerable expansion of its Third Order and in the progress of its Observant reform. Again, it was in Gaelic Ireland that the different elements in Franciscan renewal developed their momentum. The Conventual Franciscans acquired their first native Irish minister-general in 1445. The Observant Franciscans had their autonomy confirmed by Pope Pius II in 1460 and thereafter their heads were likewise from Gaelic Ireland. It was very characteristic of the Franciscan Observants that their continental links remained strong. It was no less characteristic that the Observants gradually won over the majority of the Franciscan houses, including the Anglo-Irish ones. It was a victory for the restored integration of the Order. It fortified the Order for its determined resistance to the changes sought by Henry VIII at the Reformation and for its outstanding leadership in the Counter-Reformation.

V

This essay has swept through some four centuries of Irish history. No doubt my ambition has outreached my ability to communicate clearly the essentials of my interpretation of this period. Yet a case can be made that, at least initially, the Irish church continued to evolve along lines the reformers had pioneered: the pace of diocesan reconstruction accelerated; the foundation of religious houses multiplied; councils continued to press for closer observance of canon law, enhanced clerical discipline and an improved pastoral ministry. But if the papacy, and the Irish episcopate with it, in validating the English lordship hoped that it would achieve a degree of political stability in which alone reform would progress, their expectation was not fulfilled. The abundant evidence of discrimination and mutual hostility makes it clear that a new unsettling element had been added to the endemic instability of Irish politics.

Are we then to conclude that Ireland developed into a land of two adversarial, non-communicating churches, one of the Irish nation and one of the English nation? I think not. That there were differences between the two because of their different cultures and social organisation can hardly be denied. Nor can it be denied that the two communities never achieved that integration which alone would have brought lasting peace. Nor can it be denied that, on occasions, discrimination between the two nations reached scandalous proportions. Nevertheless there was no duality in Christian essentials: in the faith professed, in its sacraments administered, in the liturgy practised, in acknowledgement of the authority of the See of Peter and common membership of the universal church. And there was no lack of leadership seeking a *modus vivendi* in common Christian purpose. I believe this was achieved to a degree which strengthened the Irish church when the great challenge of Protestantism came to be met.

CHAPTER FIVE

Lay female piety and church patronage in late medieval Ireland

Mary Ann Lyons

Lay men and women in late medieval Ireland, as elsewhere in Europe, participated in a vibrant culture of popular piety. Comprising an array of old and new rituals, rites, feast days, pilgrimages, confraternities, miracle plays, processions and devotions, this culture at once addressed the spiritual and social needs of lay members of the church. Like all Christians, the laity in Ireland were concerned with maximising their prospects of salvation and demonstrated a strong desire to harness new channels for expressing pious sentiment, most notably through their foundation of lay confraternities, churches and monastic houses in the fifteenth and early sixteenth centuries.[1] In essence, all women and men in Ireland, regardless of their ethnic or social origins, subscribed to the same set of religious beliefs and practices. This chapter focuses specifically on the role played by one section of the laity, namely wealthy lay women, in the church in both Gaelic and colonial areas of Ireland in the pre-Reformation era. The nature of their religious beliefs, pious practices, church patronage, funeral customs and attitudes towards death and salvation will be explored.

Sources for the study of female piety and church patronage in late medieval Ireland are scarce and those that have survived offer limited insights. In the case of Gaelic women, one is obliged to rely heavily on the work of annalists, rare manuscripts such as Máire Ó Máille's 'book of piety' (1513-14), and fragmentary remains of funerary monuments and monastic records. Consequently, the coterie of Gaelic women under study is very small, being restricted to members of leading aristocratic dynasties who had the resources to commission such texts and tombs. The absence of a body of wills militates against a study of the nature of post-obit bequests made by Gaelic women. The material for colonial women is only marginally better in terms of quality and quantity, with wills, funerary monuments, cathedral, estate and monastic record collections being the most fruitful sources. In all, less than thirty wills of women who were mainly resident in Co Dublin between the 1450s and 1480s have been uncovered for the purposes of this study. These women were drawn from various social strata, ranging from the gentry to farming stock and cannot therefore be readily compared with

Gaelic aristocratic women in respect of pious observance and church patronage. In addition, a sizeable amount of the surviving material in cathedral and estate collections pertains to post-obit provisions made by women in the colony. Consequently, the sample is restricted to Dublin-based women of means and the sources are more informative concerning the provisions that these women made for the remembrance of their souls after their deaths than they are in respect of their pious observance and church patronage during their lifetimes. These limitations notwithstanding, similarities and variations in the pious practices of women from both Gaelic and colonial areas of the island will be highlighted at apposite junctures throughout this chapter.

I

It was commonly believed in late medieval western European society that women were, in the main, more profoundly religious than men, their emotional nature leaving them particularly inclined to mercy, pity, compassion, piety and devotion. Renaissance theorists admitted to few areas where the female sex excelled the male but a significant number of scholars acknowledged that devotion, prayer and church attendance was one such area.[2] Clerics throughout Europe preached the virtues of a noblewoman's disciplined lifestyle of prayer, abstinence, hospitality and charity.[3] In Norman Ireland, women were praised for their civilising influence on society, and in the fifteenth and early sixteenth centuries, Gaelic annalists frequently singled out the piety of Gaelic noblewomen as one of their most praiseworthy traits.[4] Piety is represented in almost formulaic terms as a quality that complemented their other virtues of hospitality, patronage of the learned class, charity to the poor, and their humanity.[5]

Their pious observance and church patronage addressed the intertwined social and spiritual needs of these women themselves and of the wider community. In a society in which the majority of noblewomen had very limited influence over political affairs, religious observance and church patronage represented the most important of the few acceptable alternative channels through which they could assert independent authority and initiative. Both were crucial outlets for women to demonstrate publicly their fulfilment of the prescribed obligations of a noblewoman, in the process enhancing their standing in society. The subordinate role of onlooker played by Calvagh Mór Ó Conchobhair Failghe, lord of Offaly, while his wife, Maighréad (d. 1451) led a procession to their parish church one feast of Da Sinchell is emblematic of the inversion of gender authority roles that characterised church patronage in pre-Reformation Gaelic society. Religious observance also fulfilled the important function of affording Gaelic noblewomen acceptable reasons to break free of strictures that normally governed their behaviour; for example, pilgrimages offered one of the few acceptable excuses for women such as Maighréad, wife of Ó Conchobhair Failghe, to travel beyond their patrimonies.[6]

In the case of certain religious ceremonies in Gaelic society, notably funerals, women were invested with distinctive roles, which at once addressed the spiritual and social needs of their congregations. It was the remit of Gaelic 'keeners' to express the entire community's lament for the loss of the noble man or woman, and also its members' reluctance to accept the final separation of the deceased from a congregation. Richard Stanihurst, the sixteenth-century Old-English historian, described the antics of these 'keeners' in the following account:

> [they] shout dolefully through swollen cheeks, they cast off their necklaces, they bare their heads, they tear their hair, they beat their brows, they excite emotions on all sides, they spread their palms, they raise their hands to the heavens, they shake the coffin, tear open the shroud, embrace and kiss the corpse and scarcely allow the burial to take place.[7]

Apart from the tradition of 'keeners', in terms of their pious observance Gaelic noblewomen adhered to the same practices and appear to have shared the same beliefs as their contemporaries in the English colony in Ireland and their peers in English and western European society. They expressed those beliefs through the conventional channels of attending religious ceremonies, performing good works, founding and endowing churches and monasteries, bestowing gifts on clerics and religious, making charitable donations to the poor and the sick, joining convent communities, and making provisions for the cure of their souls after their deaths.

As Christians were expected to give practical expression to their religious devotion through good works, and driven by the belief that charity was operative in both the present world and in the afterlife, Gaelic noblewomen partially fulfilled their pious obligations by performing corporal works of mercy.[8] These typically took the form of generous hospitality and almsgiving to the poor and to orphans and the bestowal of patronage on those religious who sought their assistance. More munificent benefactors of the poor met their obligations of penance and of charity by combining large, impersonal benefactions with donations to individuals with whom they came into direct contact.[9] Donors do not appear to have differentiated between pious and charitable donations. Certain women excelled in their demonstration of Christian piety and charity, making independent donations of alms to the poor and publicly patronising the clergy. Their benevolence was celebrated in the annalists' commendation of them as renowned among contemporaries for their generosity and piety.[10]

Significantly, while Gaelic noblewomen appear to have subscribed to the commonly held belief that their largesse ought to reach as many beneficiaries as possible for the good of their souls, they showed little interest in drawing distinctions between recipients of the alms they distributed. Maighréad (d. 1512/13), daughter of Conchobhar Ó Briain and wife of Eóghan Ó Ruairc, was acclaimed by annalists for her humanity and charitable entertainment of 'the weak and the wretched and all, whether mighty or outcast, who stood in need thereof'. Her generosity of spirit earned her a reputation as 'one who never as long as she lived denied any man craving a boon'.[11] Similarly, Mór (d. 1527), daughter of Maelsechlainn MacCába and wife of Ó hAinlige, was hailed as a woman of 'good repute ... piety and virtue, the bestower of alms and charitable gifts of food and clothing to God's poor and needy and to all who stood in need thereof'.[12] By contrast, in late medieval London, alms were generally only distributed among those deemed the 'deserving poor'.[13]

It was usual for Gaelic noblewomen acting in their own right to include local clergy and religious, as well as churches and monasteries, among the many beneficiaries of their patronage in order that it might increase their chances of attaining salvation. Gormlaith (d. 1524), daughter of Aodh Ó Domhnaill, and wife of Aodh Ó Néill, was typical in that she sponsored religious orders and churches alongside the literary and learned professions.[14] Like their peers in the colony, many Gaelic noblewomen were responsible for more than one major donation to a monastic community or a church of their choice and frequently donated furnishing or funds to meet the cost of repairs to churches in their locality. Consequently, their patronage is often acknowledged in figures of women carved in stone, wearing secular costumes, which feature prominently above doorways of churches.[15] Wealthy women in conjunction with their husbands also commissioned pieces of church furnishings; for example, in the fifteenth century, Cornelius, son of Seán Ó Conchubhair, head of his sept, and his wife, Eibhlín, employed a smith to create a silver gilt processional cross found at Ballymacasey in Co Kerry.[16]

Given that there were many areas of Gaelic Ireland in which the laity did not have access to parish churches for worship, monastic communities fulfilled an important role in ministering to the local population. It was therefore usual for noble men and women to cultivate close associations with particular religious orders of which they became generous sponsors. A handful of wealthy women were personally responsible for the foundation of religious houses. Bibiana, wife of Molrony Ó Cearbhaill, lord of Ely, founded the Franciscan friary at Roscrea, Co Tipperary, c.1490.[17] It was in response to a request made by Richard Nangle, an Augustinian friar, that Margaret Athy, wife of a mayor of Galway, initiated the construction of an Augustinian friary at Galway c.1500.[18] Similarly, Maighréad (d. 1512/13), daughter of Conchobhar Ó Briain and wife of Eóghan Ó Ruairc, sponsored the construction of a wooden church for the friars of the Observant Franciscan friary at Dromahair in Co Leitrim that she and her husband had founded.[19]

However, it was more usually in their capacity as the wives or mothers of noblemen that Gaelic women were instrumental in initiating such grand patronage schemes, though the motivation of both parties appears to have been the same.[20] Aodh Ruadh Ó Domhnaill's mother, Nuala, and his wife, Fionnuala, urged him to establish the Observant Franciscan friary at Donegal in the 1470s. Together, Edmund MacCostello and his wife, Fionnuala, founded St Thomas' Dominican priory at Urlaur in Co Mayo in the early 1430s.[21] Such was the strength of the ties between some Gaelic families and religious communities that several Gaelic noblewomen joined their preferred order and were interred in the community's church or cemetery. Fionnuala, daughter of Conchobhar Ó Briain (d. 1528), spent twenty-one years as a sister of the Franciscan Order 'practising piety and charity and good works'.[22] More generally, Gaelic noblewomen demonstrated their associations with religious houses through ongoing financial support, frequenting the churches of those houses for Mass and other religious rites, and perhaps most telling of all, through their electing to be buried within the monastery's church or cemetery. Undoubtedly while several of these women were, in part, driven by a desire to provide for the increase of divine service for their fellow parishioners,[23] they were ultimately inspired by one basic concern, the good of their souls.[24] In an era when a good death was seen as a reflection of a good life and a promise of eternal reward, annalists stressed that Gaelic aristocratic women who had been pious, hospitable and humane during their lives died 'with victory of unction and penance' and were 'honourably' interred.[25]

Securing a suitable burial place for oneself and one's descendants was, therefore, uppermost in the minds of all women and men in this era, both for spiritual and social reasons. Mendicant spirituality held a particular appeal for women in fifteenth-century western Europe, and Gaelic noblewomen were no exception. Interment in a friary was believed to offer several important advantages over burial in one's own parish. The constant presence of the friars near the deceased patron's tomb and the body's proximity to the altar were regarded as beneficial to the soul in purgatory. Moreover, the notion that intercession was more efficacious when entrusted to the extremely specialised group of professed religious (particularly the Franciscans) and the separation of the deceased's body from the rest of the secular community held strong appeal.[26] From the surviving fragmentary evidence it is clear that many of the leading noblewomen of Ulster and north Connacht in the pre-Reformation era, like their peers in England, had a particular preference for honourable interment in monastic houses, and more specifically, Franciscan friaries.[27] The friary at Elphin was the resting-place of Sadhbh[28] (d. 1447), daughter of William FitzConnor MacBranan, and wife of Maoilín Ó Maoil Chonaire, and also of Mor[29] (d. 1527), daughter of Maelsechlainn MacCába, and wife of Ó hAinlige. Aristocratic women, including Catríona, daughter of Ó Duibhgeannáin (d. 1525), Judith (d. 1535), daughter of Conn Ó Néill and wife of Mánus Ó Domhnaill, and Maighréad (d. 1498), daughter of Mág Uidhir and wife of Gilbert Ó Flanagáin of Tuath-ratha, requested that they be buried in the Franciscan monastery in Donegal.[30] Their opting to be interred at the monastery of the Franciscan Observants reflected these women's growing preference for more austere orders, a trend that was also manifest among their peers in contemporary London.[31] Indeed, lay attachment to a particular order could override parochial affiliations as evidenced by the case of Maighréad and Gilbert Ó Flanagáin of Tuath-ratha, both of whom chose burial at the Franciscan monastery in Donegal, despite their having built a church at Aghamore, Co Fermanagh.[32]

Gaelic noblewomen often went to considerable lengths to ensure that they died in a state of optimal grace and that they were interred in monastic churches or adjoining cemeteries. Many female benefactors, usually widows, retired to the religious houses that they had endowed and lived there for several years before their deaths. As an elderly woman, Gormlaith (d. 1437), daughter of Dáithi Ó Duibhgeannáin and wife of Brian MacAedacain, embraced a powerful element in medieval piety, namely the idealisation of renouncing the world, by electing to become a hermit. Following her death, she was buried in the monastery of the Premonstratension house on Trinity Island, Lough Key, Co Roscommon.[33] Fionnuala, daughter of Calvagh Mór Ó Conchobhair Failghe, lord of Offaly, and of Maighréad (d. 1451), on the death of her second husband, Aodh Ó Néill, 'assumed the yoke of piety and devotion'. She spent the remaining forty-nine years of her life living 'chastely, honourably, piously, and religiously' as a member of the monastic community at Killaichy, Co Offaly.[34] Undoubtedly women of such social standing were warmly received by the religious orders, particularly as the community stood to receive all or part of their substantial possessions. Ailbhe, daughter of Aodh Mág Uidhir, for instance, on joining the Augustinian monastery at Lisgoole, Co Fermanagh just one year before her death in 1476, donated all of her property to that community.[35]

Familial attachments with certain houses also determined the choice of burial place for some women such as Máire Ó Máille (d. 1522/3) daughter of Eóghan Ó Máille and wife of Eóghan Ruadh MacSuibhne of Donegal. Her decision to be interred in the church of Rathmullen priory was inspired by the fact that her son, Ruaidhrí, who predeceased his parents, was buried there.[36] Burial patterns also suggest the assimilation of Gaelic noblewomen into their husband's kin as they were usually buried with their husbands.[37] It is clear that the interment of members of the laity, and particularly patrons, within the precincts of monastic houses constituted a form of inverse patronage from the religious community to local society. In the cases of both female and male patrons, their burial represented a 'gift-exchange', often marking the culmination of a succession of gifts made to the community during the patrons' lifetime and serving to enhance the status of that house.[38]

Gaelic noblewomen were acutely sensitive to the importance of the message that their tombs conveyed to the congregations of the churches in which they were interred. A minority of women commissioned elaborate tombs for their spouses and families and on the basis of the surviving evidence, no expense appears to have been spared in erecting monuments of impressive scale as befitted the deceased's elevated social status. Around 1470 Mór Ní Bhriain commissioned a tomb for her husband, Terence Mac Mathghamhna, at Corcomroe Abbey, Co Clare. The sculptor she employed was evidently highly qualified and familiar with the decorative styles and themes that were in vogue outside of Ireland. He is believed to have drawn inspiration from the Nottingham school of alabaster tables, and his Passion series on the MacMathghamhna tomb bears striking resemblance in arrangement and disposition to altarpieces in contemporary Britain and France. The vitality of the cult of St Thomas of Canterbury in Gaelic Ireland is also displayed in representations of the saint and of the head of St John the Baptist (with whom St Thomas was closely associated).[39]

Two Gaelic noblewomen in late medieval Ireland excelled in church patronage and in their pious observance. Independent of her husband, Maighréad, wife of Calvagh Mór Ó Conchobhair Failghe, lord of Offaly, was a particularly generous benefactor of the poor, the clergy, and scholars.[40] Consequently, the annalist records her death in 1451 as having been lamented by 'religious persons ... [the] mendicant or poor orders, and ... all manner and sorts of the poor in Ireland'.[41] She was also exceptionally generous in funding the construction of churches and like many wealthy women in continental Europe, she paid for the construction of several bridges, which was deemed a legitimate act of charity since the church was responsible for such building operations.[42] As was the norm for Gaelic and English women of her rank, Maighréad monitored closely the material needs of churches in her locality, supplying them with missals, chalices, and 'all manner of things profitable to serve God and her soul'.[43] Maighréad clearly prided herself on her reputation as an hospitable host and pious patron and regarded her benefactions as essentially public demonstrations of her piety. This was best exemplified during a celebration hosted by her at her residence at Killeigh, Co Offaly, one feast of Da Sinchell (26 March). Before her 2700 invited guests, and amidst much pomp and ceremony, she proceeded up to the altar of the church of Dasinchell, which was adorned with cloth of gold, and in full view of the assembly, donated two gold chalices as offerings and arranged for two young orphans to be fostered.[44]

Máire Ó Máille, wife of Eóghan Ruadh MacSuibhne, was also acclaimed in her own right as a pious noblewoman and a munificent benefactor of the church and of scholars. She was said by the MacSuibhne family's genealogist to have been 'the most generous and the best mother, and the woman of most fame in regard to faith and piety of all who lived in her time'. Máire had a particular fondness for the friars and independently founded the Carmelite priory of St Mary's at Rathmullen, Co Donegal in 1516.[45] She also extended her church patronage beyond her immediate orbit, initiating the construction of a great hall for the Friars Minor at Donegal and several churches in the provinces of Ulster and Connacht. Like her husband, she died in the habit of the Carmelite friars in their monastery at Rathmullen and is buried alongside him and their son, Ruaidhrí, in the friars' church.[46] Máire Ó Máille is one of the few Gaelic noblewomen about whose pious devotions some insights can be gleaned.[47] She is reputed to have heard Mass once daily, sometimes more. Three days a week she fasted, consuming only bread and water, and also observed the Lenten, winter and Twelve Golden Fridays fasts. In addition, Máire was responsible for employing a scribe, Ciothruadh Mag Fhionnghaill who worked in her home at Rathmullen during 1513-14 compiling a manuscript 'book of piety' featuring transcripts of mid-fifteenth-century texts. This manuscript provides valuable insights into the devotional literature that was at the disposal of literate Gaelic noblewomen in fifteenth and early sixteenth-century Ulster. Given that Máire commissioned the 'book', an examination of its composition illuminates some of her pious beliefs and practices. We find that she had a particular devotion to Saints Catherine and Margaret, both of whom were very popular with Gaelic and colonial lay women in this era. She also had an affinity with two saints who had close associations with Donegal, namely Colmcille and Patrick. The importance of local devotional practices is also evident in the inclusion of two passages on the pilgrimage site of St Patrick's Purgatory with which Máire was undoubtedly familiar.

Her reading material comprised a mixture of devotional and prescriptive passages. The manuscript contains texts on spiritual death and Christ's infancy, stories concerning characters in both the Old and New Testaments, a treatise on the Blessed Eucharist, a copy of the gospel of Nicodemus, a version of the vision of Paul, and verses on the invocation of certain angels. Significant proportions of the texts focus on Christ's passion and offered Máire practical guidance in relation to the proper practice of her faith. These include passages detailing favours received by the hearer of Mass, the conditions necessary for a good confession and a general confession of sins, both mortal and venial. Others relate to the Twelve Golden Fridays, which Máire is known to have observed. The 'book of piety' also features lists designed to keep the reader on a straight path to salvation. These itemise three reasons why God shortens the sinner's life; four things which prevent holiness; three things which lead to heaven and three which lead to hell, three reasons why one should trust in God and three why one should despise the world. Words of advice to the pious, maxims for holy living, passages on hypocrisy and a parable about a woman who was in the habit of using bad language are also featured. In addition, the 'book' contains an indulgence of Clement V (1305-14), granted for the reading or hearing of St John's gospel, and another of Urban V (1362-70), though it is significant that the manuscript features none of a more recent date. While reading her 'book of piety', Máire was obliged to pray for the souls of the scribe and his wives, and was assured that she would gain salvation for herself and three people to whom she was closest.[48]

II

In late medieval Ireland, aristocratic and gentle women among the colonial community sought outlets for expressing values that all noblewomen of the time were expected to possess, the most important being hospitality, generosity, virtue and piety. Eleanor MacCarthy Reagh, for example, was acclaimed in Raphael Holinshed's chronicle as 'a paragon of liberality and kindness, in all her actions virtuous and godly'.[49] Although there is no evidence of colonial noblewomen hosting great feasts similar to those of their Gaelic counterparts, figures such as the wives of the earls of Kildare extended hospitality to clerics, poets and musicians who visited their homes. As in Gaelic Ireland, the church was one of several beneficiaries of patronage bestowed by women of that rank.[50] Their motives for church patronage were the standard ones of optimising their prospects of salvation, enhancing the existing provisions for the 'increase of divine service', and legitimating and reminding others of their privileged position in society. The channels through which noblewomen, gentle women, merchant citizens and farmers within the colonial community expressed pious sentiment by and large resembled those of their Gaelic and west European counterparts. The wives of the colony's leading aristocrats and particularly wealthy gentlemen were co-founders and generous patrons of monasteries, churches and cathedrals in their localities. More generally, the women of the colony, whether of modest or substantial means, were generous alms-givers and sponsors of priests and religious both during their lives and following their deaths.

A small number of particularly wealthy aristocratic and gentle women of the colony, together with their husbands, founded monastic houses and churches.

In line with the trend in Gaelic areas and in England, these patrons displayed a particular attachment to the mendicant orders and specifically the more austere orders of Observants. For instance, Edmund Butler and his wife initiated proceedings in the early 1460s for establishing the Augustinian friary at Callan in Kilkenny which became the centre of the order's Irish Observant Congregation.[51] Johanna Fitzgerald (d. 1486) and her husband, Thomas, seventh earl of Kildare, founded the church of St Michael Archangel of the Friars Minor at Adare, Co Limerick in 1464,[52] while the Franciscan Third Order Regular house at Slane, Co Meath (est. pre-1512) owed its foundation to Elizabeth Stuckly and her husband, Christopher Fleming.[53] However, in contrast to their Gaelic peers, there is little evidence of these noblewomen engaging in independent large-scale sponsorship of churches and monastic houses. Instead, it was usually in their capacity as wives that they were involved in granting land and other patronage to monastic houses.[54] As in Gaelic areas of Ireland, close associations between aristocratic and gentry families of the colony and religious communities in their vicinity inspired many women to spend their lives as members of those communities. The practice of widows joining monasteries in which they ultimately died and were buried was also common in colonial areas: Ellina Butler, a member of the noble family in Kilkenny, entered the convent at Killayhyn in the diocese of Ossory prior to 1478 following the death of her husband.[55]

Albeit fragmentary, surviving evidence points to the existence of a vibrant popular pious culture in the colony on the eve of the Reformation. Important elements in that culture were confraternities and guilds. Admission usually extended to aristocratic and gentle women in their capacity as wives rather than as individuals. Guilds were for the spiritual benefit of the members whose souls were prayed for in perpetuity by guild chaplains. In addition to their spiritual functions these bodies engaged in charitable enterprises, including the provision of education and relief, and provided women with an acceptable social outlet. In the fifteenth century several religious guilds were founded in Dublin. Down to the 1530s women featured prominently in the confraternity of the Holy Trinity, Christ Church Cathedral, Dublin, and the guild of St Anne at St Audoen's Church, Dublin, founded in 1430, also had several female members. Aristocratic women also became members of confraternities overseas. Egida Butler, along with her husband, Edmund, was admitted into the Confraternity of Scala Caeli in Rome by Angelus, abbot of St Anastasius, in 1460. Sadhbh Kavanagh was admitted into the Confraternity of the Hospital of the Holy Spirit in Saxia in Rome by Rory, abbot of Mothel and general proctor of Ireland in 1501, presumably on the strength of her status as widow of Sir James Butler. That privilege was also extended in 1509 to Lady Margaret Butler and her husband, Sir Piers who

joined the Confraternity of the Convent of Osenet, near Oxford, at the invitation of the abbot and convent community. In the case of women who were
not members of confraternities but whose male relatives were, the blessings
of the confraternities were extended to them and their children, and a general commemoration of parents and benefactors was held once every year.[56]

While very little is known about the devotional literature in circulation in
late medieval Ireland, literate women had access to a range of devotional and
religious literature in their husbands' private libraries.[57] In Maynooth Castle,
Elizabeth Zouche, first wife of the ninth earl of Kildare and 'a woman of rare
probity of mind', had at her disposal one of the finest library collections in
Ireland which included copies of the Bible, the psalter of Cashel, prophesies
of St Berehan, lives of the saints, and works of St Anthony, St Gregory, St
Jerome and St Augustine. Beyond this, however, we are afforded only glimpses
of the more intimate manifestations of the pious sentiment of colonial
women in the way of holy water pots in their homes and their wearing of
pieces of jewellery displaying the crucifix.[58]

In an era of 'luxuriant flourishing of devotion to saints', colonial women
of all ranks subscribed to the widely held belief that their preferred saint
would protect them and their community in life and death if duly honoured.[59] The designs of the tombs of several of the colony's wealthiest women
also testify to their strong belief in the collective power of the apostles and
the saints to protect them in death and to intercede for their salvation. The
funerary monuments of Maud Plunket at Malahide (c. 1450), Joan Cusack at
Killeen, Co Meath (c. 1450), Anne Plunket at Howth (c.1462), Marion Cruise
at Rathmore, Co Meath (1471), Margaret Janico at Kilcullen, Co Kildare
(1496), Ellen Butler at Clonmel, Co Tipperary (c. 1530-40) and Margaret
Fitzgerald at Kilkenny (c. 1539) all feature sculptures of the deceased's
favourite saints and conform to contemporary style in their heavy emphasis
on Christ's crucifixion.[60] The array of saints on these women's tombs represents the extended family of heaven, bound together by their sainthood and
mirroring the bonds of lordship on earth. The women's effigies were designed
to console their living relatives and the wider community through the depiction of the deceased in a state of suspended animation between the earthly
and the heavenly worlds. Carvings of those saints to whose care the living
community entrusted their souls were aimed at inculcating a belief that these
deceased women passed from an earthly, extended family network to another,
celestial family.[61] While Christians throughout the whole of Europe honoured female saints, women were more enthusiastic in their loyalty to them.
In Ireland, both Gaelic and colonial women displayed a particular devotion
to the Blessed Virgin Mary, Saint Catherine, and to a lesser extent, Saint
Margaret of Antioch.[62] The belief of some women in the superior interces-

sional powers of female saints is especially evident in the case of certain widows and vowesses whose tombs feature a greater number of female than male saints.[63]

Like their menfolk, colonial women expressed their devotion to particular saints by paying for candles to be burned before statues of saints both during their lifetimes and after their deaths. They venerated relics, attended devotions and some went on pilgrimages. Invariably they bequeathed their souls to God, the Blessed Virgin Mary and 'all the saints' and expressed their wish to be buried in chapels named after particular saints or in close proximity to a statue of their preferred saint in a church. For instance, in 1473 Jenet Cristor, wife of a small farmer, requested that she be buried before the image of St Mary in the nave of the parish church at Glasnevin. Frequently testators left chalices, towels and robes as gifts to be placed near statues of their favourite saints. In her will dated 1472 Alice Cassells of Lusk, wife of a small farmer, exhibited her particular devotion to the Virgin Mary by leaving a robe to adorn the statue of Mary in the chapel of St Maurus in her parish church. Dame Margaret Nugent, wife of Sir Thomas Newbery, who was mayor of Dublin on several occasions, had a strong devotion to the Virgin Mary. In her will, dated 1474, she specified that her surplus possessions were to be donated to St Mary's chapel in St Michan's parish church in Dublin where she was to be buried. Her money was to be spent on ornaments or other items that might be needed for that chapel.[64]

Women in colonial areas shared the general intense preoccupation with ensuring that they would 'die well' and, like their counterparts in England, they demonstrated greater concern about making specific burial provisions than did lay men.[65] In their lifetimes they sponsored the installation of ornamental widows and donated money towards the erection of belfries in local churches and cathedrals in the belief that these would serve as constant reminders to the congregation to pray for their souls after their deaths.[66] In return for their generosity, they were assured of being remembered in the special prayers of remembrance offered by the congregation on feast days and on the anniversaries of their deaths.[67] The few surviving wills of gentle women, spouses and relatives of merchant citizens and farmers in Dublin archdiocese in the late fifteenth century show that even women of modest means made arrangements for their funeral ceremonies and for remembrance of their souls among their communities prior to their death in order to maximise their prospects of salvation. These wills indicate strong similarities in the pious beliefs of women in colonial areas and their counterparts in parishes throughout England. They also shed light on colonial women's beliefs about the most effective means of gaining salvation, and their perception of the contribution of the clergy, both secular and regular, to their achievement of that goal.[68]

The laity in late medieval Ireland were convinced that the manner of one's burial was directly related to one's prospect of salvation. Not surprisingly, therefore, down to the early sixteenth century, women in the colonial districts of Ireland made very specific provision for the format of their funeral service and for the adornment of the church in order that their obsequies might maximise their chances of securing salvation. Convinced that a large number of clergy officiating at a funeral service increased one's chances of salvation, several women of means were prompted to provide for specific numbers of priests and clerks to officiate. Hence, in the early 1470s we find Alice Bennet of Santry, a small farmer, allocating funds for eight priests to officiate at her funeral service while Joan White, another small farmer, left money for four priests and their clerks to preside at her funeral Mass.[69] As it was believed that the number of candles burned at the ceremony increased one's prospects of salvation, testators were intent upon ensuring a well-lit funeral.[70] Regardless of their wealth, it was customary for female testators to allocate sums of money for wax and candles for their funeral ceremony. Approximately one-third of the women of Dublin archdiocese in the mid- to late fifteenth century whose wills have survived either left modest amounts of money for the purchase of wax or they bequeathed a block of wax, typically three or four pounds, to be burned at the funeral service. The belief that candles left alight in the church after the funeral ceremony increased the deceased's prospects of salvation inspired women such as Joan Drywer to provide accordingly. In 1475 Joan, widow of a small farmer, left ten shillings to keep the three lights lighting in the church of the Virgin Mary in Crumlin where she was buried.[71]

In Kildare, Kilkenny and Tipperary, aristocratic couples such as the FitzEustaces, the Purcells and the Butlers resembled their peers in England and in Gaelic Ireland in electing to be buried away from their parish communities within the secluded precincts of Franciscan friaries of which they were benefactors.[72] In Co Dublin, one of the wealthiest female members of the aristocracy, Maud Plunket, Lady Talbot (d. mid-fifteenth century) chose to be removed from her wider parish congregation by being buried in the private grounds of her estate.[73] However, the majority of women and men in counties Dublin and Meath in the fifteenth and early sixteenth centuries opted for a form of burial that was 'public and communitarian',[74] aristocrats and farmer's wives alike exhibiting a strong preference for interment within the familiar surrounds of their cathedral or parish church or adjoining cemetery.[75]

As in contemporary England, long term post-obit arrangements made by women in the colony were twofold – provision for services or for donations.[76] Those women who were fortunate enough to have been in a position to endow a chantry were usually buried in the associated chapel; Anne Plunket was buried alongside her husband, Christopher St Lawrence in their chapel in St Mary's Abbey at Howth in the mid-fifteenth century. Others were buried in the centre of the chancel, in the nave, in the sacristy, under the church tower or by the interior of the church walls.[77] In the case of women who were poor, burial in the parish cemetery was the best they could hope for. However, women of modest or even substantial means were also interred in the parish cemetery. Joan Stevin (d. 1481), widow of a small farmer, chose burial in the cemetery of her parish church in Crumlin as did Margaret Janico who was buried with her husband in the graveyard of New Abbey, Kilcullen, Co Kildare.[78] Equally, while wealthy women generally expressed a wish to be buried in the church of their choice, this privilege could also be extended to less well-to-do parishioners. Even then, however, social distinctions were maintained by consigning poorer women to lesser locations such as the church porch.[79] A desire to be buried with one's husband or family also dictated women's choice of burial place.[80] As in Gaelic areas, many women in the colony opted for burial in the chapels and cemeteries of the religious orders, Franciscan monasteries proving especially popular. Margaret Janico and her husband, Sir Roland FitzEustace, co-founders of a Franciscan monastery at Kilcullen, Co Kildare, elected to be buried there. The couple exhibited their fondness for the friars by incorporating on their tomb-surrounds a figure of St Francis, clad in his Franciscan habit, showing the wound of the stigmata on his right side and a knotted girdle at his waist.[81]

It was common for women to make provision in their wills for prayers of remembrance to be said for their souls both in the church of their burial and elsewhere after their interment. Obituarial prayer was driven by a belief in purgatory that prompted Christian men and women alike to assuage the punishment due for their sins and those of others by making provision for Masses to be celebrated after their deaths either for a fixed term or in perpetuity.[82] Frequently even women of modest means left money for Masses to be said for their souls. In 1471 Alice Bennet, a farmer, left thirty pence for thirty Masses to be said by the priest in her local parish church in Santry. Some women specified the Mass that was to be celebrated in remembrance of them. Alice Cassells of Lusk, a farmer's wife, left ten shillings to the priests of her parish church in 1472 to celebrate the Trental of St Gregory (a set of thirty Masses said on thirty consecutive days) for her soul following her burial. In addition, in the pre-Reformation era, the month's mind and the annual anniversary Mass were popular means by which the deceased elicited the prayers of the living for the redemption of their souls.[83]

Members of a cathedral or parish congregation were enticed to approach the tomb of deceased women and their husbands and to pray for their souls. On the tomb of Katherine White and her husband, James Shorthall, lord of

Ballylarkin and Ballykeefe, in St Canice's cathedral, Kilkenny the following inscription appears: 'An indulgence of eighty days is granted to everyone who says the Lords' Prayer and the Hail Mary for their souls and the souls of their parents'.[84] It also appears that the tombs of the deceased, such as the Plunket-Cusack monument at Killeen, Co Meath (c. 1450), served as assembly points for the family of the deceased in conducting remembrance ceremonies, again maintaining a link between the deceased couple and their interceding community. Such monuments seem to have incorporated an iron frame that was adorned with a hanging or tent and with candles on occasions such as the deceased's month's mind.[85]

Those women who were of sufficient social standing to belong to cathedral congregations had their deaths commemorated through their enrolment in the book of obits, ensuring that prayers were offered for their souls by the prior and canons and the congregation on their anniversaries.[86] By virtue of their wealth, several married aristocratic and gentle women in the colony in conjunction with their spouses were also in the privileged position of being able to invest substantial sums in the creation of chantries, usually in their local church. These endowments, which proliferated throughout western Europe towards the end of the Middle Ages, were special funds derived from property income to pay one or more priests to say or sing Mass for the souls of the benefactors and their relatives.[87] Joan Cusack and her husband, Sir Christopher Plunket (d. mid-fifteenth century) founded a chantry of four priests to pray for their souls in the chancel of their parish church at Killeen in Co Meath in the early fifteenth century.[88] Particularly wealthy couples such as Sir Christopher Fleming and his wife were significantly more ostentatious in their endowments. They founded a chantry college at Slane, Co Meath in 1512. This purpose-built college was designed to accommodate four priests, four clerics and four choristers who were paid to pray for the souls of their benefactors.[89] Similarly, prior to 1500, the St Lawrence family constructed a college at Howth to house four priests attached to their family chantry in St Mary's church.[90] Chantries were preferred as the most efficacious provision since they invoked not only the specialised intercession of the professionals, the secular clergy, chantry priests or chaplains, but also the parochial community as a whole. The foundation of chantries within parish churches served as a constant reminder to the congregation to intercede for the salvation of the deceased patron's soul.[91]

A minority of women of means established modest, informal and shorter-term chantry endowments in their own right. For instance Molinda Whitechurch, a widow from Drogheda, Co Louth, who made her will in 1456, specified that a proportion of her goods was to be entrusted to a local religious, William Kyton, who was to buy a missal and chalice which he was to use for the rest of his life in praying for her soul. At the end of his life Kyton was to pass the missal and the chalice to a cleric of his choice who would then pray for him, for Molinda, her deceased husband and for all the faithful departed.[92] Other women assigned land to generate sufficient income to pay for a priest to be employed to say Mass for them and nominated a family member to ensure that the Masses continued.[93] Ten years prior to her death in 1517, Catherine Owen entrusted all of her land and appurtenances in Co Dublin to a chaplain and a yeoman. Both were to ensure that her daughter Rose paid a priest to pray for the souls of Catherine and her deceased husband in St Brigid's church, Castleknock for a period of seven years.[94] Even in the case of chantries founded exclusively by men, female relatives were often nominated as beneficiaries of chantry endowments. When in 1488 John Estrete, gentleman, made provision for the entire convent and choir of Christ Church cathedral, Dublin, to sing Mass of the Holy Ghost every Thursday, he stipulated that it was to be sung not alone for himself but also for his wife and daughters.[95]

However, chantries were, in the main, the preserve of the rich as they required considerable sums of money. Less well-to-do women supplemented their provision for post-obit services by donating moveables (liturgical equipment, vestments or church furnishings), usually to their parish church. For example, in 1473 Janet Cristor, wife of a small farmer, left money for the purchase of a cope for the clergy of her parish church in Glasnevin, and Alice White, a small farmer from Garristown in north Co Dublin, commissioned a chalice for her parish church. Like their counterparts in late medieval Bristol, women in the colony left towels, overcloths for the altar, or sums of money to pay for gilding the chalice in the church in which they were buried. Some left household items such as cups to be converted into chalices or money for the repair of the church.[96] Others donated money to meet the cost of works carried out on churches with which they were associated. During the 1470s, Agnes Lawless, wife of a small farmer, left four shillings to meet the cost of works to Glasnevin parish church where she was buried and also to St Katherine's church, and Margaret O'Bern, a small farmer, donated the modest sum of twelve pence for the repair of St Kevin's church near Dublin where she was laid to rest.[97] While their parish church and clergy tended to be the greatest beneficiaries of female testators in the colony, it was also common for women to share their bequests among several churches with which they had been associated during their lives. In addition, in recognition of their special affection for certain religious orders and out of a desire to increase their prospects of salvation by gaining the continuing prayers of those communities, women of means in English areas of Ireland distributed gifts of money or other commodities among a number of communities and individual religious.[98]

Even women of modest wealth made provision in their wills for charitable donations to be made posthumously for the salvation of their souls. Through alms-giving in particular, these women contrived to place as many as possible in their debt, thereby soliciting maximum intercession from beneficiaries following their deaths. However, like their counterparts in England but unlike their Gaelic peers, wealthy women of the colony were discriminating in making their bequests of money to the poor. In 1471 Alice Bennet, a small farmer, donated five shillings and one penny to the poor catered for at St John the Baptist without the Newgate in Dublin.[99] As in the case of London, substantial bequests or perpetual endowments for the relief of poverty are rare among Dublin's laity and non-existent among its female members.[100] However, donating gifts to debtors was a common charitable practice of testators in both cities. In 1476 for instance, Joan Steven of Crumlin, widow of a small farmer, remitted all debts due by the poor and by people unable to pay.[101] The belief that their largesse ought to reach as many members of the deceased's community as possible prompted several women to leave household items including pans and troughs to be used for good works in the hope that they would remind their fellow parishioners to pray for their souls. Occasionally wealthy widows were entrusted with responsibility for administering poor relief in their community for the good of their own souls and those of their deceased husbands. For instance a small farmer, Nicholas Delaber (d. 1476) of Balrothery in north Co Dublin, left a large pot and skillet in the charge of his wife who was instructed to leave these items at the disposal of the poor in the locality for as long as she lived.[102] In addition, the majority of women who made wills charged their executors to put their possessions to 'pious uses' for the salvation of their souls.

The last testament of Joan Douce of Dublin, dated 22 May 1381, is one of the finest illustrations of the discriminating manner in which women of means in the English colony went about maximising their prospects of salvation by combining ecclesiastical patronage with provision for post-obit services and alms-giving. During her lifetime Joan had fostered close ties with the priory of St John without the Newgate in Dublin where she opted to be buried. As a sign of her affection for St John's she bequeathed money to the altars of the churches of St Audoen and St Mary and to the individual chaplains ministering in the priory church. However, she also had close ties with St Audoen's church as evidenced by her donation of money to the chaplains, the four scholars and two parish clerks based there. She bequeathed money to help fund the work of a large number of religious communities and clergy with whom she had clearly developed relationships over the course of her life. Also featured among Joan's beneficiaries were the abbess and nuns of the abbey of St Mary de Hogges, the clergy of St James', St Olave's, St Nicholas',

St Brigid del Poll, and St John's church without the Newgate, the friars minor, the Holy Trinity, the Carmelite and Augustinian friars, and the friars preachers, all of whom were ministering in Dublin. She made a separate donation of forty shillings to each of the four mendicant orders and left modest sums to two male religious and to the priest who ministered in St Sepulchre's prison. In addition, she paid for a bell to be erected in St Nicholas' church, the tolling of which would stimulate a wide audience to intercede for her soul. She was very specific in allocating money for marginalised members of society. Her bequests included donations of money to help pay for feeding the sick at the hospital of St John the Baptist without the Newgate and also for the sick at St Stephens' leper hospital. Modest sums were also bequeathed to the inmates of three of the city's prisons and twelve pence for a cripple who lay opposite Nicholas Seriaunt's inn in the city.[103] By the late fifteenth century, however, such bequests to hospitals and prisons in Dublin city and county appear to have declined.[104]

III

Anthony Lynch remarked that 'despite the disorder of the late medieval church, there were certain signs of a yearning among many of the laity to have their spiritual needs attended to, and a more determined effort at self-help in this regard'.[105] While the evidence of lay women's piety in this era is poor, such glimpses as can be garnered from contemporary sources intimate a significant level of active and frequently independent, female participation in a vibrant culture of lay piety that characterised both Gaelic and English districts of Ireland on the eve of the Reformation. The role of wealthy lay women was perhaps most spectacularly demonstrated in their sponsorship of church and monastic foundations, and to a lesser extent in their corporal works of mercy and their membership of confraternities and guilds. Clearly they attached enormous significance to ritual, to the externals of religious observance and to public displays of piety, charity and church patronage. Yet they were discerning in their approach to all three as is manifest in their expressed preferences for certain funeral rites, for favourite saints, and for conferring sponsorship on mendicant orders.

Like all Christians in western Europe, women in late medieval Ireland were obsessive about ensuring that they exploited as many options as possible, both during their lifetime and afterwards, in order to maximise their prospects of salvation. They therefore displayed a pragmatic, utilitarian outlook on religion which is most evident in their readiness to invest substantial sums of money in church patronage and charity. They were preoccupied with 'dying well' and with ensuring that their pious activities during their lifetime, as well as their funerals and the remembrance of their souls, would be judged by contemporaries as entirely in keeping with their social position.

Distinctions in burial locations between and within churches and cemeteries reflect the social stratification that existed within both Gaelic and English communities in Ireland. The privileged access of wealthy women and men to burial places of particular spiritual potency demonstrated that the church in late medieval Ireland as elsewhere afforded religious sanction to their social dominance. In spite of sermons preaching that all souls were equal after death, clear social distinctions were maintained through the location of burial sites.[106] Both lay women and men made a significant financial and practical contribution to their parishes and to monastic communities on the eve of the Reformation, which compensated to 'an indefinable but certainly not negligible degree' for the depredations of the institutional church.[107] The potency of the laity's belief in purgatory directly contributed to the amelioration in local liturgical and spiritual standards, providing them with scope to satisfy their own spiritual and social needs throughout Christendom. Ireland was no exception.[108]

CHAPTER SIX

The Reformation in Ireland

Brendan Bradshaw SM

The history of the Reformation in Ireland is heavily marked by irony. In the first place it can be claimed that the introduction of the Reformation to Ireland in the sixteenth century was due in no small way to the donation of the island to the King of England in the mid-twelfth century by Pope Adrian IV in the Papal Bull *Laudabiliter.* That Bull provides one of the circumstances that brought English colonists flooding into Ireland from 1169 onwards and that justified the claim of the English king to the island as a patrimony of the English crown. Ironically again the reason for the papal grant was stated in the Bull to be the reform of the Irish church which, the pope was persuaded, had degenerated into a state of barbarism. Henry II showed no great interest in reforming the Irish church and it was left to his successors in the sixteenth century to take a livelier interest. However the reform then introduced was not at all to the liking of successive popes of the sixteenth century. The final irony is that the sixteenth-century Irish showed more loyalty to the pope than the pope had to them in the twelfth century. They resolutely resisted all attempts to force them to comply with the state religion. The reformed Church of Ireland appropriated the plant of the Irish church, its economic resources and its parochial churches, but an underground Counter-Reformation church established itself in opposition, and to this the vast majority of the population conformed. Down the centuries until their final emancipation in 1829 the Irish remained committed to Roman Catholicism, and so it continues to this day. Ireland then constituted an exception to the pattern that established itself throughout Europe in the aftermath of the Reformation whereby sooner or later the people and their rulers adhered to the same religion, *cuius regio eius religio*, as the formula devised at Augsburg in 1555 has it. In that sense Ireland was not a confessional state. The religion of the prince and the religion of the people diverged. It is to explain how that came about, how against all the odds the Counter-Reformation triumphed over the Reformation in Ireland that this essay is concerned. The explanation has to do in the first instance with the set of circumstances encountered by the reformers in conducting their campaign in Ireland, circumstances which distinguished the Irish situation from that encountered by the reformers in either England or Wales, the two other territories that made up the patrimony of the Crown in the sixteenth century.

One difference relates to the condition of the late medieval church in Ireland. No doubt the state of religion in Ireland at the onset of the Reformation presents in most respects the same dismal aspect as it does in England and Wales: that of a deeply traditionalist not to say hidebound cultural ethos; the laity in thrall to quasi-magical ritualism; parish cures everywhere served by simple massing priests who neglected to preach or to provide religious instruction; the monastic orders in steep decline, with lax observance the norm, vocations dwindling and downright immorality by no means rare. Nevertheless the comparison draws attention to a beacon of light in the Irish case which distinguishes it from the situation in England and Wales, one moreover that assumes heightened significance when viewed in the context of the struggle between the Reformation and the Counter-Reformation as will later appear. Its source was a vigorous movement of reform among the mendicant orders, especially the Augustinians, Dominicans and Franciscans. Whereas in Wales this Observant reform, as it came to be called, does not seem to have taken hold at all, and even in England numbered only seven foundations among its adherents – all of them Franciscan – it flourished in Ireland. Introduced from the continent to the native (Gaelic) territory in the west in the mid-fifteenth century, it expanded steadily throughout that area. At the turn of the century it had established itself in the colonial area to the east as well as in the colonial port towns and was gaining ground within the Pale itself, the seat of the English Crown's government around Dublin. Three decades later, when the Reformation burst upon Ireland, Observantism claimed forty Franciscan convents – two-thirds of what was the largest and most dynamic of the orders of friars in Ireland. By then also eight of the twenty-two Augustinian communities were Observant and elsewhere among the Augustinian conventuals it had many individual adherents: the prior of the conventual community in Dublin when the Reformation was introduced in the 1530s, who was also their provincial superior, was an Observant. Again in the case of the Dominicans the impact of the movement was clearly greater than the bare statistics might seem to indicate. When the Order of Preachers established a separate Irish province in 1484 its first provincial superior was an Observant, and six of the conventual communities went over to the reform in the course of the following twenty years; no small testimony to the vigour of the movement in the new province. Meanwhile the friars also gained vigour in the island in the fifteenth century through the spread of the Franciscan Third Order Regular. This lay order, devoted mainly to supporting the diocesan clergy in the task of evangelisation, spread again from the west. In the course of the fifteenth century forty foundations were established, mostly in Ulster and Connacht.

The significance of the reform movement among the friars for the response to the Reformation in Ireland hinges on three related considerations. One is that it provided the late medieval Irish church with a clerical spiritual elite, numerous and widely dispersed both throughout the colonial territory and the native area. Second, the Observants' manner of life and their strong pastoral orientation ensured them a voice that commanded a special moral authority among the laity. A dispatch of the imperial ambassador in London in 1534, coinciding with the inauguration of the state-sponsored Reformation in Ireland, informed the Emperor in a tone of obvious astonishment that according to reports the cordelliers (the Observants) were held in such veneration among the 'wild Irish' that they were feared, obeyed and almost adored such that even their lords submitted to physical chastisement from them. Third, in consequence of the Observants' pastoral involvement they took to exploiting the vernacular as a medium of evangelisation. In the process they became associated with those professional families whose task it was to preserve and cultivate the native cultural heritage. In this way religion became rooted in the culture of the people. What emerges from all of this is that the ambience into which the English Reformation was introduced in Ireland differed significantly from that of the Crown's other dominions not only politically but also in religious terms. Ireland uniquely possessed in the Orders of friars a spiritual elite – the fruits of the reform movement – numerous, widely dispersed, pastorally dynamic, respected by the laity of all social degrees, and well attuned to the vernacular as a mode of evangelisation. It is clearly significant then for the outcome of the Reformation in Ireland that the friars for the most part took a stand against the religious innovations from the outset and mounted a campaign of resistance.

Nevertheless the failure of the Reformation in Ireland cannot be accounted for purely in these terms. Ultimately the issue was decided in the course of the struggle between the Reformation and the Counter-Reformation itself and, it would seem, at some point subsequent to the reign of Henry VIII. It is necessary, therefore, to examine, against the background outlined above, the circumstances that operated in the course of the struggle itself to clinch the matter. Ironically it will be seen that the key is provided by a feature that the Reformation in Ireland shared with the Reformation in England and Wales and that accounts in no small part for its success in those places. This was its extension to the island as the ecclesiastical complement of the Tudor reform of government. What made the difference is that the effect of the political reform in Ireland, in contrast to the benign experience it provided in Wales, was to confirm the medieval experience of the local elite of reforming initiatives from London as a threat to their heritage of privileges and liberties, and an affront to their sense of the independence of their polity from England. For the effect of the Tudor reform of government was to introduce certain departures from the system whereby the Irish Lordship was governed in the late medieval period which, given the volatility of relations between the regime in England and the local elite in Ireland at the time, could hardly have been better calculated to ignite the powder keg. These innovations came to be adopted as central aspects of the strategy by which the Tudors sought to pacify and reform the Irish polity. Far from doing so, the effect of the strategy was to engender certain flashpoints which permanently destabilised Anglo-Irish relations not only under the Tudors but so long as and to the extent that Ireland retained its British connection.

The first effect of Tudor reform was to terminate the late medieval system of devolved government whereby a powerful local magnate was deputed to head the administration as the king's Lord Deputy and given a free hand in filling virtually all other offices. Instead a system was now put in place whereby the local Lord Deputy and his clients were replaced by an English official and by a bevy of new English administrators. With one exception, a colonial magnate was never again to be appointed to head the Irish administration down to the establishment of the Free State in the twentieth century. The potential of this Tudor 'new departure' to destabilise the Irish polity, it is important to bear in mind, derived not only from the resentment of the local elite at the loss of independence and of power and patronage. Equally, if not in greater measure, it derived from the threat posed in consequence to the established socio-political structure. For as English administrators and soldiers availed of the opportunity of a tour of duty in Ireland to advance their careers and fortunes, they transformed themselves in increasing numbers from transitory professional state servants to settlers greedy for estates on which to set themselves up as patriarchs. The result was to set a transformation of the socio-political structure in motion whereby over the next century or so these New English, as they came to be called, first challenged the dominance of the existing elites – colonial (Old English) and native (Gaelic) alike – and then ousted them altogether. This 'anglicisation' of Crown government in Ireland and the challenge it presented to the old order constitutes the first of the flashpoints engendered in Anglo-Irish relations by the Tudor reform of government.

The second flashpoint was engendered as a corollary of the first. Hitherto the Crown had relied for the purposes of defence and security on a local feudal host mobilised as occasion required by whichever colonial magnate was favoured at the time with the office of Lord Deputy. The alternative now provided to a feudal host recruited locally was a garrison force sent from England. In the course of time this garrison increased enormously in numbers and its locations were multiplied throughout the island. In the course of time also the garrison was transformed from an instrument of pacification and reform to in effect an army of occupation engaged upon a conquest. As such, needless to say, it was heartily resented by the Gaelic natives. The colonists in the Pale and in the feudal lordships were also bitter. They resented the economic burden that fell upon them of maintaining the army. Furthermore the soldiers behaved no better than any early modern undisciplined and underpaid army, living off the country, scavenging and extorting, and generally seriously disrupting the civil order. The English garrison therefore constitutes the second of those flashpoints that resulted from the innovations introduced into the government of Ireland by the Tudors. It may be added that this Tudor new departure, like the anglicisation of the administration, became a permanent fixture thereafter as a central feature of the system by which the Irish polity was governed down to the establishment of the Free State in the twentieth century. The combined effect of these two Tudor innovations was that the system of Crown government in Ireland constituted a much-resented exception to the system whereby the British conglomerate generally was governed. Elsewhere the Crown relied almost exclusively on civil methods and on locals to staff its administration. These deviations from the norm therefore go far towards explaining the continuing instability of the Irish polity within the British state system. To the increasingly politically aware and ever more disadvantaged Irish, the garrison in particular came to represent an emblem of subjection. Meanwhile the immediate effect of the two was to fuel the mounting tension between the Crown and the local elite in the sixteenth century and to further entrench the perception of reform from the centre as not only inimical to Ireland's interests but as a violation of long-cherished liberties.

The third flashpoint resulted from the new 'enterprise culture' now emerging in England in the second half of the sixteenth century. As the number of English officials and soldiers settling in Ireland multiplied, a plantation policy gained increasing favour. The theory was that strategically placed settlements of civil English subjects in Ireland would provide oases of loyalty and have a leavening influence on the natives. Meanwhile the attention of adventurous fortune-seekers generally in England was attracted to Ireland as an easily accessible land of opportunity to colonise, more attractive because easier to reach than the newly discovered, remote, overseas territories. The snag was that colonisation added a new dimension to the challenge posed to the existing pattern of land distribution, all the more so with the increasing tendency of new English officials and soldiers to remain on as settlers. For the plantations necessarily encroached upon the lands claimed by the old elites as theirs by ancient inheritance. Ultimately the effect was to spark a chain of rebellions of increasing scale and intensity as the ruling kindreds became increasingly persuaded of the need to combine under a common banner to defend their territories. The common ground on which the rebels chose to take an ideological stand was that of religion.

The potential of religion as an emotive rallying cry had become apparent to the forces of opposition to Tudor reform even before the plantation policy got under way. When the Fitzgeralds of Kildare, the most powerful of the old colonial noble families, staged a protest in arms in 1534 against the loss of their traditional monopoly of Crown government in Ireland, they proclaimed their rebellion as resistance to a heretic king and appealed – unsuccessfully – for assistance to the emperor and the French king, the two most powerful Catholic monarchs in Europe. In doing so they established a trend that was to become increasingly marked in rebellions in Ireland throughout the century. As the century progressed also the rhetoric of the militant Counter-Reformation came to suffuse the protests of the rebels ever more fully. The rebellions of 1569 and 1579 led by James Fitzmaurice Fitzgerald of Desmond mark an important point of transition in that regard. The propaganda of the rebels was not only suffused with the rhetoric of the militant Counter-Reformation – that rhetoric was suffused in turn with patriotic sentiment. The cause of the Catholic religion and the cause of Ireland were now becoming identified. Appealing to the ancient heritage of the Irish, the rebels proclaimed themselves to be defending Roman Catholicism as the faith to which the Irish had been converted by the revered St Patrick in the fifth century. Meanwhile the arrival of a small force of papal mercenaries to assist the rebellion in 1579 marks the point at which Ireland can be claimed to have become a participant in the European wars of religion. These trends reached their consummation in the Nine Years War that convulsed the island at the end of the century. The Ulster earls who, led by the great Hugh O'Neill, were the backbone of the resistance waged the war, as they constantly reiterated, in defence of 'faith and fatherland'. That rallying cry proved sufficiently powerful to attract the majority of both the native and the old colonial communities, though the Old English of the Pale, traditionally the most loyal of all the Crown's subjects in Ireland, still held out contriving to maintain a dual loyalty to the English Crown in politics and to the pope in religion. At the same time the Irish struggle became more closely identified with the cause of the Catholic struggle in Europe when Philip II sent substantial aid, both munitions and soldiers, to assist the Irish insurgents. All to no avail. The submission of the Ulster earls in 1603 and their flight to the safety of Catholic Europe in 1607 brought the Tudor conquest to completion. However, that victory was secured at the cost of alienating the vast majority of the two historic communities of the island, the Gaelic natives and the Anglo-Irish colonists. Further, the traditional animosity between the two communities was now being eroded. Instead a sense of solidarity was developing between them as alike the victims of conquest and colonisation and as loyal adherents of Catholicism against the English Reformation. As the seventeenth century progressed that sense of solidarity gradually had the effect that the two communities merged under the common identity of the Catholic Irish.

Meanwhile the three flashpoints – the anglicisation of the personnel of government, the militarisation of the system of government, and plantation pursued as a strategy of social reform – increasingly exacerbated the tensions between the local elite and the regime at the centre as the campaign on behalf of the Tudor Reformation in religion proceeded. As such they go far towards explaining the chequered history of the campaign and its anomalous outcome. As the prejudices of the elites against reform from the centre were increasingly confirmed by bitter experience so their attitude towards the Crown's ecclesiastical innovations hardened from initial ambiguity in the reign of Henry VIII to tacit and finally forthright resistance in the reign of Elizabeth. Thus the government legislation enacting the Royal Supremacy under Henry VIII encountered little opposition from the laity when it was introduced in the Irish parliament in 1536. Further, the oath prescribed by law to the Supreme Head was generally taken when presented to the people in the course of the ensuing Reformation campaign in the dioceses of the colony. On the other hand, the lower clergy mounted a campaign of resistance both in parliament and among the people. However, this relatively receptive climate had changed by the reign of Elizabeth. True the relevant Reformation statutes were enacted in the Irish parliament in 1559 but the circumstances in which this occurred are suspiciously shrouded in mystery. Thereafter the evidence of opposition quickly mounts. The leading ecclesiastic of the reformed Church of Ireland, Archbishop Loftus of Dublin, discovered on investigation in 1566 that the laws enjoining attendance at the services of the reformed church were everywhere quietly ignored. The situation deteriorated rather than improved subsequently. Local officials brazenly refused to take the oath of supremacy, as they were required to do on entering office. And when the government tried to have more severe penal laws enacted to overcome the opposition, the Irish parliament could not be persuaded to enact them. On the contrary, the effect was to provoke opposition to the government's civil legislation as well and to reduce parliament to chaos.

The non-cooperation of the lay elite was crucial in undermining the campaign on behalf of the Reformation in Ireland. The Crown was dependent on them as instruments of local government. It was on the local elite therefore that the Crown relied to secure conformity to the religion by law established. However, far from securing conformity to the Reformation the elite led the way in resistance. As already noted they increasingly evaded and eventually outrightly refused to swear to the royal supremacy over the church or to participate in the rites prescribed in the Book of Common Prayer. Likewise they neglected to impose the stipulated fines on others for failure to conform to the ecclesiastical decrees. Conversely, as their attitude towards the Reformation hardened, so their attitude to the Counter-Reformation became increasingly receptive. They allowed the missionaries of the Counter-Reformation free movement among the people and permitted the friars to reoccupy the religious houses from which they had been expelled by government. Increasingly they actively promoted the Counter-Reformation mission, according its clergy a social status quite above anything shown the lower clergy in the medieval period. They ensured that their children were soundly instructed in the Catholic religion by sending them to school to masters of a reliably Catholic persuasion and for higher studies to Counter-Reformation centres on the continent in preference to the now tainted Oxford and Cambridge. As the reign of Elizabeth advanced, a new generation of leaders of the two historic communities of the island came to the fore, deeply committed to Roman Catholicism and to its propagation. Their children in turn provided ready recruits for the armies engaged on the Catholic side in the European wars of religion and for the priesthood as candidates for the Counter-Reformation mission in Ireland. Needless to say, where the local elite led the people followed in a social environment highly attuned to deference.

That much said, the credit for ensuring the triumph of Roman Catholicism as the confession of the broad mass of the Irish people, must go ultimately to the missionaries themselves. Their achievement was to avail of the opportunity offered them by the local elite to root their creed within the living Irish tradition while at the same time undermining the credibility of the state-sponsored Reformation as an alien innovation. Here the contribution of the fifteenth-century movement of reform among the friars assumes major significance. Unlike their continental brethren the Observant friars in Ireland for the most part stood out against the Reformation from the beginning. Thus they were singled out in reports of those attempting to promote the officially sponsored Reformation campaign in the colonial territories in the 1530s and 1540s as playing the leading role in an underground counter-campaign designed to maintain loyalty to the pope and to the old religion. At the same time in the Gaelic territories they preached up the rebellion of the Geraldine League as a Catholic crusade, promising eternal salvation to all those who should die fighting against the heretic monarch. Their efforts did not abate subsequently. By the 1560s they were reported to be swarming all over the western territories evangelising and re-establishing themselves in the convents which the government had earlier forced them to abandon. By the 1580s they were filtering back into the area of the Pale. It was the friars also who sought to establish links with the incipient Counter-Reformation movement on the Continent. Early on, the papacy showed that it realised the value of the friars in Ireland, adopting a policy of favouring them as nominees for episcopal benefices. The most important contribution of the friars was to succeed in rooting Roman Catholicism in the native culture as the religion of 'faith and fatherland'. Crucially in this regard as natives themselves they evangelised in their own language; they were also to the fore in the translation and publication of Counter-Reformation texts in Irish. In this matter the Franciscans were especially prominent, centred at their College of St Anthony's in Louvain. In contrast, the Reformation movement made the great tactical error of endeavouring to evangelise the Irish on behalf of the Reformation in English. For the most part they remained wedded to the imperialist doctrine, classically expounded by the poet Edmund Spenser, which held that cultural anglicisation was the necessary precondition of religious anglicisation. A few enthusiasts for evangelisation in Irish among them were left to their own devices or even actively discouraged and thwarted. However, evangelisation in English to an overwhelmingly Irish-speaking population was futile; even in the old colonial territory the vast majority of the inhabitants were monoglot Irish speakers. So it transpired in Ireland that the Counter-Reformation mission, not the Reformation campaign, was conducted in the language of the people. Even the missionaries recruited from the old Anglo-Irish elite, despite their ingrained cultural prejudice regarding the 'wild Irish', sooner or later came to realise the importance of the Irish language as a medium through which to propagate their message. So it was that Counter-Reformation Catholicism became entrenched in Ireland as the religion of faith and fatherland. Tridentine Roman Catholicism was presented as the religion of the ancient Celtic church, the cherished heritage handed on through the centuries since the conversion of the Irish by St Patrick in the fifth century. Conversely the state-sponsored Reformation was denounced both as a heretical and an alien innovation.

What emerges from all of this is that the religious situation encountered by the Reformation in Ireland differed in one significant respect from that prevailing at the same time either in England or in Wales. Unlike these, Ireland possessed in the Orders of friars a dynamic, numerous, widely dispersed and highly respected spiritual elite who directed their formidable resources to subverting the state-sponsored religious innovations from the outset and linked the resistance with the Counter-Reformation just then developing on the Continent. The high repute gained for the friars in pre-Reformation Ireland by the Observant reform movement ensured that the voice of dissent carried special moral authority among the laity. Their place in the esteem and affection of the Irish community was to remain secure through the dark era of religious persecution on which Ireland was now soon entering.

Thus the Counter-Reformation friars reaped where the fifteenth-century reform movement of the Observants had sown. In short, the fifteenth-century reform among the friars played a crucial part in ensuring that by the end of the sixteenth century Tridentine Roman Catholicism had come to be adopted as the religious confession of the Irish and the English Reformation rejected, the will of their prince notwithstanding, as a heretical foreign innovation. For that reason, therefore, the movement earns a special place in the story of the Reformation in Ireland, a story that affected the entire course of modern Irish history.

CHAPTER SEVEN

Religious wars in Ireland: Plantations and martyrs of the Catholic Church

Colm Lennon

The return to Ireland of Catholic bishops who had attended the closing session of the Council of Trent marked the tentative start of the Counter-Reformation in the island. Sanctioned by Rome, their missionary aims of catechising and disciplining the Catholic clergy and laity ran counter to those of the official ecclesiastical regime which since 1560 had been headed by Queen Elizabeth as Supreme Governor of the Church of Ireland. Although they operated mostly in the western and northern dioceses which were as yet outside the effective control of the English administration, the very presence of these Roman Catholic bishops was offensive to the religious supremacy of the monarchy. And although they might profess political loyalty to the state, it was inevitable that the mounting pressure of events in Ireland and elsewhere would give rise to conflicts between allegiances to London and Rome. The fate of the Catholic archbishop of Armagh, Primate Richard Creagh, is reflective of this predicament. Throughout his career, he asserted his loyalty to Queen Elizabeth, but he spent almost twenty years as a prisoner in Dublin and London because he was regarded by the authorities as 'a dangerous man to be among the Irish'. He died in the Tower of London in 1586 and was soon reputed to be a martyr for the Catholic faith in Ireland.

The case of Archbishop Creagh is perhaps emblematic of the fate of the Catholic church in Ireland in the century and a half between the Elizabethan Reformation and the era of the penal laws. The implications for her Irish Catholic subjects of the excommunication by Pope Pius V of Queen Elizabeth are worthy of investigation. Although not necessarily ruling out a *modus vivendi* between them and the Protestant monarch, the excommunication gave credibility to the political analysis of those Irish Catholic leaders, clerical as well as lay, who argued for a transfer of sovereignty from England to a Catholic monarchy such as Spain. Warfare and insurgency in Ireland which stemmed primarily from opposition to the colonial policies of the state, including plantation, came to encompass a religious dimension, a phenomenon most clearly at work in the warfare of the 1590s and 1640s. There was nevertheless an alternative Catholic strategy to holy war which bears scrutiny. Based on models applied elsewhere in Europe, Irish Catholic leaders worked out a position of political acceptance of the regime and the eschewing of foreign intrigue in return for practical toleration of their religion. The proposed Catholic reform envisaged a kind of Catholic plantation of civility and social stability which would, it was hoped, be acceptable to the Stuart monarchy. But hardening politico-religious ideologies, based to a large extent on the interpretation of recent Irish history including the story of its martyrs, obtruded upon the discourse of toleration, with especially violent force in the 1640s. The outcome was the triumph of the Protestant plantation in Ireland at the expense of the envisaged Catholic one, and the image of the martyred church with its beleaguered Catholic community became a grim reality by the end of the seventeenth century.

I

With the promulgation of the bull of excommunication, *Regnans in excelsis*, by Pope Pius V in 1570, the Catholic subjects of Elizabeth I in England and Ireland were relieved of the moral obligation of political obedience to the queen and instead were freed to work for her overthrow. As a consequence, the state authorities could in theory view all members of the Catholic community as potential traitors. In practice, however, the vast majority of leading Catholics adhered to the path of political loyalty while dissenting publicly or privately in their religious practice. The desire of the early Counter-Reformation prelates such as Archbishop Creagh to 'render to Caesar that which is Caesar's, and to God that which is God's' was matched by the preference of most of the laity for a system of dual allegiance, to the pope in religion and to the English monarch in politics. This was especially true of the Old English in Ireland, those whose ancestry and outlook were English but who dissented from the Protestant Reformation. Those churchmen who eschewed politico-religious agitation received a boost when, in 1580, Pope Gregory XIII, at the request of the English Jesuits, suspended the provisions of *Regnans in excelsis*, allowing Catholic subjects of the queen to seek some *modus vivendi* with the state government. Complementing this gesture was the failure of the Tudor administration to pass any further anti-Catholic legislation through the Irish parliament after 1560. Thereafter, in an atmosphere of *de facto* toleration, the foundations of Tridentine pastoral reforms were laid particularly among the populations of Connacht and Ulster. Also, in the continental colleges Irish youths were being trained in the principles of Tridentine Catholicism from the 1580s onwards, first in existing institutions and then in colleges specially established for Irish students from both Gaelic and English communities.

There was an alternative analysis of politico-religious relations being canvassed among a significant minority of Irish Catholics in the late Tudor period. In the opinion of Maurice MacGibbon, archbishop of Cashel and agent of the Geraldine insurgent, James Fitzmaurice, to the Spanish court in 1569, Elizabeth I had forfeited her right to rule Ireland because of her heresy. Ireland had been granted as a lordship to the medieval English monarchy by the papacy on condition that the welfare of the church would be promoted there. By their rejection of the papacy, therefore, the Tudor monarchs, Henry VIII and Elizabeth, had debarred themselves from sovereign rule in Ireland. On that basis, MacGibbon brought an offer of the sovereignty of Ireland to King Philip II of Spain on behalf of a confederacy of leading Irish ecclesiastics and aristocrats. In James Fitzmaurice's later rebellion in Munster, rejection of the Elizabethan government's political jurisdiction was combined with a Catholic crusade under the benediction of a papal indulgence and a papal emissary, the Jesuit Nicholas Sanders. Fitzmaurice's aim, and that of a contemporaneous Old English rebellion of Viscount Baltinglass on the outskirts of the Pale, was the overthrow of Elizabeth's government and the official restoration of Catholicism. While Philip of Spain was cautious about becoming embroiled in warfare in Ireland, he did dispatch a company of several hundred Spanish troops to join with a small papal force to the south-west of Ireland where the entire company was massacred in 1580.

A significant factor in uprisings against the English Crown in late Tudor Ireland was the irruption of newcomers from England into the regions and localities. Plantation entailed the appropriation of land for the purpose of settling individuals and families who would implant there English social, economic and cultural institutions. In some places these lands fell to the English Crown due to the dissolution of monasteries or the failure of families to produce heirs, but in others the territories were seized from Irish families mostly of Gaelic origin who had been engaged in rebellion. In all cases, the objective was to establish colonies of Englishness, involving agricultural and economic changes, which would serve as models for the surrounding native populations. The trouble was that in many instances the lands to be planted were not free of inhabitants and great resentment was caused by the arrival of new claimants. Another aspect was the religious complexion of the newcomers. Thus plantation helped to establish islands of Protestantism among the Irish, as the vast majority of the settlers professed the reformed religion. This distinguishing mark of the New English was to be exploited more forcefully by them as the natives, whether of English or Gaelic origin, found their Catholicism increasingly becoming a barrier to political and economic progress.

Thus the expansion of English institutions and colonies into the provinces elicited opposition from aristocratic figures among the Old English and Gaelic communities. In response to such insurgency, the state authorities regularly meted out rigorous punishments. Among the victims of retribution were some who claimed to be religious dissenters, caught up (inadvertently or otherwise) in political upheavals. These included two bishops, Patrick O'Healy of Mayo and Dermot O'Hurley of Cashel, both tried by martial law and condemned and executed for alleged treasonous links with the Munster rebels in the early 1580s. Many of the Baltinglass rebels were hanged as traitors around the same time and Archbishop Creagh was put to death by poisoning as a dangerous dissident in the Tower of London in 1586. Soon after the deaths of these Catholic figures the cult of their martyrdom began to be recorded in writings in Ireland and on the continent. For the status of martyr to be accorded to them, the hatred of their antagonists for their religion (*odium fidei*) had to be established. There was thereby introduced into the historiography an ideological strain which was to be countered by Protestant historians. As a consequence, while religious identities in Ireland were becoming more clearly defined, there occurred a concomitant deepening of divisions between the confessions.

By the late 1580s, leading Catholic ecclesiastics and laypeople were to the fore in rallying opposition to a perceived attack on their faith. Seven bishops from the northern and western dioceses, led by the two metropolitans, Edmund MacGauran of Armagh and James O'Hely of Tuam, formed a confederacy to give backing to a native resistance movement in Ulster and to sue for Spanish assistance. Although Archbishop MacGauran was killed in a skirmish in south-west Ulster in 1593, Archbishop O'Hely went to Madrid to canvass aid for a Catholic crusade, representing himself as an agent of the northern chieftains. With the emergence of Hugh O'Neill, earl of Tyrone, as leader of the confederacy by the mid-1590s, the issue of religious toleration for Catholics became central to the prosecution of the Nine Years War. He demanded that 'all the inhabitants of Ireland may have free liberty of conscience or at least ways the benefit of her Majesty's positive law'. In his proclamation and articles of 1599, O'Neill fused the aspirations to religious freedom and national sovereignty, adopting the ideology of 'faith and fatherland'. The essence of O'Neill's position was that the terms of the 1570 excommunication of Elizabeth should now be fulfilled. Posing as a champion of the oppressed liberties of his 'patria', he issued the twenty-two articles of 1599 which formed an agenda for national independence (nominally under the English crown) and liberty of conscience. This combination of national and religious freedom within an inclusivist Irish commonwealth would, he asserted, eradicate the 'infinite evils' of 'barbarity and incivility' which the Tudor reform programme of plantation had fostered rather than eliminated.

In justifying his rebellion against the tyrannical sovereign, Hugh O'Neill was most anxious to woo the clergy and laity among the Old English of the

Pale and towns to his side, and he issued a proclamation ordering them to comply with the aims of his campaign. But despite their adherence to the Catholicism of their ancestors, they were loath to acquiesce in rebellion against their anointed prince, still less to countenance the mooted transfer of allegiance to a Spanish Habsburg one. To bolster his ideological stance, O'Neill enlisted the help of Peter Lombard, himself an Old Englishman from Waterford, and later to be archbishop of Armagh. Lombard's *De regno Hiberniae, sanctorum insula, commentarius*, dedicated to Pope Clement VIII, written at Rome in 1600 but not published until 1632, was a justification of O'Neill's stance and an attempt to win the pope's support for an Irish crusade. Although Pope Clement was prepared to grant to O'Neill a crusading indulgence similar to that which James Fitzmaurice had gained in 1579, the pope failed to order the excommunication of those Catholics in Ireland who did not rally to the cause of the Ulster leader. Thus Gregory XIII's suspension of the bull *Regnans in excelsis* remained in force, allowing Elizabeth's Catholic subjects in Ireland to continue to assert their stance of dual allegiance to London and Rome.

Lombard's *Commentarius* was the first extended and considered, if highly engaged, historiographical foray by a Catholic churchman into the field of explanation and justification of his co-religionists' position. As the new post-war reality of the early seventeenth century dawned, the canon of literary discourse produced by Catholic churchmen reflected their response to the changing politico-religious circumstances. Accepting the Stuart succession to the English and Irish monarchy in 1603, these writers were engaged in a process of forging under its aegis an Irish Catholic identity, transcending old ethnic divisions within the island. Central to much of the canon is the exploration of political issues of concern to the Catholic community: constitutional models for the kingdom of Ireland in the wake of the Reformation; relations between state and church and specifically between Catholic church and Protestant authorities; dual loyalty to the monarchy and to Rome; administration, the law and land in a Protestant state with a Catholic majority; and the efficacy of Catholic reform and education under the early Stuarts. There were real hopes that James I (and VI of Scotland) would revert to the Catholic faith of his mother, Mary, Queen of Scots, or at least grant practical toleration of Catholic practice within his Irish realm. These aspirations were boosted by the protracted negotiations between the Stuart and Spanish royal houses in the later part of James's reign for a wedding between Charles, the heir to the throne, and a Spanish princess. In the expectation of a marriage agreement, the Irish Catholic leadership campaigned for an alleviation of civil disabilities imposed upon their co-religionists and for the open profession of Catholicism in Ireland.

Under the aegis of a complaisant regime, then, the Counter-Reformation missioners aspired to establish a very different kind of plantation among the Irish population. They were imbued with zeal for Tridentine reform and discipline among clergy and laity, and the envisaged reforms were just as threatening to the established social and religious mores of the native inhabitants as were the reforms of the Tudor and Stuart governments. In other words, the Counter-Reformation missioners aimed at reforming institutions such as marriage, baptism and funerals, and at replacing the recourse to private distress with the operation of civil law. Their firmness of purpose was based on the confident belief that the seeds of Christianity which had been sown by St Patrick had been nurtured by the papal jurisdiction during the medieval period in Ireland, and that the Roman Catholicism of the people of the island was deeply rooted, albeit in need of refreshment and renewal. Thus the Catholic agents had a vision of a Catholic plantation which would nurture the spiritual values and heritage of the Irish people, while helping them to advance to the norms of civil living. The latter were not too dissimilar from those of the English government.

The success of the Catholic reform movement in Ireland was based on the development of a system of pedagogy and culture for catechising and inculcating the discipline and ideals of the Counter-Reformation. Beginning with the efforts of Archbishop Creagh, Bishop Thomas Leverous, Dean Peter White, and the Jesuits, William Good and Edmund Daniel, all of whom were grammar-schoolmasters in the early Elizabethan period, a network of Catholic schools was established in the urban centres of the southern half of the country. Among the graduates were the leading ecclesiastical figures of the first Counter-Reformation generation such as Peter Lombard and David Rothe. Despite the failure of the efforts of Creagh and others to found a tertiary institution for the formation of a Counter-Reformation priesthood within the island, the momentum was present for the setting up of colleges on the Continent for the higher education of young Irish people. While stemming from the older English parts of Ireland, Catholic reform embraced both the vernaculars of Irish and English, and the catechising of the population was very much a bilingual affair. This was especially aided by the printing programme of the Irish colleges of Leuven and elsewhere which produced catechisms, saints' lives and martyrologies designed to bolster the pride of the Irish in their faith. Thus hagiography, history and martyrology were combined to render Irish Catholics sensitive to their proud heritage. It was a version of the past which stressed the unity of the professors of the Catholic faith in one national grouping counterposed with the English as outsiders and heretics.

The way was clear for such an ideology because the Protestant reformers made ineffectual attempts to nativise the Reformation in Ireland. From an early stage of the Tudor ecclesiastical changes the emphasis had been on the Reformation as a tool of anglicisation. Thus few attempts were made to provide printed material for the evangelisation of the Irish in the reformed religion through the medium of the Irish vernacular. Instead there was envisaged a thoroughly anglicised population hearing the word and worshipping in the Anglican mode in the English language. Because of scarce resources and low prioritisation, educational initiatives were slow to develop. Tudor parliamentary acts for parochial primary schools and diocesan grammar-schools were implemented very sporadically, while the foundation of a university at Dublin (1592) to foster Protestant evangelisation through the provision of a sufficient ministry came a generation too late to prevent the alienation of the majority of the population from the state church. When the graduates of the new Trinity College did emerge to take up their leadership of the Church of Ireland they were for the most part dedicated to the ideal of an English Reformation. The concentration tended to be on ministering to the settled colonies of Protestant newcomers rather than converting the older populations of English and Gaelic origin.

While the leading Catholic and Protestant scholars such as David Rothe, Luke Wadding and James Ussher may have shared an interest in the history of early Irish Christianity and its saints, they were operating in very different cultural milieux. Ussher, for example, was a fine Gaelic scholar but he baulked at the use of the language in the preaching and teaching of Protestantism. Irish on the other hand was the favoured medium of those Catholic writers who wished to instruct their fellow-countrypeople in the Tridentine norms. Both Gaelic clerical writers such as Colgan, O'Clery and Keating (who was of Gaelic culture though of English descent), and Old English such as Messingham, Tirry and Fitzsimon all identified the Catholic religion with the Irish heritage. Theological issues were obviously divisive but so too was the burden of recent Irish history. Especially contentious was the biographical corpus devoted to the lives and deaths of the Catholic martyrs in the Elizabethan and Jacobean periods who were portrayed by their biographers as having suffered because of their commitment to the faith and the hatred of their demonic persecutors, the agents of the English state and church. Therefore there was a growing cultural dichotomy which tended to separate even Irish-born people on confessional lines. Much of the writing on both sides was propagandist in its force and intention. When the prospects of a *rapprochement* between the Catholic community and the state broke down in the 1630s, the background ideology emerged to give a bitterness and sharpness to the wars of the 1640s. Out of that period and the 1650s there grew the distinctive martyrologies on both sides.

II

The military and political ferment in Ireland in the 1640s was part of the war of the three kingdoms and took place against the backdrop of the final phase of the Thirty Years War. For the Gaelic Irish and Old English rebels the issues were land and religion. The latter group had been particularly agitated by the ongoing plantation schemes of the newcomers, especially the plans for Connacht. Large companies of Irish soldiers who had served under the Spanish flag on the continent and who had assimilated Spanish ideas on the religious nature of the European conflict returned to aid the insurgents. As the fighting intensified Catholic leaders made it clear that they were in arms against the unjust regime in England and Ireland which threatened their religious and civil rights but that they were still the loyal subjects of the king. The Confederate Catholics set up an administration at Kilkenny and throughout the 1640s negotiations dragged on between the Confederate leaders and the king's representative in Ireland, the marquis of Ormond, over the terms of an agreement which would see Irish troops fight for Charles I in England and an alleviation of the ills of the Catholic subjects in Ireland. Principal among the Catholic terms were the question of freedom of worship and the rights to ecclesiastical lands and offices. Should toleration of the Catholic faith and practice be at the behest of the king or should the religious freedom of the Catholic community be enshrined in law? In the circumstances of King Charles's mounting difficulties in the face of parliamentary military successes, it was inconceivable for the king to do anything but promise to allow a practical toleration of Catholicism by turning a blind eye to breaches of the acts of supremacy and uniformity.

Positions hardened in the late 1640s as divisions in all three kingdoms of the British Isles deepened immeasurably. With the very survival of the monarchy at stake and the growing radicalism of the army in England and Scotland, the search for a compromise became increasingly desperate. Into this arena came the archbishop of Fermo, Giovanni Battista Rinuccini, as nuncio of the newly-elected Pope Innocent X. From his arrival, Rinuccini made it clear that his aim was to work for the restoration of Catholicism as the established religion of Ireland and to this end he aligned himself with Irish clergy and military personnel who were opposed to any compromise on the question of full religious toleration for Irish Catholics, even if this meant placing Ireland under a French or papal protectorate. In doing so, he alienated the Old English leaders who were prepared to bargain on the basis of *de facto* toleration from the English king. The fundamental issue of Catholic allegiance to Rome and the state was thrown into the sharpest possible relief by the agonised debates and mutual recrimination among the confederates at the end of the 1640s. A treaty known as the Ormond peace which promised a review of the position of Catholics within the state was signed just as the king was being put on trial in 1649.

After Charles's execution, the campaign of Oliver Cromwell in Ireland cut across all such negotiations aimed at reaching an agreement on toleration of Catholicism. In fact Cromwell refused to allow any Catholic worship, and priests and bishops were banished from Ireland on pain of death for themselves and their abettors. In the Cromwellian war there were many killed among the clergy and laity who were later regarded as martyrs for Catholicism. Moreover the terms of the act 'of Adventurers' were applied in the 1650s whereby parliamentarian soldiers were to be recompensed with Irish lands. The lands seized for this purpose were those of Catholic proprietors and the period saw a massive transfer of property to Protestant landowners. The starkness of the Commonwealth regime's view of Catholicism was formed to a large extent by the belief in the propaganda surrounding the massacres of Protestants in the early phase of the rising of 1641. The decades of the 1640s and the 1650s were decisive in the ideological separation of the communities in Ireland into Protestant and Catholic, the members of the latter, the Old Irish and the Old English, being taken together by the Cromwellians as equally implicated in popish conspiracy and therefore indistinguishable politically or socially.

The Restoration of the monarchy under the son of Charles I in 1660 effected a moderate change of fortune for the Catholic church in Ireland. The institution had been thrown into huge disarray under the Commonwealth and the dislocation of ecclesiastical organisation was to be seen at all levels. With the Restoration the Catholic episcopate was reinstated and the number of priests recovered throughout the island. The practice of the Catholic faith was barely tolerated under the royal prerogative of Charles II but there was no guarantee of security or stability in the longer term, as the execution in 1681 of Oliver Plunkett, archbishop of Armagh, for alleged involvement in a treasonous plot against the government, showed. Due to the virtual absence of a Catholic landholding class, Roman Catholics lacked patronage and protection. The Catholic proprietors had been swept away under Cromwell and very few were restored under Charles II. By contrast the Protestant community in Ireland, comprising now the older planters of the pre-1641 period and the Cromwellian newcomers, was established as a political and social ascendancy and was alert to the preservation of the Protestant holding and interest in the country. If the numbers of Catholics converting to the state Protestant church did not represent more than a small minority, the dominant ruling elite was not too perturbed, as the revolution in landholding had rendered the Catholic majority politically powerless.

For a few brief years under the Catholic King James II the Irish Catholic community seemed to be on the verge of recapturing the initiative which it briefly possessed at the end of the 1640s. The hope was that more than a mere prerogative toleration would be assured under James whose complaisance was taken for granted. Short of establishing a complete Catholic restoration, the Irish Catholic leadership asserted a position of religious equality with the Protestants under the rule of the Stuart monarchy. The Old English element among the Catholic population were set to be restored to the political nation on terms which they considered acceptable. But the 'glorious revolution' and its aftermath in Ireland in the form of the Williamite wars cast all in doubt and the terms of the treaty of Limerick signed in 1691 were ominously vague and ambiguous. This promised Catholics such freedom of worship as was consistent with the laws of Ireland and such as they had enjoyed under Charles II. In the event the treaty was in effect abrogated by a series of laws which underscored the exclusion of Catholics from political life, being accompanied by the final, fateful transfer of remaining Catholic property to Protestants. The era of the penal laws had dawned.

The ultimate failure of Irish Catholics to sustain a position of dual loyalty to Rome and London was thus starkly demonstrated. Since the Reformation legislation of 1560 the practice of the Catholic religion was heavily dependent on the goodwill of the monarchy. Periods of relative harmony in Catholic-state relations, during which hopes were raised of more permanent toleration, were punctuated by warfare which stemmed primarily from grievances over the confiscation and plantation of land by newcomers who were predominantly Protestant. It was mostly during these phases of politico-religious belligerency that executions of clergy and laypeople who were later accounted as martyrs took place. Their deaths were written up in the work of contemporary historians who used their saintly lives to galvanise their co-religionists into defending their faith and resisting the evangelism of the Protestant church. The resultant ideological division within official circles caused a fundamental mistrust to fester which prevented a rapprochement between the New English Protestant interest and the older Catholic inhabitants. In eventually losing their lands to the newcomers, the Catholic elite forfeited their political power and, concomitantly, their bargaining power as negotiators for the right to freedom of conscience, let alone freedom of worship.

CHAPTER EIGHT

The Irish contribution to Counter-Reformation theology in continental Europe

Declan M. Downey

The general historiographical approach to Irish Catholic ecclesiastical history in the early modern period has focused on matters such as the question of the Reformation's failure and the relative success of the Counter-Reformation in Ireland; on the survival and reorganisation of the *Ecclesia Hibernica* under the aegis of Propaganda Fide; on the relationships between Catholic clergy and their community and between Catholic clergy and the Protestant state authorities.[1] Generally speaking, it could be said that scholarship concerning the Irish Counter-Reformation movement has tended to concentrate on affairs and events within Ireland in isolation from affairs and events which affected the Counter-Reformation movements on the continent. While some scholars have studied the nature of collegial life and the academic syllabi in the various Irish colleges and seminaries in Europe and the influence of such experiences on the Catholic clergy returning to Ireland,[2] it is only recently that some academic studies have directed our attention to the contribution of Irish philosophers and theologians to the Counter-Reformation in continental Europe itself.[3] This essay will endeavour to highlight such contributions, particularly in the development of Scotism and Augustinianism in Habsburg Spain and Flanders. Until very recently, too, the historiography of the early Counter-Reformation in Ireland assumed that it was Roman in its cultural-juridical character.[4] However recent work has argued that in the spheres of education, clerical allegiance and episcopal appointments, the Irish Counter-Reformation was more influenced by the rigorist Spanish Catholic mentality, and owed its impetus to Habsburg Spain and Flanders rather than to the papacy.[5] Due to the constraints of space, this essay will concentrate on providing a brief and general introduction to the pre-Reformation links with Spain upon which a Counter-Reformation corridor was constructed, and on Spanish and Flemish influence on the Irish Catholic clergy in the theological developments of Augustinianism, Scotism and Regalism.

I

In 1563 the Council of Trent decreed the establishment of seminaries in every ecclesiastical province. Unlike her sister churches in Spain, Flanders, France and the Italian States, the Catholic church in Ireland did not possess the benefits of legal status or indeed the resources to ensure such structures for clerical education. Her clergy had to be educated in Catholic Europe. It was not until the 1590s and early 1600s that the full effect of seminary-priests was felt in Ireland. Until then there was, nevertheless, a strong presence of clergy formed in the spirit of the earlier Catholic Reformation. This movement had prominent advocates in the Spanish church, and in Ireland its promoters were mainly friars of the Observant reform: Augustinian, Carmelite, Dominican and Franciscan. The last were particularly effective since they were the largest and most popular of the mendicant orders in Ireland. The Franciscan Observants enjoyed the esteem of, and close rapport with all social levels of the laity in both Gaelic Irish and Old English communities. More importantly these friars understood the mentality of their fellow countrymen. The surviving evidence from the eve of the Henrician Reformation indicates large-scale investment and endowment of existing churches and friaries and the foundation of new mendicant houses by nobles, merchants and craftsmen-guilds. This is in itself a testimony to the success of the Catholic Reformation in Ireland represented by the Observant movement.[6] Furthermore there is nothing to suggest the infiltration of Hussite, Lutheran or Zwinglian ideas through Irish ports prior to 1535, nor their reception among the urban population as had been the case in England, Scotland, France and the Netherlands.[7] The ideas, which did enter Irish ports during this period, were not from Basle, Zurich or Wittenberg, but were from Alcalá, Salamanca and Leuven. This may be explained by the fact that the bulk of Irish overseas trade was conducted with Spain, Portugal, France and Flanders, whereas trade with the Hanseatic League was limited.[8] It was upon these well-established shipping-routes that the Counter-Reformation corridor to Ireland was constructed.

There was a centuries-old tradition of Irish mercantile activity with the ports of Bruges, Bordeaux, Bayonne, San Sebastian, Santander, Bares, La Coruña, and Lisbon. From these continental points of contact, not only merchandise but ideas arrived at the Irish ports of Wexford, Waterford, Youghal, Cork, Castletownbeare, Dingle, Limerick and Galway. Not confined to intellectual or religious affairs only, these ideas also extended to architecture, naval engineering, etiquette and even interior décor.[9] Significantly, the Franciscan Observance spread rapidly in the Gaelic and Hiberno-Norman territories where it established its power-base. Its arrival via France and Spain through the southern and western ports, and its subsequent proliferation coincided with the Gaelic resurgence in literature, the arts, music and architecture, which flourished during the fifteenth century. Friars such as the poets Tadhg Camchosach Ó Dálaigh (fl. 1400) and Pilib Bocht Ó hUigínn (ob. 1487) brought to this Gaelic renaissance ideals and motifs of contemporary Spanish, French and Flemish Christian humanism. A surviving inventory of the library at Youghal friary in 1491 lists many works of Italian, French and Spanish provenance.[10] By 1530 the Observant reform had become well rooted in the English-controlled cities and enclaves.[11]

The migration of Irish students to Spain predated the Henrician Reformation. During the reign of Henry V (1413-22), a restrictive policy on the admission of Irish students was enacted at Oxford and Cambridge in response to claims that the Irish had been involved in rioting. This restriction coincided with an increased frequency in Irish trade with the Iberian Peninsula and thus many Gaelic scholars sailed south to the Spanish universities.[12] The surviving medieval registers of the universities of Salamanca, Alcalá, Paris and Bologna contain the names of Gaelic *autoditati*, *jurisconsulti*' and *'literati*', many of whom were laymen. Among the clerical scholars most were friars of the Observant reform. The increased trade with Spain brought larger numbers of Irish pilgrims to Santiago de Compostella. Gaelic Franciscans seem to have been most numerous among the *'hibernes'* admitted to Salamanca having paid their devotional respects at the shrine of St James.[13] The most prominent Gaelic-Irish Franciscan theologian in Europe during the late fifteenth century was Maurice O'Fihely. He had been a student at Oxford, Salamanca and Bologna. Known to his contemporaries as *'Flos Mundi',* he prepared a four-volume edition of the works of John Duns Scotus with commentaries, which was published in Venice in 1506. He was appointed archbishop of Tuam but died in Galway on 24 June 1513 before reaching his see.[14] The foregoing would suggest that friars abroad kept their *confrères* in Ireland informed of the contemporary intellectual and spiritual climate on the continent. This was an important line of communication for the early Catholic Reformation to the *'ecclesia inter Hibernos'*.

Irish scholars in Spain during this period experienced the great cultural and intellectual flowering of the Spanish church under the direction of the Cardinal Primate, Francisco Ximénez de Cisneros, archbishop of Toledo and friar of the Franciscan observance. His *alma mater*, Salamanca and the University of Alcalá de Henares, which he founded in 1498, became centres of classical and scriptural scholarship and of Christian humanism in the Iberian Peninsula. Their influence soon percolated throughout the Habsburg Empire and to Ireland.[15] The theological revival at Salamanca was led by distinguished Dominican intellectuals such as Francisco de Vittoria (1480-1546), Melchor Cano (1509-60), and Domingo de Soto (1494-1560). Under their influence, many Salamancan scholars (including Irish students) were formed.

This intellectual influence was evident among canonists and theologians from Alcalá, Salamanca and Leuven who led the debates on defining Catholic doctrine and discipline at the Council of Trent.[16] It is important to note that the Crown initiated the reform in Spain independently of the papacy. This increased the power of the monarchy in ecclesiastical affairs and this situation had long-term implications for Hispano-Papal relations even with regard to Ireland.[17]

Early manifestations of Spanish reformist influence in politico-religious terms emerged in the vehement opposition of the Irish Observant Franciscans to the Reformation of Henry VIII.[18] The friars were prominent in the Kildare Rebellion (1534-35), as propagandists and as contacts for the envoys of Emperor Charles V to the rebel leader Lord Thomas FitzGerald. When appealing to Pope Paul III for the excommunication of Henry and support for the revolt, the earl of Kildare's chaplain, Charles Reynolds, Dean of Kells, invoked the legal theological arguments for the lawful deposition of a ruler then being expounded by the Salamancan jurist-theologian, Francisco de Vittoria.[19] Simultaneously, Charles V consulted Vittoria concerning a justification for deposing Henry VIII either by Imperial invasion or assisting the rebels in Ireland and England.[20] The friars re-emerged in the diplomatic and politico-religious activity of the Desmond Wars of 1569-75 and 1579-84. The latter war was proclaimed and recognised as the first Counter-Reformation military crusade in Ireland.[21] The Observant Franciscans continued their involvement in such activities during the Nine Years War of 1594-1603 (the final conflict in the Anglo-Spanish War, 1585-1605). This campaign led by the Ulster lords received a formal justification and an extrapolation of the Crusader's Indulgence from the University of Salamanca.[22]

The Counter-Reformation mission began in Ireland with the return of the Limerick-born Jesuit, David Woulfe, in 1561. He had been prominent in the Catholic Reform of the Imperial territories in northern Italy and in the Valtelline. Formed in the spirit of the Spanish theological school, Woulfe was accredited papal nuncio to the Irish church. His most significant contribution to Irish Catholicism was to organise the effective recruitment of candidates for the priesthood and to arrange for their education on the continent. Through the ports of Munster and Connacht, these recruits embarked for studies in Spain and its Flemish-Burgundian territories.[23] Significantly, the early Irish seminaries and colleges were established under royal instead of papal supervision and protection at Douai, Leuven, Alcalá, Valladolid, Salamanca and Santiago de Compostella. It was not until well into the seventeenth century that Irish colleges were finally established in Rome.[24]

In addition to his work in the ecclesiastical sphere, Woulfe engaged in the less spiritual activity of espionage. Though he owed obedience to the papacy, his political loyalties inclined towards the Spanish-Habsburg monarchy. Through his ambassador to Portugal, Don Juan de Borja, Philip II commissioned Woulfe to write a *Description of Ireland* for Spanish military intelligence.[25] Woulfe's missions benefited from his good relations with the Marian Catholic clergy who had helped stem the Protestant tide and were now resisting Elizabethan innovations.[26] Nuncio Woulfe consolidated the Catholic position by introducing a committed Counter-Reformation episcopate. That he had little difficulty in finding suitable candidates is a good indication of the presence of Catholic reform-minded clergy prior to his mission. Significantly, Woulfe recommended Observant friars for Irish sees including those occupied by Queen Elizabeth's Anglican appointees. Among his nominees were Thomas O'Herlihy of Ross, Donal MacCongail of Raphoe, Eugene O'Hart of Achonry and Andrew O'Crean of Elphin. These prelates had been educated in the Spanish school and three of them attended the closing sessions of the Council of Trent following their episcopal consecration. Perhaps Woulfe's most important nomination (and certainly the most formidable who enjoyed the personal esteem of Ignatius de Loyola) was that of his fellow Limerick man, Richard Creagh, to the primatial see of Armagh in 1564. During the 1540s both Woulfe and Creagh had studied for the priesthood in the nascent Counter-Reformation seminaries of Europe. This in itself is an indication of the ethos prevalent in Limerick during the mid-sixteenth century.[27] Creagh, who had received a burse from Emperor Charles V, studied at the Standonck and Pontifical colleges in Leuven. During the 1550s Creagh returned to Limerick where he ministered as a priest and schoolmaster. Nuncio Woulfe, archbishop Creagh and their fellow prelates are pivotal figures in that they constructed the Irish Counter-Reformation on the foundation of the Catholic Reform initiated by the Observant movement.[28]

While Gaelic Irish students had attended Salamanca since the mid-fifteenth century, Anglo-Irish names began to appear with increasing frequency on its registers and on the registers of Leuven from 1548 onwards.[29] Leuven had been enriched by the return of its graduates as professors from Salamanca during this period. It soon emerged as the centre for Augustinian theology north of the Pyrenees. Foremost among its professors were Michael Baïus and Jacobus Jansonius.[30] Within a year of Elizabeth I's accession (1558), over a hundred scholars left Oxbridge to pursue their studies at Leuven, Salamanca and Valladolid.[31] Within a decade the numbers of Anglo-Irish students in Spain and Flanders had swelled into hundreds.[32] In the words of Robert Bellarmine SJ, Leuven had become a 'citadel of wisdom, almost beyond compare in the number of its students, the fame of its doctors and the wealth and convenience of its instruments of learning'.[33]

The facility with which the Irish, especially Gaelic scholars entered the prestigious universities of Spain and their immediate reception of Spanish citizenship may be explained by their identification with Spain's culture and people. The fact that they received such privileges and sympathy reveals reciprocal fellow feeling from their hosts. In Spain the Irish were regarded as 'Northern Spaniards'.[34] The accommodation of the Irish in Spain may be further explained by the concept of 'Old Ordered Society'. Both Gaelic and Spanish aristocracies maintained similarly strict hierarchical structures and codes of etiquette which differed from the norms of contemporary European social structures, then in transition from feudal to early-modern systems.[35] Hence the easy passage of Irish priests, scholars, professionals and military officers into important positions in the Spanish Monarquia from the sixteenth to the eighteenth centuries.[36]

From 1558 onwards the increasing numbers of Irish émigré students were lodged privately or in monastic houses of study.[37] It was not until the 1580s that Irish Jesuits such as Thomas White and Christopher Cusack established hostels specifically to accommodate Irish students at Douai and Valladolid. These were the nascent Irish Colleges.[38] Due to their precarious financial existence, support was sought and obtained from the Spanish Crown. In August 1592, Philip II had the Irish students at Valladolid transferred to the university of Salamanca where they were housed and incorporated as a distinct Irish College under the patronage of the Crown. In 1610, Philip III who bestowed on them the title 'Collegio Real de San Patricio de los Nobles Irlandeses, Salamanca', reaffirmed their royal collegial status and privileges.[39] Within a short time other royal Irish colleges were established at Alcalá, Evora and Lisbon (1593), Douai (1594), Antwerp (1600), Santiago de Compostella (1605), Leuven (1606), Lille (1610), Seville (1611), Nieupoort (1627) and Madrid (1629). Significantly Spanish ecclesiastics and nobles were equally well disposed to the émigrés, which is a testimony to the Spanish affinity with the Irish. The Irish College at Alcalá was founded by Count Jorge de Paz y Silveira whose mother was descended from the Gaelic Irish dynasty, the MacDonnells of Antrim. The Irish College at Seville was founded by the Archdeacon of Seville, Don Felix de Guzman and a local nobleman Count Jerónimo de Medina Farragut.[40] The Salamancan graduate, Florence Conry, obtained the patronage of Philip III and the Archdukes Albert and Isabella in the foundation of the first Irish Franciscan continental college at Leuven (1606). This *Koninklijke College de S. Anthonius van der Ierscher Franciscaner, Leuven* (Royal College of St. Anthony of the Irish Franciscans), was incorporated into the university of Leuven.[41] It soon rose to academic prominence of European significance, especially in the development of Augustinianism and Scotism. Three years later at the behest of Philip III and Hugh O'Neill, exiled earl of Tyrone, Conry was appointed archbishop of Tuam (1609-1629).

The foundation of these royal Irish colleges coincided with the emergence of Irish expatriate merchant and military communities in Spain and Flanders. An Irish Counter-Reformation laity was formed through the ministrations of the Irish colleges. In particular the colleges provided chaplains to the Irish regiments in the army of Flanders, and it is a testimony to these chaplains that a large number of retired or decommissioned Irish officers and soldiers later studied for the priesthood in these colleges. Close family ties also existed between the Irish military and religious émigrés.[42] The Hispanophile English Jesuit, Robert Persons, in a letter to Philip III in 1605, commented on the émigré collegial-military relationship, that the soldiers undergoing catechesis would 'return as Catholics to their homeland' and spread the faith.[43] The Spanish authorities gave practical recognition to this link by frequent contributions to the Irish colleges from military funds.[44] As the Council of State advised Philip III in June 1600, Ireland could be the 'English Flanders'[45] The English authorities were also acutely aware of this Irish factor in Spanish interests and policies.[46]

II

This Irish dimension in Spanish politico-military designs would also affect relations between Madrid and Rome and the subsequent development of Regalism in the Irish colleges in the Spanish-Habsburg Monarquia. In this respect, the background to the foundation of the Royal College of the Noble Irish at Salamanca provides an interesting case-study. At the time when the Irish college was founded at Salamanca Philip II with the support of Castilian Jesuit Provincial, Jose de Acosta, was seeking to remove the Spanish Jesuit provinces from the centralised authority of the Father General in Rome, Claudio Aquaviva.[47] In such a Regalist climate, Acosta at the king's request directed the formation of the Irish college at Salamanca despite Aquaviva's disapproval. For the first ten months of its existence the college was governed by Thomas White, a secular priest, with James Archer SJ, as vice-rector and spiritual director.[48] The following year, White entered the Castilian Jesuit novitiate and Archer became the first Jesuit rector of the Irish college. Although Aquaviva disapproved he did not oppose the situation since he desired reconciliation with the Castilian province having defeated the royal challenge earlier that year.[49] Nevertheless Aquaviva remained wary of the Spanish monarchy's Irish adherents such as Archer, lest they endanger the Society's Irish mission with their Regalism.[50] The divergence between Papalist and Regalist Jesuit interests arose again during the Nine Years War (1594-1603), when some Spanish-educated Irish Jesuits led by Archer defied Aquaviva's warning against involvement with the Spanish-Irish alliance by their promotion of Ireland's investiture in the Spanish-Habsburg monarchy.

Regalist in its politics, the Irish college at Salamanca also reflected Spanish culture, etiquette and attitudes in its discipline and character. Archer modelled the formation of the Irish students on standard Spanish Jesuit practice. Students were obliged to be of legitimate Catholic parentage, of noble or gentlemanly status and of sound morals. They were also required to swear allegiance to the faith, the Spanish monarchy and the Irish mission. These rules provided the model for other Irish colleges in the Spanish monarquía.[51] Graduates of these colleges were spiritually, academically, culturally and politically formed in the milieu of Regalist Spanish Catholicism. Between 1590 and 1615 it is estimated that three hundred priests (diocesan and regular), were ordained from the Irish colleges in Spanish territories.[52] Since its foundation, three hundred and eighty-nine alumni had been ordained and had returned to Ireland from the Irish college at Salamanca by 1652.[53] The effectiveness of these colleges was reflected in the draconian legislation against 'all seminary priests and Jesuits', and the prohibition on foreign education by the Stuart monarch, James I.[54]

III

During the first fifty years of the Irish colleges' existence, the theological focus of the great universities was concerned with the 'Salvific Question of Grace'. It was a major influence on the mentality of the Counter-Reformation and early modern European thought.[55] The problem arose of reconciling divine prescience and predestination to salvation or damnation with the dogma of divine will to universal salvation. Salamanca became the cradle of controversies concerning 'Grace'. The main protagonists were the Rigorist School, which developed and used Augustinianism, and the Laxist School, which employed the writings of the Jesuit, Ludovico Molina. The Dominicans were concerned that both Augustinians and Molinists might undermine the Thomist-Scholastic approach by their literalism and fundamentalist scriptural exegesis. Augustinianism had become pre-eminent in the University of Salamanca by the late 1580s after initial Thomist opposition during the 1560s and 70s. Irish students attending the university studied under the great theological masters of the age such as Luís de Léon OSA, Alonso Gudiel, Martin Martínez de Cantalapiedra and Francisco Sanchez de las Brozas, 'el Brocense', of the Augustinian School; Michael Banez OP, and Melchor Cano OP., of the Thomist School; and the Laxist exponent Ludovico Molina SJ. While students of the Irish college and the Dominican houses were well briefed in the latter two systems, it appears that Irish Franciscan scholars inclined towards Augustinianism.[56]

Foremost among the first generation of Irish Counter-Reformation Franciscans influenced by Spanish Augustinianism and Regalism were Florence Conry, Hugh MacCaghwell, Robert Chamberlain, Hugh Ward and

Luke Wadding. Significantly they were professed in the Observant province of Santiago de Compostella and educated at Salamanca.[57] Their Franciscan lectors and tutors at their friary were of the Augustinian School. Their Irish pupils rose to great distinction in the Augustinian tradition. Conry became a leading authority on the doctrines of St Augustine. He also distinguished himself as a diplomat under Philip III and Philip IV.[58] MacCaghwell, an outstanding Scotist, employed Augustinianism to develop the theology of the fourteenth-century Irish Franciscan philosopher-theologian John Duns Scotus and like his confrère Luke Wadding, he used these systems to develop and defend the theology of the Immaculate Conception of the Virgin Mary, a subject dear to the Spanish Crown.[59] Chamberlain was a leading professor of Augustinian theology at Leuven and Wadding a prominent scripture scholar and theological consultor to the Spanish embassy in Rome and to the Holy Office.[60] MacCaghwell, Chamberlain and Ward having received their doctorates went to Leuven where they lectured and assisted Conry in the foundation of the Anthonianum.[61] While *en route* to Flanders, Ward stayed awhile in Paris as secretary to his former tutor, the queen's confessor, Arriba, who was then writing *De Auxiliis Gratiae*.[62]

Augustinianism had been professed at Leuven before the arrival of the Irish Franciscans from Salamanca by Michael Baïus and his disciple Jacobus Jansonius whose rigorism was opposed by the Jesuits led by Leonardus Lessius SJ.[63] Jansonius was a friendly benefactor to the Irish at Leuven. For almost twenty years before the establishment of the Irish Franciscan (1606) and Pastoral (1623) colleges, Jansonius accommodated and supported Irish students in the university. He taught many of them. Among his protégés were the Irishmen Peter Lombard, Edmund Dungan and Dutchmen, Cornelius Jansen and Philip Rovenius.[64] Lombard, Jansen and Rovenius opposed Molinism and supported their university against Jesuit attempts to obtain greater influence in, if not control of, the theological faculty. Among the intellectual elite of the Counter-Reformation in Europe, Lombard rose to prominence. He had a distinguished career in Leuven as a theologian and later as a diplomat and theological *peritus* at the papal court. In 1598 Lombard was sent to Rome by the university as its commissary to counteract Jesuit machinations. He was soon employed by Hugh O'Neill to represent the Irish-Spanish political cause. In 1601 he was appointed Archbishop-Primate of Armagh at the behest of Philip III and O'Neill. From 1602 to 1607 Lombard was chief episcopal theologian in the 'Congregatio De Auxiliis' and with its consultor, the aforementioned Juan de Rada, he consistently opposed the propositions of Molina.[65] Lombard also opposed the Jesuit control of the Irish Colleges of Salamanca, Alcalá, Lisbon and Santiago.[66] After distinguished studies in Leuven and Pont-à-Mousson, Edmund Dungan became

Bishop of Down and Connor (1625-1629).[67] Philip Rovenius, a renowned advocate of Augustinianism and friend of Conry, became Vicar Apostolic of the Northern Dutch Provinces (1614-1651).[68] Cornelius Jansen was certainly the most famous (or infamous) of the rigorist Augustinian School. He was the first rector of the Dutch *Collegium Pulcheriae Mariae Virginis* at Leuven (fd. 1617), situated opposite the Irish Franciscan college, and lectured in the theological faculty.[69] The writings and opinions of Jansonius and Conry had considerable influence on Jansen's theological development.[70] His controversial book *Augustinus,* concerning predestination, was published posthumously in 1640. Jesuit accusations of its renewal of Baïanist errors and neo-Calvinism led to its condemnation in 1642 by Pope Urban VIII's bull, *In Eminenti.* In the following year the University of Leuven contested the bull and sent its representatives, Dr John Sinnich, an Irish priest and later Rector Magnificus of Leuven, and Dr Cornelius de Paepe, to present the university's defense of *Augustinus* in Rome.[71] Interestingly, it was not until 1651 that *In Eminenti* was finally promulgated in Spanish Flanders. Nevertheless, it aroused major division in the church during the seventeenth century and led ultimately to schism in 1704.[72]

St Anthony's Irish College at Leuven became a confluence for the Augustinian streams of Spain and the Low Countries. Its founder, Conry, widely regarded as the most important Rigorist of the age, incorporated the systems of Léon, Pastrana, Herrera, Baïus and Jansonius with his own erudition in his writings concerning grace.[73] Conry was the central link in the chain of leading Spanish, Dutch and Irish Rigorists and Regalists as much as he was a leading advocate of Irish incorporation in the Spanish monarquía. His theological significance lies in the fact that he was one of the very few to have published on the 'Salvific Question' despite the Roman Inquisition's prohibition in 1611, following the dissolution of the 'Congregatio De Auxiliis' by Paul V in 1607.[74] With the support and protection of the Spanish Crown, Conry published his *Tractatus de Augustini sensu circa beatae Mariae Virginis Conceptionem* (Antwerp, 1619).[75] As we shall see, this major treatise gave intellectual weight to the efforts by the Spanish monarchy to obtain a doctrinal definition concerning the Immaculate Conception of the Blessed Virgin Mary. Cornelius Jansen in his correspondence with the Abbé de St Cyran (a leading French Rigorist and chaplain to Louis XIII) sheds interesting light on his relations with Conry.[76] On 4 November 1621, Jansen wrote that Conry despaired of obtaining papal approval for his treatise dealing with original sin and redemption.[77] This work *Peregrinus Jerichuntinus,* was later bequeathed by Conry to Jansen and published posthumously in 1641.[78] Nevertheless, Conry had done everything he could to promote the Augustinian teaching on 'Grace'. We know from Jansen's correspondence with St Cyran that Conry pushed against the limits of the Inquisition's pro-hibition by treating this subject subtly in another work. Using pseudonyms identified by the distinguished French historian Jean Orcibal, Jansen wrote:

'Gemer' [Conry] burns with desire to bring to light a certain work, 'De Poena Parvulorum post hanc vitam', believing that it will breach the fort-ifications of 'Porris' [the Molinists]. It touches indirectly the affair of 'Pilmot' [Grace], as you well see by the teaching of 'Leonius' [St Augustine]...[79]

Having obtained the support of Augustinian divines at Salamanca and of Alfonso Cardinal de la Cueva, Spanish ambassador at Brussels,[80] Conry pre-sented his treatise to the Spanish Cardinal Protector in Rome, Gabriel de Trejo, as Jansen informed St Cyran:

The treatise which 'Gemer' [Conry] sent to Rome to Cardinal de Trejo for consideration, *'De Poena Parvulorum'*, contains succinctly what 'Seraphy' [St Augustine] defended as an article of faith, that they [deceased unbaptised children] are damned to sore punishments, in truth to fire, although he dares not say it openly, and consequently they are Pelagian who deny it...[81]

However, Conry modified this grim interpretation, and with approbations from Leuven, Douai and Salamanca he published *Tractatus de Statu Parvulorum sine baptismo decedentium ex hac vita iuxta sensum D. Augustini* (Antwerp and Louvain, 1624). Dedicated to Cardinal de Trejo, this work dealt with the state rather than the penalty of the unbaptised deceased infants. Using St Augustine's writings and scriptural exegesis, Conry com-bated what he perceived as a neo-Pelagian error that these infants were exempted from hell. He maintained that the laxists had a misguided sense of compassion, that the reality was that there was no salvation outside the church. While not suffering the fate of evil-doers, the unbaptised children did not enjoy the beatific vision either; they were in a state of reserve until the Last Judgment.[82]

It is interesting to note that before Conry published his tracts Jansen revealed that the students in the Irish college requested that his writings on 'Grace' be read to them at dinner in the refectory.[83] In 1618, the Rector, Hugh MacCaghwell, published his rigorist treatise on Penance, *Speculum Poenitentiae,* translated into Irish *Sgathán Shacramuinte na hAithridhe* (Louvain, 1618). It followed the publication by his confrère Bonaventure O'Hussey of *An Teagasc Críosdaídhe* (Antwerp, 1611 and Leuven, 1614), the first catechism published in Irish print. It also has a rigorist flavour.

Augustinianism among the first generation of St Anthony's graduates was well reputed and among the doctoral theses from the college, two were particularly distinguished.[84] John Barnewall of St Patrick defended his thesis *Universa theologia iuxta mentem Doctoris Subtilis* on 13 November 1620. It was dedicated to the newly appointed Archbishop-Primate of Mechelen (Malines), Jacques Boonen, a rigorist and friend of Conry.[85] Another John Barnewall achieved distinction in the University of Leuven with the defence of his thesis *Sententia D. Augustini Eximii Ecclesiae Doctoris de gratia libero arbitrio, praedestinatione et reprobatione* on 9 September 1627. According to the Jesuit theologian, Adriaan Crom, Jansen desired the publication of this thesis in order to prepare public opinion for the reception of his own forthcoming work, *Augustinus*.[86]

Apart from Conry's important contribution to the Augustinian movement in Europe, there was the publication of an authoritative edition of St Augustine's writings with scholarly commentaries by members of St Anthony's Irish College, the *Opera Omnia D. Augustini* (Louvain, 1630). This provided a major work of reference for Augustinian theological studies, for patristics and for scriptural studies in the theological faculties of seventeenth and eighteenth-century Catholic Europe. Irish theologians also played a significant role in a major Spanish doctrinal cause, the definition and defence of the Immaculate Conception of the Virgin Mary. They were specifically requested by the Spanish Crown to assist this cause.[87] Significantly, the matter was initiated by Philip III and not by the papacy and Augustinian-Scotist theology provided the system for definition rather than the Thomism of the Dominicans.[88] The Old English Franciscan, Luke Wadding, a prominent theologian and scriptural scholar at Salamanca, whose work on the origin and use of Hebrew, *De Linguae Hebraïcae origine praestantia et utilitate* (Rome, 1621)[89] provided a major contribution to biblical linguistic and scriptural scholarship in the early modern period, was appointed theological consultor by Philip III to the Spanish deputation in Rome in 1616. In 1618 this mission, led by Bishop Antonio de Trejo, formally presented the case to the pope. The Augustinian treatise on the Immaculate Conception, published by Conry in 1619, provided theological support.[90] Significantly, this was the first major work to be published on this subject since the cause was formally initiated in Rome and was an important reference work in subsequent writings on the matter. Conry received from Wadding his report on the Spanish legation and had it read in the refectory at St Anthony's.[91] Conry also acquainted members of the University of Leuven and the Council of Brabant with it.[92] Through their influence Wadding published his *Legatio Philippi III et IV Hispaniorum Regum ad Sanctissimos Paulum V, Gregorium XV et Urbanum VIII, Pro definienda controversia Conceptionis B. V. Mariae* (Antwerp, 1624); it was dedicated to Bishop de Trejo. Both Wadding and MacCaghwell revived and promoted Scotism by using Augustinianism as a theological system in

Leuven, Paris and Rome.[93] Bonaventure Magennis, one of MacCaghwell's pupils and future bishop of Down and Connor, publicly defended his mentor's writings in 1623. Another disciple, Malachy Fallon founded the Irish college in Prague in 1630. Significantly it was dedicated to the Immaculate Conception.[94] Furthermore, Wadding's colleague in the Spanish legation, Joseph de Bergoigne, Commissary General of the 'Natio Germano-Belgica' Franciscan province (1625-1638), imposed Scotism on the theological curriculum of Franciscan novitiates and colleges worldwide at the Order's General Chapter in Toledo (1634).[95] One of the most distinguished advocates and disseminators of Scotism in the Tyrol, Austria, Bohemia and Bavaria in the mid-seventeenth century was the Gaelic Irish Franciscan, Bonaventure O'Connor Kerry. Though based at Bolzano (Bozen), O'Connor Kerry had lectured at Innsbruck, Prague, Eichstatt and Marienberg. Among his publications were two major works on Scotism the *Elenchus Encomiorum ....* *Ioanni Duns Scoti* (Bolzano, 1660), and *Lumen Orthodoxum* (Bolzano, 1661), and one Scotist treatise on the Immaculate Conception entitled *Quintuplex.* *Pentekaedechyris Mariana* (Trent, 1658), and a treatise on the Portiuncula Indulgence entitled *Jubilaeum Jubilum* (Prague, 1664).[96]

In 1661, the Irish Franciscan annalist, John Punch, who was based in Paris, recorded that since the beginning of the seventeenth century there were at least seventy Irish Franciscan theologians, philosophers and canonists of high distinction who had held professorial chairs and lectureships in the major universities of Counter-Reformation Catholic Europe.[97] These Irish philosophers and theologians of the Augustinian and Scotist schools contributed much to the intellectual life of the Catholic Counter-Reformation in Europe and further afield. Their teaching in the great universities of Salamanca, Leuven, Innsbruck, Salzburg and Paris (*inter alia*), helped form the intellectual development of generations of Counter-Reformation Catholic clergy in early modern Europe. This is quite a notable testimony to the Irish theological contribution to the Catholic and Counter-Reformation movements.

CHAPTER NINE

The religion of the Protestant laity in early modern Ireland

Raymond Gillespie

To understand something of the religious world of Protestants in Ireland from the Reformation until the nineteenth century two different approaches are possible. The first stresses the institutional structures, which people created to give expression to their beliefs, and the second focuses on those beliefs themselves. The lived experience of religious belief in the early modern world was the product of the interaction of these two manifestations of religion. This essay will consider each of these aspects in so far as they were revealed within the community of non-Roman Catholics in early modern Ireland.[1]

I

From the perspective of religious ideas, it is clear that the Reformation in Ireland progressed only slowly. Protestant doctrines were slow to be fully adopted even among those who described themselves as such. The late sixteenth-century will of Sir Thomas Cusack of Lismullen in Co Meath, for instance, opened with a long theological preamble in which he declared his Protestant credentials by proclaiming himself one of the elect, saved by the blood of Christ. However he also took the precaution of providing money for a month's mind, building a chapel at Trevet where he was to be buried and arranging for a priest to be paid £4 to sing the service. These arrangements strongly resemble the establishment of a chantry chapel and thus were contrary to Protestant doctrine.[2] Whereas this example illustrates that personal theology could be rather confused in an era of change, in administrative contexts it is less difficult to identify a break with older arrangements.

In May 1536 the Irish parliament, following its English counterpart, passed an act recognising Henry VIII as 'supreme head in earth of the whole church of Ireland' and appeals to Rome were forbidden. A significant body of legislation and administrative changes followed. In the parliament of 1537 acts were passed 'against the authority of the bishop of Rome' and for the dissolution of some small monasteries. By the 1540s the dissolution campaign widened and all the Irish religious houses within the sphere of English authority were dissolved or transformed into secular churches. A reformed Church of Ireland, independent from that of Rome had been created and had in one action acquired the property and clergy of the older pre-Reformation church. The central issue here was not doctrine but authority. Those who did not subscribe to the new order would be termed 'popish' or 'papists' because of their allegiance to the authority of the church of Rome.

Reaction to these changes was muted. Many of the great Irish lords, such as the Butlers, earls of Ormond, or the O'Neills of Tyrone, were happy to embrace the administrative changes. More difficulty was experienced over the issue of religious practice. Despite the administrative changes, the Mass continued to be celebrated, though the destruction of relics in the early 1540s became a cause of concern for many. While the native Irish annals record the destruction of relics at Trim and in Dublin in 1538 in their account of the coming of the Reformation, the same relics are mentioned again in the seventeenth century. It seems likely that the best-known relics were not destroyed but rather removed from public view and retained in secret by the laity. In Limerick the property of dissolved religious houses was also retained in lay hands.[3] This may also have been true in Dublin since during the brief Catholic restoration under Queen Mary in the mid-1550s the former Augustinian canons of the cathedral of Christ Church were able to produce pre-Reformation ecclesiastical dress, which suggests it had been carefully stored.[4]

By the time Henry VIII died in January 1547 a conservative style of reform had been achieved in Ireland, mainly in institutional terms. His son, Edward VI, introduced more radical reforms before his early death in 1553.[5] Unlike his father, Edward redrafted the liturgy twice in two Books of Common Prayer in 1549 and 1552, although the second book does not seem to have been used in Ireland. While the revised liturgy was used in some parts of Ireland, including the cities of Limerick and Kilkenny, it does not seem to have struck any popular roots. Alterations in the liturgy produced more opposition than had been seen previously in regard to administrative changes. Old traditions survived unaltered well into the 1560s. The feast of Corpus Christi continued to be celebrated publicly in Dublin, and in Kilkenny some of the nominal members of the new church demanded that their bishop 'have a communion in honour of St Anne'.[6]

The death of Edward VI in 1553 and the accession of his Roman Catholic sister, Mary, were perceived by some as the end of the Church of Ireland and the flirtation with reform. The Protestant bishop of Ossory, John Bale, described with annoyance the speed and enthusiasm with which the old order was restored. The Marian interlude was, in turn, to be a short one with the death of the Catholic queen in November 1558 and the accession of the Protestant Queen Elizabeth. At first it was not clear what form Elizabeth's settlement would take but the parliament of 1560 restored the supremacy of the crown in ecclesiastical matters, imposed an oath of supremacy in recognising this and introduced a new prayer book, of which a Latin version was to be allowed as a concession to non-English speakers.[7] Of considerable importance for the newly established church was the introduction of the oath of supremacy since many of the more conservative clergy found themselves unable to take the oath and so were deprived of their livings. In this way a new cadre of more committed Church of Ireland clergy began to emerge. This, however, took time and it is worth remembering that in 1580 the bishop of Clonfert, Roland Burke, held his see both by papal provision and Crown appointment.

In the early stages of Elizabeth's reign the religious settlement remained uncertain and much depended on the survival of the queen. As the reign continued it became clear that the Church of Ireland was set to establish itself as an enduring presence in Ireland most notably among those associated with the English administration. What was worrying was that the church was failing to attract converts among the indigenous population. The reasons for this are complex. Lack of resources in poorly-endowed parishes, an increasingly dilapidated stock of buildings, a shortage of clergy prepared to work outside the area of English influence and an unwillingness to use the Irish language as part of the evangelisation process have all been advanced as reasons why the Church of Ireland lacked dynamism in the later sixteenth century.[8] In addition by the early seventeenth century it was facing a newly resurgent Counter-Reformation church that was rapidly reorganising in Ireland. What the late sixteenth century saw was a slow retreat of the state church from being a truly national one to being the church of a colonial minority. Ireland became almost unique in Europe in that the principle of the Treaty of Augsburg (that the religion of the ruler should be the religion of the people) did not apply.

That retreat was both prompted by and in turn shaped the theology of the Church of Ireland into the seventeenth century. Like its sister church in England, the Church of Ireland was quick to adopt a Calvinist theology of election.[9] However, influenced by its position as essentially the church of a minority community, it went further in its 1615 articles of belief, stating explicitly what had only been implied in England, that the pope was antichrist. As well as adopting a hardline position on the concept of the elect these articles went further than their English equivalents by accepting double-predestinarianism, i.e., the predestination both of the damned and the saved. Culture and religion as a result became hopelessly confused. The failure of the native Irish to anglicise in matters of language, dress and manners became a mark of their barbarity. Their failure to convert to a church which, because of its theology of election, did not envisage converting them all, seemed to reinforce the idea that they were incapable of being part of the elect. Around these assumptions the scholarly archbishop of Armagh, James Ussher, built an intellectual edifice in the early seventeenth century which gave the Church of Ireland a coherent identity. His work drew on European models of the history of the church to prove that what had happened in the 1530s was not a new departure but simply a purging of the church of St Patrick from its medieval corruptions.[10]

The conception which the early seventeenth-century Church of Ireland had of itself had important implications for worship and liturgy. The focus of worship lay not in a communal liturgy drawing together the people of a parish, but rather in the sermon preached to a group who considered themselves among the elect. The Eucharist was celebrated infrequently outside the major cathedrals and the value placed on the ceremonial surrounding worship was low. In some respects this approach to worship served the Church of Ireland well. In the years after 1609 large numbers of Scots migrated to the northern part of Ireland as part of the Ulster plantation. The ecclesiastical background of these men and women was different from that of the Church of Ireland because they came from a country where a Presbyterian church had effected the Reformation. Given the 'puritan' emphasis within the Church of Ireland, the only issue which separated these newcomers from the established church, was church government. The minority position of Protestants meant that agreement on broad issues became more important than 'externals' and an accommodation resulted by which various Presbyterian practices were countenanced by Church of Ireland bishops in order to maintain a rather uneasy Protestant unity.[11]

Such unity was not, however, to last. In the 1630s a group of churchmen in England, led by Archbishop Laud of Canterbury, began to remodel the theology and practice of the Church of England. Drawing on the ideas of Jacob Arminius they denied the existence of a predestined elect, stressing instead the importance of the Eucharist as the main channel for sacramental grace and emphasising also the importance of the parish as a unit of worship. Allied with this was an enhanced role for the church. Its rights and privileges were to be reinforced, its property rights enhanced and the fabric of its buildings beautified as a fit setting for worship. The appointment of Laud's ally Thomas Wentworth as lord deputy of Ireland in 1633 saw these ideas introduced to Ireland through the appointment of a number of Laudian bishops and clergy.[12] Those who rejected this agenda, including the Ulster Presbyterians, were forced out of the Church of Ireland by the imposition of an oath declaring the king to be head of the church. By 1640 Irish Protestantism had begun to fragment.

That fragmentation worsened over the following twenty years. The outbreak of rebellion in Ireland in 1641 and civil war in England in 1642 had long-term consequences for the Irish church. In 1647 the 'puritan' forces of the English parliament triumphed in Ireland. With their victory came the disestablishment of the Church of Ireland and the prohibition of its liturgy. The inflow of parliamentarian troops from England brought with it a wide range of Protestant sects including Presbyterians, Quakers, Baptists and Independents who for the first time established a small but very significant presence in Ireland.[13] The result of this was that, after 1660, Protestantism would never again be coequal with the re-established Church of Ireland and differences that had been patched over before 1640 became occasions for public dispute within the Protestant community.[14] Moreover, dissent lacked a unified set of doctrines and was itself seriously split in the seventeenth and eighteenth centuries.[15] The situation was further complicated by the propensity of the Irish dissenting churches, especially the Presbyterians, to subdivide in response to centralising tendencies. Between 1700 and 1800, for instance, the Presbyterian church, located mainly in the north of Ireland, witnessed three major splits.

In 1660 with the fall of the Cromwellian protectorate the Church of Ireland was restored as the established church. Ideas that had seemed radical in the 1630s when Archbishop Laud propagated them had now acquired the patina of respectability. New patterns of worship were gradually established. Monthly communions became the norm in Dublin by the 1680s and this pattern gradually extended to the countryside.[16] In terms of devotion and doctrine, the ideas of the 'Caroline divines', pre-eminently Jeremy Taylor, bishop of Down and Connor, became dominant in the Church of Ireland into the eighteenth century. With the exception of the crisis of 1688-90, the position of the Church of Ireland seemed secure after 1660. It has been argued traditionally that this security lapsed into apathy during the early eighteenth century. However, if the eighteenth-century church is judged not as a national church but rather as provider of pastoral services to a Protestant minority within Ireland then its record is rather more credible.[17]

By the end of the eighteenth century the Church of Ireland, which had managed to hold diverse interests together for most of its existence, began to show signs of strain. The issue on which it divided was its response to resurgent Catholicism. In the closing decade of the seventeenth century and the first two decades of the eighteenth a series of laws, usually termed the 'penal laws', had been passed. These were designed to restrict the actions of Catholics whom the government felt to be disloyal and churchmen felt needed conversion. By the latter part of the eighteenth century sentiments were changing and for reasons of practical politics as well as ideological shifts some in the Church of Ireland were prepared to support a relaxation of that legislation. Conservatives, spurred on by fears generated by agrarian violence, felt this amounted to an attack on the church and rallied against their liberal co-religionists. Dangerous as the situation might have been, no outright split took place and the issue was defused.[18]

By 1800, when the Church of Ireland and the Church of England were formally joined under the terms of the Act of Union, the institutional side of Protestantism in Ireland had evolved greatly since the first appearance of the reformed institution in the 1530s. The Church of Ireland still existed but it was only one among many Protestant sects and churches. In 1831, the date of the first religious census in Ireland, out of a population of 7.9 million, 1.5 million (or 19 per cent) designated themselves as Protestant. Approximately 0.8 million (or about half of all Protestants) described themselves as members of the Church of Ireland. By doing so they were making a series of statements, both political and religious. The institution had become a marker for a particular group identity in Ireland but it was also underpinned by a set of real beliefs about the supernatural world and how it was made manifest in daily life. It is to those that we now turn.

II

Perhaps the best way to begin an exploration of the ideas of religion espoused by the laity in early modern Ireland is to listen to what some of the laity themselves had to say about their beliefs. Such statements about belief are not plentiful. Irish people's religious ideas were usually formed early in their lives, and were integral to their understanding of the world in which they lived. Because of this, they rarely wrote down those assumptions on paper. It therefore is important that we pay close attention to those few comments that survive.

From the surviving evidence, four individuals who have left some personal record of their religious belief can be selected to stand for many others. The first is Eleanor Stringer, the wife of a carpenter from Cork. In 1642 when asked by a Catholic priest what religion she belonged to she replied, 'she was of that religion wherein she had been bred and would live and die'.[19] The second individual, a Mr Dean, was also from Cork. In 1645 when he asked some of the Catholic Irish rebels why he was being persecuted they answered:

> he was a Protestant and a Roundhead. He replied I take it upon my death I know not what those words mean but I am of the religion that both the king and the Lord Lieutenant General of Ireland profess which is the true Protestant religion and if I suffer I know not what I die for...[20]

The third person is another woman, Mary Burrill, a member of a Godly congregation meeting at Christ Church cathedral in Dublin in 1651. Speaking before the congregation she declared:

I have had in my dreams two terrible conflicts with Satan by all which I have been much assured of God's love for that I always had the better, the victory. O, I love the saints of God! His word! and all his ways! and I rest on Christ Jesus alone! and on nothing of self! and I do desire your prayers to God for me to grow in grace etc.[21]

The final example comes some years later in 1686 when two Church of Ireland members of the Irish gentry, Henry Piers, a Westmeath landowner, and Sir James Leigh, talked about religion. Leigh suggested that saints and angels could intercede with God and could be prayed to. Piers told him that this was a ridiculous idea. He said saints and angels could not hear our prayers. Leigh retorted that 'in this I was contrary to our own divinity. I told him that I had never met with anything in any of our divines that would favour the doctrine.' He advanced the proposition based on Matthew 11:28 that Christ invited those who were burdened to come to him for rest, 'but find not that he invites any to address in this case to his mother or any other saint'. He quoted Augustine to support the case. Leigh countered by dismissing Augustine as a Catholic and replied to the text from Matthew with one from Paul. The discussion became confused and ended when the men agreed to consult a bishop when next they were in Dublin.[22]

A good deal can be gleaned from these cases, and from other similar exchanges which have survived from early modern Ireland. At the simplest level they reflect a wide range of religious experience among the Protestant laity. For Eleanor Stringer religion was something of a custom; for Mr Dean it had overtones of political loyalty, while for Mary Burrill it was a highly emotionally charged experience. Despite this diversity, a number of general points emerge. First, when lay men and women were asked what they believed they did not naturally turn to the formulations of belief articulated by the institutional church. The creeds or the catechism, which most of the laity may have been expected to be familiar with, were not central in shaping their beliefs. When the laity entered theological discussion they were often ill equipped to do so. The dialogue between Henry Piers and John Leigh, two literate and well-informed Protestants, demonstrates this. Laymen and women did not think of religious belief in terms of discussable philosophical concepts or collections of ideas. They wanted to understand how faith affected daily life; personal and communal systems of religious thought were devised to be workable, not intellectually tidy. As a result, at the level of belief, there were many tensions between different theological ideas and customs. Protestants, such as Sir James Leigh, can be found articulating what seem to be Catholic beliefs. At a non-elite level, for instance, Protestants might visit holy wells. Even as late as 1838 those writing about the state of the parish of Ballymartin in Co Antrim for the Ordnance survey project recorded that there was a holy well in the parish and that there were '2 old men (Presbyterians) who believe in the properties of this well and are in the habit of using it'.[23] Again from a Catholic perspective there were those whose understanding of belief came very close to what might seem to be a Protestant position. Thus some Catholics in Wicklow in the 1660s told Capuchin missionaries that the Eucharist was the grace of God; others said that it was a picture of God. At the level of belief the boundaries between confessional groups could be permeable. When belief was linked to institutional affiliation, and issues of authority came to the fore, then clearer boundaries emerged.

The second general conclusion which we might draw from our four examples is that at the heart of lay religiosity, however expressed, was a belief in the existence of God, and a belief that he was at work in the everyday world. This may seem so obvious that it is not worth stating but it remains a central feature of the belief system of early modern Irish Protestants. When called to demonstrate the fact most people referred to creation, but other illustrations were also used. The most important were actual experiences of God at work in the world. Contemporaries described such instances as providence or more commonly as wonders. The ordinary providence of God kept the world working but special providences were more dramatic. Some understood their wealth to be the result of God's active intervention in the world on their behalf. Thus the earl of Cork took as his family motto 'God's providence is mine inheritance'. In times of war, such as the 1640s or the 1690s, many Protestants described their experience in terms of God's providential intervention on their behalf. The sovereign of Kinsale, Tristram Whetcombe, described the settler victories in the early months of the war of the 1640s:

> Thus we see that by divine providence our policy and weak means do prosper to the astonishment and destruction of our enemies and to the perpetual exaltation and obligation of all true Protestants who ought not to tempt God by neglecting the means in due time of sending over sufficient ammunition, money and men to succour our distressed friends and suppress the enemy who (with God's blessing on these means) may be justly extirpated or reduced to their obedience to the crown of England.[24]

More dramatic were individual escapes from potential death recorded as the direct intervention of God. Thus one woman in Cavan claimed that in 1642 a rebel was preparing to burn the local town of Virginia when 'it pleased God to command and work with the rebels to out rule him'. Many survivors explained their fortune using phrases such as 'God delivered me' or that he came to a safe settler town 'by God's providence'. Some saw their lives transformed by such providences and chronicled their experience in spiritual autobiographies which recounted the dangers they had faced and how they had been delivered from them.

Such events were not always easy to understand. In the confessional battle which characterised early modern Ireland, much of the action revolved around claim and counter-claim about whose side God was on. One aspect of this was a suspicion by Protestant clergy, at least, of strange occurrences which some people might attribute to providential intervention. These episodes, they feared, were manufactured by Catholic clergy who would later claim them as miracles in support of the Catholic cause. One example of the efforts made to establish the veracity of strange occurrences is that of the woman who claimed in 1687 to weep corn. One of the most distinguished Irish scientists of the day, Thomas Molyneux, was called to investigate. Careful enquiries at the episcopal visitation in November included tying the woman up and keeping her in the bishop's house for two days. Still, the grain continued to flow from her eyes. Finally it was concluded that she was not a fraud and the phenomenon was 'an effect of supernatural power'. How, then, could Protestants try to understand the workings of God in their world if they were surrounded with possible fraudulent events? (One diarist noted 'the devil can work miracles ... so therefore the works of Satan are called lying wonders'.)

There were two tools at their immediate disposal. The first was the text of the Bible and the second was prayer. These were the building blocks of Protestant religiosity and need to be considered in some detail. Writing in 1609 the Protestant polemicist Barnaby Rich urged 'when thou hearest tell of a vision or miracles ... bring them to the touchstone and compare them with the Word of God'. During the seventeenth and eighteenth centuries this was a feasible proposition since the Bible was a common text in Protestant Ireland. In the 1640s, for instance, there are numerous reports of Bible burnings in Ireland and when book-owners listed their losses in the depositions taken after the rising of 1641 many recorded only a Bible. Nevertheless, not everybody was sufficiently literate to read the text for themselves. Many people had access to the words of the Bible in other ways. At worship on Sunday large portions of the Bible would be read to the congregations, and people might also read extracts from the Bible to illiterate members of their family or friends. By the later seventeenth century hymns and metrical psalms made the biblical text accessible in other ways. However, reading the Bible was difficult since it was clearly not a straightforward text and was pregnant with political meaning.

Protestants read their Bibles carefully, making use of the verse divisions first introduced in 1553. In practical terms this involved interpreting specific verses by comparing them with extracts from other parts of the scriptures, which might yield further light on the text. The Dublin Presbyterian minister Robert Chambers, for instance, urged his catechumens to 'be very diligent in comparing one scripture with another'. Ministers, according to another Dublin minister Joseph Boyse, were not sparing in their use of concordances to facilitate comparisons between similar scriptural passages. This scriptural paper chase was an activity to be pursued not only in private but in church also. Sermon listeners were encouraged to participate, and many brought their own Bibles to church. Thus 'a great part of the time [during the sermon was] spent by the people consulting and comparing various parts of the word of God'. Even this might not yield the full meaning of the text. One Killileagh Presbyterian who kept notes of his Bible reading from the early eighteenth century read in three ways simultaneously. First his notes contain passages taken from the Bible for their literal meaning; second he recorded typological meanings in the scriptures in which Old Testament figures are seen as types or equivalents of those in the New Testament. Third he saw symbolic meanings in the text. The Bible, while a central text for Protestants, was not always easy to deal with. Some people dealt with it in less literal ways. For example, in Antrim, some Presbyterians used the Bible as part of a divination ritual. They saw no harm in it since it was simply a way of understanding the will of God in the world.[25]

If the Bible provided one way of understanding the providence of God the second technique was prayer. The nature of prayer makes it difficult to reconstruct much of its history. In the formal context of worship a liturgical form shaped prayer, whether described as such or not. More important was family prayer which seems to have been more frequently encountered among dissenting households than among those of the established Church of Ireland. However, in the seventeenth and eighteenth centuries most gentry houses held communal daily prayers, which were heavily influenced by ministerial styles of prayer. The young William King, later archbishop of Dublin, spoke of the prayers in the Presbyterian household in which he was brought up as being conceived 'in words and phrases in a manner peculiar to those times and sect'. Whatever about the detail of the experience of prayer it is clear that people had high regard for prayer as a way of understanding the power of God. One Presbyterian minister in 1625, for example, who consulted one of his flock about a sick horse was told:

> there was need of no other means to be used but prayer whatever ailed soul or body, young or old, corn or cattle ... I need not use any other help but to go to my chamber and pray for him [the horse].

Prayer was used as a remedy for a range of problems including troublesome tenants, illness and poor harvests. When George Wilde, bishop of Derry, began his campaign against the Presbyterians in his diocese in 1661, he complained they 'do pray against me in their pulpits'.

In the final analysis the Bible and prayer were ambiguous guides to the experience of the world. They needed to be constantly interpreted and refined to meet the realities of the time. One way of doing this was to consult a professional interpreter, one of the clergy. Clergy had at their disposal two main means of clarifying belief. The first was a range of printed works, including devotional books, biblical commentaries and catechisms. The use of catechisms was particularly well developed among dissenting Protestant clergy. As a Dublin Presbyterian minister, Joseph Boyse, observed in the 1690s:

> ministers of the north of Ireland ... do (speaking generally) outstrip all others that we know of in the Christian world as to their unwearied diligence in catechising those under their charge.

Likewise, the minister at Larne, Thomas Hall, described catechising as 'one part of my work'.[26] Parishes were divided into districts, often called quarters, and each district was catechised at least once a year, usually at the house of an elder. Knowledge of the catechism was a requirement for admission to communion on the first occasion.[27]

In Dublin, Boyse noted that catechising was done publicly on Sundays and the catechism was gone through least once a year.[28] The catechism used was not necessarily the *Shorter Catechism of the Westminster Assembly*, drafted in the 1640s, although the Independent ministers in the Dublin area during the 1650s had recommended the *Shorter Catechism* 'unless some particular brother shall think some other catechism more convenient for his congregation'.[29] By the 1680s there were a variety of Protestant catechetical resources in the city including reprints of English catechisms by Thomas Lye and John Wallis undertaken by the strongly anti-Catholic bookseller Joseph Howes. By 1700 others had been reprinted in Belfast.[30] Before the 1680s there was a lack of Protestant catechisms in Dublin. The early seventeenth-century catechism of James Ussher, the archbishop of Armagh, was the main one in use and some clergy composed their own. Something of how these works were used can be traced in the activities of Robert Chambers. According to John Cooke, one of his congregation, Chambers

> did so constantly and earnestly apply himself to [catechising] and that in so peculiar a method that he always had before him publicly in that exercise a number of very ripe years and understandings, many standing in the rank to their very marriage day.[31]

Chambers' technique was to distribute, each week, 'papers' containing the questions and answers to those who were to respond the following week. These 'papers' were eventually assembled into his 1679 'Explanation of the Shorter Catechism' which, it seems, he intended for publication.[32] On the basis of that text the papers contained not only the relevant question and answer from the Westminster *Shorter Catechism* but a host of subsidiary questions which expanded on the earlier questions. In this way the bare questions and answer structure was developed into a systematic theology. That this method was widely used is also suggested by the format of a catechism composed by the minister of Larne, Thomas Hall. Here too there is the text of the Westminister *Shorter Catechism* but also 'questions raised from the answers of the catechism', although, to judge from the typography, these were probably of lesser importance. The largest font was reserved for the text of the Westminister *Shorter Catechism* with smaller type sizes and italics being used for the subsidiary questions.[33] Thus catechesis became not simply a bare repetition of simple questions and answers but the setting out of a complex theological position. It is likely that those of 'ripe years and understanding' were expected to understand the finer points of theological debate rather than merely memorise the basis of belief.

The second tool which ministers might deploy to help their followers was preaching, a trademark of dissenting Protestant clergy. Dissenting ministers saw preaching as a central part of their work and the sermon formed a focal point of almost every act of dissenting worship from the normal Sunday service to special occasions, such as fasts. At least one sermon was preached every Sunday. At Burt in Co Donegal and in some congregations in Dublin city, two or three Sunday sermons were the norm.[34] These varied in length from half an hour to much longer sermons. Dublin dissenting meetings in the 1660s, for instance, could last between three and four hours, most of that time being taken up with the sermon.[35] Indeed this emphasis on preaching became one of the grounds on which the dissenters were both criticised and satirised. Edward Wetenhall, the precentor of Christ Church cathedral, wrote in the 1670s of dissenting preaching which was the

> whole business of the ministry and hearing all the religion of the people as if ... [one] were only to be ever learning and never come to a knowledge of the truth, to have itching ears and an unstable heart.[36]

Such preaching was a genuinely popular activity. As the Larne session noted in 1701 'it is considered that unless there be a sermon they will hardly meet'. Edward Synge, the rector of Summerhill in Co Meath where the landlord was a convinced Presbyterian, saw the possibilities of this. He wrote to his bishop in 1683 noting the poor attendance at afternoon catechesis and evening prayer but the inclusion of a sermon in the proceedings 'brought so great a congregation after as before noon' who would then proceed to listen to another sermon by the Presbyterian minister later.[37] It was by the standard of this performance that people judged their ministers and a powerful preacher was an important draw to worship. The London bookseller John Dunton's sermon-tasting in Dublin in the 1690s repeatedly stressed this. Nathaniel Weld, Independent minister of New Row, was 'a person of sobriety, learning and solid judgement and much admired and followed for his preaching' he being 'a pious and excellent preacher'. Meanwhile he described Alexander Sinclare, a Scottish Presbyterian minister preaching in Bull Alley, as 'a most affectionate preacher'.[38] While many dissenting clergy used notes when preaching they did not read sermons from prepared texts.[39] Dissenting commentators were scathing about those of the Church of Ireland who adopted this practice. In 1681, for instance, it was reported from the diocese of Derry that tradesmen would read either shorthand notes or printed sermons to their families and then 'laugh at the bishop and boast that they have done as much as the bishop himself'.[40] Dissenting preaching, by contrast, was more about performance than reading. The difference was emphasised by Robert Chambers who claimed that 'there is much difference between hearing and reading, between a lively voice and breathless lines as much as is between cold meat and hot'.[41] Church of Ireland clergy preferred a different style of preaching, less dramatic in presentation and satirised their dissenting counterparts for their style. Edward Wetenhall, later bishop of Cork, preaching in Christ Church, Dublin, in 1672, pilloried the 'inward titillations of griefs, hopes or joys' which formed the core of the dissenting conversion experience and was stimulated by the sermon. He observed:

> because novelty had this effect especially if it set up (as was the custom) with some mimic gestures and tones [they] therefore could hear sermons and long winded prayers all their days. Nor were they concerned to understand or remember them, much less to practise them. It was enough if they were moved and wrought upon by the present hearing of them ... I am far from censuring all non conformists of this weakness but the event shows it to have been a good many who will say they have wondrously profited by such a sermon of which they are not able to tell you two words ... they mean their affections were tickled and stirred by it.[42]

William Sheridan, bishop of Kilmore, in 1685 likewise attacked dissenting clergy for 'bawling loud and making faces and thumping the pulpit and holding forth for two of three hours and preaching off [the] Book such stuff as it is impossible for a considering person to write'.[43]

Whatever the style of preaching or the zeal for catechesis, at least some of the laity paid little attention to it apart from its apparent entertainment value. Churches were often empty on Sundays, some preferring to remain in bed or sample the alternative attractions of the alehouse. For those who did attend, their behaviour was sometimes less than the standard demanded by the clergy. Some slept, others gazed around them. One preacher claimed that many went to church to find 'table talk'. In 1683 Bishop Edward Wetenhall of Cork complained of those who 'too often heedlessly mutter over' prayers read by the minister 'with what understanding appears (commonly) by their repeating what they should not (the minister's part, absolutions etc), as well as what they should'. During lessons they whispered and observed strangers or their neighbours and the sermon had barely begun before 'some have plainly and designedly composed themselves for sleep' while others censured the preacher or were engaged in 'mutual caresses'.[44] In the area of catechesis the result was little better. In the 1690s Bishop King and the Presbyterians debated the importance of the catechism in the formation of faith with rather disappointing results. Even the Dublin Presbyterian Joseph Boyse had to admit that out of 2,400 in the Derry congregation of Templemore only about a quarter could repeat the Westminister *Shorter Catechism*.[45] This does not reflect a lack of interest in religion among the laity but rather a different perception of what constituted belief, most being more interested in devotion rather than doctrine which seemed to have little practical application to daily experience.[46]

While some of the laity read their Bibles, prayed and took the advice of their clergy on how to interpret their experiences, they were also prepared to make their own mind up on the best way to interpret the everyday world within a religious framework. One example might help to illustrate this. In the mid-1660s a Waterford farmer, Valentine Greatrix, began a remarkable series of miraculous healings. He preached no new doctrine and claimed that his powers came from God through 'an impulse or strange persuasion in my own mind ... which did very frequently suggest to me that there was bestowed on me the gift of curing the king's evil'. He emphasised his orthodoxy by adopting biblical models for his healing rituals; his use of spittle in cures, for instance, was reminiscent of the same method used by Christ in Matthew 7:33 and Mark 8:23. Despite this profession of orthodoxy, the archbishop of Dublin ordered him to cease cures because his actions failed to conform to Church of Ireland teaching that the age of miracles had passed. The lay reaction was rather different and many people who witnessed the miraculous cures 'adore[d] him as an apostle'. The Protestant Lord Broghill, initially sceptical, later wrote: 'Mr Greatrix was here some four or five days and did many cures before my father and I do now believe he can do miracles'. The result was, as Greatrix noted, 'Sir Henage Finch says that I have made the greatest faction and distraction between clergy and laymen than anyone these 1,000 years'. Most people cared little for that. Whatever their clergy thought, lay Protestants could accept as orthodox experiences which seemed to manifest the power of God in the world. Greatrix's practical demonstration of that power was valued more than the abstract teaching of the clergy.[47]

III

This essay has tried to tackle the problem of what it meant to be a Protestant in early modern Ireland at two levels. At the institutional level the pattern was one of fragmentation over time. What began as one institution in the 1530s had become many churches and sects by 1800. In part this was inherent in Protestantism with its strong emphasis on individuality but it was also created by practical political and theological shifts within the Irish church itself. At another level, that of belief, the story is rather different. The religious life of the Protestant laity of all institutional backgrounds in early modern Ireland was powerfully shaped by the realities of everyday life rather than the doctrinal formulations of their clergy. The power of God at work in the world offered a practical solution to day-to-day difficulties. People were interested in accessing that power. They were not interested in an intellectual response to it. Their experiences drove them to their Bibles and to prayer in search of explanation. Often their interpretation was at variance with that of the clergy but that did not hinder them from pursuing their own path to salvation.

CHAPTER TEN

The Presbyterian Church in Ireland

Finlay Holmes

Irish Presbyterianism is largely the result of a movement of population from Scotland to Ireland in the seventeenth century. Presbyterianism emerged in sixteenth-century Europe as part of a process of renewal and reformation in the church that came to be called Protestantism. Reformation brought new life but it also brought division when traditional patterns of authority, belief and practice were challenged. Presbyterianism involved radical re-ordering of the church's doctrine and life in obedience to what reformers like John Calvin in Geneva believed to be the guidance of scripture. It alone, they held, rather than the tradition of the church, was to be authoritative in questions of belief and practice. At the centre of Presbyterianism is the Word of God in scripture. The name Presbyterian comes from two words in the Greek New Testament, *presbuteros*, a presbyter or elder, and *presbuterion*, a council of presbyters or elders, and relates to the organisation or government of what became known in Europe as the Reformed church. The idea was to emphasise that reformers like Calvin were not founding a new church but reforming the one, holy, catholic and apostolic church. Presbyterians hold firmly to the historic creeds of Christian antiquity which define the fundamental doctrines of the Christian faith. The hierarchical government of the church by bishops, archbishops and popes was replaced by a hierarchy of courts or councils from what became known as the consistory or kirk session at congregational or parish level through presbyteries which governed an area corresponding to a bishop's diocese, to a representative synod or general assembly as the supreme governing body of a provincial or national church. One of the distinctive offices of Presbyterianism was the ruling presbyter or elder to share with the teaching presbyter or elder, the minister of Word and Sacrament, in the spiritual oversight of the church. Presbyterians believe that, in the New Testament, bishops and presbyters are interchangeable terms. Ruling elders, as members of kirk sessions, presbyteries, synods and general assemblies, provide an important lay element in the government of the church.

A fundamental principle of Presbyterianism is found in the early Christian affirmation that Christ is Lord. Presbyterians insist that the Lord Jesus Christ is the sole king and head of the church and they are opposed to Erastianism – state control of the church – in any form. Sixteenth-century monarchs, who had long been accustomed to exercise some control over the church through judicious episcopal appointments, disliked Presbyterianism. James VI of Scotland, later James I of England in succession to Elizabeth I, resented being told by Presbyterian reformer, Andrew Melville, that in the church he was neither a king nor a lord nor a head but simply a member. The fact that in Scotland reformation in the church was led, not by the Crown, as in England and Ireland, but by churchmen like John Knox, a great admirer of Calvin's Reformation in Geneva where he had been an exile, and by lay-men, the so-called Lords of the Congregation of Jesus Christ, who no doubt had their own agenda, contributed to the success of Presbyterianism there. Another characteristic of Presbyterianism is the ideal of simplicity. Elaborate ritual and ceremonial were suspect. Only two of the church's seven sacra-ments were retained, the Lord's Supper and baptism, believed to have been instituted by Christ himself.

Presbyterianism was brought to Ireland by English and Scottish immi-grants. In Ireland the Reformation introduced by Henry VIII had been little more than an act of state but when, under Edward VI and Elizabeth, it became clear that the established church in Ireland would be Protestant, the disaffection of a majority of the Irish people, who had remained Roman Catholic, grew. Religion gave a new justification for resistance to English rule in Ireland and a last-ditch struggle to preserve the old Gaelic order was led by the Ulster chieftains, O'Neill and O'Donnell. Their defeat in 1603, after nine years of war, left Ulster devastated and depopulated, ripe for colonisa-tion from Britain. Elizabeth had been succeeded by James VI of Scotland, which meant that Scots settlers, hitherto unwelcome in England's Ireland, could share in the new colonisation.

The Reformed Church of Ireland had made little headway in Ulster and faced a serious shortage of clergy. The fluidity of the ecclesiastical situation, James VI having restored episcopacy in Scotland and Scotsmen originally ordained by presbyteries in Scotland having become bishops in Ulster, enabled Scottish Presbyterian ministers to become parish ministers in the Church of Ireland whose 105 Articles of Religion were emphatically Calvinist. Thus in 1634 a report on the diocese of Down and Connor stated that it would be difficult to find a dozen Anglican prayer-books in the dio-cese! Inevitably this was a temporary situation and when the Church of Ireland, under pressure from Charles I, James I's son and successor, and his archbishop of Canterbury, Laud, who was attacking puritanism in any form in the churches of these islands, began to enforce Anglican episcopal discipline, the Presbyterian ministers were driven out of their parishes. Before that hap-pened they had been involved in a religious revival among the hitherto Godless settlers, beginning in the Six Mile Water valley in Co Antrim, anticipating similar revivals of religion in colonial America a century later. An American historian, Marilyn Westerkamp, researching the origins of American revivalism, claims to have found them in the seventeenth-century revival on the Ulster colonial frontier.

The deposed ministers were forced to return to Scotland or go underground in Ulster. When one of them, John Livingstone, who had ministered in Killinchy in Co Down, became minister in Stranraer in Ayrshire some Ulster Scots settlers made the short sea crossing to attend his communion services and have their children baptised. There might never have been a Presbyterian church in Ireland had not the autocratic policies of Charles I and Laud in church and state provoked rebellion in Scotland in 1638, providing an example followed by the Catholic Irish in 1641, before England was convulsed by civil war in 1642. Attempts to impose an Anglican type church order and liturgy upon Scotland led Scots to assert their national and ecclesiastical independence in the National Covenant of 1638. Charles responded with military force which the Scots resisted successfully and a Presbyterian national church was restored in Scotland. Irish Roman Catholics followed their example and their rebellion in 1641 threatened the future of the Anglo-Scots colony in Ulster. A Scots army in the pay of the English parliament was dispatched to Ulster to crush the rebellion and the chaplains of that army, with some officers who were ruling elders, formed the first presbytery on Irish soil in 1642. This presbytery was formed to provide for the spiritual needs of the Scots army but regiments raised by the Scots settlers also appointed chaplains who became members of the presbytery which was soon faced with appeals for ministrations from parishes in which kirk sessions had been formed, the structures of the Church of Ireland having been largely swept away in the chaos of the rebellion. The General Assembly of the Church of Scotland was reluctant to assume spiritual responsibility for the Ulster colonists but some ministers were provided on a temporary basis, including men like John Livingstone who had been ministers in the Church of Ireland in Ulster. Soon ministers were being ordained and installed in Ulster parishes and Patrick Adair, ordained and installed in Cairncastle in Co Antrim in 1646, observed in his *True Narrative of the Rise and Progress of the Presbyterian Church in Ireland,* 'There began a little appearance of a formed church in that country.' The history of the Presbyterian Church in Ireland had begun.

Also ordained in 1646 at Billy (modern Bushmills) in Co Antrim was Jeremy O'Cuinn, the first native Irish Presbyterian minister. O'Cuinn was from Templepatrick in Co Antrim and the Templepatrick kirk session records, which date from 1646, reveal many Irish names among the members of the Presbyterian congregation, showing that some native Irish people were finding a spiritual home in the infant Presbyterian Church.

The Templepatrick kirk session minutes illustrate how Presbyterian structures and discipline gave their communities cohesion and contributed to their self-awareness as a distinctive people – a people of God. The kirk sessions enforced what was believed to be the law of God. It was not only cases of personal delinquency which were dealt with – fornication, drunkenness and adultery – but fraud and dishonesty in business and conflicts in personal relations. The charity of the community, its care of widow and orphan, were also the responsibility of the session whose representatives linked the local congregation with the wider community through the presbytery. Many difficulties faced the infant church. Armed conflict continued throughout the 1640s. The Scots army, which Patrick Adair saw as the instrument of providence in the beginnings of Presbyterianism in Ireland, suffered defeat by Eoghan Roe O'Neill's Irish forces in 1646 and came to be regarded by some settlers as oppressors rather than deliverers as, starved of pay and resources, they lived off the people they had come to defend.

Cromwell's victories in Britain and Ireland brought peace but did not end the difficulties of the Ulster Presbyterians. They put themselves on the wrong side of the new regime by protesting against the execution of Charles I in 1649 and the toleration being given to Protestant sects of all kinds. They saw this as a betrayal of the Solemn League and Covenant of 1643 between the Scots and the English parliament which they understood as an agreement to establish Presbyterianism in Britain and Ireland on the Scottish model. Their protest earned them the invective of John Milton, Latin secretary of the Westminster parliament, who ridiculed them as 'the blockish presbyters of Clandeboye', 'a barbarous nook in Ireland'. Milton, like Cromwell, disliked Presbyterianism, famously declaring that 'New presbyter was but old priest writ large.' Ulster Presbyterian prospects deteriorated further when some Scots supported Charles II against Cromwell and were defeated. Irish history might have been very different if plans to transplant the Ulster Scots to Munster – as far as possible from Scotland – had been implemented. In the end some seventy or eighty Presbyterian ministers were among those, including some former Church of Ireland clergy, who were given official recognition and paid salaries by the state to provide a preaching ministry in the parishes of the now outlawed established church. In spite of the regime's opposition to Presbyterianism, the original presbytery of Ulster, as the army presbytery had become, was subdivided into five 'meetings' of presbytery, local presbyteries in embryo – Antrim, Down, Route, Tyrone and Laggan, in the west of the province, providing oversight for the growing church. Also in this period associations of ministers – some former Church of Ireland and some independent ministers – were formed in Cork and Dublin, marking the beginning of what became southern Irish Presbyterianism. The background of most of these ministers and their congregations was English rather than Scottish, and Phil Kilroy in her recent *Protestant Dissent and Controversy in Ireland, 1660-1714,* differentiates between what she calls English Presbyterians in southern Ireland and Scottish Presbyterians in Ulster. Although in time both were embraced in what became the Presbyterian Church in Ireland, differences in theology and churchmanship persisted between northern and southern Irish Presbyterians.

The restoration of monarchy and the episcopal established church in 1660 put a new question mark over the future of Irish Presbyterianism. Very few Ulster Presbyterian ministers conformed and some seventy were evicted from their parishes. Nonconformity was made illegal and once more ministers had to go underground or return to Scotland. A few favoured open resistance like the Covenanters in Scotland and one or two may have been involved in the quixotic attempt by Colonel Blood to seize power, but the unheroic quiescence of the majority and the realities of the political situation, in which the minority Irish colonial government could not afford to alienate completely the majority Protestant population in Ulster, led to a precarious toleration of dissent and even a small official financial support in the *regium donum* or royal bounty in 1672. This policy was rewarded when the Presbyterians supported William III and the Irish Protestant establishment against James II in the British colony's crisis in 1688-90. William's victory brought them some improvement in their position as Dissenters and an increased *regium donum,* though William did not attempt to establish Presbyterianism in Ireland as he did in Scotland in 1690.

After 1690 the five Ulster presbyteries met as a Synod of Ulster, the records of which have been preserved and published. New immigrants from Scotland swelled Presbyterian numbers to the great concern of the Church of Ireland which was forcibly expressed in an attack on Presbyterianism by William King, successively bishop of Derry, 1690-1703 and archbishop of Dublin, 1703-29, to whom the erudite Joseph Boyse, minister of the Wood Street congregation in Dublin, replied. There were now five flourishing congregations in Dublin and in 1710 a group of wealthy Dublin Presbyterians established a fund to support and encourage Presbyterianism in the south and west of Ireland. Every effort was made by the Irish Protestant establishment to prevent Presbyterian expansion and in the last year of Queen Anne's reign the payment of *regium donum* was stopped but immediately restored and increased by the new Hanoverian regime.

In the eighteenth century Presbyterians continued to suffer disabilities as Dissenters. The Test Act of 1704 restricted public office to those who took communion in the established church, increasing the tendency of Presbyterian landlords to conform, thus enhancing the leadership role of ministers in their communities. The majority of Ulster Presbyterians were tenant farmers who began to suffer increasing economic hardship with rising rents, poor harvests and tithes to pay to support the established church. Many emigrated to colonial America where they contributed to the growth of American Presbyterianism, whose founding father, Francis Makemie, had been ordained for ministry in Maryland by the Laggan presbytery in 1682. Ulster Presbyterianism was weakened in the eighteenth century not only by emigration but also by theological conflict and division. The conflict was between conservative Calvinists, known as Old Lights, and theological liberals, or New Lights, and frequently centred on the question of subscription to the Westminster formularies by ordinands, the Synod of Ulster having followed the Church of Scotland in adopting the formularies of the Westminster Assembly of Divines – the Confession of Faith and catechisms – as its official doctrinal statement. Classical Calvinism had come under attack in Europe and Scotland and in Ulster Old Light conservatives resisted the advance of New Lights giving support to Scottish conservative Dissenters, Seceders and Covenanters, who established congregations, presbyteries and eventually synods in Ireland.

The wider intellectual context of Irish Presbyterianism's theological tensions was the European Enlightenment which was subjecting the political and social structures of the old order in Europe to rational criticism. Irish Presbyterians who studied in Glasgow and Edinburgh were taught by Enlightenment luminaries like Francis Hutcheson, son of an Ulster Presbyterian minister, that oppressive and unjust regimes should be overthrown and the purpose of government was to provide 'the greatest good of the greatest number'. The American revolution in which many Ulster Presbyterian immigrants were involved, and later the French revolution, inspired some Ulster Presbyterians to become leaders in a revolutionary movement in Ireland. In 1791 the Society of United Irishmen, aiming to unite Protestants, Catholics and Dissenters to achieve radical change in Ireland including separation from Britain, was founded in Belfast, its committee all Presbyterians. When advance by constitutional means was blocked the movement ended in rebellion in 1798. Presbyterians, both ministers and people, were involved in the rebellion in Antrim and Down and its accompanying sufferings. They were condemned by the Synod of Ulster which had always made it clear it could only approve of constitutional means of achieving change.

In the nineteenth century Ulster Presbyterians were profoundly influenced by evangelicalism with its emphasis on experience of Christ as living Saviour and Lord. The century-old controversy between Old and New Lights exploded in open conflict as the Rev Henry Cooke, a formidable champion of orthodoxy, led a vigorous and ultimately victorious campaign against the liberal New Light minority in the Synod of Ulster, some of whom, including their leader, the Rev Henry Montgomery, were self-confessed Arians or anti-trinitarians. Montgomery led seventeen ministers and congregations out of the Synod of Ulster and later joined with the non-subscribing presbytery of Antrim and the Synod of Munster, who were also non-subscribing, to form the Association of Non-Subscribing Presbyterians, which, in 1919, became the Non-Subscribing Presbyterian Church in Ireland with strong Unitarian associations. Though small, it maintains its witness to the radical New Light tradition in Irish Presbyterianism. The Synod of Ulster, in 1835, restored the practice of obligatory subscription to the Westminster formularies for ordinands, opening the way for reunion with the Seceders, who, in a little less than a century, had formed 141 congregations. The resulting General Assembly of the Presbyterian Church in Ireland embraced 433 congregations, 33 presbyteries and some 650,000 souls. The Covenanters or Reformed Presbyterians remained and have remained outside the General Assembly, maintaining their witness to what they believe to be the permanent obligations of the great seventeenth-century Covenants. Today 35 congregations serve some 3,000 members who still eschew the use of hymns and instrumental music in worship.

The new Presbyterian Church in Ireland displayed considerable creative energy in outreach at home and abroad, initiating a foreign mission which was quickly followed by Jewish, colonial and continental missions. New congregations were formed and old congregations revived. Earlier attempted outreach in the south and west of Ireland through the medium of the Irish language had been unsuccessful, partly because of the Church of Ireland's opposition, but now, in the context of a wider Protestant crusade in Ireland, sometimes called the Second Reformation, Presbyterian congregations were formed in the south and west of Ireland, in places like Fermoy and Ballina. The Rev John Edgar, founder of the Irish Presbyterian temperance movement, appealed effectively in his *Cry From Connaught* for aid for the famine-stricken peasantry of the western province in the 1840s and industrial schools were established to train young people in useful and productive skills. Evangelicalism reached an explosive climax of influence in Irish Presbyterianism in the Year of Grace, the great religious revival of 1859 in Ulster, recalling the seventeenth-century Six Mile Water revival.

Industrial and agricultural revolutions in Ulster brought new challenges for Presbyterians as for other Christians. Provision of new churches could not keep pace with the population explosion in Belfast which grew from 20,000 in 1800 to 300,000 a century later. A town, later city, mission provided spiritual ministrations for the unchurched, underlining the fact that Irish

Presbyterianism was becoming increasingly middle-class. Sunday schools were promoted by a Sabbath School Society and an Orphan Society and the Kinghan Mission to the Deaf and Dumb represented Presbyterian responses to urgent social needs, while John Edgar's temperance movement challenged the widespread abuse of alcohol. Having relied upon the Scottish universities to provide ministerial training in the seventeenth and eighteenth centuries – attempts to provide theological education in Ulster having proved short-lived – Irish Presbyterianism founded two colleges in the nineteenth century, one in Belfast in association with the government's new Queen's College, the other, a college of arts and divinity in Londonderry, bearing the name of its major benefactress, a minister's widow, Martha Maria Magee.

It is often alleged that, after 1798, Irish Presbyterians abandoned their political radicalism and became tories. This is not the whole truth. Like most Irish Protestants, Presbyterians came to believe that their rights and interests were best safeguarded by the parliamentary union between Britain and Ireland, which had followed the 1798 rebellion. It was feared that a restored Irish parliament, following the admission of Roman Catholics to full civil rights in 1829, which Presbyterians supported, would be anti-Protestant. Having suffered under a Church of Ireland ascendancy, Presbyterians had no wish to experience a Roman Catholic ascendancy. Thus, while most Presbyterians supported the Liberal party in politics and such reforms as tenant-right and the disestablishment of the Church of Ireland, they opposed Gladstone's proposal in 1886 to concede Home Rule to Ireland. Ulster Presbyterian opposition to Home Rule played a significant part in bringing about the partition of Ireland in 1921 which left Presbyterians the majority Protestant population in Northern Ireland. The Presbyterian Church remained a united church in a divided Ireland although the overwhelming majority of the church's congregations and members are in Northern Ireland. After partition and the violence which preceded and accompanied it, there was a great loss of Presbyterian numbers in southern Ireland, but by the end of the twentieth century that process seems to have been arrested and may be beginning to be reversed. A new church building for a growing congregation in Kilkenny and a new youth centre in Lucan are evidences of advance instead of retreat. Most Presbyterians in what is now the Republic of Ireland regard themselves as Irish, not British, while most Presbyterians in Northern Ireland see no contradiction in being both Irish and British, of which they are equally proud. All Presbyterians, if they are true to their principles, should be good citizens of the state in which they find themselves unless it requires them to disobey their lord and master, Jesus Christ.

Presbyterian membership statistics have fallen since the General Assembly in 1840. There are now more congregations than in 1840 but they serve a membership of less than half the 650,000 of 1840. Movements of population from rural areas into towns and cities, and more recently from inner Belfast to the outer suburbs and surrounding towns have caused the decline of older congregations and some fifty new congregations have been formed under the General Assembly's church extension programme. Church House, built in the centre of Belfast at the beginning of the twentieth century, with its spacious and recently refurbished Assembly Hall in which the annual meetings of the General Assembly normally take place, symbolises the increasing importance of the central agencies of the church. The church's work at home and abroad, in education, social service, for young and old, its publications and women's organisations are administered and resourced from offices in Church House.

Education and concern for children and young people have always been important responsibilities for Presbyterians as for all Christians. Educational issues often figure largely on the agenda of the General Assembly which has specialist committees to inform and guide the church in this as in other important areas of Christian responsibility. As well as Sunday schools, organisations for young people like the boys' and girls' Brigades, scouts and girl guides have proliferated. More recently youth clubs and councils have multiplied and the church's youth office provides resources and guidance for those engaged in youth work. Links are fostered with young people of other churches and traditions and there are residential youth centres at Rostrevor, Lucan and Castlerock. Teams of young people become involved in outreach at home and abroad in raising funds to meet human need worldwide, material and spiritual. The church's two theological colleges were united in 1978 as Union Theological College in Belfast, though the tradition of ministerial students going abroad for part at least of their theological education, chiefly to Scotland and America, persists. Participation in the Institute of Theology in Queen's University and increasing numbers of non-ministerial theological students have widened the context in which ordinands, an increasing number of whom are coming from secular work experience, are being trained. Recognition that Christian ministry involves all church members has led to the establishment in 1981 of Magee Christian Training Centre to provide a wide range of training courses to office bearers and members of the church.

Women have always played a vital part in the life of the Presbyterian church, particularly in the work of overseas mission, but they were debarred from membership of kirk session, presbytery, synod or general assembly until the twentieth century. In 1908 the first Irish Presbyterian deaconess began training and since then deaconesses have contributed much to the church's ministry. Since 1920 women have been ordained as ruling elders and since 1976 as ministers of word and sacrament in the Irish Presbyterian Church.

Irish Presbyterian concern for the church's mission in the world continues today. More than eighty Irish Presbyterian missionaries are currently working in some nineteen countries in the world, including India, Jamaica, Malawi, Indonesia, Nepal, Kenya, Israel and Brazil. Many more Irish Presbyterians are abroad in interdenominational missions and Christian agencies and in partner churches in Europe. Like other Christians Irish Presbyterians have had a ministry to disadvantaged members of society through a variety of institutions. The nineteenth-century Orphan Society and Kinghan Mission to the Deaf and Dumb have continued and developed their work. Since its foundation in 1896 the Shankill Road Mission has combined social service and evangelism. Recent initiatives have been the Clifton Street Centre in an area of high unemployment in Belfast and Carlisle House providing residential accommodation for those with alcohol or drug problems. The Scots Centre in Dublin was founded to offer resources and guidance for Presbyterian ventures in social service in the Republic of Ireland. In Thompson House in Belfast ex-offenders and other homeless young men find a home while the Presbyterian Residential Trust provides a growing number of homes for the elderly.

Presbyterians have been involved in a wide range of relationships with other churches in Ireland and beyond through the World Alliance of Reformed Churches, the Conference of European Churches and the Irish Inter-Church Meeting. Today relations between different churches are much better than in past centuries although Irish Presbyterians remain wary of relationships which could compromise their distinctive Reformed witness, leading in 1980 to the church's withdrawal from the World Council of Churches and failure to join the Council of the Churches of Britain and Ireland. The Presbyterian Church in Ireland, like most churches, has suffered decline in membership in face of growing secularisation and hostility to institutional Christianity. Some Presbyterians are attracted to new forms of Christian community and worship often associated with the modern charismatic movement which has influenced and challenged all churches. In response some Presbyterian ministers and congregations are experimenting with new forms of worship, and house groups for prayer and Bible study provide the greater intimacy of fellowship some seek. Irish Presbyterians have shown themselves eager to bring their church up to date in response to the challenges of witness and service in an increasingly secular world and in the circumstances of sectarian conflict in Northern Ireland. Within the existing political context in Ireland they seek to promote peace, justice and reconciliation between its divided peoples. In 1990 and 1997 residential general assemblies were held in the University of Ulster in Coleraine to express repentance for the sins and shortcomings of the past and to seek a way forward in effective Christian witness and service.

A time of reform: from the 'penal laws' to the birth of modern nationalism, 1691-1800

Hugh Fenning OP

The era of the wars of religion, plantations and martyrs closed with the Battle of the Boyne (1690) and the fall of Limerick (1691) when the Protestant King William of Orange defeated the Catholic King James II. King James, already rejected by his subjects in England, then fled to France, never to return. His defeat set the stage for the entire eighteenth century, during which 'the Protestant interest' reigned supreme in church and state, leaving the Catholic majority without wealth, political power or social status. So far as the Catholic clergy were concerned, the 'War of the Two Kings' was soon followed by a decree of banishment in 1698, which sent the bishops and regular clergy into exile. Disastrous as this situation may have been, it did guarantee two centuries of peace, disturbed only by the rebellion of 1798, and helped to dissolve old differences. No longer would the church be troubled by quarrels between Old English and native Irish (Gaelic), nor would it be unduly controlled by a Catholic nobility. The decline of the Catholic aristocracy, gradually deprived of its lands, enabled the church to become slowly more egalitarian in root and branch until, in the early 1800s, few could deny the emergence of an 'Irish Catholic nation'.[1]

The chief object of the penal laws was to secure the Protestant ownership of land. Land and only land was the source of wealth and political power. This also inspired the strict legislation forbidding the marriage of Catholic and Protestant. Religion as such was a secondary consideration. The penal laws, as they were gradually framed in the early decades of the eighteenth century, fell accordingly into two categories: those concerning the landed gentry and those relating to the exercise of religion. The prohibitions against carrying arms or owning a horse of any value were precautions against rebellion. All Catholics were excluded from public office and parliament unless they took two oaths: one of allegiance to the British Crown – difficult for those still loyal to the Stuarts; the other to the royal supremacy – rejecting even the Pope's *spiritual* authority, denying transubstantiation and rejecting thereby the sacrifice of the Mass – an oath impossible for any genuine Catholic to take. A Catholic might not accept a bequest of landed property from a Protestant. Nor might he buy land or lease it for more than thirty-one years. Worse still, if his eldest son became a Protestant, the son became owner of the estate, thus making his own father a tenant for life. Another provision, called the 'gavel act', provided that on the death of a Catholic, his estate would not pass to the eldest son, but be divided among all his children. The effect of these laws was to destroy the Catholic aristocracy. Most of them went to the continent, taking up military careers, or found a humbler but more rewarding role as merchants.[2] The penal laws concerning land remained in force and were always strictly applied. In consequence, the proportion of land in Catholic hands fell between 1700 and 1780 from fourteen per cent to a mere five per cent. The Catholic majority of the population were thus left simply as tenants or landless labourers, political nonentities, excluded even from the legal profession, hampered in their trades, and forbidden to have their own schools. The slow process of dismantling this penal code began in 1759 but was marked by no significant progress until the 1770s. For a more general 'emancipation', as it was called, the people had to await the passing of a final act of parliament in 1829.

In 1697, all Catholic bishops, vicars general, deans and all members of the regular clergy were ordered by parliament to leave the kingdom within a year. Thus began a period of religious oppression which did not cease until 1746. That was the year of the battle of Culloden in Scotland in which the English decisively defeated the supporters of James III and put an end to the pretensions of the House of Stuart. This success brought great relief to the Protestants of Ireland who began to worry less about the likelihood of rebellion at home. Another reason for the end of religious persecution was that Protestant England, in the context of international politics, still needed the political support of Catholic Austria.[3]

At full strength the Irish episcopal hierarchy numbered about twenty-six bishops grouped in four ecclesiastical provinces: Armagh, Dublin, Cashel and Tuam. In 1700, however, shortly after the exile, only two or three bishops remained in the country. By 1707 there was only one and he was a prisoner in Dublin. Few of the exiled bishops ever returned, and it took another forty years to fill all the vacant dioceses. The restoration of the hierarchy was the work of the Roman Congregation *de Propaganda Fide* which took care of all Irish disputes and other ecclesiastical business until as late as 1908.[4] The life of a bishop in Ireland during the first half of the century was very difficult. At least one died in jail; another was brought to court but released. A third, James Gallagher of Raphoe, was obliged to leave his diocese altogether, though he was humble enough to accept another. They had to lie low, use the utmost secrecy particularly concerning correspondence, and could scarcely rebuke a wayward priest in case he might betray them to the government. Many were non-resident, living usually in Dublin; partly for safety, and partly because they could not find a 'safe house' in which to lodge within their dioceses. One of their greatest difficulties was that James III, the Stuart king, then living in exile in Rome, had nominated each and every one of them.[5]

Those who framed the penal laws seem to have anticipated the principle later expressed by Napoleon: 'a parish priest is more effective than ten policemen, and costs far less to support'. Thus, almost 1,100 secular priests were allowed to register in 1704 for their respective parishes throughout the country. They, at least, were free from persecution, though they were forbidden to employ curates or schoolmasters. They also faced great difficulties in obtaining sites and leases for new chapels. Sometimes for want of any shelter they said Mass in the open air. The practice grew up of offering Mass in private houses, the so-called 'station masses'. A further law in 1709 obliged the secular clergy to take the oath of abjuration, rejecting the Stuart king. When, almost as a body, they refused to do so, they too lost their legal status and made themselves liable to prosecution. Practically all these secular priests had studied in Irish colleges abroad, mostly in Spain, France and the Low Countries. There was also a college in Rome, but the greatest concentration of Irish clerical students was at Paris where the Collège des Lombards was the Maynooth of penal times. Many priests were ordained secretly in Ireland before beginning their studies, a practice which led to the occasional choice of unsuitable candidates.

The regular clergy who were almost exclusively friars (Franciscans, Dominicans, Augustinians and Carmelites) returned within fifteen years from their exile but then faced not only the hostility of government but also that of the secular clergy. The government whenever possible arrested and transported them again. The longstanding antipathy of the diocesan priests was based to some extent on theological grounds, the secular priests being 'Gallican' in consequence of their training at Paris, and the friars so 'Ultramontane' that they were derisively called 'the Pope's dragoons'. On a more material level the two rival groups were competing for the meagre alms of the poor. Nonetheless, the friars began to restore their convents throughout the country – although with great difficulty in Ulster – accepted novices for education on the continent, and returned to their life of itinerant preaching while questing for their food. Even the bishops seldom favoured the friars over whom they had little control, for the friars could always appeal to their papal privileges and exemptions. One bishop in Munster, finding a friar absolving sins and censures which he could not absolve himself, for they were reserved to the Pope, exclaimed in exasperation: '*Ecce plusquam episcopus hic*' ('Behold, we have more than a bishop here').

Here, then, despite all persecution, was a flourishing church, largely composed of a Gaelic-speaking and illiterate peasantry. But it was a church with many weaknesses and, from a canonical point of view, quite dishevelled.

Fortunately, the Pope of the time was Benedict XIV (Lambertini, 1740-58), a decisive, energetic man who happened also to be an able canonist. Thanks to him a special visitator, John Kent of Leuven, was sent to Ireland in 1742 to report on every aspect of the situation.[6] Kent's movements in Ireland were minimal; he was alleged to have seen only as much of the country as might be observed from the window of the coach on which he travelled from his native Waterford to Dublin. His comments also were weighted in favour of the diocesan clergy to whom he belonged. That said, his thorough report formed the basis of some drastic decrees framed, though not promulgated, by *Propaganda Fide* in 1743. Eventually, a shadowy group called the 'zelanti di Dublino' sent their own spokesman, Fr John Murphy, to Rome in 1750. Thanks to his intervention a large number of reforming decrees were promulgated for the Irish church in 1751. Most of the 1751 decrees intended for the secular clergy were addressed to the bishops. They were ordered to reside in their dioceses and submit reports to Rome every two years. They were forbidden to exact levies, the 'first fruits', on priests newly collated to parishes, or to accept payment for dispensing from the banns of marriage. Confessors, too, were forbidden to accept alms in the confessional or to impose as a penance the giving of stipends for Masses they would later say themselves. Both bishops and priests were strongly urged to teach catechism to the young. Several Irish bishops felt insulted by these decrees, partly because they had not been consulted beforehand, and partly because they were now implicitly accused of abuses which they had always condemned.

The eight decrees framed in 1751 for the regular clergy were more draconian. All religious living outside the houses of their respective Orders were subjected totally to the bishops. Friars coming to Ireland without letters of obedience were to be treated as apostates and expelled by the bishops from the country. The bishops might now tell religious priests exactly where they were to work. Religious superiors were forbidden even to remove a subject from one place to another without the prior consent of the local ordinary. Finally, the regular clergy were prohibited from giving the religious habit to candidates in Ireland. Those wishing to join religious orders would henceforth have to do so abroad. These measures, which showed so little understanding of religious life, brought about what has been called 'The Undoing of the friars of Ireland'.[7] Small country convents began to disappear; the friars themselves, on becoming curates or parish priests, increasingly tended to blend with the diocesan clergy while their overall number went into an apparently terminal decline, dropping from about six hundred in 1751 to some three hundred and fifty at the end of the century. This decline was relatively much greater than it appears, because over the same period both the population and the number of diocesan priests steadily increased.

Throughout the period, the church in Ireland carried a political millstone about its neck in that the bishops were nominated by James III, the Stuart pretender, in Rome.[8] Since this was well known to government, opponents could all too easily question the loyalty of Catholics to the British Crown. Benedict XIV considered that problem too, and from 1750 the right of nomination claimed by the exiled king was limited to the approval of candidates chosen for him by *Propaganda Fide*. On the death of James III in 1766, the Holy See refused to recognise his successor, the former 'Bonny Prince Charlie', famous in Scottish history, recognising instead the Hanoverian succession. The Irish church was thus finally released from an incubus which had long weakened its own attempts to find a *modus vivendi* with Dublin Castle, residence of the lord lieutenant and seat of political power. The rulers of the country, having taken the land and persecuted the religion of the Catholic majority, expected also their unswerving allegiance to the Hanoverian king. Although the 'oath of abjuration' of the Stuarts had been long available, that formula continued to be objectionable in many respects even when the power of the House of Stuart was no more. The oath also rejected the pope's supposed power 'to depose rulers and dispense subjects from their allegiance'. As early as 1724, Catholics did their part in the search for a more acceptable oath of allegiance. The person most prominent in that search was Cornelius Nary, a parish priest of Dublin and author of many works of controversy. Yet even he achieved nothing in this area before his death in 1738.[9] The question was revived with no greater success in 1756 when parliament again envisaged a registration of 'popish priests'. It was not in fact until 1774 that the matter of an oath for Catholics was finally settled with the passing of an act 'to permit his majesty's subjects of whatever persuasion to testify their allegiance to him'. The oath then prescribed was taken by the vast majority of Catholics, both lay and clerical, who had any expectation of social or political advancement, either under the act of 1774 or under later relief acts in 1778, 1782 and 1793.[10]

From 1746, the year of the decisive battle of Culloden, one begins to notice the frequent publication in Dublin of pro-Catholic pamphlets calling for justice on the mildest humanitarian grounds. A layman, Charles O'Conor of Belanagare, wrote most of them, and continued to do so through the 1750s and 1760s.[11] In his view, the Catholics of Ireland were worse off than the natives of Muscovy or Tartary. The Tartars at least were not forced to support a Protestant church to which they did not belong. Besides, the establishment injured even the economic well-being of the country, for it penalised through increased rents any who sought to improve the land they leased. O'Conor, the apologist, was helped by his friend and fellow author John Curry, a medical doctor, whose contribution was to challenge Protestant myths about the

Irish rebellion of 1641 – a pivotal event on which the Protestant paranoia about Catholics was popularly based. In 1756 O'Conor and Curry established a 'Catholic Committee' to further their aims. The Committee languished for decades because the clergy, particularly those of Dublin, could not agree among themselves on the exact wording of an 'oath of allegiance', nor on loyalty to the Stuarts, nor on the 'Pope's deposing power', and thought the wisest course of action was to do nothing. The clergy after all enjoyed the toleration of government; it was the laymen of property, like O'Conor, who were technically at the mercy of any vindictive 'discoverer', or indeed of their own children should one of their sons become a Protestant and claim his father's land. Besides, the early members of the Catholic Committee were landlords and professional men. In later years Catholic merchants came to dominate the Committee which became a powerful lobby, almost an alternative 'parliament', in the 1790s.

The problems of the laity were gradually resolved by successive relief acts which owed much to rebellion in the American colonies and to the growth of patriotic spirit among Irish Protestants. Military necessity breached the dyke in 1759 when Catholic recruits were first admitted to the British army, though not as officers. Then economic considerations, such as the need for drainage, took effect and in 1771 Catholics were allowed to lease small portions of bog for sixty-one years. Wealthy Catholic traders might now invest their money in land rather than invest it abroad. The earl of Charlemont remarked in his memoirs on the extraordinary increase in tolerance within the Irish parliament between 1772 and 1778. In 1772 it decisively rejected his proposal to grant Catholics a short lease of land sufficient for a cabin and a plot of potatoes. Yet six years later, without any opposition, the same parliament permitted Catholics to take out leases of lands of any extent for 999 years: 'The spirit of toleration', remarked the earl, 'was lately gone abroad and had spread itself through all the polished nations of Europe ... I should rather suppose that it took its rise from fashionable deism than from Christianity, which was now unfortunately much out of fashion.'[12]

The noble earl might also have mentioned as another result of this change of heart that from 1774 parliament had permitted Irish Catholics to take the oath of allegiance. Under the Quebec Act of 1774, Britain made generous concessions to her new Canadian Catholic subjects. In British Canada, Catholics might now hold civil offices, they constituted the established church, and were given an oath of allegiance. This legislation was passed at London in the same month as that permitting an 'oath of allegiance' to be taken in Ireland.[13]

A more extensive emancipation act in 1792 allowed Catholic barristers and solicitors to employ clerks, and even permitted barristers to marry

Catholics. The ban on 'mixed' or interfaith marriages, which held them to be invalid in civil law, was removed. These concessions being very limited, the Catholic Committee organised a national convention in Tailors' Hall, Dublin, a meeting of delegates from all over the country which came to be known as the 'Back-Lane Parliament'. Bypassing even the lord lieutenant, this convention took the bold step of sending a delegation directly to the King in London. The result was a much more extensive emancipation act, passed in Dublin in 1793, by which Catholics regained the right to vote in elections for parliament provided they held land in freehold worth at least forty shillings. By this act they also gained the right to hold civil and military offices, to be admitted as freemen to trade guilds, and to become members of city corporations.[14] After 1793 Catholic landowners and merchants might prosper as they pleased, but for another three decades they were still forbidden to sit in parliament or even as judges in the courts of law. So far as the clergy were concerned, the most important of these concessions came in the relief act of 1782. This legislation removed almost all restraints on public worship and on the activities of the clergy. More importantly, it also permitted the establishment of Catholic grammar-schools and colleges, though subject to the consent of the local Protestant bishop.

Since the process of church reform depended so much on the bishops, it did not begin in earnest until about 1748 when, finally, each diocese had a bishop of its own. Thereafter even the quality of the bishops themselves improved, thanks to the new policy of *Propaganda Fide*, initiated in 1750, whereby bishops were chosen from short lists of candidates prepared well in advance of any vacancy. Among the first duties of a bishop was that of enforcing or framing diocesan statutes which were essentially regulations for the clergy. Such legislation had indeed been issued for the dioceses of Dublin, Limerick and Cashel long before there was any relaxation of the penal code. Yet it is interesting to note that four other sets of statutes – for Kildare, Ossory, Kerry and Killaloe – were all framed in 1748, and one of them was explicitly dated from 'the treaty of Aix-la-Chapelle'. That treaty, signed in November 1748, marked the end of the war of the Austrian Succession which had ravaged much of Europe for eight years. The coming of peace, coinciding with the end of real persecution and the promulgation of the new Roman decrees for Ireland in 1751, at last made it easier for reforming bishops to set about their work. Though working in isolation, they did occasionally meet at provincial synods, at least in Munster and Connacht, while the four metropolitans began to hold regular meetings in 1772.

In order to meet his clergy and understand their needs, the reforming bishop set off each year on visitation. Usually he kept a special register for that purpose but few such records have survived. The earliest is a rather short one of 1753 for the diocese of Ferns. The next, much more extensive, is that of the archbishop of Cashel, covering the period from 1759 to 1774.[15] The best known of all visitation records are those of Patrick Plunket of Meath, begun in 1780 and continued annually for forty-six years.[16] During the 1760s Bishop John O'Brien of Cloyne conducted a few parish missions with the help of some twenty priests. He was horrified to discover that two or three of his parish clergy were guilty of flagrant misconduct. Worse still, there was little he could do about it for the culprits were protected by wealthy Protestant relatives who might invoke the law against the bishop. The result of the mission was not the punishment of the guilty priests but the departure of Bishop O'Brien for Paris where he died in exile. The bishops, in the course of visitation, insisted on the keeping of parochial registers for baptism and marriage. Wherever they found tattered vestments they promptly tore them up and if the chalice was a battered one of base metal, they ordered its immediate replacement. Every effort was made to have baptisms performed in the chapel rather than in the parents' home. This led to the installation of baptismal fonts in chapels, but it took rather longer for pulpits to appear. Chapels were forever being improved, mud walls giving way to stone and thatched roofs being replaced by slate. It was a slow process, particularly where the congregation was poor, and one which continued well into the middle of the nineteenth century. Some penal restrictions remained as late as 1800. No chapel might have a bell, nor be erected on a main street. Even in the twentieth century, some chapels stood well outside the towns they served, simply because the landlord had refused to grant a more convenient location.

The bishop, while on visitation, made sure that catechism was being taught every week and that each parish had at least one school. He kept an eye also on clerical education, basically through the holding of conferences in each deanery. If the local parish priest could not or would not preach, he was told to use the 'prone' of the diocese: a set of sample sermons or points for sermons of a kind still published. Another concern of bishops and priests was to put an end to abuses arising from wakes, patterns, and stations. The 'wake' was a gathering of family and neighbours around the dead body of a loved one on the night before burial. Whenever the deceased was elderly, or not much missed, this 'wake' was marked not only by the consumption of whiskey but also by obscene games of pagan origin.[17] The 'pattern', so called from the word 'patron', was ostensibly a gathering of pilgrims at a holy place on the feast-day of the local patron saint. Naturally, while many came to pray, the occasion attracted others more interested in enjoyment, usually with the aid of drink, which led to broken heads and other irregularities.[18] Stations, as they were called, centred on the celebration of Mass in a private house, preceded by the hearing of confessions and followed by a good dinner. The clergy then withdrew, but the ensuing party regularly lacked decorum. For that they too were discouraged.

With regard to popular devotion, one cannot speak of 'reform' but rather of revival, because most devotions of this kind had been practised in Ireland during the seventeenth century whenever conditions were favourable. One devotion, that of saying the Rosary, was known in Ireland as early as the sixteenth century, if not in late medieval times. It continued to be popular during the 1700s. In Dublin from about 1725, the four or five religious orders in the city had their own confraternities or sodalities, with the devotions peculiar to each order. Paradoxically, it was easier to organise such groups in full view of Dublin Castle than it was in the countryside. From the same early date they also observed Exposition of the Blessed Sacrament. After about 1748 one begins to find evidence of evening sermons and sung Vespers on Sunday afternoons. Generally speaking, one may say that continental devotions were practised in Ireland, at least in towns and cities, wherever the friars or the Jesuits had established themselves. In Wexford, for instance, the Franciscans were already promoting the Stations of the Cross in 1746 and had the appropriate images or paintings on their chapel walls. For their part, the Jesuits of Dublin encouraged devotion to the Sacred Heart and their novena in honour of St Francis Xavier. Both official and popular devotion conformed to what is styled the 'Tridentine model'. So too did the organisation of parishes and dioceses, certainly by 1782, except that there were as yet no seminaries in Ireland, nor indeed cathedrals.

Most priests studied in foreign colleges before returning to the mission, though a significant number, attracted by comfortable chaplaincies in Catholic Europe, never returned at all. Some colleges were badly affected by the suppression of the Jesuits in 1777 but there was no substantial loss until the outbreak of the French Revolution in 1789. The Irish colleges in France and Flanders were then despoiled, as were even those in Rome under French occupation in 1798, and in Spain and Portugal during the Peninsular War. Encouraged by the relief act of 1782, a few bishops began to think of creating seminaries or at least preparatory colleges in their own dioceses. The bishop of Elphin was planning one as early as 1786, and it enjoyed a brief existence in Athlone. Three others were founded in 1793: the successful colleges of Carlow and Kilkenny, with another in the far north which the enthusiastic Bishop Anthony Coyle of Raphoe set up in his own house in Letterkenny.[19] The greatest achievement, however, owed almost everything to the Protestant government itself. At war with France and wishing to guarantee the loyalty of the Irish clergy, parliament provided funds for the establishment of a seminary at Maynooth near Dublin in 1795. In the short term, these colleges did not provide enough priests to serve a rapidly increasing population, but in the end they prevailed.

Though greatly reduced in numbers, the regular clergy too made a modest recovery after 1777 when they were again permitted to receive novices at home. Since these novitiates were fewer in number and more strictly controlled than those forbidden in 1751, one may say that the regular clergy also had been reformed. Freedom from direct persecution enabled religious superiors to control their subjects better. But they had already lost many of their small houses in the countryside, and were to lose many more because the bishops continued to take religious away for parish work and could, if they wished, effectively limit their number by granting diocesan faculties only to a few. The friars still had their own colleges abroad which functioned successfully until they too were lost or rendered useless by the French Revolution.

One should also mention the foundation of congregations of religious sisters: the Ursulines and Presentation sisters in Cork, founded by Nano Nagle (d. 1784), and the work of Teresa Mullaly (d. 1803), foundress of the Presentation Sisters in Dublin. A Franciscan, Lawrence Callanan, gave Nano Nagle every support he could over many years of struggle in Cork. Some Jesuits were no less helpful to Teresa Mullaly in Dublin. Both these foundresses spent their lives in the education of poor children, despite every obstacle which the penal laws or anxious relatives threw in their way. Thanks to their schools, and to those conducted in every parish, the number of literate Catholics increased. This factor, apart from more obvious benefits, enabled Catholic publishers to print more devotional literature than ever before. It also meant that the bishops could more easily reach their people through printed pastoral letters.

In general, it may be said that the work of recovery began first in the cities and large towns, especially, and paradoxically, in Dublin. The actual rate of progress was slower in rural areas, depending on the richness of the soil and the corresponding wealth of Catholic tenant farmers. The provinces of Leinster and Munster fared best. To the west, in Connacht, there was immense poverty; hence fewer chapels and a slower rate of improvement. Reform and recovery in Ulster, the northern province, came more slowly than anywhere else, partly because the eastern counties had a heavily Protestant population, while to the west, where the land was poor, most Catholics lived close to destitution.[20] The gradual improvement steadily achieved by the church during the eighteenth century was seriously threatened by the rebellion of 1798. Had that rebellion been successful, assisted as was intended by the timely landing of French troops, the patient work of a century might have been overthrown. In the event, though 30,000 died and many chapels were burned, Ireland was spared the attentions of the French revolutionary army, which had already brought such destruction to the church on the continent and was soon to do still more harm in Spain and Italy.

CHAPTER TWELVE

Irish Methodism

Dudley Levistone Cooney

The Methodist Church developed from the work of the Rev John Wesley, a priest of the Church of England, who in 1739 began to form a chain of religious societies within the Church of England. The name was originally applied in derision by Oxford undergraduates to a small group which Wesley led, and which methodically applied itself to the study of the Bible and other Christian works, the observance of the feasts and fasts enjoined by the Book of Common Prayer, and works of charity. The unsympathetic accused them of believing in 'method'. It was not Wesley's intention to form a separate Christian denomination but to gather societies which would provide encouragement and support for those who wished to practice devotion and holiness without withdrawing from ordinary life.

It was not on the initiative of Wesley that the Methodist work crossed the Irish Sea. Those who joined the Methodist societies in England were generally members of the artisan and working classes created by the social revolutions which began in England in the first half of the eighteenth century. From these classes the junior officers of the British army were recruited and when sent with their regiments to Ireland they sought, if they were Methodists, to sustain their own religious commitment by gathering people of like mind from the regiment and from the civilian population into Methodist meetings. Thus Methodist societies were formed in various parts of Ireland, the first in Dublin in 1745.

This development led Wesley himself to come to Dublin in 1747. The society, which he met in Marlborough Street, was, shortly after his departure, attacked by a mob, and its furniture burned. Wesley sent his younger brother Charles, also a Church of England priest, to Ireland to support the Irish Methodists until such time as he could come again. Charles gradually withdrew from active participation in the Methodist work, but his greatest contribution to it lay in the thousands of hymns which he wrote, some of which the Methodists and others have been singing ever since. This not only facilitated worship in the Methodist societies but provided a readily memorable way in which the members could learn their Christian doctrine. His hymns were saturated in biblical language and allusion.

John returned to Ireland again and again, eventually spending a total of about five and a half years in the country, visiting almost every county, and supervising and disciplining the societies. His twenty-first and last visit was in 1789, when he was eighty-six. However, the pioneering work in Ireland was not done by Wesley himself.

We have already noted the contribution of the army officers. The work also spread as Methodists moved from town to town for commercial reasons. The chief pioneers, however, were Wesley's preachers. These were laymen whom Wesley recruited from his societies, who were possessed of a remarkable enthusiasm and the gift of speaking in public in a plain and direct manner without oratorical flourishes. Often derided as illiterate, they were in fact possessed of a basic education which enabled them to read the best Christian authors, and whatever grace they lacked at the beginning they acquired through the programme of reading which Wesley demanded of them. Moved from place to place annually at Wesley's direction, it was they who carried the Methodist system into new areas. In Wesley's time they were always called 'preachers' for that was their task. As numbers of both members and of preachers increased, they developed a pastoral role, and by the middle of the nineteenth century were being described as 'ministers'.

Wesley drew from a variety of sources for the administration of his societies, and the language which he used is still that in which the Methodists describe their organisation. The Methodists meeting in one place are still officially called 'a society' rather than a congregation. Originally each society was divided into 'classes' of about ten or a dozen members, men meeting separately from women and young people separately from the older members. They met weekly for mutual examination and exhortation to encourage one another in holy living. One member of each group was the Leader, responsible not only for the conduct of the class meeting, but also for the pastoral care of its members. Thus, from the beginning women played a very significant role in Methodist work, leading the women's classes. A group of societies were placed under the care of one or more preachers, who visited each in turn. When they had visited each society and any other place where meetings were held, they repeated the round or circuit. The basic Methodist administrative unit is still called a circuit and not a parish, though ministers are now able to visit their preaching appointments much more frequently – usually at least weekly. When in the early years the circuit preacher was not present, meetings were led by one of the members who was recognised as having a particular gift for this and who was called a 'local preacher'. The term is still used for lay people authorised to conduct public worship.

During his lifetime Wesley directed the Methodist societies but each year he called the circuit preachers to meet with him and discuss the work. These meetings were called Conferences and were intended to advise Wesley, with whom the ultimate decision lay. After his death the Conference became the governing body of Irish Methodism, and so continues, meeting annually. Originally Wesley moved his preachers freely between England and Ireland, but as the Irish work developed and the number of Irish preachers increased this became too expensive, and English and Irish preachers remained in their own countries. So the English (British) and Irish Conferences developed independently, though there was never any formal break.

The early members of the Irish Methodist societies were largely recruited from the Church of Ireland or the nonconformists. Names of English, Scottish, Welsh, Huguenot and German origin are more likely to be found in the membership lists than those of Irish origin. Socially, in the cities and towns the membership was likely to be drawn from the artisan and upwardly aspiring commercial classes, and in rural districts the larger tenant farmers. An unusual feature of the work in Ireland was the degree of encouragement given by some of the lesser gentry. These were quick to recognise that joining the Methodist society led their tenants to attend the Established Church services more faithfully, and encouraged industry and thrift. If they encouraged their tenants to join, only a few felt the need to do so themselves.

However, the early Irish Methodists did not have an easy time. The authorities were deeply suspicious of any new movement, fearing Jacobite risings to overthrow the religious and civil establishment. In some places Established Church clergy resented the rise of a group which seemed to imply that they had failed to do their work properly. The Dublin mob attack on the Methodists was not repeated but there were attacks elsewhere in the country, and in the city of Cork the Methodist society underwent a sustained persecution for more than a year.

II

Wesley died in 1791, and within a few years the Methodist Conference in England authorised the administration of the sacraments of baptism and the holy communion in their chapels. In effect this was recognition that the Methodists were a separate denomination. In Ireland the Methodists preserved their link with the Established Church for a further quarter of a century. On Sundays the members were expected to go to both the Established Church services and to the Methodist meetings. They were encouraged to go for holy communion to their parish church as often as possible, and to have their children baptised there. Under the civil law marriages were not allowed in Methodist chapels. This became possible in 1845 as a result of a change in the civil law. However, the civil registrar was required to be present for the ceremony to be legal. In 1863 there was a further change, and Methodist chapels were registered for marriages. Since then the Methodist ministers have been able to register the weddings of their people.

The first crisis to face the Methodists in Ireland after Wesley's death was the succession of risings and the French invasion of 1798. The Methodists, with very few exceptions, none of them in leading positions, remained on the side of the government. When the Conference met in 1799 it responded to the situation by establishing a General Mission, funded by the Wesleyan Methodist Missionary Society in England. Three preachers, James McQuigg, Charles Graham and Gideon Ouseley, were set apart to tour the western half of the country preaching in English and Irish. It was the first instance of the Irish Methodist Conference taking the Irish language seriously. In time these men were replaced, and the number of general missionaries increased. The work continued into the early years of the twentieth century.

As the nineteenth century dawned and the proportion of members in the Methodist societies with any real affinity with the Established Church declined, insistent demands for the administration of the sacraments in the Methodist chapels began. In 1816 the Conference gave permission, and there was an immediate secession. About one third of the membership withdrew and formed the Primitive Wesleyan Methodist Society. The larger body was now called the Wesleyan Methodists, and acknowledged that it was a separate denomination. The Primitive Wesleyans continued the old pattern of attendance at the Established Church services and sacraments and at their own meetings. This they maintained until the Irish church was disestablished in 1870. After some years of negotiation the two bodies re-united in 1878. At various times in the eighteenth and nineteenth centuries a number of British Methodist groups began work in Ireland, including the Countess of Huntingdon's Connexion, the Methodist New Connexion, the Primitive Methodists, the Wesleyan Methodist Association, and the Welsh Calvinistic Methodists. The work of these groups was generally confined to small areas, and during the twentieth century they either passed their work to the Irish Methodist Church or simply closed.

The Great Famine of the second half of the 1840s affected Methodists in the same proportion as it did the general population – about one quarter of the membership of the Wesleyans and Primitive Wesleyans was lost through death or emigration. The greatest loss among Methodists was in the county Fermanagh and parts of the adjoining counties. In most parts of the country the Methodists were able to afford a varied diet, and so were not dependent on the potato. Deaths among them were generally from the fevers which they contracted from their neighbours who were starving, and whom they were trying to relieve.

The principal political issue in Ireland at the end of the nineteenth century and the beginning of the twentieth was Home Rule which developed into a demand for independence from Britain. The great majority of Methodists were unionist, and this was the position taken publicly by their leaders. There were, however, dissentient voices in various parts of the country. The partition of Ireland in 1921 became a practical reality for Methodists as for everybody else. However, the Methodist Church itself never divided its administration, and like all of the Christian denominations and religious groups has functioned as a unit within two political jurisdictions. This has created some complications, but they have been accepted, and the work of the church has continued. With quite remarkable rapidity in some places, the Methodists in what is now the Republic of Ireland adapted to the new regime, and began to play a role in the political, cultural, economic and social life of the new state.

III

It was the realisation that many people, particularly of the new working classes, were not attending churches that led Wesley and his early preachers to preach wherever they could gather a crowd. This practice came to be known as 'field preaching' though the venues might not always be fields. Crossroads, market squares, fairgrounds and any other convenient spaces were equally welcome. Preaching at fairs continued until the middle of the twentieth century, and the tradition is still maintained in some places by the holding of annual field meetings, now usually attended by Methodists and their friends rather than the general public. The later years of the nineteenth century saw the flourishing of the 'cottage meeting', so called whether the building used was a small cottage or a substantial farmhouse. Cottage meetings were held regularly in each place on a certain day of the month, and the Methodist family who owned the house would invite neighbours to attend. The company would fill the ground floor of the house, and the service would be much less formal than that in the chapel. These had the effect of spreading Methodist influence beyond its own membership.

When the Methodists began to build meeting places for themselves Wesley was anxious to avoid the words church and chapel, which might have suggested that he was trying to rival the Established Church. On the other hand, the term meetinghouse was linked to Dissent, and he was equally anxious to avoid that connotation. The buildings were therefore called preaching houses. By the middle of the nineteenth century this term was falling into disuse, Methodists being now a separate denomination, and the word chapel came into general use. It was towards the end of the same century, as these buildings became more elaborate in design, and more like the parish churches, that the word church came into general use.

The late nineteenth century also saw the introduction into Irish Methodism of organisations designed to serve particular groups. The first of these was the Women's Department of the Methodist Missionary Society, which encouraged women in support of foreign missions, by prayer, fund-raising and making items for use by the missionaries. In the second half of the twentieth century, this group broadened its interest and changed its name to the Methodist Women's Association, welcoming into its membership other women's meetings. The Young Women's Association was formed to cater for younger women. Most of the youth organisations were interdenominational. Christian Endeavour was a devotional group. Boys' and girls' Brigades catered for those children who enjoyed wearing uniform and following a programme of physical exercise. Some circuits formed boy scout and girl guide troops. The Wesley Guild, designed on much the same principles as Christian Endeavour, was favoured in places where the minister thought that the youth group should be distinctively Methodist.

IV

Wesley was concerned not only about the education of his preachers but also about education in general. He wished the Methodists to be a reading people, and therefore published a monthly magazine containing pious articles and a certain amount of news of Methodist work. His Christian Library was designed to introduce them to more serious reading and contained extracts from and condensations of Christian authors of many periods. This was not taken up as widely as he would have wished and he lost money on the project. When the Methodists in Dublin built their first chapel at Whitefriar Street, part of the building was used for a boys' school. A school for orphan girls was added later. In most circuits throughout the country schools were established, sometimes meeting in the chapels and sometimes being provided with separate buildings. These welcomed boys and girls of all denominations, and taught the basic subjects of reading, writing, arithmetic, and some of the skills which the children would later need in the home or on the farm. Religious instruction was an important part of the programme.

In 1841 the Board of National Education in Ireland was founded. For some time the Methodists hesitated to participate in its system but eventually recognised the benefits to be derived from it. In 1865 sixty-five schools were transferred to it. The schools in Northern Ireland were eventually transferred to the Department of Education there but in the Irish Free State/ Republic they continued with Methodist management under the Department of Education there. Economic factors led to the amalgamation of small schools and the resulting larger schools were generally under Church of Ireland management, though some established interdenominational boards. The only primary school in Ireland continuing with Methodist management is that at Rathgar in Dublin. Between 1858 and 1872 the Methodists operated a training college for primary teachers at Hardwick Street in Dublin. It was closed when an arrangement was made with the Model School in Marlborough Street for Methodist teachers to be trained there. In 1845 the Wesleyan Methodists opened what they called the Wesleyan Connexional School on St Stephen's Green, having three boarding pupils and nine day pupils, all boys; George Bernard Shaw was educated there. In 1879, the school moved to a new site on the same side of the Green, and because the Wesleyans and Primitive Wesleyans had reunited in the previous year it was renamed Wesley College. In 1911 it admitted girls for the first time. The college was one of the first to plan a move out of the city centre in the 1960s. It transferred to its present campus at Ballinteer in 1969.

The bulk of Methodist membership was in Ulster where the city of Belfast was growing rapidly in size and commercial importance. In 1868 the Wesleyan Methodist Collegiate Institution was opened there. One wing housed a theological hall for the training of Methodist ministers; otherwise the college was for the secondary education of boys. In 1885 the name was simplified to Methodist College. The first headmaster, Dr Robert Crook, almost immediately persuaded the board to admit 'young ladies' so that Methody, as it was affectionately called, was co-educational almost from the start. In 1882 the sports grounds and preparatory department were transferred to Pirrie Park. Methodist College has developed into one of the largest colleges in the United Kingdom. In 1918 the theological hall was moved to a house at the end of Lennoxvale called 'Edgehill'. The move resolved the tensions which had existed between the interests of the hall and those of the secondary school. In 1928 the hall was formally separated from the college, and became a distinct entity as Edgehill College. In 1951 it became a recognised college of Queen's University, and since then there has been increasing co-operation between it and the Presbyterian Assembly's College, enabling Presbyterian and Methodist ministers to share one training course.

After the Second World War economic conditions in the Irish Republic led to a great deal of emigration, particularly from the rural areas. It was in the hope of enabling young people to earn a better living on the land that in 1947 the Methodist Church founded Gurteen College, located in the north of Co Tipperary, for the teaching of agriculture. It then had forty-one students. As with other Methodist educational establishments, Methodists were always a minority among the students. At first recruitment was among the Protestant families throughout the Republic and beyond but in 1970 the first Catholic student was received, and the college now welcomes students of all denominations, other religions and none. The changing economic situation in recent years has reduced the number of students seeking agricultural courses, and the college is now developing other studies. Always the intention is, as it first was, to encourage people to remain in the rural areas by enabling them to make a good living there. The capacity of the college in terms of student numbers continues to grow.

V

Early Methodist charity took the form of individual response to individual need, though collections were made for the relief of impoverished members, and also for debtors who had been imprisoned until such time as their debts were paid. The first charitable institution which they founded was the Methodist Widows' Home for which two houses were built in Dublin's Whitefriar Street. The first residents, twenty in number, were provided with their own beds but shared rooms. They were allowed coal and candles, and a small sum of money to enable them to buy their own food. The home was moved to other locations from time to time, and is now at Palmerston Park where it has been renamed Eastwell Residential Home. Conditions have greatly changed, and each resident now has her own room but it still caters only for women. It was a Methodist, John Dedrich Ayckbown, who proposed that a similar provision should be made for men but this was undertaken as a joint project by the Protestant churches in Dublin. The Old Man's Asylum was opened in 1808 on Northbrook Road, and continued to cater for elderly men for more than a century and a half. The Strangers' Friend Society, formed in 1786, was an association of Methodists who undertook to relieve the poor in their own homes. Each applicant was visited by one or other of the members who then assessed the need and recommended an appropriate grant. The objective of this society was to put people in the way of helping themselves. Long-term support was not generally given. Those who were assisted were more likely to be members of other churches but all were asked to bring a recommendation from a priest or minister. A similar society in Waterford, the Association of Friends of the Sick Poor, had a shorter life but did very useful work. It was very much involved in the foundation of the city's fever hospital.

The Methodist Female Orphan School was opened in Whitefriar Street in 1806, making provision for up to twelve girls. It too had more than one address in Dublin before it was finally closed and the money used to establish a trust fund to pay grants for the education of orphan girls in Wesley College. The terms of this trust were later expanded to allow grants to be paid for boys as well as girls. Changing circumstances had a similar effect on the Methodist Orphan Society, established in 1870 to make grants for the maintenance of the orphaned children of Methodist parents. In the later years of the twentieth century it was recognised that the death of either parent was not the only cause of hardship for children, and the terms of this trust were varied to take account of new needs. In 1985 the name was changed to the Methodist Child Care Society.

In the 1890s a new work began developing in the cities. City Missions had been established in several cities by the English Methodists, using premises that did not look like churches and had seats instead of pews. It was thought that the poor of the city centres would feel more comfortable in such places. To the worship programme were added a wide variety of activities designed to improve physical health and to relieve poverty. The first of these to be developed in Ireland was the Belfast Central Mission in 1889. It was soon joined by others in North Belfast, Dublin and Derry. An East Belfast Mission was established in 1985. All of these missions have adapted their work to meet changing needs, and their major contribution to the welfare of the community in the late years of the twentieth century was the building of sheltered housing projects. Though not operating as missions, churches in Limerick and Cork have done the same.

VI

Methodists hold no doctrines which are not held by other Christians; their difference lies in their emphases and their ethos. The basis of their teaching is, of course, the Bible and they subscribe to the historic creeds which express the Christian faith in short form. They stand within the traditions of the Protestant Reformation. Their principal emphases are the availability of salvation through Christ to every person, the belief that each person may be assured of his or her salvation, and the understanding that salvation is expressed in a way of life – in scriptural holiness. In the outworking of that way of life Wesley urged his people to industry, simplicity, integrity and thrift. Always practical in his thinking, he could not but recognise that there were circumstances in which people were obliged to look to others for support but it was always his idea that the need for such support might be short-term. Ideally, by personal industry the Methodist would not only earn enough to maintain him or her self but also to give to others who were in need. Preaching on the use of money, he called on people to 'Earn all you can (provided you do it honestly); save all you can; give all you can.' This last clause is the key to Wesley's philosophy of manners. It was the privilege of the Christian to give as much as they could, and so money was not to be wasted on the unnecessary. He abhorred waste and extravagance, and advocated a simplicity of life and dress. His chapel in London and other buildings which he praised, indicate that he had an eye for beauty and grace but he did not favour elaboration of ornament. The same held for his views on dress. Clothes could be of good material and elegant, but they need not be luxurious or fussy. Most Methodists followed this simplicity of style. None of them, however, went to quite the length that he did in giving, else there would have been no such thing as a wealthy Methodist. As it was, the ethic of industry, integrity and thrift enabled many of them to develop very successful businesses.

It was the same ethic which lay behind their rejection of gambling. To gamble was to seek money without earning it. To this day even the mildest forms of gambling are excluded from Methodist premises. In the popular mind it is the exclusion of alcohol that is regarded as distinctively Methodist. However, this is not so. It is an expression of Methodist evangelicalism, and as such is shared by evangelicals of all denominations. It comes as a surprise to many Methodists to learn that Wesley was not a total abstainer, and that total abstinence as such did not find strong acceptance among Irish Methodists until the last quarter of the nineteenth century. Temperance was always advocated, partly to avoid unnecessary extravagance, but more so because drunkenness rendered people unemployable and therefore unable to achieve the ethic.

In 1940 the Conference set up the Council on Social Welfare to examine matters of social concern and to help to form the mind of the church on them. In the beginning it addressed itself exclusively to the Methodists themselves but during the years of conflict in Northern Ireland after 1968 it began to find a new role, and increasingly it proposed statements and reports which the Conference accepted and addressed to governments or to the community at large. Obviously most of these statements were concerned with the tensions in the community and the violence resulting from them but time was found to address other important issues. Quite lengthy reports were published on homosexuality, abortion, euthanasia, divorce, punishment, the role of women and leisure. In 1993 the name of the Council was changed to accord with a change in the usage of the word welfare. It is now the Council on Social Responsibility. Cooperation with other churches in Ireland developed considerably in the last three decades of the twentieth century. The Methodist Church in Ireland belongs to several ecumenical organisations and councils of churches, and happily cooperates with other Christian bodies in worship, service and mission.

We have noted that women played an important role in the life of the early Methodist societies, chiefly as class leaders. In England, Wesley in fact allowed a number of women to preach, and encouraged Alice Cambridge in Ireland to do the same. After his death the Conference was more conscious of the scandal which would be caused by women preaching to men, and actively discouraged it. Anne Lutton, who exercised a valuable preaching ministry mostly around mid Ulster in the nineteenth century, confined herself to women's meetings. In the middle of the twentieth century a number of women began to serve as local preachers, and in 1976 the first woman was accepted as a candidate for the ministry. She was the Rev Ellen Whalley.

VII

The Irish have a long history of missionary enterprise overseas, and this has been equally true of the Methodists among them. In the earlier years their contribution to the worldwide spread of Methodism was not so much deliberate as consequential. Methodists were among those who emigrated from this country to America, Australia and South Africa. It is a source of pride to the Irish Methodists that the first Methodist preachers in what was to become the United States of America were from Ireland. From that small beginning has grown a church of seventeen million people. Where Irish emigrants were not the pioneers, they often gave significant leadership. When in 1814 Dr Thomas Coke inaugurated his mission to India, two Irishmen were among those who travelled with him. Coke died on the journey but his companions went on to begin work in India and Ceylon. Considering the number of Methodists in Ireland (never more than 60,000) the Irish were very well represented in missionary work in the years that followed. They served in every part of the world where the Methodist Missionary Society worked. In recent years the number has declined as the churches in other lands are assuming control of their own work, but Irish people are finding a new vocation as mission partners working alongside local Methodists.

The Catholic Church in Ireland in the age of the North Atlantic Revolution, 1775-1815

Dáire Keogh

The period of the North Atlantic Revolution represents a critical epoch in the development of the Catholic Church in Ireland. In those years the church emerged from the catacombs of the penal era and adopted the features which were to make it such a formidable institution in the centuries which followed. These years of emergence, however, were not without trials and while the general tensions of the period facilitated the Catholic revival, those same pressures threatened to undo the great achievements of the age and represented a threat which was in many ways more significant for the church than that of the Tudor Reformation centuries earlier.

I

Debate continues as to whether the penal laws were a draconian code, or merely 'reasonable inconveniences', as has been suggested by recent commentators.[1] Nevertheless, it is increasingly clear that the story of the Catholic community in the eighteenth century is more one of 'endurance and emergence', than of blanket persecution as was previously accepted.[2] The Catholic Church had experienced isolation and dislocation under the penal laws, as discussed by Hugh Fenning in chapter 11, but by the outbreak of the French Revolution in 1789, the Catholic revival was well under way. Significantly, that recovery had been facilitated by the loyal stance adopted by the Catholics throughout the American Revolution (1775-83). While Ireland's Protestant patriots and volunteers chose the war as an opportunity to press the government for greater independence for their cherished Dublin parliament, Ireland's Catholics saw in the crisis an appropriate occasion to stress their reliability and obedience to the Crown. This pragmatic stance proved successful and resulted in a series of important concessions from the government: the relief acts of 1778 and 1782 which removed most of the penal restrictions regarding religious practice. The lessons of the episode were clear – loyalty brought results – and the implications of this experience dictated the response of the Catholic hierarchy and gentry to the radical challenge of the 1790s.

With the bulk of the penal legislation removed, reforming bishops, especially James Butler II of Cashel, John Troy of Dublin and Patrick Plunket of

Meath, set about re-establishing order and discipline within the church. Regular meetings of the four metropolitans were resumed in 1787. The younger bishops engaged in frequent visitations of their dioceses, correcting abuses and bringing practice into line with the Roman ritual. There were by then 1,800 priests in the country. Clerical conferences became increasingly common and the emphasis placed on catechesis is reflected in the revival of the confraternities, particularly the Confraternity of Christian Doctrine. The ecclesiastical revival is also reflected in the spate of chapel building, which characterised the period, with many of the new churches rivalling those of the Church of Ireland in both scale and grandeur, the splendid cathedral in Waterford (1793) being perhaps the best example. Further evidence of this renaissance may be seen in the impressive lists of religious and devotional material printed in the period, Hugh Fenning's analysis of which has forced a rethink of the so-called 'devotional revolution' of the mid-nineteenth century.[3]

This revival, however, was seriously threatened by the outbreak of Revolution in Europe. The progress of 'the French disease' had serious implications for the hierarchy. In France, the Catholic Church had been abolished under the terms of the Civil Constitution (1790) and throughout Europe the spread of revolution made serious inroads into institutional religion. The bishops were well aware of European affairs and nowhere is the urgency of the situation clearer than in the voluminous correspondence between John Troy, archbishop of Dublin, and his Roman agent, fellow Dominican Luke Concanen.[4] The Revolution and its associated Irish radicalism created a nightmarish scenario for the Irish bishops. Catholic loyalty had been their trump card since the late 1770s. The relief measures of 1778 and 1782 had arguably been promoted by London in an attempt to recall the Irish patriots to their senses, but those concessions had come from the benevolence of the Crown and not from any sense of justice or right. In the 1790s the bishops feared that these concessions would be repealed, or that future relief would be restricted by imprudent agitation by the laity. Apart from these concerns, the bishops were haunted by the images of the devastated church in France; it was the excesses of the French rather than the political principles of the United Irishmen *per se* which inspired their pastorals throughout the 1790s.

Along with this, the crisis brought a novel convergence of interests between the British government and the Catholic Church and their mutual concern created a new atmosphere of trust and dialogue. The Catholic Church, with its renewed institutions, became the perceived bulwark against Jacobinism in Ireland, while British arms offered the only hope of salvation for the continental church. As the decade progressed, and the revolutionary armies threatened the Papal States, the Irish bishops came under intense pressure from Cardinal Antonelli, Prefect of *Propaganda Fide*, to urge loyalty and obedience to the British Crown. At a diplomatic level, improved relations between Great Britain and the Holy See were reflected by the presence of informal representatives in their respective capitals: Monsignor Charles Erskine in London and Sir John Cox Hippisley in Rome. Underlying both the appeal from the administration and Rome was the assumption that the hierarchy was in a position to control their people but the Catholic community had been transformed and the bishops were at best only able to motivate a *willing* flock.

The Catholic Committee, which had represented Catholic interests since the 1760s, had undergone great change in the 1780s, as confident middle-class members emerged to challenge the traditional aristocratic leadership. French revolutionary influence accelerated this development and, in December 1791, Lord Kenmare and the old guard withdrew, relinquishing the leadership to John Keogh, Thomas Braughall and the other advanced radicals. This renewed leadership demanded redress for Catholic grievances as a right, rather than as a reward to be sought with deference from the Crown. This schism within the committee was a bitter one and the decision of the bishops to side with Kenmare resulted in their humiliation. Throughout the country their attempts to gain signatures to the loyal address resulted in a paltry response and it became increasingly clear that either the clergy joined with the people or the people would go it alone. A resolution of the General Committee of Catholics in January 1792 spoke of the divide in the Catholic body, the attempts of the seceders to 'seduce the ... clergy from the laity' and the conversion of 'the ministers of the gospel into instruments of oppression'.[5]

The lessons of the 'Kenmare episode' were not lost on the radicals who throughout 1792 and 1793 exploited episcopal weakness to the limit. The bishops were now in an unenviable position with both the radicals and the Dublin Castle administration vying for their support. Their position became even more acute in 1792 as the bitter debate on Hercules Langrishe's relief bill incensed the sensitivities of the Catholic Committee. They particularly resented the 'shopkeeper and shoplifter' jibes hurled in their direction, and the questions about their political reliability, which had been raised by the so-called 'ultras', conservative Protestant Members of Parliament. The Committee's immediate decision was to present a declaration of their civil and religious principles in an attempt to dispel the notion that Catholics were incapable of living in liberty, but more significantly they called a grand convention in an attempt to display once and for all their truly representative nature. The Committee decided to muster the assistance of the Catholic clergy to secure maximum support for the declaration. Archbishop Troy at once rallied to their side. This prompt response was inspired by his desire to bring his isolation from the Committee to an end. No doubt he was also aware of criticism that the bishops appeared more concerned with government approval than with the sufferings of their people.[6] The Committee's success in obtaining so many signatures to their declaration was largely due to their effective marshalling of the clergy through the country. There is, however, little doubt that the clergy were in some cases intimidated into supporting the venture against their own judgement; in Wexford Bishop Caulfield was threatened with a revival of the Rightboy tactics of withholding dues, while John Keogh, one of the leading members of the Committee, confirmed that 'the people seem well inclined to give them [the non-cooperating clergy] the French cure'.[7] In the same way, it was the Committee's exploitation of the renewed institutions of the church, which made the convention possible. The reform congress of 1784 had failed because the high sheriffs in the counties were unwilling to cooperate in the election of delegates, but the Catholic convention of 1792 had been a success precisely because the Committee had used parish structures and the clergy in building a broadly democratic and representative convention.

The appearance of Archbishop Troy and Bishop Francis Moylan of Cork at the convention, or 'Back Lane Parliament' as it was called by its critics, and their promise to rise or fall with the Committee seemed to place the hierarchy inextricably at the head of this great swell. Such perceptions, however, were misleading since the bishops were *following* rather than leading their people. Nevertheless, this distinction was lost on the Dublin Castle administration and ultra-loyalists. They retained the memories of the parish meetings, which gave the impression of a powerful church, one capable of exerting real influence over its members. As one recent commentator has observed, if the convention was proof of Catholic ability to organise in support of their publicly declared aims, their ability to plot rebellion could also be assumed.[8] However, the reverse of this was that if the institutions of the church could be harnessed by the administration rebellion could be prevented.

In this way the church became the object of attention for both radicals and loyalists. The Convention Act of 1793 made overt political activity impossible but the republican United Irishmen found a surrogate for their meetings in the large number of debating societies and political clubs spread through the country. In a similar way the radicals turned their attention to the church and took advantage of the many proselytising opportunities offered by its renewed structures. Chapel meetings were a constant feature of both urban and rural radicalism in the 1790s and the level of reports reaching Dublin Castle reflects the anxiety which the meetings generated. Leonard McNally, the United Irish lawyer and informer, claimed that the Defenders, an elusive radical proletarian organisation, had originated in these parochial meetings, but his information as usual was vague and tended towards sensationalism.[9] The notorious spy, Francis Higgins, claimed that the Dublin charitable societies were entirely composed of United Irishmen and that they were formed for no other purpose than to carry out sedition.[10] The large chapel congregations also provided the radicals with opportunities to disseminate their propaganda; broadsheets were frequently posted to chapel doors and handbills passed out among Massgoers. The religious confraternities, which had formed an essential part of the Catholic revival, provided ideal opportunities for covert association. From Rush, in north Dublin, came warnings of meetings supposedly held for religious purposes but 'too frequently to disseminate their traitorous principles and to form plans for outrage'.[11]

Scapulars, too, became symbols of identification and badges of sedition. James Little, the Church of Ireland rector of Lacken, in his diary recording the events of 1798 in Mayo, pointed to the use made of scapulars and confraternities by the radicals in mobilising the people; 'after undergoing the cookery of scapularism' he declared, the people were enticed to feast upon 'the dishes of atheistical libertinism'.[12] In Edenderry, the behaviour of a prisoner was attributed to his enthusiasm for the 'popish mania' of the 'rosary or scapular of the Blessed Lady' which had spread amongst the lower classes, particularly in the Defenders.[13] Significantly, Fr James McCary, the United Irish emissary and later government spy in the Ards peninsula in Ulster, described himself as organiser of the White Scapular Confraternity in the diocese of Down and Connor. Amongst the subscribers to his devotional 1797 tract, *The Sure Way to Heaven*, were prominent radicals, the Teelings and the Dublin United Irishman Hugh MacVeagh.[14] In the wake of the rebellion, the Orange historian Richard Musgrave devoted considerable hostile attention to the use made of scapulars by the United Irishmen. In 1799 the Catholic archbishop of Tuam published a pastoral against scapulars which he believed had become not only objects of superstition but had been used as banners by the rebels.[15] Religious processions and funerals also became transformed into United Irish rallies and displays. The initial symptoms of this were seen at the funeral of a freemason in Dungannon, Co Tyrone, in November 1796. The first of the Dublin United Irish funerals took place in April 1797 when five thousand, including the 'Marats of Pill lane' marched in procession behind the remains of Edward Dunn.[16] There were also incidents of mock funerals, but these high-profile funerals attracted adverse attention from the Castle authorities and much of the cover which the confraternities and clubs had provided for the United Irishmen was now gone. The government prohibited such political displays, but the United Irish *Northern Star* humorously reported on the repressive regulations concerning funerals, declaring that in future people must literally follow the Lord's instructions and 'let the dead bury the dead'.[17] Clerical involvement in the

United Irish cause was significant even though the numbers of priests involved was very limited. The Armagh man, James Coigly, remains the most celebrated of these priests. He was active amongst the Defenders; he had helped radicalise workers' combinations in England and was eventually hanged in Kent for his part in an attempt to secure a French invasion of England.[18] In a similar way Frs John Martin OSA of Drogheda and the Dominican James McCary of Carrickfergus exploited the opportunities their priesthood provided in propagating the United Irish gospel.[19]

Loyalists too, alarmed at the often bizarrely exaggerated accounts from informers, attempted to tap the potential of the church. On one level there was a fear in government circles that the financial dependence of the clergy on their people was bound to expose them to contagion. It was this consideration which had made a state pension for the clergy so attractive since the notion was first mooted by the Viceroy's private secretary, the former seminarian Thomas Lewis O'Beirne who had conformed to the established church in 1782, but even in the crisis of the 1790s the Catholic hierarchy successfully resisted this and the proposal to establish a Royal veto on episcopal nominations. The foundation of the Royal College in Maynooth with government support in 1795, however, successfully detached the episcopacy from any further flirtation with Catholic out-of-doors politics. The foundation of the college, Ireland's national seminary, deepened the divide between the bishops and their people since the latter regarded it as a sop for the failure of Henry Grattan's emancipation bill of the same year.[20] The bishops, however, were undeterred and continued to urge their flocks to loyalty and passive obedience in the growing crisis.

In spite of these divisions the chapel meetings and petitioning of the 1790s presented a powerful, if mistaken, image of Catholic unity to outsiders. Thus, prior to the rebellion many magistrates emulated the radicals and attempted to exploit the potential of the church in an effort to instil loyalty. Just as the radicals raised petitions, so the magistrates orchestrated loyal resolutions, often choosing a chapel in which to administer oaths of allegiance. Andrew Newton of Coagh, Co Tyrone, claimed to have been the first magistrate to encourage Catholics to enter into these resolutions. Newton began his campaign at Ardboe where the priest and 678 parishioners signed a loyal declaration. He repeated this through much of mid-Ulster and was confident that his efforts had made a 'split between them [the Catholics] and the Presbyterians'.[21] Newton's example was adopted elsewhere, and published resolutions provide an interesting barometer of regional tensions in late 1797 and early 1798.[22] The earliest addresses are mainly from Antrim, Down and other parts of Ulster, but from early 1798 they appear in the south, with the Catholics of Richard Musgrave's parish of Cappoquin, Co Waterford, being amongst the first to publish a declaration.[23] Petitioning reached a peak in March 1798 and it generally formed part of a wider campaign, as was the case of Bishop Caulfield's pastoral, delivered in the context of Lord Mountnorris's drive against the United Irishmen in Wexford. Such resolutions were viewed with scepticism in some loyal quarters. It was suggested that they provided a cover for the true sentiments of the people, but while the Marquis of Downshire had little faith in them he believed they 'did no harm' and might at least be useful in separating 'some of these poor deluded fools from the general conspiracy'.[24] Arthur O'Connor's radical *Press* condemned the petitioning as 'the most thoroughly abominable' scheme ever employed by the 'abandoned administration', claiming that the resolution from Rathlin Island had been misrepresented to the people there as a petition to bring the Armagh magistrates to justice for their treatment of Catholics.[25]

Many priests joined with local magistrates in urging their people to surrender arms. Some like Fr Patrick Ryan, pastor of Coolock, Co Dublin, and subsequently bishop of Ferns, were more than willing to lend their support to the loyal effort but in other instances the magistrates and militia, like the radicals, intimidated the clergy. Immediately prior to the rebellion the loyalist *Dublin Journal* praised the efforts of Captain Swayne of the City of Cork Militia who had addressed the congregation of Fr John Lynch of Ballysax, near Kilcullen. So successful was his exhortation that five hundred pikes and vast quantities of arms were 'voluntarily surrendered' over the next two days.[26] While the *Dublin Journal* carried the sanitised official account of the proceedings, William Farrell, a Co Carlow United Irishman, recalled a more brutal, if equally embellished memory of Swayne's visit to the chapel of Fr Higgins at Prosperous, Co Kildare. According to this account, the captain interrupted Mass and ordered the people to bring in their arms. Then, turning to the old priest who later became a target of the United Irishmen, Swayne warned, 'if you don't have it done I'll pour boiling lead down your throat'. Farrell recalled that the congregation dispersed 'in sullen and silent indignation, whispering their wrongs and insults and breathing vengeance at any hazard'.[27] In Higgins' case, then, we see a concrete example of the 'battle for affection' as the curate was subject, in turn, to loyalist and United Irish intimidation.

Similarly the hierarchy were subjected to pressure from both parties. In the spring of 1798 Troy, described by Patrick Duignan as 'a steady loyalist', was criticised by the lord lieutenant Camden for his timidity in failing to call the people to their senses.[28] The radical press, on the other hand, lampooned the hierarchy for their supine support of the administration. At Christmas 1797 *The Press* carried a seasonal reflection with striking parallels between Judea and Ireland:

The PRIESTHOOD and the Government of the province where he

[Jesus] had his birth, found his doctrines incompatible with the foreign yoke which their tyranny imposed.[29]

In a measure of the success of this campaign the bishops were forced to address these specific criticisms in their pastorals, as did government ministers in parliament.

Such was the 'battle for affection' or the race for the support of the Catholic clergy run between the radicals and the administration in the 1790s. Once the rebellion broke out in May 1798, the great majority of the clergy remained steadfastly loyal. Only seventy of their number joined the rebel cause. But in the bitter post-rebellion polemic, there was a sense in which both sides were justified in their criticism of the clergy. On the one hand, Richard Musgrave believed that the rebellion sprang from 'the envenomed hatred with which the popish multitude [were] inspired from their earliest age by their clergy' towards the Protestant state and British connection. On the other, the United Irishman Miles Byrne railed against the clergy for their 'pious assiduity and earnest endeavours' to keep the Irish in thraldom. It was only this, he believed, which saved 'the infamous English government in Ireland from destruction'.[30]

The aftermath of the rebellion proved equally difficult for the Catholic hierarchy. While Archbishop Troy and his confrères had opposed every manifestation of the 'French disease' in Ireland, the prominence of a substantial number of clerics amongst the rebels was sufficient to feed interpretations of the rising as a 'popish plot'. Memories of the massacres of 1641 were revived; once more loyalists rallied to the call for revenge, giving rise to a backlash and polemic as vicious as the rebellion itself. Significantly, it fell to the bishops to lead the defence of the general Catholic body. The Catholic Committee was already dissolved but now the leading Catholic radicals, tainted by their association with the United Irish cause were forced underground; many in prison, others in fear for their lives or property. In their absence, Troy became the acknowledged voice of Irish Catholics, a development which placed him in an unenviable and ironic position, given his steady loyalism throughout the decade.

The hierarchy were compromised by the rebellion – this vulnerability explains, in part, the willingness of the bishops to cooperate with the Viceroy, Lord Cornwallis, in his project of a legislative Union of Ireland and Great Britain. Cornwallis was known for his conciliatory approach to Irish affairs and it appears the bishops saw in him some protection against the backlash of the ascendancy and the feared reimposition of penal legislation; indeed Bishop Francis Moylan of Cork described him as 'the saviour of Ireland'. In any event, Catholic Ireland had little affection for the Protestant parliament in Dublin – as Bishop Hussey of Waterford and Lismore put it, he would prefer a union with the 'Beys and Mamelukes of Egypt than being under the iron rod of the Mamelukes of Ireland'. Nationalist historiography has criticised the hierarchy for their acquiescence in the passage of the Union and the annihilation of Ireland's parliament. As one recent commentator put it, 'Archbishop Troy conspired with the murderous viceroy [sic] Castlereagh for the Act of Union'.[31] Troy's stance on the measure was not without qualification, however. In the past he had assured Castlereagh that no arrangements to pacify Ireland would be effective so long as Roman Catholics remained excluded from the benefits of the constitution.[32] In 1799 he supported the Union in the belief that the measure would clear the way for emancipation.

The Catholics may have carried the Union; certainly they were in no position to oppose it.[33] There is no clearer illustration of the compromised position of the bishops than their willingness to allow government interference in the internal workings of the church. Indeed, it was an irony that the peculiarities of the penal era allowed the church to exist free from state control; so while many European churches were hindered by the terms of concordats the Irish bishops enjoyed unfettered authority. The bishops jealously guarded that freedom, but in the aftermath of the rebellion they were forced to concede a limited crown veto on episcopal nominations. Confiding in his Roman agent, Troy confessed:

> we all wish to remain as we are, and we would so, were it not that too many of the clergy were active in the wicked rebellion or did not oppose it ... If we had rejected the proposals in toto, we would be considered as rebels ... if we agreed to it without reference to Rome we would be branded schismatics. We were between Scylla and Charybdis.[34]

Emancipation, however, did not follow the Union. Protestant opinion in Ireland prevented Cornwallis from coupling the two issues while the king's known antipathy towards Catholic relief made it an impossibility. In this failure was found the fatal flaw of the Union which historians have argued transformed Britain's Catholic question into an Irish Question.[35] The veto, too, remained a thorny and divisive issue, which dogged Catholic politics and delayed the delivery of the final measure of Catholic Emancipation.

CHAPTER FOURTEEN

The Catholic Church in the age of O'Connell

Donal Kerr

For Irish Catholics the early nineteenth century brought many changes. During much of that period the powerful voice of Daniel O'Connell, the 'Liberator', resounded through the land and drew many Catholics into the major politico-religious movements of the age. Catholics read the speeches and pamphlets of bishops of outstanding quality – James Warren Doyle, John MacHale and others – who gave public voice to their grievances and, at the same time, saw them make determined efforts to modernise and reinvigorate the Irish church. Charismatic leaders and founders of religious congregations arose who not only made available new forms of consecrated life but also were geared towards providing for the needs of the Catholic population. The state introduced important social reforms that mainly benefited the poorer classes and, under sustained Catholic pressure, the penal code was finally eliminated. Zealous evangelical Protestants made one more determined effort to promote the Reformation and to unite the kingdom religiously as well as politically. These stirring events wrought important changes in the position and expectations of the Catholics of Ireland.

I

In 1790 the population was probably 4.5 millions; by the time of the Great Famine it had almost doubled. A census of 1834 showed the population of Ireland at 8 million at a time when the population of England and Wales was 13.9 million. Of that 8 million, some 6.5 million (80%) were Catholic, Anglicans 853,000 and Dissenters, mainly Presbyterians, 665,000. Four-fifths of the Catholics lived on the land – seven out of eight lived in the country or in towns of less than 2,000 inhabitants. As striking as the size of the Catholic population was its poverty. There were Catholics in all grades of society – prosperous farmers, particularly in the eastern half of the country, wealthy Catholic business people, merchants and some professional men in towns and a small Catholic gentry. Most Catholics, however, were poor, often indescribably poor and the rapid increase in population made their lot more desperate. The great poverty of those millions must always be taken into account when describing the church. Sharp regional differences existed. In Connacht and in Ulster Catholics were too poor to build chapels in the way that the more prosperous eastern and southern dioceses could. In Ulster, too, the presence of a large Protestant community forced them to keep a low profile. The peasants at the bottom end of the social scale constituted the majority of Catholics. In general they lived in huts, cabins or two-roomed farmhouses, with little or no furniture but well heated by peat fires. Their sustenance in most of the country was potatoes with perhaps a little milk. Visitors, and there were many, who saw them from their carriages on the roads or met them in the villages were struck especially by their miserable attire, often no better than rags. Poor though they were, they were attached to their little plot of land knowing that if they lost it they and their families would become beggars on the roadside. The endemic rural violence had most to do with land for desperate peasants organised into secret societies, Ribbonmen or Moonlighters, to protect their 'rights'.

It is difficult to assess accurately what their religion meant to those millions, for the faith and the spiritual life of a person or group is difficult if not impossible to discover. Devotional practice provides some external measure. If the many visitors to Ireland are to be credited, the people were devoted to their faith. Count Charles de Montalembert, visiting Ireland in 1830, wrote of the faith of the people kneeling in the mud and rain to hear Mass: 'I cannot imagine anything more worthy of respect than the faith of the Irish people'.[1] Count Aléxis de Tocqueville and his companion, Count Gustave de Beaumont, who visited Ireland twice in the 1830s wrote simply: 'The Irish people are in their church'.[2] Other French writers, Edouard Dechy and Adolphe Perrault, later a cardinal, all expressed the same admiration for the faith of the people. Besides sympathetic French visitors others too were impressed. The German Lutheran visitor, Kohl, wrote in 1844: 'the Irish are the most genuine Catholics in the world'.[3] The English novelist, Thackeray, a sharp critic of Catholicism, wrote of the cathedral in Waterford: 'A much finer ornament to the church … was the piety, stern, simple and unaffected, of the people within. Their whole soul seemed in their prayers, as rich and poor knelt indifferently on the flags.'

In devotions the regional differences were marked. In the countryside Irish was the language of probably the majority of the peasantry. The language had a rich oral tradition of religious poetry, narrative and prayer together with extensive copies of favourite authors. The *Pious Miscellany* of Tadhg Gaedhealach Ó Súilleabháin reached its fourteenth edition in 1832. The Holy Trinity, the Passion of Christ, the Blessed Virgin, figured largely in the prayers.[4] There were many blessings; before meals, at work and on meeting someone. These devotions tended to be somewhat syncretic. The cluster of beliefs and practices that constituted their religion, in addition to the Mass – always held in high esteem – the Rosary, called the *Páidrín Páirteach,* that is, the little shared prayer, fasting, and prayers for certain occasions, also included devotions connected with patterns, pilgrimages to holy wells and wakes. Belief in the 'little people', fairy forts, changelings, curses, and cures was widespread. Wakes, particularly, often had games with strong sexual overtones, relics of paganism and satire of the clergy.[5] As elsewhere in Europe those practices were under attack from a reforming Tridentine church as either superstitious or giving rise to insobriety, immorality, and other abuses. Another element which Irish Catholics had in common with much of western Europe was a type of millenarianism. Many Catholics, sensing in the rousing and triumphalist words of O'Connell a forthcoming victory over their oppressors, related it to the prophecies of Pastorini which foretold that the faithful would see their persecutors perish under the terrible hand of the Almighty.[6] Many Protestants believed that Catholics had even decided on Christmas Day 1824 as the day they would rebel and massacre them.

Attendance at Sunday Mass was much less regular than it was to become later in the century, as David Miller's pioneering studies of the figures given in the Report of the Commissioners of Public Instruction in 1834 indicate.[7] His recent carefully revised estimate is that in most areas north and west of a line from Dundalk to Killarney, Mass attendance was less than forty per cent, whereas to the east and south of that line attendance was over forty per cent. Towns with a catchment of 5,000 had a very high attendance. The interpretation of this report presents problems, however, and many historians believe that the Mass attendance figures should be revised upwards.[8] Nevertheless, it is clear that attendance was much lower than in the post-Famine period. Factors existed which help explain the low Sunday Mass attendance. Many of the churches were small and the parish was often too poor to extend them or build new ones. As late as the 1830s and later, in parts of Connacht and Ulster, many Masses were celebrated in the open air at Mass-rocks. In many dioceses priests were forbidden to say more than one Mass. Often, too, people had not got appropriate clothes to go to Mass. In the 1850s, a distinguished French visitor, Fr Perraud, learned that in Co Donegal 4,000 people went barefoot in winter, that rarely had a man a warm shirt, and there were families where five or six grown women had between them only a single dress to go out in.[9] They would take it in turn to go, as often there was only one Mass on Sunday. The practice of stations, where all the people of the neighbourhood assembled for Mass and confession and often for some instruction, constituted an important substitute for the Sunday Mass in the parish chapel. To attend the station the faithful had to travel no further than a neighbour's house and they did not need to be as well clad as for church on Sunday. Fr Thomas O'Carroll, curate in Clonoulty, Co Tipperary, mentions going to stations as often as four times a week during certain parts of the year and spending four or more hours hearing confessions.[10]

The poor attendance at Sunday Mass may not be too readily seen as non-practice. For the bishops and clergy of the time the fulfilment of the Easter duty appears to have been the criterion by which they judged the religious adherence of the faithful. The reports regularly prepared by the parish clergy for the bishops' visitation never mention Mass attendance but list the numbers who have not made their Easter duty. Very few missed out on this. Bishop Kinsella told Tocqueville: 'It is nearly unknown in the towns and still less in the country that a Catholic fails to make his Easter communion.'[11] The Easter duty, apparently, was for the clergy the touchstone of Catholic practice. The devotional life of the people in the cities and towns and in the more prosperous east and southeast of the country, which included much of Leinster and Munster, was different from that of the countryside. Attendance at Mass was quite high. Devotional life was more in line with the reforms of the Council of Trent (1545-63) or late eighteenth-century France. A list of devotions for the diocese of Dublin included devotions to the Sacred Heart, to the Immaculate Heart of Mary, novenas for the feasts of the Virgin, of St Francis Xavier, Stations of the Cross, Three Hours agony devotions on Good Friday and Bona Mors devotion. This was true of other towns. Catholics were catching up with nineteenth-century devotions more in keeping with the spirituality of continental Europe and more adapted to their modern lifestyle. Soon an Italian lithograph of the Sacred Heart took an honoured place in every Irish Catholic home.

Pious and well-to-do city and townspeople who had absorbed this more modern devotional life and regarded it as the norm, endeavoured to bring it to the rest of the country. The period saw a major phenomenon of many well-educated wealthy men and women devoting themselves to caring for the poor, religiously and socially. Nano Nagle had made a beginning in Cork in 1775 and her Sisters of the Presentation there visited and instructed the poor. In 1802, Edmund Rice, a wealthy Waterford merchant, had founded the Christian Brothers to provide education for poor boys, and in 1820 they secured official Roman approval. The work flourished with schools in Waterford, Cork and Limerick. In 1828 Daniel O'Connell laid the foundation stone of the Catholic Model School, later known as O'Connell School in Richmond Street in Dublin. Daniel Delaney, bishop of Kildare and Leighlin, gathered as catechists to the poor in Mountrath and Tullow a group of pious women, who later became the Brigidines. Later he formed a group of men catechists who became the Patrician Brothers. Both small groups provided education for the poor in the diocese. James Warren Doyle, bishop of Kildare and Leighlin, began an important and successful scheme of catechising the poor by frequent classes and the use of libraries, book societies and so forth.[12] The coadjutor archbishop of Dublin, Daniel Murray, also founded and encouraged the founding of schools. He persuaded two well-to-do young women, Mary Aikenhead and Teresa Ball, to establish two very important congregations – the Sisters of Charity to cater for the poor and the Loreto Sisters to cater for the better-off.[13] When, in 1814, Pope Pius re-established the Jesuits, Peter Kenney, an Irish Jesuit, trained in Naples, revived the order in Ireland, with chapels, communities and a college at Clongowes Wood, Co Kildare. Education, indeed, was a priority for church leaders. Half the Catholic laity had no formal education and the children of the rural poor received little instruction of any sort.[14] The education provided by the 'hedge-schools' was inadequate. Since 1811, the schools of the Kildare Place Society provided good, nondenominational education but by 1820 Catholics became convinced that that they were aiding proselytism and boycotted them. The efforts of bishops like Murray, Doyle and the teaching orders of Brothers and Sisters improved matters but they, too, were unable to cope with the problem of the vast number of poor children who, particularly in the countryside, were deprived of any education.

If the Irish church faced many problems it was also sharing in the general religious renewal in Europe. In France the Catholic Church was engaged in active restoration of religion as clergy and people endeavoured, with considerable success, to repair the damage inflicted by the French Revolution and a string of new religious orders were springing up. The long reign of Pius VII who had suffered so bravely under Napoleon, restored much of the papal prestige and the church was once more respected by the ruling nations. Pope Leo XII (1823-29) came to the papal throne committed to a programme of reform. One of his earliest measures was to announce a jubilee for 1825 calling on nations and their rulers to make it an occasion for deepening their faith. Irish bishops used the jubilee as an occasion to bring people to the sacraments of penance and communion. The jubilee was a catalyst in many dioceses. A Dublin parish priest, Fr James Meagher, recorded that 'to the fidelity with which the graces of the holy year were husbanded, was due the amazingly increased frequentation of the sacraments' in the Dublin diocese.[15]

The bishops continued the reorganisation that had begun in the middle years of the eighteenth century. The involvement of many priests in the rebellion of 1798 had created shock waves and made the hierarchy nervous in their dealings with the government, but a decade later, the twenty-seven Catholic bishops formed a powerful and independent body. A combination of circumstances had made them remarkably autonomous. On the one hand, the state had first persecuted them, then ignored them and now had no say in the nomination of bishops as did the Catholic Princes of Europe, the voltairian Napoleon Bonaparte or even the Protestant King of Prussia. On the other, Rome, forbidden by English law to have contact with Catholics in the

United Kingdom, was ill-informed of what was going on there and when it did interfere the Irish bishops, while professing great deference to the Holy See, often simply ignored its injunctions on the grounds that it did not understand the situation in Ireland – which was often true. As the Irish church was directly under the Congregation of *Propaganda Fide*, there was no nuncio in Ireland to curtail the bishops' power. In 1829 a system for the selection of bishops was finally agreed on. The parish priests and canons chose three names in order of merit. The bishops could change the order of the list, eliminate one name but not add any. Rome, where the final decision was made, kept to the list. Since the arrangement provided adequate local participation, it satisfied bishops, priests and nationalists. Up to the 1820s all the bishops had trained for the priesthood at Paris, Salamanca, Rome or the other Irish colleges on the continent. Increasingly from the 1820s the new bishops trained at Saint Patrick's College, Maynooth. The earlier generation of bishops was influenced by the ideas of the *Ancien Régime*, remembered the penal laws and tended to be grateful to the state for small concessions. The newer generation contemplated more forceful ways to remedy grievances. Before long a type of Irish-style 'Liberal Catholicism' developed.[16]

As Dáire Keogh's chapter illustrates, in the key diocese of Dublin Archbishop John Thomas Troy had successfully steered the church through the difficult years of the 1790s. He had also initiated many reforms. Until his death in 1822 he was still running his diocese although he was gradually conceding place to his chosen successor, Archbishop Daniel Murray. A very pastoral bishop, Murray did much to enrich the diocese with new foundations. As a reformer, he was closely associated with the rising star among the bishops – the brilliant young, determined bishop of Kildare and Leighlin – the Augustinian, James Warren Doyle. Doyle marks a transition from the timidity of the penal era to the more assertive role of the Catholic Church in the 19th century as even his 'illegal' assumption of the acronym JKL, 'James of Kildare and Leighlin' indicated. Doyle, a brilliant and fearless controversialist, highly respected by friend and foe, intellectually formidable, had raised the consciousness of Catholics by writings which were bolder far than any Catholic had dared publish to date. His writings, in particular his *Vindication of ... Irish Catholics* and *Letters on the State of Ireland,* together with his spirited exposé of Catholicism during a four-day examination in 1825 before two parliamentary committees, as Gladstone later admitted, won over many enemies of Catholic Emancipation. He put the Catholic case in bold and convincing terms and his publications often caused a sensation. Up to his early death in 1834, Doyle's powerful voice was raised on matters of public concern from education and the Poor Law to voting rights and repeal of the Union. Another and more strident voice, if not yet as influential, was that of John

MacHale, professor at Maynooth College and later archbishop of Tuam. MacHale, O'Connell's chief supporter in the movement for repeal, was a powerful popular leader. In an era when democracy was barely respectable, MacHale drank public toasts 'To the People, the source of all legitimate power' and 'Civil and religious liberty for the whole world'. Revered by the faithful of Tuam, feared by governments, he was regarded as a maverick by many of his fellow-bishops.

The bishops had begun to hold annual meetings. This important development was quite unusual. Throughout Europe neither governments nor Rome liked such meetings, governments fearing that the bishops might constitute a state within a state, Rome fearing that the meetings might give rise to a gallican or national church. Although the decisions taken at those meetings were not binding on the bishops, a co-ordinated policy emerged which strengthened their bargaining power with the government for they used the meetings to petition the government for concessions they wanted or to restate publicly their opposition to unwelcome measures. The meetings also increased their authority over both people and clergy. In penal times, when the bishops' presence in Ireland was illegal, their control over their clergy was limited and on occasion a priest in dispute with his bishop could denounce him to the authorities. During that time priests depended for their support on their own family and often lived with them. As a result, if the bishop tried to move the priests from their family parish both the priests and their relations might offer forcible resistance. As late as 1836 Dr Francis Maginnis, professor of theology at Maynooth, in a letter to his colleague, Charles McNally, later bishop of Clogher, described the parish priest of Aghnamullen, as 'a rude leader of a rude host, he is surrounded by a strong, well-armed body-guard of determined ruffians to prevent forsooth by force, his desertion of them and any attempt to acquiesce in the commands of the bishop'.[17] At a meeting on 18 October 1817, in Cavan, in the diocese of Kilmore, Michael O'Reilly, the parish priest of Kilmore, did not mince his words concerning his bishop, Dr Farrell O'Reilly. 'On the administration of the diocese since the arrival of his present Lordship, I do not wish to be very particular, but I dare say that the clergy were never so dissatisfied and disquieted.'[18] By the 1820s, however, the bishops united to reassert successfully their control over appointments to parishes to the extent that McNally complained, 'the bishops have formed themselves into a corporation whereby the clergy are even precluded from the benefit of an appeal to distant Rome against such a phalanx'.[19] The bishops reduced the power of the parish priests in another manner – the provision for curates. Up to then the curates were totally dependent on the parish priest and were usually quite poor. The bishops decreed a fixed stipend and a fairer provision for them and the parish priests accepted it.

Important for the organisation and efficiency of the diocese was the provision of a diocesan centre. 'We had neither a respectable nor central residence for the bishop nor a seminary where the candidates for the sacred ministry could be trained' wrote Bishop James Browne to the faithful of Kilmore diocese in his pastoral letter of 1838. It was much the same in other dioceses. There was no cathedral town and when bishops were appointed they often simply remained in the parish in which they were or moved to a better one if the parish priest there would allow them. The bishops now began to establish a diocesan centre in the principal town of the diocese which included a cathedral, residence and sometimes a seminary. As with other reforms, the introduction of a settled residence varied from diocese to diocese and took place earlier in Leinster and Munster than in Ulster. James Browne of Kilmore had lived in lodgings in Cavan for a short while, then in Drung, and later in Cootehill. In 1839 he was able to tell Paul Cullen, rector of the Irish College in Rome and agent of the Irish bishops, that he had solved his problem: 'I have purchased a splendid house in Cavan ... to the great astonishment of that Protestant town.'[20] The property he bought was to serve for a bishop's residence and a seminary. The establishment of a diocesan centre made for better administration and the seminary nearby facilitated the preparation of candidates for the priesthood. When these candidates had finished their studies in the diocesan college, most proceeded to the national seminary of St Patrick's College, Maynooth.

By 1826 students for the priesthood numbered 651 of whom 391 trained in Maynooth College. By 1844 the number of students in Maynooth College had increased to 438 and the college was providing some 66 priests a year. Parliament made an annual grant for the upkeep of the college to the anger of ultra-Protestant members of parliament. Aware of its dependence on the state the staff of Maynooth avoided politics. The students were in general the sons of 'middling' or strong farmers. The students' training was geared to produce pious, obedient priests sufficiently versed in the rather static theology of the time. Their courses were mainly in moral theology and were intended to help them hear confessions and to preach. The textbook in use up to the 1850s was the eight volumes of Louis Bailly's *Theologia dogmatica et moralis*, published in 1789.[21] Bailly, like most French theologians, was not a Jansenist but like them he had inherited from Jansenism its pessimistic approach to morality and was 'rigorist' in his theology. His textbook took a stern approach to sin, especially in sexual matters. A change was heralded when, in his Jubilee address of 1825, Pope Leo XII strongly advocated a milder approach along the lines of the theology of Saint Alphonsus Liguori, but this change came quite slowly.

II

While the church was reforming and reconstructing itself internally, events were taking place that affected the public image and status of Catholics and their sense of identity. Catholics had been led to believe that the Act of Union would usher in Catholic Emancipation, and its denial angered their leaders and created the conditions for mass Catholic nationalism. At first a controversy broke out concerning a royal veto on the appointment of bishops, at the root of which lay the broader question of how the church should be governed and what role, if any, the crown should exercise. Although English Catholics, together with Monsignor Quarantotti in charge of *Propaganda Fide*, Cardinal Consalvi, the Secretary of State and Pope Pius VII himself, were prepared to concede a veto, the Irish hierarchy who would have accepted it, if reluctantly, at the time of the Union, rejected it in 1808 and again in 1815. The popular party of which Daniel O'Connell was one of the leaders also rejected it forcibly. The bishops sent Archbishop Murray to Rome to put their case. The popular party sent the Franciscan, Fr Richard Hayes, who was later forcibly expelled from the Papal State. The long drawn-out controversy was divisive and when Henry Grattan, who for so long had championed the Catholic cause in parliament, died in 1820 the Catholic struggle for equality seemed at its nadir.

This was to change in the 1820s when the veto question was overtaken by the struggle for Emancipation. The veto issue may have passed over the heads of peasants living outside of the cities and towns and concerned more with eking out a living. Emancipation did not. It became the great question of the day. In 1823 O'Connell set up the Catholic Association and to involve everyone he decided to collect a subscription from even the poor who were asked to pay a penny a month – the Catholic Rent.[22] All, rich and poor, now felt involved. Importantly too he enlisted the clergy, persuading them that Emancipation was their cause and placing part of the Catholic Rent at their disposal to fight the agents of the New Reformation. Early on Bishop Doyle of Kildare and Leighlin came out in favour. His friend and metropolitan, Murray of Dublin, a universally respected, prudent and pastoral bishop, followed his example. Soon all bishops and priests joined. The clergy's support was vital for the priests could collect at the chapel doors from the poor in every country parish and from the thousands of poor Catholics in the towns. The Association quickly became a national movement which included all Catholics from Lord Kenmare to the poorest peasant – a non-violent mass movement led by O'Connell, the uncrowned king. O'Connell's influence reached out to all parts of the country as he held meetings in the villages to which the peasants flocked. Adroitly using the press, he also broadened the issue, attacking any abuse of power by landlords and other members of the ruling class. He founded his own thrice-weekly newspaper, *The Pilot,* where reports of the Association's activities were published and read out aloud at gatherings all over the country so that even the unlettered peasant knew and delighted in what O'Connell and the Association were doing on his behalf.

The Waterford election of 1826 was a vital break-through. Waterford Catholics led by Thomas Wyse and Father John Sheehan, with O'Connell's support, gave a startling display of Catholic political power when they persuaded the forty-shilling voters to reject the all-powerful Beresford candidate. In 1828 came the Clare election. The re-election of William Vesey Fitzgerald, a popular landlord, was a mere formality, or so it seemed. Suddenly, it was announced that O'Connell, a Catholic, was going to stand. The astonishment was great and in Britain and Ireland all eyes turned to Co Clare. Voting was open and the peasants had always voted for their landlord's candidate; that was the pattern of rural dependence and deference. During the three days of the Clare election the landlords and the government rallied to the support of Vesey Fitzgerald. The priests supported O'Connell. At the hustings the people rejected their landlords and followed the priests. Emancipation swiftly followed O'Connell's victory. Although it allowed Catholics to assume most public offices and sit in parliament, socially, Emancipation did not change much. The peasant was as badly off as ever. As O'Connell had told one of them, 'you will still break stones'. Yet it was a psychological boost to all Catholics. It was greeted with bonfires all over the country. The poet, Thomas Moore, acknowledged his pleasure at being finally able to stretch his 'emancipated legs'. Catholics had recovered a sense of self-esteem. The masses had an idol they could look up to and, in return, they provided O'Connell with a formidable power base.

III

County Clare was not the only county to gain celebrity in the 1820s. County Cavan, too, became famous for it was there that the Second or New Reformation achieved its most notable successes. The New Reformation was a crusade to accomplish what the first Reformation had not achieved. This crusade is often dated from the charge of the evangelical archbishop of Dublin, William Magee when in 1822 he described Catholics as possessing a 'church without what *we* can properly call a religion' and 'blindly enslaved to a supposed infallible ecclesiastical authority'. Religious antagonisms were never far beneath the surface and now during the 1820s they boiled over. No less than five societies had been founded in Ireland to distribute Bibles and religious tracts to Irish Catholics. Zealous missionaries of the New Reformation vigorously preached the gospel in villages and at fairs throughout Ireland, distributed religious material and denounced the priests as standing between the people and the pure word of God. The Catholic clergy saw this missionary endeavour as proselytism and, led by Doyle, MacHale, O'Connell and many others, hit back vigorously. O'Connell's support for the clergy, less versed in scripture than the evangelicals who descended on their parishes challenging them to public dispute, made the priests his stoutest supporters during the Emancipation campaign and after. The evangelical crusade scored its most significant gains in Cavan where, with the enthusiastic support of Lord Farnham, it won over several hundred Catholics. The hierarchy became alarmed and in 1826, in an unprecedented move, they sent a delegation of bishops to Cavan – Patrick Curtis, the Primate, William Crolly, bishop of Down and Connor, James Magauran of Ardagh and John MacHale, coadjutor bishop of Killala. MacHale and Curtis addressed large crowds in Cavan chapel. When the bishops left they declared that the people were enthusiastic Catholics and denounced in the vituperative language of the day Farnham's converts as 'worthless vagrants, strolling beggars, prostitutes with their illegitimate children, idle schoolmasters … disguised Protestants'. Although it does appear that many of the converts were poor and that most of them later returned to the Catholic faith, the Catholic Church had been shaken.[23]

These years were marked by religious controversies and public disputations in many parts of the country. One of the most celebrated was a six-day dispute at the Dublin Institute in Sackville Street between Fr Tom Maguire and the evangelical, Rev Richard Pope. Little good came of these 'spiritual cockfights', as Richard Whately, Anglican archbishop of Dublin, called them, except to deepen religious animosities. In evidence before the Lords' Committee on the State of Ireland in 1825, Doyle attributed the deterioration of relations between Catholics and Protestants to the proselytising efforts and O'Connell complained that the Catholics of north Dublin were 'a prey to the baleful and destructive influence of nearly forty fanatical and proselytising establishments'.[24] Yet relations between many of the bishops remained good. In Dublin, Daniel Murray and Richard Whately, the Catholic and Anglican archbishops, had a good relationship and the same applied to the two bishops of Limerick, John Ryan and John Jebb. In December 1829 William Crolly, the Catholic bishop of Down and Connor, presided over a Catholic meeting in St Patrick's chapel, Belfast which was addressed by Henry Montgomery, moderator of the Presbyterian Synod. Despite the initial hopes it inspired among the evangelicals, by 1827 the New Reformation was petering out.[25]

IV

The pace of reorganisation and reform quickened after Emancipation. Since 1829 the church had a more acceptable system for appointing bishops. At their 1829 meeting, the bishops set up a committee to examine the discipline of the church and shortly afterwards a series of synods promulgated reforms. The faithful were reminded how essential it was to make their Easter duty. Priests were told to administer the sacraments only in the chapels and to hear confessions only in confessionals where possible. They were warned not to take excessive stipends from the faithful. They were to avoid dining at the houses of parishioners at stations because of the burden it placed on the parishioners and lest they give bad example, particularly if alcohol were taken. Abuses in popular religious practices were condemned. By now, too, the practice, common enough in the eighteenth century, of marriages performed illicitly by 'couple beggars' or 'silenced' priests, had virtually ceased. In general, what was taking place was that the bishops were restoring discipline to the church and introducing more and more the Tridentine reforms. This process had begun in the eighteenth century but by the 1820s times were more propitious.

Apart from the work of the diocesan church, religious sisters, brothers and priests continued to make contributions to the spiritual and social life of the faithful. In 1830 Irish Trappists came from France after the July Revolution to found the first monastic community since Henry VIII suppressed the monasteries in the 1530s. The people came parish-by-parish, one each Sunday, to contribute a day's labour. In 1831 a group of women who were working for 'poor female children and the instruction of young women', became the congregation of the Sisters of Mercy. Their leader, Catherine McAuley, who had opened a house in Baggot Street, Dublin, in 1827 as a school and asylum for the poor, was one of the century's most charismatic religious founders. In 1832 a group of four young priests with Fr Philip Dowley, dean at Maynooth College, came together to found what was to become the Irish Vincentians who engaged in teaching and in mission work. In 1835 Mary Aikenhead's Sisters of Charity broke new ground when they founded the important hospital of Saint Vincent's, 'the first hospital in Dublin to be founded, owned and managed by women'.[26] Older orders expanded their work. In Dublin, Father John Spratt, provincial superior of the Irish Carmelites, founded an orphanage, a night refuge, and an asylum for the blind. In 1846 the Domincan Sisters established a school for deaf and dumb children in Cabra, in north Dublin. The Poor Clare Sisters who had opened a school and orphanage at Harold's Cross established a large convent in Newry in 1830 to cater for poor girls. In teaching religion and providing schooling, nursing, caring for the abandoned and other social services, those religious had a notable impact in raising the level of care and instruction available to the poor. There was, as always during this period, an economic constraint. However economically they did their work, the sisters and brothers needed financial support and in the impoverished Ireland of the mid-nineteenth century this support could not be found outside of the towns and cities and it was to those areas that they were forced to confine their activities.

A tangible sign of the people's attachment to their faith and of the zeal of their leaders is the number of churches Catholics built in the decade after Emancipation. The novelist, William Makepiece Thackeray, spoke of 'the many handsome cathedrals for their [the Catholics'] worship which have been built of late years … by the nobler contribution of the poor man's penny and the untiring energies and sacrifices of the clergy'.[27] Kohl, the German visitor remarked: 'the Catholic churches are beginning to tower over those of the Establishment … and all over the country Irish Catholics are vying with English Protestants in the zeal with which they build new churches and repair old ones'.[28] In 1842, the diocese of Elphin claimed that 'twenty-six slated chapels have been erected since 1825' and Achonry diocese maintained that new chapels had been built in every parish in the ten years from 1831 to 1841. According to Archbishop Cullen, the elderly Patrick MacGettigan, bishop of Raphoe from 1820 to 1861, claimed to remember the time when there was not a single church in his diocese.[29] Perhaps the bishop exaggerated but certainly the diocese of Raphoe was well provided with churches and religious institutions at the time of his death. When Murray became archbishop of Dublin there was only one convent; by the time of his death in 1852 there were twenty-nine. The archdiocese had but one school for girls and one or two for boys; by 1852 it had some 220 schools suitable for Catholics. Up to a hundred churches had been built or refurbished. The *Catholic Directory* claimed in 1844 that 'within the last thirty years, nine hundred Catholic churches have been built or restored'. Many of the new churches were quite large such as Saint Mary's and Saint Andrew's in Dublin and the cathedrals in Carlow and Killarney. Built mostly after 1829, often on land provided by Protestant landlords, those churches had begun to transform the external image of the church.[30]

Poor though most Catholics were, the amount they contributed towards the church in this period is quite remarkable. According to a submission Archbishop MacHale and William Higgins, bishop of Ardagh, made to the Congregation of *Propaganda Fide* in 1847, the church's outlay over the previous thirty years amounted to almost £22,000,000 which included £18,000,000 for the maintenance of the clergy and £4,000,000 for the building of churches, convents, colleges and schools for the poor. A rich Catholic bourgeoisie that had developed since the eighteenth century provided most of that money. O'Connell's successful movement for Emancipation had made them more conscious of their religion and they provided funds for schools, orphanages and hospitals as well as churches. Among those families were the Ball family, the Corballis family, the O'Briens and the More O'Ferralls.[31] Not merely did they endow new religious congregations but they often provided the personnel. This was so with Frances Ball who founded the Loreto Sisters, and Mary Aikenhead who founded the Sisters of Charity.

Official relations with Rome during this period were good. Pope Gregory XVI (1831-46) had been Cardinal Prefect of *Propaganda* and so had a better knowledge of Irish affairs than his predecessors. The British government through their agents in Rome sought with some success to influence episcopal appointments. In 1834 the possibility arose that MacHale, coadjutor bishop of Killala, would be appointed archbishop of Tuam. The prime minister, Lord Melbourne, later related that the government asked Rome not to appoint MacHale, *'anybody but him'*. Government agents in Rome redoubled their efforts to exclude MacHale. They won over the Secretary of State, Cardinal Bernetti and brought prolonged pressure to bear on Gregory XVI. The pope, however, complained that no piece of preferment of any value ever fell vacant in Ireland that he did not get a nominee from the British government for the appointment, and insisted on appointing MacHale. Later Gregory supported the bishops in their rejection of state salaries and quashed the fear that the Holy See would enter a concordat with Britain behind their backs. When the government demanded that the Holy See censure priests involved in O'Connell's Repeal movement, Rome, while warning the clergy to abstain from politics, was careful not to offend national opinion in Ireland.[32] The government's reluctance to accept MacHale was well-founded for he was to cause the state authorities, and many of his fellow-bishops, continual trouble until his death in 1881. A fiery O'Connellite, a cultural nationalist, a leader of men, and an outspoken critic of all British governments, he wielded a powerful, if vitriolic pen.

Pope Gregory's influence on Irish Catholics was largely responsible for the increase in mission activity in the 1830s. Gregory, who had been prefect of the Congregation for the Propagation of the Faith and had thoroughly re-organised it, retained an intense interest in foreign missions. In 1834 he appointed Bede Polding, an English Benedictine, vicar apostolic of Australia and Tasmania. Polding came to Maynooth College in 1836 to preach the retreat and in 1837 seven students went to Australia to join him. The following year saw an even more remarkable development, this time as regards India. Since the Catholic Church in that subcontinent was languishing under Portuguese royal patronage, Pope Gregory decided to take decisive action and created five new vicariates. He appointed the Augustinian, Daniel O'Connor, vicar apostolic of the vicariate of Madras in 1832. When O'Connor's health began to fail Patrick Carew, professor of theology at Maynooth College, was named coadjutor. When Carew left Ireland for Madras in 1838 he brought with him five Maynooth priests and one student. In 1840 Carew was transferred to the vicariate of Bengal to replace Robert St Leger, an Irish Jesuit. Rome then appointed to Madras another Maynooth staff member, John Fennelly, who remained vicar apostolic until 1868. He was succeeded by his brother, Stephen, who was vicar apostolic until 1881. John Fennelly brought with him to India in 1841 three Presentation Brothers and four sisters. The Irish Presentation Sisters were invited by Carew to Madras to care for Irish children orphaned after Afghans defeated the British in 1841 when some 20,000 soldiers died many of whom were Irish. The Loreto Sisters went to Calcutta to teach and to care for orphans. In 1838 Murray introduced into Dublin the *Society for the Propagation of the Faith*, a dynamic mission association founded in Lyon which involved the laity in raising funds and occasionally providing personnel for the missions.[33] Before long the diocese was to have one of the Society's most generous branches in all Europe. In 1842 John Hand, aided by Murray, set up the College of All Hallows in Dublin, which over the past 160 years provided thousands of priests for the Irish emigrant community in the United States and elsewhere. With the provision of priests, religious and sisters that the development of All Hallows, the Sisters of Mercy, Sisters of Charity and Loreto Sisters represented, and the involvement of the laity in fund-raising, the Irish Catholic Church was poised to take on that outstanding missionary role in the Americas and the British Empire which was one of its main characteristics in the 19th and 20th centuries.

A major reason why the clergy supported O'Connell was his determination to channel the expression of grievances away from crime into legitimate and often successful protest; as one priest put it, 'the national spirit was weaned by O'Connell away from the midnight folly of rebellion – it was taught by him the secret of moral power.'[34] When the Young Irelanders challenged O'Connell on the legitimacy of physical force, the clergy weighed in against them. Bishop Cantwell of Meath declared publicly that 'to pursue a course of physical force would prove fatal to the temporal and eternal welfare of the flocks committed to our care.'[35] Archbishop Murray, who remembered only too well the slaughter during and after the 1798 rebellion, played a role in minimising the extent of the Young Ireland rebellion of 1848. The clergy used O'Connell's prestige to persuade people of the folly of violence. Robert Peel's initiative in establishing an effective police force was another factor in reducing crime. Faction fighting though not uncommon diminished considerably during this period though it was not until 1855 that the notorious Donnybrook Fair was suppressed.

Drunkenness was a common cause of crime and domestic unhappiness. A number of Protestant clergy in Cork, Wexford, Dublin and Belfast and also the Carmelite, Fr Spratt, tried to meet the problem by founding Temperance movements. Most successful was the total abstinence society which a Capuchin friar, Fr Theobald Mathew, aided by the Quaker, William Martin, launched in 1838. Soon O'Connell used it as part of his moral force movement. The tax returns on alcohol dropped by a third and it is claimed that between 1838-42, five million Irish (in Ireland and the USA) took the pledge.[36] The German visitor Kohl commented: 'it may be questioned whether history can present a parallel to this great moral revolution, or whether any ever acquired so great and bright a name in so short a time'.[37] Lord John Russell called it 'a moral miracle'.

The country was sick, Bishop Doyle declared, and 'poverty is the leprosy that covers it'.[38] As the population increased the rural poor became poorer. A plethora of benevolent societies of all denominations attempted to aid the poor, but what they could do was limited and confined to the towns. Charity sermons, which Murray, Doyle and others organised or preached, raised very considerable sums of money for the poor. In 1844 an important French organisation began a branch in Ireland. This was Frederick Ozanam's Society of Saint Vincent de Paul. Its first Irish branch was in Dublin and some of the leading men in public life took part, including John O'Connell, the Liberator's son and political heir, and Charles Gavan Duffy. Two years later another branch was founded in Cork. The Society, heavily subsidised by the parent body in Paris, provided much relief during the Famine. It is clear, however, that the church had not worked out a coherent social welfare programme; in view of its limited resources it would be too much to expect one. Doyle saw clearly enough that only state provision for the poor could meet the problem. It was the state's duty, he argued, otherwise it would be guilty of the deaths of its own citizens. Some of the wealth of the established church, he believed, could be appropriated for that purpose. Although he fought hard for a Poor Law, Doyle was opposed to the harsh, humiliating system of workhouses, where the strict regime separated even members of the same family. After Doyle's death, the Anglican and Catholic archbishops of Dublin, Dr Richard Whately and Daniel Murray, took part in a commission that recommended state provision for the poor, but when in 1838 the state did introduce a Poor Law it did not follow their recommendations. This Poor Law included the workhouses.

The clergy's dependence on the generosity of the faithful was a burden on the poor but neither the clergy nor the national leaders wanted a state-paid clergy. From France Lamennais, who with Montalembert followed Irish affairs closely, approved, commenting that the only way to free the church was to be free from the state:

This is what Irish Catholics had rightly felt, who have many times rebuffed the efforts of the English government to impose it. As long as we do not follow their example, Catholicism will have a precarious and feeble existence among us ... The scraps of bread thrown to the clergy are the title deeds of her subjection ... It was not with a cheque drawn on Caesar's bank that Jesus sent his apostles out into the world.[39]

Yet there was a disadvantage in refusing state support as Murray, Archdeacon O'Sullivan and others perceived. Priests felt it hard to have to squeeze money out of an impoverished people and many of them, especially the curates, were badly off. Furthermore, the lack of money meant that the number of priests was insufficient to minister to the growing population. Again and again in the 1830s and 1840s the bishops petitioned the Lord Lieutenant to increase the grant to the national seminary of Maynooth, claiming that double the number of priests was needed to cope with the growing population but that distress in the country so affected 'that middle class of society from which the ... priesthood are usually presented, that there has been a ... reduction in the numbers who pay for their support'. The bishops' claim that double the number of priests was needed was no exaggeration. On average, there was one priest for 3,000 people but in some of the poorer areas it was 1:4,000. Already in 1825 Fr Michael Collins, parish priest of Skibbereen, told a parliamentary committee that the number attending religious duties had fallen because of the inability of the overworked clergy to give instructions or to catechise the children.[40] Bishop McNally of Clogher informed O'Connell that the conditions required for gaining the jubilee indulgence – the confession of one's sins – 'could be fulfilled only with great difficulty because the clergy were overworked and there were no order priests to help them'.[41] Murray, too, complained that 'they [the priests] are obliged to shorten the time [in confession] allotted to each, on account of the great number they had to attend to and the comparatively small number of clergy'.[42] The well-informed John O'Sullivan, archdeacon of the Kerry diocese and parish priest of Kenmare, reflected in the privacy of his diary that the people were ill-instructed and ascribed the failure to the lack of priests:

The number of priests to attend to them is too small, the parishes too extensive; with a population of over 10,000 and an area of near 60,000 statute acres, how could myself and my curates come at all the calls, and attend to the instruction of the people ... What can one of my curates do this day who has a [sick] call thirteen miles from here more than go and return?[43]

The low ratio of priests to people is a major factor to be taken into account in evaluating the state of the church in Ireland in the first half of the nineteenth century. The failure of the clergy to provide adequate instruction for the increasing rural population meant that their religion retained its mixture of sacred and profane, orthodox and unorthodox, Christian and pagan. It also left Catholics open to what the clergy denounced as proselytism. Peel's measure in 1845 increasing substantially the grant to Maynooth was a generous effort to meet the bishops' request.

Some other means of evangelising the people existed. In France the chosen instrument of the church for reconverting the people after the desolation caused by the French Revolution was the mission. For a few weeks priests came from outside the parish to preach to all the people a complete course in religion, with emphasis on confession, penance, communion. In Ireland missions did not take off until the 1840s and then slowly and mainly as a reply to the evangelical crusade. Regular clergy or congregations – Vincentians, Redemptorists, Jesuits, and Passionists – usually gave the missions. Luigi Gentili, a noted Italian Rosminian priest, died of famine fever caught while hearing confessions during a mission in Dublin. Whatever about the faithful's grasp of doctrinal issues their moral life was of a high standard, a fact remarked on by visitors, friendly or hostile.[44]

As in much of western Europe, education was seen as the panacea for many of society's ills. Doyle, Murray and the other bishops, with support from O'Connell and the influential Anthony Blake, had pressed in vain during the 1820s for an educational system acceptable to Catholics. When the Tories went out of office, the Whig government in 1831 brought in the National System of Education whereby a state-supported primary school was established in every parish. This was a highly important reform. Though not a 'Catholic' system, provision was made for the teaching of religion on one or two days a week. The system as it worked out put primary education in the control of the different churches. In most cases, the parish priest was the school patron, a position that increased greatly his standing in the community. Although it had limitations, especially in its neglect of the Irish language and culture, the National System of Education proved of great benefit to the mass of poor children. The scheme has endured to this day.

O'Connell held the balance of power in parliament for some years and used his position in parliament to obtain other concessions. Opposition by Catholics to paying tithes to the Protestant clergy resulted in a Tithe War in the 1830s with skirmishes between peasants and police. At Doon in Co Limerick 19 people were killed and 36 wounded; 12 at Newtownbarry in Co Wexford and 12 at Carrickshock, in Co Kilkenny. The Tithe Commutation Act of 1838 removed many of the causes of grievance. A modest Municipality Act enabled O'Connell to be elected Lord Mayor of Dublin, in itself an event that boosted Catholic morale. A Church Temporalities Act, though fierce

Tory opposition managed to have it shorn of the vital clause decreeing the appropriation of surplus funds to education and other social uses, was an indication that the government would reduce the power of the established church. The Whig administration in Ireland, especially the undersecretary, Thomas Drummond, gave Catholics a fairer administration to the point where Archbishop Murray told the Irish government that for the first time Irish Catholics believed they were being fairly treated.

Religious matters figured high in the values of the early nineteenth century. During the 1830s and 1840s a remarkable development within the established church in England attracted attention in Ireland. This was the Oxford movement where leading Anglican divines, including John Keble, John Henry Newman and Edward Bouverie, initiated a re-evaluation and a defence of the Catholic elements in Anglicanism. Pusey, who with Newman, headed the movement, visited Archbishop Murray in Dublin whom he found 'apologetic' and 'ecumenically minded'. The movement led to the conversion to Catholicism of a number of Anglicans, many of them clergy of high standing. Among the more notable were John Henry Newman, and Henry Edward Manning in 1851. In that year, too, the Irish poet, Aubrey de Vere, converted to Rome. Although the main thrust of the movement was to reclaim Catholic elements in the Anglican Church, many enthusiastic Catholics in Ireland and elsewhere professed to see in it the beginning of a general movement towards Rome and every conversion was noted and recorded in the Irish *Catholic Directory*. All in all the later 1830s and early 1840s were years when Irish Catholics began to feel a greater sense of their worth.

On the political field O'Connell resumed in 1841 a spectacular campaign for the repeal of the Union with Britain. He tried to involve Protestants and was supported by the Young Irelanders, many of whom – Davis, Mitchel and Smith O'Brien – were Protestant. Nevertheless, the movement depended in great measure on the organising power of the clergy. Like the Emancipation movement, O'Connell's Repeal movement boosted Catholic morale. Although it proved unsuccessful it did push Peel's Conservative government to grant concessions to Catholics – a more equitable charitable bequests act, a colleges act, and the grant to the national seminary of Maynooth, in effect a type of endowment of the Catholic Church. Peel's insistence, despite a revolt of his own party, on forcing the Maynooth grant through parliament impressed many Catholics of the government's efforts to do them justice. Partly as a result of this concession Peel fell from office in 1846. Lord John Russell, who then came into power, nourished an even more ambitious programme of concessions to Irish Catholics. In effect, he would give the Catholic Church a type of concurrent establishment with the Established Church and allow wealthy Catholic landlords to replace insolvent Protestant ones. Opposition from within his own party and from nationalist bishops like MacHale, his own irresoluteness and, above all, the catastrophe of the Famine shattered his efforts.

V

While the official position of the Catholic Church improved during all this period, the rural poor were still living from hand to mouth. The potato crop partially failed in 1816, 1821 and 1830. It was in 1845 that the Great Famine struck Ireland and in the spring of 1847 people were dying by the thousand. On 15 May Daniel O'Connell died in Genoa on his way to Rome, reportedly saying, 'My heart to Rome, my soul to God and my body to Ireland.' In the stricken Ireland he left behind some million and a quarter died of the Famine. Many voluntary relief workers and organisations including the British Association and the Quakers did admirable work. Protestant and Catholic clergy laboured endlessly on behalf of the famine-stricken. International relief came too. In England Protestants and Catholics gave willingly. Dominic Barbieri, the Passionist who had devoted himself to the English mission, told his confrères when deciding to sell their little silver chalice to raise relief money that 'it is lawful to sell the sacred vessels of the church to relieve the poor, who are the real vessels of election'. The rector of the Irish College in Rome, Paul Cullen, whose own family in Ireland and Liverpool were extraordinarily generous towards the victims, organised relief. Pope Pius IX and the cardinals of the curia as well as the Italian bishops sent aid. In March 1847 Pius, saddened by the continuing distress, appealed to Catholic bishops throughout the world to pray for Ireland and to collect funds for famine relief. English, French, Belgian, Dutch, German, Austrian, American, Canadian and other bishops channelled relief money towards Ireland. O'Connell's campaigns, too, played a part for they had aroused an understanding and sympathy for Ireland among many European nations. The network of Irish clergy, from South Africa to Canada and from Argentina to Australia threw themselves into the work of raising funds for the famine victims. In the United States, as the Society of Friends who organised relief testified, it was the Irish emigrants, many of whom had but recently arrived, who were most generous, sending home millions of hard-earned dollars.[45] In Ireland, England and Canada, many clergy, Catholic and Protestant, including seventeen Sisters of Charity in Montreal, died bringing consolation and relief to the famine-stricken.

Side by side with such generosity were the usual problems that attend a catastrophe. Although strong farmers were often generous, many were able to improve their holdings. Accusations of proselytism, too, particularly as regards the use of food and clothing as enticements, abounded. Some were true, many exaggerated but true or false they roused bitter feelings. Father John O'Sullivan, who was a moderate in politics and on good terms with Charles Trevelyan who had charge of government relief policies, gave vent to the extremes to which he would go to oppose 'souperism' as Catholics labelled proselytism:

> Now I am no agitator ... If souperism were to invade my parish in the morning, before evening Father John would become the greatest agitator in the country ... He would be a Tenant Right man, ... a repealer, anything, everything to stir up and excite the people.

He admitted that his own preaching stirred up the people to break the doors and windows of the Protestant church and to beat the parson 'to an inch of his life'. It was not an ecumenical age.

Other dissensions arose. The bishops, so united before, divided over attitudes to government policies. When Queen Victoria visited Ireland two of the three archbishops made clear their anger at the soaring number of evictions and at the government's failure to do more for the famine-stricken. MacHale declared that protest was 'the expression of those evangelical duties to our flocks, suffering from famine and cruelty, on which Christian bishops could not be silent'. The synod held in Thurles in August 1850, the first national synod since the seventeenth century, confirmed the reforms of the synods of the 1830s. It also, however, brought out sharply the differences between the group of bishops led by Archbishop Murray of Dublin and those led by the Roman-trained Paul Cullen, who had been appointed papal legate and archbishop of Armagh in 1849. These latter included the other two archbishops, John MacHale of Tuam and Michael Slattery of Cashel. The main bone of contention was whether to accept the non-denominational university colleges offered by government or to reject them as dangerous to Catholics. Cullen, who fought to have the government's offer rejected, won by a small minority and Rome supported him, even reprimanding Murray for his refusal to condemn the colleges. Behind the debate on the colleges lay the more basic question of what attitude the hierarchy should adopt towards the government. Within a few weeks of the close of the Synod of Thurles Pius IX's establishment of a Catholic hierarchy in England and the manner in which Cardinal Wiseman announced it, roused violent anti-Catholic agitation in England. Responding to it the government introduced an Ecclesiastical Titles Bill, a penal act that weakened Murray's case for trusting the government. When Murray died early in 1852 leadership of the Irish church passed into the hands of Cullen whose attitude to the government was one of distrust.

A country, which had lost over a few years a million and a quarter of its people through famine and another million and a half through emigration, a percentage proportionately perhaps as great as any population loss in recent times, could never be the same again. The suffering, spread over three or four years, was enormous and the psychological shock profound. The Famine eliminated the cottiers, destroyed the old Gaelic culture and with it much of popular religious practice. 'The socially deprived were culturally deprived', for with the decline of the language, the culture was lost and religious values were at the heart of that culture. The devotional life of rural Catholics became more and more assimilated to that of the towns. Thanks to the religious sisters and brothers and especially to the National Schools, many more people could read about their faith – Richard Challoner's *Garden of the Soul or a Manual of Spiritual Exercises and Instructions*, which nourished a devotional life that was individualist, meditative and instructional, and other writings such as *The Key of Heaven, Think Well on it* and *The Imitation of Christ*. The changes in Irish Catholic devotions brought it closer to continental Catholicism. In discipline, too, the Irish church became more like the continental churches for the bulk of the legislation of the Synod of Thurles restated and expanded the decrees on the administration of the sacraments and clerical life, as laid down by the reforming synods of the 1830s. A crucial factor in facilitating the reforms was the improved ratio of clergy to people. As the population sharply declined the number of priests and ecclesiastics increased. More priests from religious orders became available to give missions and, especially in the decades after the Famine, this both strengthened the faith and made the practice more in keeping with the European churches.

A summary of the development of the church from the early decades of the nineteenth century needs to take into account the many changes. Apart from the devotional and disciplinary developments, political changes were also significant. Clergy and laity, drawn by O'Connell, had become more involved in public affairs. O'Connell did not create what Tocqueville and De Beaumont called the 'indescribable unity between clergy and people' but by having them work together in his two great mass movements, and by constantly extolling that unity as the basis of Irish nationality, he strengthened it immensely. His campaigns constituted the birth of democracy in Ireland and, schooled by him, Irish Catholics became a political force to be reckoned with in Boston, New York and elsewhere. In this as in many other ways, Irish clergy and laity were already influencing the international church and leaving a permanent mark on its style in all English-speaking countries.

CHAPTER FIFTEEN

The Catholic Church after the Famine: Consolidation and change

Gerard Moran

The Great Famine of 1845-50 was a watershed in Irish history, leading to major social and economic transformation that had significant implications for the Catholic Church in Ireland. The post-Famine decades were a period of consolidation and change for the Catholic Church, which must be examined on two fronts: the dynamics within the hierarchy itself and the relationship between the clergy and the laity. The Famine could have crippled and divided the Irish church; instead more than any other institution in the country it emerged stronger and adapted better to the changing Ireland.

I

Prior to 1845 the principal challenge facing the church was that of finding sufficient priests to minister to the burgeoning population. Between 1821 and 1841 the population of Ireland increased from 6.8 million to 8.2 million and Catholics represented about 80 per cent of the total population. By 1841 there were 2,996 Catholics for each priest in Ireland but there were great regional variations in their distribution. While the more affluent dioceses, such as Ferns, had one priest for every 1,941 Catholics, at the other extreme the diocese of Tuam had only one priest for every 4,199 Catholics. The bishops were desperately trying to address this problem, but despite the provision of almost 800 seminary places at Maynooth and the Irish Colleges in Rome, Paris and Louvain, the church was fighting a losing battle in its attempts to provide an adequate number of priests to minister to the people. However, the impact of the Famine and the subsequent exodus from the country saw the population decline to 6,552,000 in 1851 and to 4,704,000 in 1891. As a result, the ratios improved so that by 1871 there was one priest for every 1,560 Catholics in Ireland. Indeed, by the 1870s the Irish church was able not only to meet its own clerical needs but was increasingly providing priests for Britain, the United States, Canada, Australia, New Zealand and India. Often a newly-ordained priest found it difficult to secure an appointment in his own diocese and was 'lent' to a foreign bishop until a parish was found for him in Ireland. Many of the bishops in these countries were Irish-born: John Hughes, archbishop of New York was a native of Co Monaghan; the Co

Carlow-born Patrick Moran was archbishop of Sydney; John Ireland from Co Kilkenny became bishop of St Paul and Thomas Croke, from Co Cork, became archbishop of Auckland in New Zealand.

The changes in the Catholic Church after 1849 can be attributed largely to Paul Cullen who had served as Rector of the Irish College in Rome in the 1840s and who was appointed archbishop of Armagh in 1849. Three years later he was translated to Dublin and in 1866 he was appointed the first Irish cardinal. Between 1849 and 1878 he dominated the Irish church as a loyal servant of the pope. When he arrived in Ireland in 1849 he inherited a divided church with many problems. The greatest external threat came from the Second Reformation and the attempts of evangelical Protestants to proselytise the Catholic population, especially in the poorer regions of the west and southwest. The biggest internal problem throughout the 1830s and 1840s was the division among the bishops, two groupings clashing over issues such as politics, national education and the subsequent recognition of the Queen's Colleges. These rival groups were headed by Archbishop John MacHale of Tuam and Archbishop Daniel Murray, Cullen's predecessor in Dublin.

One of Cullen's first actions was to convene a National Synod at Thurles on 22 August 1850, the first to be convened in Ireland since the seventeenth century. The synod enjoyed the backing of Rome; it aimed to ward off dangers confronting Catholics and to preserve and strengthen the faith in Ireland. It also intended to foster divine worship, to spread devotion to the sacraments, to define the duties of the clergy and to settle bitter controversies, many of which were in the field of education. The synod decreed that the sacraments of baptism and marriage could only be administered in churches, that marriages between Catholics and non-Catholics were to be discouraged, and that a register of marriages and baptisms was to be kept in each church. Sodalities were to be established for the laity and Catholic books were to be published to help strengthen the faith. It took time for the decrees to win acceptance and even among the clergy there was some dissension since the regulations in some quarters were seen as an erosion of the independence of individual clerics and bishops. Priests were forbidden to issue personal denunciations of people or movements from the altar.

The issue which concerned the bishops most in the decades after the Famine was that of education. Throughout the 1830s and 1840s the hierarchy had been divided on the question of both primary and university education. With regard to the National Education System, the Synod of Thurles acknowledged the authority of each bishop within his diocese, and while the majority were prepared to exploit the system, others refused; John MacHale of Tuam was the most vocal of the opponents. The alternative to the state system was that run by the Catholic religious orders. The church was fortunate that there was a major increase in vocations to the religious life after the Famine and this resulted in schools being opened in most urban centres in the country by the Mercy and Presentation Sisters and the Irish Christian Brothers. By 1867 the Irish Christian Brothers, which had been founded in 1802 by Edmund Rice, were educating 28,000 boys in sixty-seven schools throughout the country. In the diocese of Tuam alone there were five schools under the control of the Sisters of Mercy, one under the Presentation Sisters and eleven conducted by the Third Order of St Francis.

However, the provision of university education proved more difficult. While the three Queen's Colleges had been established in 1845 by the British Prime Minister, Sir Robert Peel, to meet the demands for a Catholic system of higher education, they were non-denominational colleges and as such were condemned by the Catholic hierarchy at the Synod of Thurles and by Rome in 1851. The bishops refused to allow Catholics attend the colleges and the bishop of Clonfert, John Derry, refused the sacraments to parents who allowed their children to enter the colleges. Throughout the second half of the nineteenth century the bishops sought an alternative: a distinctly Catholic university complete with an endowment and charter. Towards this end, Cullen was behind the formation in December 1864 of the National Association which attempted to secure a charter for the Catholic University of Ireland which he had established in 1854 and placed under the rectorship of John Henry Newman. However, the bishops' endeavours were a failure despite the high hopes that they placed in the Liberal administration of W. E. Gladstone, in whose support they had been conspicuous during the 1868 general election in Ireland in the expectation that his return to power would bring about a satisfactory conclusion to the education issue. The only attempt that the Gladstone administration put forward was the ill-fated Fawcett university bill in 1873 which aimed chiefly at the abolition of religious tests in Trinity College Dublin and the reconstruction of its governing body. The bishops opposed this legislation and it resulted in the Irish Liberals withdrawing their support for the government and bringing about its downfall. It was not until 1908 when the National University of Ireland was established that the demands of the Catholic hierarchy were satisfied. The bishops were then given a major role in the governing body of each of the three constituent colleges at Dublin, Cork and Galway.

While the decline in population helped redress the imbalance in the priest-population ratio, other problems remained. One of these was the provision of churches. Dioceses such as Dublin and Kildare and Leighlin had embarked on major church-building programmes before the Famine. But there were many dioceses, especially in the west and the south-east of the country, which did not have the resources to build or to update their chapels.

An example of the financial difficulties which many parishes encountered can be seen in Cong, Co Mayo, where the local parish priest, Michael Waldron, was forced to sell the Cross of Cong, an ancient symbol of the area's past ecclesiastical greatness, to the National Museum in Dublin for one hundred guineas so that he could put a new roof on his chapel. In other cases, former parishioners who had emigrated to England, Australia and North America sent back donations to help the programme of church renovations and church building. There were instances, too, of parish priests embarking on fund-raising missions to the United States; included in this number was the administrator of Castlebar, Co Mayo, Fr James Magee, who visited America in 1877. As a result of such exertions there were 2,322 chapels and churches in Ireland by 1867. Of course, these were dispersed unevenly across the country and some dioceses were better served than others. While Dublin had 160 chapels, the neighbouring diocese of Meath had 147; in the west Killaloe had 143, but Achonry, with a Catholic population of 105,203, had only 37.

In order to facilitate change and to stamp his authority on the church in Ireland Paul Cullen found it necessary to have bishops appointed who held similar views to himself. As a result he played an active role in the selection of bishops in the different dioceses that became vacant in the 1850s and 1860s, not alone in the province of Dublin but also in the provinces of Armagh, Cashel and Tuam. Accordingly, it was his intervention which resulted in the episcopal appointments of John MacEvilly (Galway, 1856), Laurence Gillooly (Elphin, 1856), his secretary in Dublin, George Conroy (Ardagh and Clonmacnoise, 1870), and his nephew, Patrick Moran, to Ossory in 1872. This, however, was a slow process and it took time to build up support in the hierarchy. Along the way he suffered a number of setbacks, as in 1859 when he was forced to recall to Dublin John Miley, Rector of the Irish College, Paris, and one of his supporters and confidants. Nevertheless, by 1869 his control over the Irish church was clearly visible. In that year, of the Irish bishops who attended the First Vatican Council, all supported the principle of papal infallibility with the exceptions of John MacHale and Bishop David Moriarty of Kerry.

Difficulties remained in the realm of secular politics. In this instance, too, Cullen took the lead and in 1852 he was responsible for the withdrawal of clerical support for the Independent Irish Party. This was a serious blow, since the bishops and clergy had played an important role in both local and national politics since the Emancipation and Repeal campaigns of the 1830s and 1840s. The clergy's failure to become involved in the political agitation of the 1850s was a major factor in the demise of the Independent Irish Party in 1857 but it was in keeping with Cullen's view that the church should concern itself in political affairs only when religious issues were at stake. It was not that he and the other bishops were opposed to political agitation, but rather they opposed the participation of their priests. One can sympathise with this attitude since clerical involvement at election time often resulted in embarrassment for the church, as in the 1857 election in Mayo and the 1872 Galway by-election when candidates were disqualified because of alleged clerical intimidation of voters. When the clergy did participate it was because religious issues were involved as in the 1868 general election when the principal issue was the disestablishment and disendowment of the Church of Ireland. However, the overall feature during the Cullen years was that the Catholic Church kept out of politics unless there were religious issues involved.

Of course, it was impossible for the church to ignore the threat of Fenianism. The Irish Republican Brotherhood, or the Fenian Brotherhood, was established in New York in March 1858 with the aim of securing Irish independence by military means. From the outset the Catholic bishops, led by Cullen, condemned the movement, maintaining that it was a revolutionary movement and administered a secret oath. The clergy were also concerned because they had no control over the organisation. The first indication of the conflict between the church and the Fenians occurred in November 1861 at the burial of the Young Irelander Terence Bellew MacManus whose body was returned to Ireland for reburial by the American Fenians. The Fenians hoped to use the occasion to muster support for the organisation. Cullen refused to allow his clergy to have anything to do with the event, even with the reciting of prayers at the cemetery at Glasnevin. Militant nationalists were angered by his attitude since many bishops in the United States, such as Archbishop Hughes of New York, had received the remains as it passed through the country on its way to Ireland. The MacManus incident heralded a decade of conflict between the church and Irish militant nationalism which had repercussions not only in Ireland but also for the Catholic Church in Britain and the United States. The conflict between the church and the Fenians was exacerbated by the divisions within the hierarchy over the militant organisation. Not all of the bishops were entirely opposed to its aims and its methods, most notably the nationalist prelate of Tuam, John MacHale. There were priests who sympathised with the Fenians publicly in letters to newspapers and at public meetings in Ireland and Britain. One of these was a priest of MacHale's diocese, Fr Lavelle. He skilfully argued that the Fenians did not come under the censure of the church because many were practising Catholics and he stated that they had every right to take up arms because Ireland was ruled by a tyrannical and oppressive government. Throughout the 1860s Cullen made many attempts to have Lavelle silenced, through unsuccessful efforts to have his bishop, John MacHale, suspend him and by having him called to Rome in January 1864 where he was reprimanded and suspended from priestly duties. However, his attacks on Cullen and his defence of Fenianism continued until November 1869. In the following year, Cardinal Cullen's intervention at the Vatican brought papal condemnation of Fenianism and the excommunication of its membership.

While the bishops appeared united on issues such as militant nationalism there were occasional divisions within the clerical ranks. One of the most serious episodes centred on a petition, initiated by Dean Richard O'Brien of Newcastle West, Co Limerick, which sought an amnesty for Fenian prisoners in English jails in December 1869. This initiative angered the hierarchy, since 1,600 priests, seventy per cent of the clergy, signed the petition. While most did so for humanitarian reasons, not because they supported Fenian principles, the petition suggested that the clergy were unwilling to accept the lead of their bishops. The bishops were also angered because the petition had been circulated while they were in Rome. In many ways, however, the priests were merely reflecting the mood in the country and the general rise of nationalist sentiment, which followed the execution of the 'Manchester Martyrs', Allen, Larkin and O'Brien, in November 1867. Such sentiments resulted in the merger of the constitutional and militant nationalists into the Amnesty Association which campaigned for the release of the Fenian prisoners. The gap that existed between the hierarchy and the laity was clearly illustrated at a number of by-elections in 1869 and 1870, when candidates who were nominated and supported by the bishops in Tipperary and Longford were either defeated or severely tested by popular candidates. This was an indication of the realities of Irish politics. By the 1870s and 80s, the church was no longer in a position to dictate in political matters to the laity; at best they could reach an accommodation with the people when it came to the selection of parliamentary candidates.

II

It would be wrong, however, to characterise the relationship between the clergy and the laity simply in terms of confrontation. While there were divisions over political issues, the decades after the Famine must be regarded as a period of consolidation, leadership and partnership. While recent historians have suggested that the clergy's power over their parishioners declined in the post-Famine era, this fails to take into consideration the special relationship created during the Famine. Very often, priests were the only group highlighting the plight of their parishioners and pleading with government and the outside world for relief. And while the Great Famine was the last catastrophe which hit the whole country, there were significant regional subsistence crises in the early 1860s, between 1879-83 and again in the 1890s. The western seaboard bore the brunt of these crises; many landlords were absent and took little action to relieve destitution and poverty. In their absence, the clergy assumed a leadership role, highlighting the problems of their parishioners, famine and the injustice of rackrenting landlords in letters to newspapers and to relief organisations seeking assistance for their starving congregations.

In the early 1860s when a potato failure occurred along the western seaboard, it was clerics such as Fr Patrick Lavelle in Partry, Fr Patrick MacManus in Clifden and Fr Patrick Malone in Belmullet who helped avert famine. Again, between 1879-83 the clergy showed true leadership qualities when the failure of the potato crop threatened a crisis on the scale of the Great Famine. Indeed, the situation was exacerbated by a decline in seasonal migration remittances from Britain, a decline in credit facilities available to tenant farmers and a depression in agriculture brought about by increased competition in the European markets. At the height of the crisis, almost half the total population of 2.5 million along the western seaboard was destitute and in need of relief. Catastrophe was averted by the exertions of private relief organisations such as the Mansion House and Duchess of Marlborough Relief Committees but at local level the clergy were paramount in overcoming the difficulties.

From the outset priests like Fr Patrick Greally of Carna, Co Galway highlighted the impending crisis. In December 1879, he informed a national newspaper how:

> On Christmas evening several poor, virtuous women, mothers with large, helpless families, came to me in tears asking for God's sake to give them even the price of one meal for the starving children, that they had not even a morsel of the coarsest food for the little ones on that night of Universal Joy ... that their husbands were gone for the last fortnight to England or Scotland to try and earn something to support their families at home.

Greally administered to nearly 5,000 parishioners who eked out an existence on 1,700 acres of poor, barren land, divided in units too small to provide a living. While 480 families in the parish were being assisted by the two relief organisations, the remaining families were destitute. In exasperation Fr Greally suggested that it would be better if the whole population was encouraged to emigrate. Hundreds of similar letters came from clergymen across the country and their initiative led newspaper correspondents to those areas of acute distress. In many cases, too, the priests were behind the establishment of local relief committees, acting as chairmen, secretaries and treasurers, and seeking aid from the national relief organisations. There is no doubt but that many priests worked to near exhaustion in their attempts to save their parishioners. They also worked with the Church of Ireland parsons and Presbyterian ministers in seeking aid for their local communities. The relief operations in the 1879-83 period contrasted with those of the Great Famine in that there was unity and solidarity of purpose rather than division and rancour. The question of proselytisation was not an issue on the local relief committees in the early 1880s nor in the 1890s.

While the activities of the Mansion House and the Duchess of Marlborough Relief Committees are well known, historians have neglected the efforts of the Archbishop McCabe Fund which distributed nearly £20,000 in relief to the destitute in parishes throughout the country in the 1880s. Catholic prelates in Britain, France, the United States, Canada and Australia had raised money in response to news of the crisis in Ireland. This was forwarded to Dr McCabe, who distributed it to priests in distressed areas where it was used to relieve poverty and to purchase food and seed potatoes. There is no doubt but that this intervention saved lives in many of the remotest parishes in the country.

The clergy adopted a pragmatic approach to such crises and to the social problems of their parishioners. So while they were unhappy to see the large-scale emigration of their flocks to Britain and North America, fearing for their moral well-being, they realised that such action offered the only escape from the perennial poverty and destitution that they endured in Ireland. Accordingly, about 600 priests from all over the country applied to the philanthropist Vere Foster for financial assistance to enable their parishioners to leave. Foster provided up to £2 towards the travelling expenses for each girl from the poorer parts of Ireland who wished to settle in North America. Local clergymen such as Fr Greally and Fr MacManus from Clifden were also active in the assisted-emigration schemes from their parishes in the early 1880s. Local clerical participation in such emigration schemes only ended when the Irish bishops, and in particular those in the west of Ireland, denounced the system of assisted emigration in July 1883.

The relationship between the clergy and the laity in this period must also be examined through their interaction on agrarian issues. While Paul Cullen had greatly curtailed clerical involvement in political and agrarian agitation, it would be incorrect to believe that such participation ceased. Priests were well aware of the plight of the tenant farmers and the inequities of the existing land laws. Indeed, the successive subsistence crises of the late 1870s prompted the emergence of an agrarian campaign whose objective was to secure better rights for farmers. The Land League, founded in Co Mayo in April 1879, aimed at securing lower rents and fixity of tenure. Initially clerical participation was limited, because the bishops and priests distrusted the lay leadership, but by July 1879 the clergy in the west of Ireland had become enthusiastic supporters of the movement. By October, when the Irish National Land League was founded in Dublin, fourteen of its national executive were priests. Over the next two years the local parish priest chaired most of the league meetings that were held throughout the country and there was always a strong clerical presence. Over 2,000 local league branches were established and again there was strong clerical involvement.

While it has been argued that clerical participation was motivated principally by a desire to prevent radical elements such as the Fenians taking control of the league, it is clear that many priests were committed to the objectives of the movement and empathised with the grievances of the people. Priests played prominent roles during the agrarian campaigns. Fr John O'Malley of the Neale, Co Mayo, for example, organised his parishioners and carried out the famous policy of social ostracisation against Captain Charles Cunningham Boycott. Other clerics were prepared to go to prison to defend the rights of the people, including Fr James McFadden of Gweedore, Co Donegal and Fr Coen of Woodford, Co Galway. On these occasions the Catholic Church showed that it was prepared to risk the censure of Rome. The British government was worried by the priests' participation in the agrarian campaign and its representatives at the Vatican sought papal intervention. During the Plan of Campaign in the late 1880s, Monsignor Persico was sent by the Holy See to investigate charges that the agitation and boycotting was unlawful and that the clergy were taking a prominent part. The result of his mission was a Papal Rescript, published in April 1888, in which the Vatican condemned the Plan of Campaign. This denunciation, however, had little effect. Irish Catholic political leaders immediately condemned Rome's intervention while the hierarchy was equally angered by Persico's jaundiced interpretation of circumstances in Ireland. In any event the sympathies of the hierarchy were with their people. One of the most forceful supporters of the tenants' cause was Archbishop Thomas Croke of Cashel, who went so far as to argue that the rescript was irrelevant since the condemnation was based upon a Roman misunderstanding of the land system in Ireland. What emerges from the agrarian campaign, then, was a partnership between the clergy and the laity to secure better conditions for the tenants.

The Famine could have crippled and divided the Irish church. Instead the church more than any other institution in the country emerged stronger and adapted better to the changing Ireland. Not only was it able to stamp its authority on Ireland but it was also able to contribute greatly to the emerging churches in the English-speaking world. By the time of Parnell's fall in 1891 the hierarchy was a united body, which spoke with one voice. The divisions and public splits that had characterised it before the Famine had long since disappeared. At the same time its relationship with the laity had become one of leadership and partnership. The Irish Catholic Church was now in a stronger position to cope with the changing Ireland.

CHAPTER SIXTEEN

The Parish Mission Movement, 1850-1880

Emmet Larkin

The parish mission movement was the single most important factor in making and consolidating the devotional revolution that took place in Ireland between 1850 and 1880. In literally a generation, the Irish people *as a people*, were transformed into those pious and practising Catholics they have essentially remained almost down to the present day. The first formal parish mission in Ireland was given by the Irish Vincentian fathers in the town of Athy in the diocese of Dublin in November and December of 1842. In the next twenty-five years, not only were virtually all of the thousand Catholic parishes in Ireland visited by missioners of the various Irish religious orders, but by 1880 most of these parishes had been visited again a second, and some even a third and fourth time. The cumulative effect of those two thousand missions was a remarkable national religious revival that profoundly affected both the character of the Irish people and the course of their history.

The first mission at Athy in early November 1842 had been scheduled to last four weeks. The crowds proved to be so large, however, and the numbers requiring confession so great, the mission had to be extended for another three weeks. 'Hundreds,' Father James Maher, professor of Theology at Carlow College, explained, in reporting the Athy mission to his nephew, Paul Cullen, rector of the Irish College in Rome, on February 21, 1843, 'remained all night in the chapel, and many remained in town away from their homes for five or six days waiting an opportunity of confessing':

> This extraordinary movement [he added] has confirmed an old opinion of mine that we do not always afford the people an opportunity of general confession when required. In fact we have not half [enough] Priests for the wants of the Mission, and a very considerable number of the Parrochi [Parish Priests] leave the confessional almost entirely to the curates.[1]

Indeed, the press of numbers at Athy had been so great that the parish priest persuaded the missioners at the close of the mission in December to return again the following summer when the mission was continued for another five weeks. When the mission was finally closed in August 1843, the crowds attending it were still immense.

On 30 August, Cullen's sister Margaret informed him that they had the 'Missioners' in Athy again, and that it 'would be impossible for me to describe the enthusiasm of the people'.[2] If the missioners were angels from heaven, she explained, they could not be more venerated. Work was at a standstill while the people followed them around all day and crowded 'in *hundreds* to the confessionals, many very many who had never before been there'. The missioners preached three times a day in the chapel, which was 'crowded to suffocation'. 'What a pity,' she finally concluded, 'we have not more priests in the parish. I fear a great deal of their labours will go for nothing.' 'Where,' she finally asked, 'is the opportunity for the *bulk* of the parish to approach the holy sacraments?' 'The confessions of all who presented themselves', Thomas Murphy, a Vincentian father, who later chronicled the mission, admitted, 'were not heard, but as numbers were flocking in from all the surrounding parishes, it was believed the mission would never end; and it was therefore found necessary to leave although the work seemed as yet very incomplete'.[3]

Over the next several years the Vincentians continued to give four or five missions a year, and while the work proved to be most gratifying as far as the response of the people was concerned, the numbers attending were simply overwhelming. In making his annual report to Jean-Baptiste Étienne, the superior-general of the Vincentians in Paris, on 23 November 1844, for example, the Irish superior, Philip Dowley, explained that while words were not adequate to describe the remarkable religious enthusiasm with which the Irish people embraced the missions, the task of ever being able to meet their pastoral needs was daunting.[4] 'Since the beginning of Lent,' Dowley reported, 'we have given four missions, each of six weeks. In some, six confrères labour constantly, in the others there are always five. The parish priests and the curates, who are usually two or three in each parish, also worked, still that was not sufficient; we were always obliged to send for the curates of the neighbouring parishes, so that we often saw ten and even sometimes sixteen priests confessing at the same time.' 'In spite of all that,' Dowley added, 'the poor people were obliged to remain entire days and nights awaiting their turn.'

'The parish priests,' he then further explained to the superior general, 'are delighted to see the good that is effected in their parishes; they did not at all know the deplorable state, the profound ignorance, the monstrous vices in which their poor parishioners were sometimes buried.' 'All is altered,' Dowley maintained, 'by the missions. The people proclaim in a loud voice they are in a state of damnation, the old people say before the whole world that they have never received holy communion.' 'In the last mission,' Dowley then added, 'hundreds of adults aged 18 to 80 years were prepared to receive the sacraments of confirmation and first communion.' 'The only thing that distresses us,' he then finally observed in conclusion, 'is to see that we cannot, even in the parishes where we have given missions, provide a remedy for the crying needs that surround us. We are obliged to forsake thousands whom we have not time to listen to in these vast parishes.'

The mission, however, that established the Vincentians' national reputation was that given in Dingle, Co Kerry on the eve of the Great Famine. In reporting the Dingle mission of that summer to Père Étienne on 30 November 1846, Dowley began by explaining the occasion for it.[5] 'The inhabitants of this district,' he pointed out, 'have been for several years reduced to extreme poverty because of the persecution of the landlords and their agents.' 'The demon of heresy,' he charged, 'has been fully employed to destroy the faith of these unfortunates. Gifts, houses, money were all offered to those who would turn Protestant.' 'And,' Dowley added grimly, 'a thing unknown in this country since the introduction of heresy, some hundreds of these ignorant poor sold their souls to the devil by *outwardly* renouncing the faith of their Fathers':

> Among the means advised to reclaim these forsaken poor, the first that was thought of was a mission. Towards the end of July our little band took its place on the battlefield. Instead of being received as they had been everywhere else, they only found there the absence of all religious feeling in the mass of the poor who formed the population – coldness on the part of the bishop, unconcern and jealousy on the side of the clergy for whom the presence of the missionaries was tantamount to condemnation of their own zeal and of their works. Our missionaries, however, had taken care to go only at the request of the bishop and the parish priest.

'All then, things and people,' Dowley observed, 'was opposed to the work of St Vincent. It was the first time of trial, therefore, for your children in Ireland. But thanks be to God, the difficulties began to ease.' 'At the end of the second week,' he then explained, 'the faces of those who at the beginning presented only an *attitude of unconcern* began to give the impression that the grace of the mission worked there in spite of them. The confessionals were resorted to, people came in crowds to listen to the instructions, and the demand for tickets for confession soon became so pressing that the parish priest at the request of the missionaries obtained from the bishop a reinforcement of workers, and during the last two weeks thirteen confessors laboured earnestly to reconcile these poor people, so long deprived of the consolations which religion provides for the afflicted.'

During the Dingle mission, moreover, the missionaries discovered that there were some one thousand adults who had never been confirmed. In the process of confirming these adults there occurred a most revealing and remarkable incident that speaks volumes with regard to the profound emotional response on the part of the people induced by these parish missions. 'Even at this distance in time,' the leader of the Vincentian mission in Dingle, Thomas McNamara, reported many years later in his memoirs, 'I recollect so well the difficulty there was in maintaining order amidst such a mass of people, as they came forward':

> The Bishop remained seated within the sanctuary enclosure, and the candidates for confirmation had to be brought to him two by two. The ceremony was on this account very tedious, and the patience of the people gave way. Apprehending this beforehand we engaged the services of the Christian doctrine confraternity, which we had already instituted [in the parish] to form a cordon across the entire width of the church in order to keep back the pressure, and admit those who were to be confirmed according as the Bishop could receive them. But the difficulty was in maintaining the cordon. The people pressed forward and the confraternity men pressed them back until unable to resist by any other means, they had actually to use sticks and clubs in the struggle, and what can scarcely be believed blood flowed copiously from the blows inflicted, the confraternity men feeling they had a duty to perform even to so terrible an extremity, and we who attended the Bishop right and left had to witness with his Lordship how the poor people fought their way to come forward.[6]

'Such a scene,' McNamara finally concluded, 'is only to be imagined amongst a poor rude people urged onward by their religious enthusiasm to offer, as one may say violence to heaven.'

What is to be made of this combined witness of Fathers Maher, Murphy, Dowley, McNamara, and Margaret Cullen about these early parish missions in pre-Famine Ireland? There are, in fact, at least two important points to be made besides that of the obvious spiritual destitution of a large portion of the Irish people. The first is that the remarkable religious enthusiasm revealed in these early missions indicated an extraordinary, if latent, evangelical potential just waiting to be realised among the people; and second, that before the Great Famine, at least, the Irish church was not able to realise that potential because it simply did not have the manpower necessary to deal with the enormous increase in the Catholic population that had taken place over the previous seventy years. Each of these points, in their turn, raises a very significant question. What was the cause of that remarkable religious enthusiasm, and how was that enthusiasm eventually realised? The answer to the second question of how, of course, is the subject of this paper, and I should therefore like to deal with it first, reserving the more difficult question of why there was a devotional revolution for the conclusion of the essay.

How was this devotional revolution made and consolidated? Between 1770 and 1840, the Irish church had to face a one hundred and forty-four per cent increase in the Catholic population, while over the same period, it had only been able to increase the number of priests by some fifty per cent.[7] In 1770, the ratio of priests to people had been one to 1,690, already a very heavy pastoral load. By 1840, that ratio had worsened to one priest for every 2,750 Catholics, a virtually impossible pastoral load. Then, suddenly and dramatically, in 1847, the Great Famine transformed the whole clerical-lay numerical relationship. In little more than a decade, the Catholic population was reduced by a third, while the number of priests was increased by a fifth, as the ratio of priests to people improved from about one in 2,600 on the eve of the Famine to one in 1,500 by 1860.[8] In each succeeding decade after 1860, the Catholic population continued to decline and the number of priests to increase, until by 1900 the priest to people ratio was one to less than 900. In the wake of this break-up of the logjam of adverse numbers at the Famine, parish missions began to increase at a rapidly accelerating rate over the next decade. Soon after the Famine, the Vincentians were joined by the Rosminians and the Jesuits, and then by the Redemptorists and the Passionists, and finally by the Oblates in giving missions in Ireland. The example of all these new religious congregations resulted in the older religious orders of friars – the Dominicans, Franciscans, Capuchins, Augustinians, Carmelites, calced and discalced – also eventually engaging in the good work of parish missions.

A very large part of the early and continued success of these parish missions was certainly the result of the encouragement of the singularly determined and influential archbishop of Dublin and the Pope's Apostolic Delegate in Ireland, Paul Cullen. No one among the Irish bishops, in fact, was more forward or enthusiastic in promoting parish missions than Cullen. Whatever the particular problem might have been in the Irish church – whether it was proselytising, secret societies, faction fighting, drunkenness, mixed education, or spiritual destitution – Cullen's immediate and effective response was a parish mission. One of his first acts after his translation from Armagh to Dublin in May 1852 was to endow the Vincentian community with £1,000 to fund their missions in Dublin.[9] A short time later he began to lay plans for a combined assault on the Protestant proselytisers in the west of Ireland. 'Here,' he reported, in a letter headed 'Evviva Maria,' to Tobias Kirby, rector of the Irish College in Rome on 8 December 1852, 'we are trying to enroll a large missionary body before next summer to wipe out the proselytisers everywhere.'[10] 'It is necessary to see,' he added more cautiously, breaking into Italian, 'if it will be successful, and then I will write to Propaganda. The Jesuits, Dominicans, Carmelites, Vincentians, Redemptorists, secular priests, will all join together – but.'

Although Cullen was frustrated in this attempt to launch his missionary crusade against the proselytisers in the summer of 1853, he was nothing if not persevering. Towards the end of 1853 he founded the Society of St Laurence O'Toole, part of whose purpose was to collect funds for the subsidising of missions in Ireland.[11] The first substantial work of the Society was to fund two missions in the diocese of Elphin in the west of Ireland. In the next three years, between 1853 and 1856, the various missionary congregations and orders, with the Jesuits and the Rosminians in the vanguard, conducted some fifty missions in the west.[12] By the end of 1856, in fact, the celebrated New Reformation in Ireland was well on the wane, and this was certainly in large part due to the effects of the parish mission movement. By 1861, moreover, virtually all of the religious congregations and orders in Ireland were committed to the good work of giving parish missions, and the religious face of Ireland over the next twenty years was thereby profoundly changed.

But in what did this good work consist? What was a parish mission like? How did the missioners excite such an incredible religious fervour, and what did they do to ensure that the enthusiasm generated would not prove to be merely a transitory phenomenon? In the early years because of the very large number of penitents, missions usually tended to last about six weeks with five or six missioners conducting the exercises, but as the population began to decline after the Famine, they were gradually reduced to three or four weeks with two or three missioners in attendance. The mission generally opened on a Sunday and closed on a Friday several weeks later. Physically and psychologically, it was a very strenuous experience for both the missioners and those who attended. The missioners laboured six days a week, rising at five in the morning and retiring at ten in the evening, and usually taking their day of rest on a Monday or Wednesday. The daily schedule, of course, varied with the tradition and style of each religious order but in general the pattern of the exercises was much the same for all.[13]

The most important exercises during the day were the three sermons preached in the morning, at midday, and in the evening. The morning sermon at eight, which took place after Mass and confessions, was devoted to the duties of religion especially in regard to the sacraments. The midday sermon was applied to a plain exposition of Christian doctrine as contained in the catechism, and the evening sermon at eight, which served as the climax to the day's exercises, was dedicated to one of the great truths of religion. The purpose of the preaching during the day was to heighten in a cumulative way the penitent's consciousness of sin, and bring him to a realisation of the catastrophic consequences for his immortal soul if he should die in such a state. On each succeeding day of the mission, the penitent was made more acutely aware of all of the various ways in which he might have forsaken God, and reminded that if he did not confess his sincere repentance for his transgressions, he would lose the reward of heaven and win the torments of hell for all eternity. Since no one could be sure when his end would come and death usurp all good intentions, the time for reconciliation with God was at that moment. The multitudes who flocked to the confessionals at the mission were a true witness to the effectiveness of the preaching of the missioners.

Indeed the confessional was the heaviest part of the clergy's duties at the mission. Confessions were heard not only for two hours before the morning sermon, but again for two hours before the midday sermon, and again for the two hours before the evening sermon. In the early years of the missions, the missioners often felt obliged to hear confessions again after the evening sermon until well past midnight. During the course of the day, in order to encourage greater piety and zeal, the missioners also conducted a whole series of religious devotions, usually before and after the sermons, which included matins and lauds, vespers, litany of the Blessed Virgin, benediction of the blessed sacrament, and the rosary of the Blessed Virgin, besides morning and night prayers. The religious fervour aroused during the mission by the sermons and the devotional exercises was astonishing and to none more than the missioners. They found themselves being followed about all day by large crowds asking their blessing, abasing themselves and touching or kissing their garments. The most remarkable moment of the mission, however, was its closing. During the last day a large stone mission cross, with a suitable inscription and date, was raised with great solemnity in the church or chapel yard to commemorate the mission and to serve as a visible reminder to the faithful of both their recent triumph over sin and death, and their solemn promise to persevere in their new-found state of grace.[14] In the evening after the closing sermon, the people assembled in their thousands in and around the church or chapel, each with a lighted taper, and renewed their baptismal vows by renouncing sin, evil, and Satan. When time came for the missioners to depart the following morning, they were escorted considerable distances by large crowds begging their final blessing amidst anguished tears, piteous cries, and awful heartrending.[15]

During the mission the missioners also made great efforts to consolidate the gains they had recently made.[16] On each Sunday afternoon after the mission opened, the missioners encouraged the people to enrol in confraternities and sodalities and other pious associations and institutes. They especially encouraged the Confraternity for the teaching of Christian Doctrine. The missioners exhorted the better off in the parish, males and females, to enrol in order to teach the catechism on Sundays to the children of the parish in the parish church. The missioners not only drew up rules for their guidance, but they also took care to launch the Sunday school classes before the close of the mission. Each of the various religious orders also encouraged particular religious associations. The Vincentians, for example, always attempted, wherever the materials for such associations existed, to establish the Society of St Vincent de Paul and the Ladies Association of Charity for the visiting of the sick and poor. All of the various religious orders also attempted to build on the work of Father Mathew, the celebrated Temperance priest of the 1840s, by establishing or re-establishing Temperance Societies in each parish to deal with what was undoubtedly Ireland's most serious social problem after poverty – drunkenness.

The purpose, of course, in establishing all these voluntary associations, with their dues, and rules and regulations governing pious practices, under the presidency of the parish priest or his curate, was to mobilise as many of the faithful as possible in the parish to commit themselves to preserving that religious enthusiasm excited during the mission by institutionalising it at the grass-roots. In addition, the missioners encouraged a whole series of devotional practices, all to be celebrated communally in the parish church, including the rosary, the litany to the Blessed Virgin, benediction, the way of the Cross, perpetual adoration, forty hours, the angelus, vespers, and novenas. They also recommended monthly confession and communion as well as the reading of pious books as effective means for preserving the fruits of the mission. Indeed, in a very short time the missions became marts for pious books and other devotional tools and aids, such as holy pictures, crucifixes, holy water, candles, rosary beads, medals, scapulars, and *agnus deis*, which the faithful brought to the missioners to be blessed and which they afterwards reverenced as sacred souvenirs of the mission.[17]

One of the most effective techniques for consolidating ongoing religious devotion and practice was having a Solemn Office and Requiem Mass said during the mission for all the deceased members of the parish.[18] The realisation that their deceased parents, relatives and friends could also partake of the benefits of the mission stirred up the most intense feeling among the participants. In the sermon preached on the occasion the missioner explained the obligation of all present to help shorten the time of torment of the souls of their loved ones suffering in Purgatory by praying for them regularly, applying indulgences on their behalf, and above all, by having them remembered at the Holy Sacrifice of the Mass. The missioners not only counselled the faithful to reverence their dead but they also exhorted them to strengthen the faith of the living by building churches and schools where necessary, or repairing and enlarging them if dilapidated or too small. They also urged the faithful especially in the town parishes to invite nuns and brothers to establish convents and schools in order to improve both the religious education of their children and the religious tone of the parish. Before closing the mission, the missioners in cooperation with the parish priest helped form committees of the laity to make provision for these proposed pious works.

If the experience of a parish mission is multiplied by more than some two thousand times between 1850 and 1880, the magnitude of this remarkable religious revival becomes very obvious. One measure of the magnitude of this devotional revolution was the astonishing improvement in Mass attendance. In pre-Famine Ireland only some forty per cent of the potential church-going population assisted at Mass on a given Sunday.[19] By 1880, some thirty years later, that figure had improved to about ninety per cent and in the succeeding decades continued to edge upwards.[20] A second measure of the magnitude of the devotional revolution was the enormous increase in the clerical population, both men and women, between 1847 and 1880. In 1847, the total number of priests, nuns, brothers, and seminarians in Ireland was about 4,700, while in 1880 it was some 10,200 – a nearly 120 per cent increase.[21] To put it another way, there was in 1847 one cleric for every 1,450 Catholics while in 1880 there was one for every 390, a 270 per cent improvement. This improvement was mainly the result of an absolute increase of over 300 per cent in the number of nuns, from some 1,300 in 1840 to 5,300 in 1880.

A third and final example of the measure of the magnitude of this extraordinary religious and moral transformation, which also allows an insight into how it was achieved, is the testimony of the man who did most to give drive and direction to the devotional revolution in the generation after the Famine, Paul Cardinal Cullen, archbishop of Dublin and Apostolic Delegate of the Holy See. In testifying before the Royal, or Powis Commission on elementary education in Ireland in early 1869, the cardinal was asked if he did not think that the great moral improvement in recent years in Ireland was not the result of the work of the National Board of Education, which had been established in 1831, and had been administratively responsible for the system of primary education in Ireland since then.[22] The cardinal replied that he did not think the great improvement in morality and knowledge had been, to any considerable extent, the result of the Board's work. Rather, he thought that the Catholics themselves had done a great deal by building convents, orphanages, schools, and churches. 'But there was another reason,' the cardinal then pointed out, 'for great improvement.' 'The Catholic clergy began,' he explained, '... soon after Catholic Emancipation to give "missions" throughout the country. Almost every parish in Ireland must have had a mission since that time.' 'These missions,' the cardinal insisted, 'were the cause of the greatest improvement in the morals of the country, and consequently of the utmost benefit to society.'

While all of the foregoing may tell one something about what the devotional revolution consisted of and how it was made, the crucial question still remains – why did the Irish people respond so readily to the reform of their church and become pious and practising Catholics within a generation? The

Great Famine was truly a gigantic psychological shock, and it certainly would be both neat and convenient to be able to assign so impressive a cause for so remarkable an effect. A guilt-ridden and frightened people turning more formally and fervently to their God in their hour of need makes more, indeed, than a good deal of superficial sense. The problem, of course, is that the devotional need was obviously and increasingly present before the Famine, and only the adverse circumstances of population growth and the lack of money and personnel on the part of the church prevented that need from being realised. The Famine, therefore, was as much the occasion for, as it was a cause of, the devotional revolution, and one must probe more deeply if one is to understand why as well as how this remarkable historical phenomenon occurred.

What I should like to suggest in conclusion is what I suggested more than twenty-five years ago when I first considered this subject, namely that the devotional revolution which took place after the Famine satisfied more than the negative factors of guilt and fear induced by that great catastrophe. The Irish, after all, had been gradually losing their language, their culture, and their way of life for more than a hundred years before the Famine. Education, business, politics, and communication in the written word, even more than in the spoken word, were increasingly geared to English as the Irish were being effectively Anglicised, or perhaps, more appropriately, West Britonised. There has been so much concern, for example, in the study of Irish history with the geography of emigration that it has hardly been noticed that the Irish before the Famine had nearly all become cultural emigrants, that they had in fact moved in their minds before a good many of them had actually to move in space. In a word, Irishmen who were aware of being Irish were gradually losing their identity, and this is what accounts for their becoming pious and practising Catholics in the generation after the Famine. By doing so, Irish Catholics were psychologically assured that they would never be absorbed or assimilated by the greater English culture because the historical identity of that English culture was itself profoundly rooted in its Protestantism, and could not, therefore, without becoming something other than it was, accommodate an Ultramontane and Tridentine Irish Catholicism.

CHAPTER SEVENTEEN

The Catholic Church
from Parnell to Partition

Mary N. Harris

In the years 1890 to 1928 the Catholic Church in Ireland witnessed momentous political, cultural and social change. Nationalists and unionists became
increasingly militant, their campaigns ultimately leading to the partition of
Ireland and the establishment of two states, Northern Ireland and the Irish
Free State. Cultural nationalists who sought to discover the essence of
Ireland's cultural heritage and promote an awareness of it, reinforced separatist aspirations. A different form of struggle engaged the attention of the
working classes of Belfast and Dublin, who sought improvement in their own
conditions, under the direction of Labour leaders. The Catholic Church
responded with alarm to the upsurge of radicalism and the uncertainty about
Ireland's political future. It feared that an unfavourable political outcome
would reduce its influence, particularly in the field of education.
Nonetheless, it also hoped for the emergence of a Catholic nation-state. This
essay examines the fears and hopes of the Catholic Church in the face of
major changes, the role it expected and was expected to play, and the impact
of these changes on it.

I

The responses of the Catholic Church in this period were determined by
long-standing traditions. For decades the church had involved itself in Irish
politics. Its support offered politicians legitimacy as well as the use of a widespread network of well-educated men with leadership experience. Political
involvement provided the church with an opportunity to steer movements
along peaceful lines and to promote its own interests. The cause of Catholic
education, in particular, helped to forge links between politicians and church
leaders. Furthermore, many priests and bishops were personally committed
to nationalism, their views reinforced by resentful memories of persecution
of the Catholic Church and injustices suffered in the past. The defensiveness
of the church as an institution and of many of its loyal followers was reinforced by an awareness of problems such as secularisation and socialism facing the Catholic Church elsewhere. Religious journals such as the *Irish
Ecclesiastical Record* and *Studies* devoted much space to the vicissitudes of the

Catholic Church around the world. Nationalist newspapers, in particular the *Irish Independent* and the *Irish News*, drew the attention of a wider audience to these issues. The church, for its part, was determined to guard against any incipient encroachment on its territory in Ireland. This concern was evident during a rather passionate debate in the *Irish Ecclesiastical Record* in 1900. Fr J. F. Hogan justified the publication of correspondence on the theme of French education by referring to the dangers facing Ireland. He warned, 'it is only a small rift now that might widen out in the course of years, and ultimately admit that demon of secularisation which has wrought such havoc in the fairest land in Europe' and added, 'Indeed it is more for the information of the Irish clergy that we have gone to the trouble of entering into this correspondence ...'[1]

Throughout this period the Catholic Church maintained a high public profile, assisted by the press. Bishops' lenten pastorals and statements received extensive coverage while letters of support from bishops were read aloud at political meetings and reprinted in the press. Reports of election campaigns noted clerical support for candidates and letters from priests appeared in the correspondence columns of leading newspapers. The weekly *Irish Catholic* promoted a sense of Catholic nationalism as well as discussing religious affairs.[2] The Catholic Church expounded its views and concerns in greater detail in religious journals ranging from the *Irish Ecclesiastical Record* which addressed a clerical audience, to the *Catholic Bulletin*, directed towards a wider readership.

This public profile and political involvement of the church were deeply resented by many Irish Protestants and a small number of Catholic critics. Hostility frequently manifested itself in the Protestant unionist press, particularly the *Northern Whig*, which found Catholic Church statements objectionable but newsworthy nonetheless. In the early twentieth century a number of publications appeared denouncing the role of the Catholic Church in Irish society. Both Horace Plunkett and Michael J. F. McCarthy were critical of the large sums of money channelled into the church. McCarthy highlighted the contrast between the wealth of the church and the poverty of the people by including in his *Priests and People in Ireland* (1903) a photomontage of a Catholic cathedral towering over a street lined by the cottages of the poor. McCarthy's tone tended towards the scurrilous, however, and his work did not constitute as serious a challenge as Horace Plunkett's more measured *Ireland in the New Century* (1904). Fr Michael O'Riordan took Plunkett to task in *Catholicity and Progress in Ireland* where he highlighted the church's contribution to education, training and economic life, and included a few sharp attacks on Protestants. The general trend in this period, then, was one of energetic attempts by the Irish church to promote its interests through publicity, involvement in public debate and participation in public life. While perceived by critics as triumphalist, the church regarding itself as constantly under threat had a strong sense of grievance and reacted to most changes with a combination of defensiveness and wariness.

II

1891 marks the death of Charles Stewart Parnell, leader of the Land League, chairman of the Irish (Nationalist) Parliamentary Party, and arguably one of the two greatest political leaders of nineteenth-century Ireland. During the 1880s the bishops had called on Parnell to promote Catholic education and had supported his campaign for Home Rule. Emmet Larkin has termed this understanding between the bishops and Parnell an informal clerical-nationalist alliance.[3] The alliance collapsed and the party split when Parnell's long-term affair with Kitty O'Shea became public. Nevertheless, the Catholic Church continued to play a significant role in Home Rule politics for almost three decades.[4] When the Irish Party recovered from the split in 1900, the pattern of consensus between church and party set during the Parnellite years formed the basis for a renewed understanding between nationalists and the church.

The years immediately following the split saw increased interest in Ireland's cultural heritage, in particular the Irish language, Irish sport, and a sense of Irishness based on a heroic past. The Gaelic League, founded in 1893, spearheaded the movement to preserve and promote the Irish language. Fr Eoghan O'Growney, professor of Irish at the national seminary at Maynooth, played a leading role in the Gaelic League, and a number of other clerics made substantial contributions to the movement. Priests wrote pamphlets for the League, delivered rousing addresses in favour of the Irish language, produced dictionaries, grammars and teaching materials, and participated in cultural festivals. Bishop Patrick O'Donnell, later cardinal, issued pastoral letters in Irish. Interest in the language spread rapidly among clerical students at Maynooth who formed their own organisation and produced their own publication. Such cultural developments both fuelled and legitimised separatist aspirations. The Christian Brothers' schools contributed to this growing sense of nationalism, much to the horror of Ulster unionist critics. While elite Catholic colleges run by other religious orders were sometimes berated as West British, these too became more interested in Irish culture in the early twentieth century.[5]

For some priests, Irish offered a defence against the evils of the modern world. Thus Fr Peadar Ua Laoghaire described the language as 'the strongest shield for the faith except for the grace of God itself'.[6] A more extreme view was presented by Fr Cathaoir Ó Braonáin in a pamphlet entitled *The English Language and the Faith in Ireland*:

English is the language of infidelity. It is infidels who for the most part speak English. It is infidels who for the most part compose literature in English. Infidels have most of the power in the English-speaking world ... The sooner we discard English and revive our own language, the better off the faith will be in Ireland.[7]

Such views were also held by many of the laity at a time when the nature of cheap English literature reaching Irish shores caused considerable concern. The causes of culture and religion seemed to overlap. Nevertheless, the views of highly individualistic clerical personalities involved in the movement varied, reflecting similar divisions of opinion among the laity. Philip O'Leary has drawn a distinction between nativists, who were essentialists, drawing mainly on the existing Gaelic tradition, and the progressives who accepted the need for Gaelic culture to move forward, to look to the future and the wider world, to adapt elements from its own traditions but also to assimilate elements from other sources.[8] Both tendencies found clerical supporters.

Clerical and lay opinions were also divided regarding the best medium for a modern literature in Irish. Fr Peadar Ua Laoghaire favoured the contemporary spoken language while, in opposition, Fr Richard Henebry argued in support of the classical language of the seventeenth century. The clerical and lay wings of both groups saw in the promotion of the language movement an evocation of an unsullied and noble form of Irishness, a means of moral regeneration that can be seen in a constructive, as well as a defensive light. Indeed, John Hutchinson has highlighted the 'positive' dimension of this 'invocation of the past'. 'For the cultural nationalist seeks not to "regress" into an arcadia but rather to inspire his community to ever higher stages of development.'[9] Radical nationalism was presented as a moral, political and cultural package, as illustrated in this passage from the Sinn Féin pamphlet *The Ethics of Sinn Féin*, published in 1917:

Independence is first and foremost a personal matter. The Sinn Féiner's moral obligations are many and restrictive. His conduct must be above reproach, his personality stainless. He must learn the Irish language, write on Irish paper, abstain from alcohol and tobacco ... Give good example: make examples of your life, your virtues, your courage, your temperance, your manliness, which will attract your fellow countrymen to the national cause.[10]

The promotion of language and religion did not always go hand in hand, however, and when a conflict of interests occurred, religious interests generally prevailed. Some priests refused to permit the use of schools under their management for Irish classes attended by both young men and women, fearing the moral danger of mixed classes.[11] Sexual morality was also a major concern for Fr Peadar Ua Laoghaire who considered certain works by Pádraic Ó Conaire immoral and succeeded in having them removed from the university syllabus.[12] A major clash occurred when the Gaelic League sought to have the Irish language made compulsory for entry to the National University of Ireland, established in 1908. While 850 priests signed a petition supporting this proposal opposition came from more powerful quarters.[13] Fr William Delany SJ, president of University College Dublin, rejected the proposal, fearing that Catholic students who were not competent in Irish would study instead at Trinity College Dublin, long associated with Protestantism.[14] It was his ambition, too, that the new university would become one of the foremost Catholic intellectual centres in the world, and feared that Catholics from other countries would be excluded by a language requirement. Further opposition to the proposal came from the Catholic bishops who issued a statement in 1909, registering their support for the language but opposition to compulsion. Fr Michael O'Hickey, professor of Irish at Maynooth, defiantly opposed the bishops' stance and was dismissed for flouting their authority.

Those who lent their support to the language movement were attracted by its emphasis on simple rural life as authentically Irish. As Joseph MacMahon has noted, most priests were from rural backgrounds themselves.[15] Their response to urban life and in particular urban poverty was less sympathetic, and many had little understanding of the problems of growing urban areas. Irish clerical commentators varied in their interpretations of poverty: some attributed it to a lack of discipline on the part of the poor, some emphasised the evils of alcoholism and campaigned for abstinence, others showed greater sympathy.[16] The church's perception of deprivation and its remedies was coloured by its concern at the willingness of Protestant charities to provide assistance and its suspicion that such aid would be used to win converts to Protestantism. Fr Lambert McKenna explained:

> The wretched economic conditions of our towns, insufficient wages, inconstant employment, bad housing, defective and unsuitable education, an iniquitous Poor-Law system, all these things have provided a superb hunting-ground for the proselytiser.[17]

The church had long sought to tackle poverty through a range of organisations and institutions of its own and thus sought to prevent the more vulnerable members of society, particularly unmarried mothers and orphans, from falling into Protestant hands.

In the early years of the twentieth century urban poverty presented a new challenge in the form of socialism, particularly when the labour leader Jim Larkin arrived in Ireland and organised industrial disputes in Belfast and Dublin. Cardinal Logue expressed his concerns in his Lenten pastoral letter of 1912 where he listed the errors and dangers of socialism: the subversion of religion, morality, human rights, and the peace and well-being of the community, its open profession of atheism, its renunciation of marriage and the family.[18] The conflict between labour agitation and the church reached its height during a major lockout in Dublin in 1913 during which a plan to send the children of workers to England met with the opposition of Archbishop Walsh of Dublin who argued that the children's faith would be endangered.[19]

The Irish Catholic Church's theoretical response to social questions was generally underpinned by Pope Leo XIII's encyclical, *Rerum Novarum,* which criticised both socialism and capitalism but accepted inequality as inevitable. Such issues came to public attention in 1910 when Fr Robert Kane SJ delivered a series of lectures denouncing socialism. Marxist theoretician James Connolly responded in a pamphlet entitled *Labour, Nationality and Religion* where he questioned the view that socialism and Catholicism were incompatible. Fr Lambert McKenna SJ added a further layer to this debate in 1920 when he published an analysis of Connolly's beliefs. McKenna, who had by this time published a number of pamphlets on social issues, identified flaws in Connolly's theoretical position and argued that Connolly could not have been a Marxist in the fullest sense.[20] In general, the Irish church was intensely wary of those who leaned towards the left, as the question of socialism was a recurring one in religious journals.

In the short term there was little cause for concern about socialism as it was soon overshadowed by the national question. New opportunities arose in 1912 when the British government introduced a bill for Irish Home Rule. Two previous Home Rule bills had failed: the first rejected by the House of Commons in 1886, the second by the House of Lords in 1893. By 1912 the power of the House of Lords had been curtailed and the third bill seemed to have a reasonable chance of success. The bishops, who had close contacts with the Nationalist Party, greeted the bill with enthusiasm. Bishop Patrick O'Donnell hoped for 'the gradual reconstruction of a sterling Christian nation'.[21] Nevertheless, the hierarchy sought legal advice regarding the bill's implications for education.[22] Although the bill received the royal assent in 1914, increasingly militant opposition from Protestants in the north-east raised questions about its application. These difficulties were temporarily avoided when Home Rule was postponed following the outbreak of the First World War.

The war presented new opportunities for the Irish Republican Brotherhood (IRB). Following its foundation in 1858 this revolutionary organisation had met with the general hostility of the Catholic Church. A softening of clerical attitudes was evident following an unsuccessful rising in 1867 and the execution of three Fenians, 'the Manchester Martyrs', for involvement in the killing of a policeman in Manchester. This pattern of initial ecclesiastical opposition during unrest and subsequent generalised sympathy following the imprisonment and execution of rebels was to repeat itself during later struggles. In the early twentieth century the IRB reorganised. A small number of clergy sympathised with the revolutionaries – some noted by the police.[23] Two priests in the diocese of Clogher were permitted to join the IRB without taking the oath, to avoid difficulties if their bishop later questioned them.[24] Tyrone IRB leader Patrick MacCartan later noted that these priests 'had redeemed the Catholic Church in the eyes of nationalist Ireland of the stain caused by the attitude of some priests and bishops in the days of Fenianism'.[25]

The church confronted the question of revolution again during and after the Easter Rising in 1916. Despite traditional hostility to armed rebellion, sixteen volunteers arrived at the gates of Maynooth seeking the blessing of the seminary's president before proceeding to Dublin. Dr Hogan pointed out that he did not support violence, but blessed them individually as neighbours and, in some cases, employees of the college.[26] The personal piety of the participants in the rising is well attested, and religious imagery was a characteristic of the rebellion: one of the leaders, Patrick Pearse, clearly saw himself as a redeeming Christ-like figure.[27] Another leading figure, Joseph Plunkett, composed mystical poetry on the death of Christ. The time chosen for the rebellion – Easter – reflected this line of thought. Rebels recited the rosary on the roof of the General Post Office building, headquarters of the rebellion. Countess Markievicz, who participated in the rebellion, later attributed her conversion to Catholicism to the piety of the rebels. The bishops issued no collective response to the rising, though some saw it as foolhardy. Private correspondence reveals episcopal attempts to tease out the ethical aspects of the revolt in the light of theological scholarship.[28] At a more public level, Bishop O'Dwyer of Limerick refused to discipline two priests when General Maxwell asked that he do so. His refusal and the accompanying expressions of horror at the treatment of rebels became well known. O'Dwyer was not alone. Public sympathy grew following the execution of the rebels. Over the next few years it became more radicalised, assisted by various British blunders. The death following forced feeding of hunger striker Thomas Ashe, author of a poem entitled 'Let me carry your cross for Ireland Lord', increased sympathy for the rebel cause. Attempts to introduce conscription in 1918 led to a massive protest campaign involving both moderates and radicals. The church played an important part in organising the campaign, and individual bishops were outspoken in their opposition, to the honour of its critics, some of whom suspected Roman influence.[29] In reality, however, the church's involvement stemmed from its desire to steer the campaign along peaceful lines. 'The fact is,' Cardinal Logue wrote, 'that in common with the other Irish bishops, I am trying to keep the people quiet, and to deter them from rushing into wild and rash outbreaks'.[30]

Meanwhile the Nationalist Party, unable to deliver a measure of autonomy that did not involve the partition of the country, was supplanted by the more radical Sinn Féin party. The Catholic Church's willingness to accept Sinn Féin became clear when the cardinal arbitrated on the allocation of eight northern constituencies between Sinn Féin and the Irish Party to prevent a split Catholic vote that would enable unionist candidates to win. As they had promised during their election campaign, the successful Sinn Féin candidates established Dáil Éireann as an alternative parliament in Dublin and its first meeting was opened with a prayer led by Fr Michael O'Flanagan, vice-president of Sinn Féin.

Catholic bishops and priests consistently condemned the guerrilla warfare of the War of Independence that followed, though only one bishop excommunicated the rebels. As British security policies became more repressive, the church became more sympathetic towards its own people. Bishop MacRory, later Cardinal, was particularly outspoken and asked:

> Who by all this tyranny and perfidy and denial of their rights taught their young men to distrust constitutional agitation and have recourse to physical force? If they were to find the cause of the present deplorable condition of their country they must go farther back than the last year or two and find it in the age-long denial of their unquestionable rights.[31]

Nevertheless, the armed struggle led to much soul-searching and debates on the morality of rebellion. The church found itself in a further dilemma when political prisoners embarked on hunger strikes, an issue debated from various perspectives in journals such as the *Irish Ecclesiastical Record,* the *Irish Theological Quarterly* and *Studies.*[32] English Catholic publications such as the *Tablet* adopted a hostile position. The hunger strikers themselves seemed to have had no doubts about where they stood: Terence MacSwiney, Lord Mayor of Cork, who died after 74 days without food, declared, 'it is not we who take innocent blood, but we who offer it, sustained by the example of our immortal dead, and that Divine Example which inspires us all for the redemption of our country,' reflecting the sense of martyrdom that had also been evident following the 1916 Rising.[33] A further concern for the church was the possibility that a papal condemnation of Sinn Féin would alienate many people.[34] Talks between Sinn Féin and the British government began in the autumn of 1921. The Sinn Féin negotiators attended Mass in London and were greeted by Bishop MacRory afterwards. While the negotiations were under way a number of Irish people prayed in Downing Street. The outcome of the negotiations was an Anglo-Irish settlement which provided for dominion status similar to that of Canada. It was agreed that the

Northern Ireland state, which nationalists had refused to recognise when it began to function the previous year, would remain autonomous, though the border was to be changed in conformity with the wishes of the inhabitants. The Catholic Church responded favourably to the Treaty, though expressing some concern about Northern Ireland. The agreement met with hostility from many republicans who felt that it involved an unacceptable compromise. Civil war broke out, and a few months later the hierarchy, prompted by the cabinet, issued a collective statement condemning the anti-Treaty forces. The bishops expressed horror at the murder and destruction and, reflecting the church's teaching on just war, they argued that no one was justified in rebelling against the legitimate authority, the elected government of the state. Any section of the community with grievances could resort to political measures. Clearly outraged that they themselves were the subject of criticism, they stated:

> Disregard of the Divine Law then laid down by the bishops is the chief cause of all our present sorrows and calamities. We now again authoritatively renew that teaching, and warn our Catholic people that they are conscientiously bound to abide by it, subject, of course, to an appeal to the Holy See.[35]

Indignant that the rebels claimed to be good Catholics, the bishops announced that those who persisted were excluded from the sacraments, and that any priests who approved of the campaign against the government would be deprived of their faculties. Such republican sympathisers did indeed exist among the clergy; two Capuchin fathers had been with the rebels in the Four Courts when the government decided to shell it and various clergy showed anti-Treaty sympathies in subsequent months.[36] Despite the bishops' criticisms, republicans themselves believed they occupied the moral high ground and couched their arguments in the language of Catholic piety.[37] Republicans responded to the bishops' criticism by appealing to the Holy See. Dr Conn Murphy and Professor Arthur Clery travelled to Rome with a document of over eighty pages disputing the bishops' decision.[38] A papal representative arrived in Ireland the following spring in an attempt to broker a settlement, but by that time the anti-Treaty forces were seriously depleted and the civil war almost over.

The Irish Free State that took shape when conflict ended was a Catholic state where legislation reflected Catholic values, rather than those of a heroic Gaelic past; Catholicism became the predominant badge of identity. From 1922 to 1932 it was led by W. T. Cosgrave, a devout Catholic and friend of the archbishop of Dublin. From the 1920s the Free State government sought to develop a special relationship with the Vatican, further legitimising the new government and boosting the morale of the people.[39] Catholic values were reflected in legislation. As Dermot Keogh has noted, most Irish leaders in this period shared the Catholic educational formation of their religious leaders, and shared a desire to build a state based on the philosophy of Catholic nationalism.[40] Change in the education system was largely curricular; there was no interference in the church's control of its schools. Most social problems were dealt with by the Catholic Church which, with its large numbers of religious, continued to run schools, hospitals and a wide range of other institutions: reformatories, homes for the destitute, homes for unmarried mothers, for orphans, for children whose parents were considered 'respectable', and homes known as 'Magdalen Asylums' for women of dubious moral character. When the question of divorce arose, the bishops declared their view 'that it would be altogether unworthy of an Irish legislative body to sanction the concession of divorce, no matter who the petitioners may be'.[41] Provision for divorce was ended in 1925, a change bitterly criticised by the poet Senator W. B. Yeats. The partition of Ireland had ensured that Protestants were a small minority who could not hope to influence legislation, a position shared by Catholics in Northern Ireland.

III

The position of Catholics in the predominantly Protestant north-east was unenviable. This area suffered periodic outbreaks of rioting in the nineteenth and early twentieth centuries, especially when changes in the balance of power between Catholics and Protestants seemed imminent. Belfast and Derry were particularly prone to such disturbances as the rapid increase in Catholic numbers added to their instability. On such occasions priests and bishops frequently acted as defenders and spokesmen of their community. A priest who gave evidence to a commission of enquiry following the disturbances of 1886 argued that 'Catholics were treated as if they were an inferior and conquered race'.[42]

Religious divisions were immediately apparent during the debate on Home Rule. Protestants in the north-east, who had seen their area prosper under the union with Britain, were determined to maintain the political status quo. A recurring theme in unionist literature was the influence of the Catholic Church in Irish political and social life. Fears that Home Rule would mean Rome Rule were reinforced by the *Ne Temere* decree on mixed marriages and the *motu proprio Quantavis Diligentia*, which provided for the excommunication of lay people (though not in Ireland) who took clerics to civil courts. Both pronouncements feature in anti-Home Rule literature. The Orange Order proved a serious concern for Catholics, but unionists argued that the Ancient Order of Hibernians discriminated against Protestants.

As the unionist campaign against political change became more militant, the British government considered partitioning Ireland and excluding the largely Protestant north-east from Home Rule. The Catholic Church was outspoken in its opposition to partition proposals, fearing, above all, that a Protestant-dominated administration in Belfast would be hostile towards Catholic education. Cardinal Logue argued that it would be better to wait fifty years for a solution to the Irish problem than to accept proposals for Home Rule made in 1916 which entailed partition.[43] Such fears were reinforced by proposals for educational reform involving the abolition of education boards on which the church had representation and the establishment of county education committees. Protestant enthusiasm for such changes and the Catholic Church's opposition to them left little doubt that partition would be followed by clashes on the education issue. Apart from this issue, the more politically-minded church figures saw partition as an affront to the national ideal. It was, said the bishop of Clogher, 'the grossest insult to the spirit of Irish nationality'.[44] Moreover, Catholics feared the prospect of becoming second-class citizens. Bishop McHugh of Derry, ever watchful of any possible encroachment on Catholic rights, declared, 'to become serfs in an Orange Free State carved out to meet the wishes of an intolerant minority, to this we will never submit'.[45] Such concerns were reinforced by the memory of frequent communal violence.

The church was concerned at the creation of the northern state following the Government of Ireland Act of 1920, but initially hoped it would be short-lived. During the first election campaign in May 1921 both Catholics and Protestants raised the question of education. Bishop Joseph MacRory called on Catholics to use their vote to demonstrate their opposition to partition, suggesting that measures which jeopardised Catholic education affected the eternal salvation of children. Protestant candidates referred bitterly to the way in which the Catholic Church had obstructed reform measures in the past, and looked forward to an opportunity to promote social change without hindrance in the new regime. Most Catholics remained aloof from the new system. The cardinal declined an opportunity to attend the opening of parliament in Belfast in June 1921, and also refused an invitation to nominate representatives on a committee to investigate education. Catholics awaited an alternative settlement and hoped that the Anglo-Irish negotiations of late 1921 would have a better outcome.

When preparations for these negotiations got under way, a number of northern bishops and priests were consulted by Sinn Féin on the likely implications of partition for northern Catholics. They expressed particular concern about the likelihood of gerrymandering of constituencies and reduced funding for Catholic education. While the bishops generally welcomed the outcome of the Treaty, the provision for continuing partition caused great alarm.

Nevertheless, the Treaty also provided for a boundary commission to adjust the border between north and south, leading Catholics to hope that extensive areas of Northern Ireland with Catholic majorities would be transferred to the south leaving the northern state so small that it would be liable to collapse. Furthermore, Arthur Griffith of Sinn Féin assured the bishops that safeguards for northern Catholics would follow. The new Dublin government, formed in early 1922, looked to northern bishops and clergy for advice on northern issues. Many church leaders were more sympathetic towards the Sinn Féin government than were many of the laity in Belfast who still supported the old Nationalist Party. Bishop MacRory, a staunch Sinn Féin supporter, attended a number of cabinet meetings in Dublin, but when civil war broke out in southern Ireland the fate of northern Catholics received less attention in Dublin.

Within Northern Ireland the Catholic Church played an important role in seeking safeguards for Catholics during the particularly turbulent period of 1920-22. As violence escalated in early 1922, a Catholic Protection Committee, with MacRory as president and Fr B. Laverty as chairman, highlighted attacks on Catholics. Unionists, who considered the committee's statements inflammatory, set up a unionist counter-propaganda organisation. The two organisations engaged in bitter debate as to the underlying causes of the conflict: Unionists attributed it to Sinn Féin activity, while Catholics represented the violence as religious persecution. Bishop MacRory, equally concerned about anti-Catholic feeling, sent a book of Protestant songs to the rector of the Irish College in Rome. MacRory suggested that he show it to the Pope; it would 'give some idea, though faint, of the spirit of these savages'.[46]

While the Boundary Commission was pending, most northern Catholics were reluctant to recognise the Belfast parliament. By the autumn of 1923 various acts prejudicial to Catholic interests had been passed by parliament. These included an unacceptable Education Act and legislation requiring declarations of allegiance from all those in receipt of funding from local authorities, including priests who served as chaplains in prisons and hospitals. The bishops issued a highly critical statement, referring to 'this ever-advancing aggression on Catholics' and suggesting that Catholics should organise and 'resolve to lie down no longer under this degrading thraldom'. Various meetings took place, organised by clergy. They were closely monitored by the police but no political movement materialised as a result.

In advance of the Boundary Commission many priests, at the invitation of the laity, played a leading role in preparing cases for the transfer of northern territory to the Free State. When the Commission's recommendation of minor transfers of territory was leaked in late 1925, the Free State government was outraged at the idea of any transfer of southern territory to

Northern Ireland. The leaders of the Dublin, Belfast and London governments reached an alternative arrangement which left the border unchanged and adjusted the financial arrangements between the two governments. Northern Catholics were bitterly disappointed and reacted with anger. Many found it difficult to accept Cardinal O'Donnell's suggestion that the time had come to adjust to the new reality, but in following years Catholic politicians rethought their political position.[47] In 1928 the National League of the North was founded. From the outset the Catholic Church was deeply involved; the bishops had been consulted about its establishment; the clergy were active in the organisation at a local level.[48]

Educational grievances continued to promote close links between Catholicism and nationalism. The church supported Catholic candidates in local government and parliamentary elections, relying on them to advance the cause of Catholic education. The Northern Ireland education system established in 1923 had left Catholic schools seriously disadvantaged as the church had feared. The nondenominational character of public-funded schools also aggravated Protestants who set up a United Education Committee in 1924 to campaign for Bible reading during compulsory school hours and permission to take religion into account in making appointments to state schools. Their success in rendering the state schools more Protestant in character added to Catholic resentment. The church continued its involvement in electoral campaigns in Northern Ireland up to the mid-century. When labour candidates stood for election in Catholic areas in Belfast they met with fiercely hostile opposition from the Catholic Church, nationalist politicians, and the *Irish News*. References were made to developments in Russia, Mexico and China, and voters were warned against voting for socialists.[49] The northern bishops envied the exceptionally favourable position of the Catholic Church in the Irish Free State. The sense of deprivation was acutely felt during the centenary celebrations of Catholic Emancipation in 1929. The Bishop of Dromore rejoiced with Catholics in the Irish Free State but noted the educational grievances of northern Catholics, asking ruefully, 'How can we sing the song of the Lord in a Strange Land?'[50]

IV

The Catholic Church's institutional stance in the period 1891-1928 can be summed up in the word vigilance: vigilance against proselytisers, socialists, Protestant unionists, evil literature and secularists. The need to protect hard-won gains and promote Catholic interests led to involvement in politics. The laity frequently looked to priests to adopt leadership roles. Catholic politicians viewed the bishops as a legitimate interest group and recognised their right to consultation, though their advice was not always followed. While some joint statements were issued, clerical political involvement was usually on an individual basis and driven by a sense of idealism, a sense of mission and a vision of how Irish Catholic society ought to be. Clerical involvement received much publicity and lent legitimacy to the great variety of causes and movements in question. Fr Michael O'Flanagan, an Irish-language enthusiast, became vice-president of Sinn Féin in 1917. Jesuits John McErlean and Lambert McKenna edited bardic poetry and commented on social issues. Fr Peadar Ua Laoghaire took an interest in politics, the land question and the Irish language. In addition, the religious journals of the period helped promote a wide range of interests, often publishing articles on issues relating to nationality, Irish history and early Irish literature. The Jesuit quarterly *Studies,* established in 1912, became a forum for works on culture as well as religion and society, and continues to play this role. The *Catholic Bulletin*'s sympathy for the rebels of 1916 led to its being heavily censored. The range of clerical views mirrored the range of lay views. Protestants tended to see the Catholic Church as reactionary on social issues but politically subversive. Abusive letters sent to Bishop MacRory in Belfast during the particularly violent early 1920s indicate a belief that he could curb violence if he wished.[51] This was a serious overestimation of his influence.

In reality few priests were very radical; few joined the IRB or argued that the armed struggle was justifiable. Nevertheless, the exceptions helped to prevent republican alienation from the church. Many of those who espoused republican ideology considered themselves devout Catholics and couched their arguments in religious terms. Indeed, the iconography of martyrdom evident during the 1916 rising and the troubles of 1919-23 resurfaced during prison protests in Northern Ireland in the 1970s, and again during the hunger strike of 1981. The murals of West Belfast included a depiction of Ireland crucified on a British flag and Ireland carrying a cross, reminiscent of Thomas Ashe's poem, 'Let me carry your Cross for Ireland, Lord.' Inscriptions such as 'Lord may their sacrifice like yours not be in vain' and 'Blessed are those who hunger for justice' accompanied murals.[52]

In the period under study both Catholic and Protestant churches feared the implications of new political arrangements for their religious freedom. The subsequent fate of religious minorities on both sides of the border suggests that at least some of their earlier fears were well-founded. In the past Catholic and Protestant churches tended to respond to criticism by defending their positions to their own members, often dismissing the concerns of their critics. Stereotypes and myths flourished in the widening gulf between the communities in Northern Ireland. Robert Harbinson's autobiographical *No Surrender* includes an entertaining though disconcerting portrayal of a Protestant child's perceptions of Catholics and Catholicism.[53] In recent years, attempts have been made to address such misunderstandings. Against this background it is not surprising that *Building Trust in Ireland*, a series of essays on the churches, religion and religious minorities was commissioned by the Forum for Peace and Reconciliation, a body set up in 1994 to consider ways of counteracting distrust and promoting peace and respect for both identities. Sensitivity to the religious beliefs of others has increased. As Michael Hurley notes in this volume, the Troubles promoted closer interaction between Catholic and Protestant churches. An Interchurch Group on Faith and Politics has attempted to examine and explain areas of religious divergence. Programmes in schools aim to dispel myths and misunderstandings, and to explain to children the similarities and differences between various religions. ECONI (Evangelical Contribution on Northern Ireland) has sought to examine the negative impact, in spite of good intentions, of certain religious positions. The impact of such increased sensitivity has extended also to the Irish Republic. Reflecting international interest in human rights, the Belfast Agreement of 1998 includes measures to protect the rights of citizens both north and south. It is hoped that when new structures are in place respect for rights, religious and otherwise, will no longer depend on membership of the majority community.

CHAPTER EIGHTEEN

The Church of Ireland
since Partition

Kenneth Milne

The Church of Ireland was the state church of the country for over four hundred years, and has retained the title since it was disestablished in 1869. It was accorded the title 'Church of Ireland' in the Irish constitution, until a referendum in 1972 removed the names of all churches, and also removed the 'special position' of the 'Holy, Catholic, Apostolic and Roman Church'. It is perhaps worth pointing out that the word 'Protestant' has tended to be used in Ireland to denote the established church which from the start was Anglican. To ask for 'the Protestant church' in an Irish town or village, especially outside Ulster, is, more often than not, to be directed to the Church of Ireland building. Anglicans were the original Protestants in Ireland, and the name has stuck, to the understandable indignation of other Reformation traditions, and indeed of some Anglicans.

I use the word 'Ireland' to mean the whole island of Ireland, not just the twenty-six counties of the Republic. Three-quarters of the Church of Ireland population reside in Northern Ireland, which is part of the United Kingdom, and it would be impossible to describe the Church of Ireland experience in the twentieth century without looking at its life in both political jurisdictions, north and south. 'Partition', of course, refers to that division of the island by British legislation whereby the area where Protestants predominate, the six north-eastern counties, was given the option of remaining in the United Kingdom, while the remaining twenty-six counties were accorded a degree of limited self-government within the British Commonwealth. Southern politicians skilfully turned the Irish Free State into a sovereign Republic over a period of thirty or so years, with British acquiescence.

I

In 1922, what is now the Republic of Ireland began its constitutional life as a 'free state' within the British Commonwealth of Nations. But even that limited degree of independence was uncongenial to the overwhelming majority of the members of the Church of Ireland. For, though never more than about one-sixth of the population of the island, their church had enjoyed a status of great privilege since the Reformation, and its standing as the 'established church' or 'state church' had inevitably bred an attitude of theological, political and social superiority. The Church of Ireland minority, in addition to its ownership of the vast majority of Irish landed estates until the late nineteenth century, also had enjoyed for centuries a prominent, sometimes dominant, place in the social and economic life of the country, as it had in political life. The high profile of the Protestant population in economic life was not, of course, an Anglican monopoly: Presbyterians, Methodists, and to a remarkable extent Quakers, had also made their mark. But all other Christians, Catholics in particular, had suffered from political and social discrimination at the hands of the established church. However tenable the Church of Ireland's constitutional position may have been in earlier times (Ireland was, after all, for centuries an Anglican kingdom under the English, Anglican crown), such political theory became increasingly difficult to sustain in the nineteenth century.

Yet, though the Church of Ireland had a position of privilege, a sense of insecurity was never far beneath the surface. Faced with the understandable hostility of Catholics and Protestant Dissenters, the established church clung tightly to the British connection, and more often than not, whenever British politicians were criticised by the established Church of Ireland it was because they were entertaining excessive notions of tolerance that were regarded by the leaders of the church as prejudicial to its position, and, therefore, they asserted, to the maintenance of the Protestant constitution of the state.

It is not surprising to find Catholics and Dissenters amongst the founders of Irish republicanism but it is somewhat paradoxical to find in their number men and women of Anglican background. Some, such as Wolfe Tone, comprehensively espoused the principles of the French Revolution, and could scarcely be counted orthodox members of the established church. But other revolutionaries, such as Thomas Russell, were devout Anglicans whose religious commitment was very real, despite the conflicting loyalties that must have beset them. In later generations, too, there have been Irish leaders who found membership of the Church of Ireland compatible with nationalism, even with republicanism. But several swallows do not make a summer, and the leadership of the Church of Ireland at the beginning of the twentieth century, as well as a great majority of its members, stood by the British connection. It must also be said that while the members of other Irish churches, Catholic and Protestant, had welcomed, indeed demanded, the removal of the Church of Ireland's political privileges, the other Protestant churches were scarcely less committed to the British connection than was the Church of Ireland. Most Irish Protestants, irrespective of their particular religious tradition, were devoted to the British link, but the Church of Ireland had more reason than others to treasure it. Even when its position as Ireland's state church had disappeared with disestablishment in 1869, the Church of Ireland remained very much the church of the political and social elite.

In 1922 everything changed and the leaders of the Church of Ireland found themselves in an Irish Free State. They accepted the situation, if without enthusiasm, at least with integrity, and the public pronouncements of such men as Archbishop Gregg, who was Church of Ireland archbishop of Dublin from 1920 to 1938, strongly encouraged loyalty to the new regime. To quote him:

> It concerns us all that we should have a strong, wise and capable government. And therefore it concerns us all to offer to the Irish Free State so shortly to be constituted our loyalty and our goodwill ... The new Constitution will claim our allegiance with the same solemn authority as the one that is now being constitutionally annulled.[1]

Similarly, the influential, though unofficial, journal of the Church of Ireland, the *Church of Ireland Gazette,* displayed realism (and perhaps a tinge of superiority) when it said:

> In the past we have been compelled more or less to stand aside. Our attitude towards matters of high abstract policy rendered us unpopular and suspect. But that having been settled, and settled against us, it is felt that the country now needs just those qualities which our church can give, and that the Christian spirit urges they be not refused.[2]

The religious minority in the Free State quickly adjusted to the new political situation. Some would say that it had little choice, which is true. But there was more to it than that. Enthusiasm for the new regime might have been lacking, but it brought political stability, and in some regards was sympathetic to certain Protestant values. F. S. L. Lyons contended that a major factor in reconciling the religious minority to the Irish Free State was the speedy realisation that the new government was well disposed to the business world in which so many leading Protestants were involved.[3]

None the less, the new political environment in which southern Protestants found themselves was in several ways uncongenial. Two areas of policy of the fledgling Irish Free State made it particularly so. There was, to begin with, the policy of the founding fathers that the new Ireland should be Gaelic in character, a policy most clearly expressed in their determination to restore Irish as the vernacular language of the people. To some extent this was a reaction to the neglect, not to say disdain, with which things Gaelic had so frequently been treated in the past. It was also a response to an official attitude to the teaching of Irish history in a British context that had previously prevailed. Now, pride of place was given to the Irish language in the school curriculum, and the teaching of Irish history was introduced at primary-school level with the express intention of fostering devotion to the Irish language, competence in which was made an obligatory qualification for appointment to the civil service and other sectors of state employment.[4] Members of the Church of Ireland had played a leading role in the language revival movement from the late nineteenth century onwards, notably Douglas Hyde, a co-founder of the Gaelic League, who had deplored in no uncertain terms the anglicisation of Ireland. But the subject was scarcely taught at all in Protestant primary or secondary schools. Perhaps more uncomfortable for Protestants than the imposition of the Irish language in this way was the implication, sometimes expressed as more than an implication, that to be truly Irish one must be Irish-speaking.

The other defining element in the formation of the character of the new state was its strongly Roman Catholic ethos. And if, in some quarters, to be truly Irish one had to be Irish-speaking, so in other circles to be truly Irish one had to be Roman Catholic. That a political entity with a Catholic population of over 90 per cent would be Catholic in ethos was hardly astonishing, and the fact that the overwhelming majority of Irish Protestants had wished to opt out of Home Rule was impossible to deny. Under the new regime, Roman Catholic teaching on divorce and contraception was given legal status, either through the constitution or legislation, and a rigorous censorship of publications soon made it evident that government aimed to protect the population not only from pornography but also from expressions of anti-clericalism, and from the views of such authors as appeared on the Vatican Index of prohibited reading. Furthermore, the Irish censorship board was empowered to ban literature advocating birth control, a practice that in the view of the Church of Ireland from the 1940s onwards was a matter for the consciences of married couples.[5]

In recent years historians have shown that the Irish Free State walked delicately in its diplomatic dealings with the Vatican. Many present-day citizens of Ireland, of different religious traditions and of none, read with embarrassment the protestations of loyalty to the papacy expressed by early governments on behalf of *all* the citizens. A ministerial reference to 'the well-proven affection of the Irish people for the Holy See' is a good example.[6] It begs the question, 'who are the Irish people?' The statement made in 1934 by Lord Craigavon, Prime Minister of Northern Ireland, that 'we have a Protestant Parliament and a Protestant State',[7] is well known. But de Valera, as head of the Irish government, broadcasting on St Patrick's Day in the following year, spoke of Ireland as 'a Catholic nation'.[8] Such quotations, over-familiar to many, give something of the flavour of the times in which they were uttered. In fairness to de Valera, it has to be recorded that when he framed the Irish

Constitution of 1937, he refused to give his church the status that the Vatican would have liked.

There were two *causes célèbres* bearing on this area: the Tilson case in 1950 and the Mother and Child controversy the following year. In the Tilson case it was declared by the Supreme Court that while, under the constitution, both parents had equal rights in the upbringing of their children, the written undertaking to have the children brought up as Catholics given by the Protestant partner in a mixed marriage was enforceable by the law of the state.[9] Probably the last unambiguous declaration of government sensitivity to ecclesiastical precepts came during the 'Mother and Child' controversy of 1951 when the then Taoiseach, John A. Costello, stated in the Dáil that when it came to matters of morality he had no hesitation in following the teaching of his church 'without qualification in all respects'.[10]

All of this must be seen in the context of the times. And given the enormous changes in Irish public opinion and public policy in the intervening years, one feels a certain reluctance to publicise them yet again. But it would be impossible to depict the Ireland of the 1930s, 40s and 50s without mentioning them and the enormous public debate they created. It is understandable that Catholic members of parliament and the judiciary, who held office in a state whose institutions reflected for the first time the ideals of the great majority of Irish people, should express such sentiments. It is equally understandable that the members of the Church of Ireland felt themselves to be living in a society governed by precepts that were in many respects alien, even repugnant, to them. By and large, however, they accepted the inevitability of the situation. Indeed, the voices raised against the 'confessional' character of the new state tended to be those of intellectual Catholics, though there were Church of Ireland voices criticising Protestants for their acceptance of the confessional aspects of government policy. One such voice was that of W. B. Stanford, the Trinity don, who represented the university in the Senate from 1948 to 1969, and who called for full participation by his co-religionists in the life of the new state, putting it to them squarely that the way to influence political life was to enter it.[11]

The Protestant population of the Free State was tiny, if in many ways influential in areas other than politics. But there were a million Protestants in Northern Ireland who could with some justification claim that their prognostications that Home Rule would be Rome Rule had proved correct. The avowed aspiration of all political parties in the twenty-six counties that Ireland should be united (though they might differ about the means to achieve it), was scarcely commended to unionists by the twin objectives of promoting the Irish language by compulsion and enshrining Catholic social teaching in the law of the land. The territorial claim by the twenty-six counties to suzerainty over the six, explicit in the new constitution of 1937, made even more adamant the determination of northern unionists, most members of the Church of Ireland among them, to defend their position. Northern nationalists were placed in an invidious and vulnerable situation. They could be deemed by unionists to pose not only a threat to the very existence of Northern Ireland, but also to be potential enemies of Protestant values and religious freedom.

To northern unionists, the steep decline in the Protestant population in the south represented stark evidence of the attrition under which many of them believed southern Protestants to exist. The decline was undeniable, and undoubtedly it owed something to the changed political situation. There had, indeed, been an exodus of Protestants during and immediately after what are euphemistically called 'the Troubles'. Between 1911 and 1926, the Church of Ireland population of the twenty-six counties fell by 85,000, one quarter of that figure being attributed to the withdrawal of British armed forces and their dependents.[12] The decline continued, as perhaps was inevitable given the inroads made on the Protestant population by the loss of young men in the First World War, and by the Vatican's regulations governing the upbringing of the children of mixed marriages. Hence the significance attached by Protestants to the Tilson judgment. With a steep decline in population went a decline in self-confidence. Southern Protestants have been criticised for keeping their heads down in the decades immediately following independence. But it was hardly to be expected that those who had been on the losing side in the struggle for independence would enter readily into the political structures of the new state at national or local level, even supposing that their candidature had been successful. The intellectual bastion of unionism, Trinity College, withdrew into itself for generations, and while the *Irish Times* continued to thunder, its editorialising was easily dismissed by its critics as at best ex-unionist, at worst anti-national.

The Anglo-Irish might have been, to quote Yeats's somewhat extravagant Senate speech of 1925, 'no petty people', but rather 'one of the great stocks of Europe', who had created 'the most of the modern literature of this country'.[13] Indeed Terence Brown has contrasted the pantheon of Protestant writers active in the literary revival of the late nineteenth century with the dearth of literature emerging from that community in more modern times. 'There are,' he argues, 'no works of modern literature that could be said to emerge from the complex of concerns, ideas and feelings that have preoccupied Irish Anglicanism in the period.'[14] He continued ' ... the Church of Ireland has been directly present in Irish literature throughout most of the modern period only in brief images and allusions, as a social presence that can be variously represented in fiction, drama or poetry without the need for any sustained examination.'[15] The few literary references he cites to what might be termed the psychological condition of the Church of Ireland in the south consist of melancholy lines by John Betjeman, describing an 'extinguished family' as it waits for

A Church of Ireland resurrection
By the broken, rusty gates.

Brown also finds similar, melancholy, resonances in Beckett.

Enormous changes have taken place in what is now the Republic of Ireland, largely as the result of changes in public opinion, some self-induced by the impact of greater educational opportunity on a society that was increasingly given to questioning authority, some with a little help from European institutions such as the court of human rights. Many of the social and intellectual constraints of the past have disappeared, and Protestants have come to feel themselves increasingly at home in a state in which their attitudes and values are not only tolerated, but indeed shared. Important influences on public opinion, such as Trinity College Dublin and the *Irish Times*, once regarded, and justifiably so, as organs of the Protestant ascendancy, are no longer so, yet retain, under new leadership, much of their former character and prestige. Ecumenism has been a major solvent in breaking down misapprehensions between Irish Christians, and many Catholics eagerly seized the opportunities for fraternisation that resulted from Vatican II, generally finding a ready Protestant response. Given the enormous difference in the size of the two communities in the Republic, any ecumenical movement depends to a great extent on the initiatives and enthusiasm of the Roman Catholic Church, and while ecumenism was a concept with which at least some members of the main Protestant churches were familiar long before Vatican II, the council gave it a much wider currency and, of course, a wider interpretation. Many Protestants, Anglicans in particular, had been slow to espouse an ecumenism that smacked rather of pan-Protestantism. With Rome's participation in the movement, their inhibitions diminished. It must, however, be admitted, that simultaneously the inhibitions of other Protestants increased, not least in Northern Ireland.

II

The partitioning of Ireland was so devised as to result in a unionist, that is to say, Protestant, majority in Northern Ireland. Church of Ireland members comprised a minority, albeit a substantial one, of that unionist presence, making up less than half of a 59 per cent Protestant population in the six counties.[16] Furthermore, the Church of Ireland has to a great extent been the church of the less well-off urban and rural Protestants in the north, and while, indeed, having more than its fair share of landed gentry there, it has been under-represented among the leaders of industrial and commercial life. Nor have relations between the Protestant churches been invariably cordial, a case in point being friction over educational matters at local level. But where the matter of commitment to the union with Great Britain is concerned, the Protestant churches have been at one. Five northern bishops of the Church of Ireland were among the signatories to the Solemn League and Covenant of 1912 whereby hundreds of thousands of unionists pledged themselves '[to use] all means which may be found necessary to defeat the present conspiracy to set up a Home Rule Parliament',[17] and in doing so they offended very few of their followers. In a sense, the feeling of insecurity that so consistently bedevilled the experience of the erstwhile established church in pre-partition Ireland was inherited by the Protestant majority in Northern Ireland at large, and not just by those whose allegiance was to the Church of Ireland. The phenomenon of 'Protestant fears', which observers find difficult to understand, has to be seen against the background of constitutional claims to the territory of Northern Ireland by a southern state that, until comparatively recently, was unapologetically Catholic in ethos. The perceived threat from a very large and growing Catholic-nationalist community within Northern Ireland should also be taken into account. The fact that the nationalist population and its church leaders have consistently deplored the armed struggle conducted in the name of Irish unity by some republicans cut no ice with unionists, who regarded nationalist refusal to identify wholly with the constitution of Northern Ireland, and in particular with its security forces, as tantamount to supporting the enemy within.

Such inter-community distrust and suspicion have deepened over the last thirty years but were always there, and a vicious circle of alienation and discrimination prevailed from Northern Ireland's earliest years. Nationalists were aggrieved that the Home Rule legislated for in 1914 was abandoned, as subsequently were hopes that the border would be adjusted in their favour by a boundary commission, whose work was aborted. Enemies within and without generated in the unionist community a widespread siege mentality, having resonances with the seventeenth-century Siege of Derry, which held, and still holds, an honoured place in Protestant folk memory. Discriminatory electoral and employment practices against Catholics resulted.

World War II was a time of bonding between the Protestant population of the north and the rest of the United Kingdom. The whole-hearted support given by the North's Protestants to the war effort contrasted vividly with the south's policy of neutrality. The bonding was further achieved by the participation of Northern Ireland in the social benefits of the post-war Welfare State. The devotion of the Protestant population to the union for religious reasons was now deepened, if that were possible, by the economic benefits that it brought. While nationalists, too, enjoyed the fruits of the Welfare State, as unionists were quick to point out, for many of them there were other considerations, not just their grievances in the matter of the local franchise, allocation of public housing and discriminatory practices in employment, though these loomed large in their consciousness. There was also the demand that their sense of Irishness be accorded legitimacy. It would be difficult to estimate the proportion of northern members of the Church of Ireland who claim to be Irish. Many do, but there are certainly others who claim not to be, a number that, one strongly suspects, has increased over the last thirty years. Anecdotal evidence would suggest that this is partly because Protestants in the south have espoused a particular definition of Irishness, whereas they, or many of them, in the north were only prepared to see themselves as Irish in a British context, like the English, and most of the Scots or Welsh. But northern Catholics appear to have suffered from no such identity crisis. Some may well be happily British: few, if any, would deny that they are Irish.

In the late 1960s, discontent came to a head. There were civil rights protests, demonstrations that erupted into violence, and instances of questionable tactics by the security forces. Soon, paramilitary organisations were proliferating, and the north entered a thirty-year period of political turbulence that was to see appalling acts of violence, miscarriages of justice, over 3,000 deaths and the image of Northern Ireland that is so prevalent the world over. The gulf between the Catholic and Protestant communities widened and animosities deepened. Much argument has taken place as to whether or not, like another Thirty Years War, these hostilities constituted a religious war. The very fact that one so easily equates nationalist with Catholic, and unionist with Protestant, gives substance to the claim that it was, indeed, religious. While the debate was not about the minutiae of doctrine, it did encompass issues of power and human rights, and to that extent has a theological dimension. What then, of the part played by the churches? The record of the churches has not been unblemished. Their prophetic role has frequently been inhibited by a reluctance to appear neglectful of the fears and aspirations of their respective members. Having said that, however, it is important to recognise that clergy of all the main Christian traditions have shown moral and physical courage in the face of bitter community tensions, and have, for the most part, counselled moderation and reconciliation. Probably the most trenchant criticism to be answered by the churches is that they were slow to read the signs of the times, and were blind to the consequences of the sectarian spirit that too often infused the attitudes of members of one community to another.

The annual spectacle at the Church of the Ascension, Drumcree, highlights for members of the Church of Ireland as never before the manner in which religion and politics interact in Northern Ireland. Drumcree also revealed the divergence of perspectives that have developed between southern and northern members of the church. Dr Stevens, secretary of the Irish Council of Churches, in an address to the General Synod in 1999, spoke of 'the appalled reaction of southern church members' to Drumcree. Several southern bishops had articulated this, and it can safely be said that the people in the parishes expected no less of them. Likewise, some Northern members of the church had been equally appalled by what they perceived as ill-informed and unfair criticisms from the south. Dr Stevens attributed the strength of southern reaction to the fact that Drumcree represented a threat to the hard-won belonging of Protestants in the south and the opening up of memories of that deep sense of insecurity that marked the southern Protestant position until the 1960s.[18] But southern reaction was much more than an awakening of Protestant folk memory. Recent generations of members of the Church of Ireland identify with society in the Republic. While frequently empathising with the tribulations of their fellow church members in the North in the recent past, they also empathise with the sufferings of others there. Southern church members live in a state governed according to principles with which they feel increasingly comfortable at a time when many Northern Protestants are experiencing changes in their society which they find decidedly uncomfortable. Church of Ireland citizens of the Republic have seen the development of a new tolerance of diversity, and a new willingness to subject authority, whether civil or ecclesiastical, to criticism. They would like to think that their fellow citizens increasingly share their own values. The scenes they have witnessed in the precincts of one of their own parish churches in the North, somehow associated with a Church of Ireland act of worship, have indeed appalled them. The turmoil surrounding Drumcree and the Garvaghy Road have similarly appalled many other citizens of the Republic, who, more often in sorrow than in anger, have questioned whether the Church of Ireland's much-vaunted adherence to liberal values only relates to its own interests.

The heart-searching within the Church of Ireland occasioned by these events may well presage the beginning of a process that will, in time, give new life to the church. There is precedence for such hope in the experience of the Church of Ireland in the south. In recent years, commentators have observed a new self-confidence in the Church of Ireland in the Republic and a mentality very different from that which existed thirty years ago. Some would attribute this change to the fact that the southern members of the church have confronted their history, at a time when southern society as a whole has done much the same. A broader interpretation of patriotism and a more generous definition of Irishness are now abroad, exemplified by the changes in the Irish constitution overwhelmingly approved by referendum in 1998, and which, as part of the package that makes up the Belfast Agreement of Good Friday 1998, remove the contentious territorial claim to the six counties. The Church of Ireland now tends to look at its past in the light of a fresh understanding of Irish history, recognising how its role was conditioned by political as well as theological factors, and coming to appreciate how it was perceived, and can still be perceived, by those of other Christian traditions, and why. Released from the constraints imposed by polemics, the church has gained fresh understanding of its past.[19] Positions that owed little to historical truth have been abandoned while in the process much that was neglected has been retrieved. Modern commentators, freed from polemical debate, can reflect on the history of the established church in the manner that historians would wish to. With the loss of what has been discarded has come the recovery of much that was laudable. The *raison d'être* of any church's existence, its spirituality, is receiving attention, as is the witness of what was edifying in the lives of its members – not necessarily the more conspicuous ones.

The emergence of a revised, hopefully more truly focused, view of the Church of Ireland, past and present, has come about in the south, in the context of a growing historical understanding of the society in which we live. Political circumstances in Northern Ireland have, understandably, inhibited the influence on public opinion of such reassessment there. One must also reckon with the undeniable fact that Church of Ireland members in the north have largely missed out on Irish history at school (as many of them now regret). None the less, there are encouraging signs. The report on sectarianism presented to the General Synod of 1999 made statements such as have seldom, probably never, been contained in an official Church of Ireland report before.[20] It is to be hoped that the process will gain momentum, and that the agonies of the present will result in an understanding of the past that frees rather than enslaves.

CHAPTER NINETEEN

Irish Catholicism in the Diaspora: the case of the United States[1]

David Noel Doyle

Despite a maturing sense of the diversity of their origins, a quarter of American Catholics still identify Ireland as their chief country of ancestry and almost an equal proportion name Germany. By contrast, about a fifth of such Catholics name Italy as the main origin of their forefathers. The number of Irish-American Catholics, around fifteen million (in 1995), is a marked increase on the 17 per cent, or 8.3 million Catholics reporting Irish descent in 1979, one indication, amongst others, that there has been a return to the church in Irish-American families. Between 1890 and 1920 up to a half of American Catholics were of Irish extraction despite the 'new immigration'. For a century or so (1870s-1970s) a proportion varying from a third to a half of the American hierarchy were partly or wholly of Irish descent. In the intra-church rivalries of the time, the argument as to whether Irish immigrants and their descendants had built the faith in America or, on the contrary, had largely failed to keep it, was a central one.

In 1925, Gerald Shaughnessy published a vigorous defence of the view that overall the immigrants had kept the faith, and more especially had the Irish.[2] Tall, stern, and very efficient, he later became bishop of Seattle, 1933-1950. To him, the stewardship of the American church was thus vindicated, as was its guidance (since after the Civil War) by largely Irish-American hands. So too it seemed was the relatively relaxed Irish-American approach to America itself: it was a natural place to be Catholic in. The defensiveness of Germans, Poles and others, before 1917, or the communalism of many Italians and French Canadians thereafter thus seemed unnecessary. The insistence of Irish-American and mixed-descent prelates, such as John Ireland and George Mundelein, on treating such approaches as (at best) temporary mechanisms for the uprooted, seemed fully justified. When Shaughnessy wrote in the 1920s, American Catholicism was indeed creating the pre-eminent success story of modern urban Catholicism. It was also identifying itself with the premises of American democratic constitutionalism, and championing its theistic and ethical foundations at a time when many Protestant and secular Americans, haunted by Darwin and Freud, were shifting toward a less certain, if not necessarily amoral, outlook. In short, it had succeeded as a church;

it was now guardian too of the religious and rational foundations of the republic; and it had correctly pointed nervous immigrants from Europe in sound directions.

Today, with the vast American Catholic Church fragmented by numerous fissures, many are less confident than was Bishop Shaughnessy of the vision of his generation. With Irish Catholicism today also shaken we have more sympathy for the doubts of its continental-stock rivals. After all, Germans, Italians and others came from cultures already transformed by statist rationalism and enlightenment nostrums. Many of them took the view that the Irish were naïve; and indeed they came from an island where all dangerous complexity was then subsumed under, and contained by, blanket bias against England and 'its' Protestantism. Shaughnessy understood that the numerical record of retention (or otherwise) of the faithful was the initial key to answering such doubts. Does his work survive?

Despite refinements in historical knowledge and in statistical science, his picture broadly holds up: a massive church was created out of a mass migration. The first phase of growth, from a minor church of a third of a million in 1830, to America's largest, with nine million, in 1890, coincided with the greatest Irish (and German) influxes. Shaughnessy maintained that the church then built on the lessons learnt to double its size to 18 million by 1920, by merging millions of continental immigrants, as well as American-born Catholics, into a pre-tested successful pattern. But many partly-known factors mean that his confident sweep of detail is suspect. True, his orders of magnitude as between immigrant groups broadly stand, certainly for the years 1840-1920. From Ireland majority Catholic emigration began *after* 1815, more certainly after 1830. But what is wrong with Shaugnessy's picture must be emphasised. He set all Irish immigrants at 4,360,000 between 1820 and 1920, and assumed they were Catholic in the same proportions as the Irish population at the beginning of each decade's outflow. Cumulated net Catholic immigration by decade, however, he indicates to be 2,283,791, which is markedly too low. Direct Irish immigration to America, 1815-1921, was at least 4,918,300. This recorded migration was itself an undercount, as is clear from wide discrepancies between the number of the young lost to the census at the end of each decade, and that decade's recorded emigration (see Table One).[3]

Table One
Irish Immigration to the United States, 1841-1920 in 000s

Years	Numbers*	Catholic est.§	Cohort Depletion(%)#	Depletion ('000s)
1841-50	781	531	72.7%	1,216
1851-60	914	602	48.0%	701
1861-70	436	371	42.8%	551
1871-80	437	180	35.9%	355
1881-90	655	300	42.3%	438
1891-1900	388	40	34.0%	338
1901-10	339	10	23.3%	214
1911-20	146	70	N/A	N/A

* US Immigration reports, in Blessing, 'Irish' table 1, 528
§ Shaughnessy's estimates of net Catholic immigration.
#Depletion of those aged 15-24 in each initial year, for the decade given.

Moreover, after 1845, the immigrants were at least 85 per cent of Catholic background (he put it at 78 per cent to 74 per cent). Protestant surveys found New York's Irish-born to be around 90 per cent Catholic between 1900-1906. Shaughnessy made no allowance for the changing regional patterns of the emigration. In the Famine and after, it was disproportionately from the Catholic provinces: Munster and Connacht, with 65 per cent of Ulster's emigration from Catholic areas. After 1880, it was largely from the overwhelmingly Catholic west. There was also secondary immigration from amongst the Irish Catholic populations of Great Britain and Canada.

Further, Shaughnessy assumed fairly uniform rates of natural increase within the general American population, and not radically dissimilar rates amongst its Catholic ethnic subcomponents. This was quite incorrect. He also assumed that Catholic birth rates and rates of increase (where they did differ) would not be radically out of line with populations left behind in Europe. This was more accurate. In 1900, immigrant Irish women (married between 10 and 19 years) had borne the same number of children as equivalent immigrant Italian women, and almost twice the number of children borne by US born women of American-born parents. And US-born daughters of Irish immigrants had sustained that pattern. For the Irish, overall marriage and birth rates were *higher* in America than at home, even controlling for different age-pyramiding; thus so too were natural rates of increase. And the emigrant population was disproportionately youthful as well, adding considerably to this difference. Young women emigrated in numbers similar to those of young men, and few of either returned to Ireland (around 10 per cent). Before 1920 in America, then, both Catholic Irish immigration and natural increase rates were considerably higher than Shaughnessy supposed. So too, incidentally, were inter-ethnic marriage rates (at least from 1880): for quite a few Irish, the flight from Ireland became a flight from the choice of Irish spouses. Less than a fifth at mid-century, but over a third or so from the 1880s, selected non-Irish partners if often also Catholic ones (usually American-born Irish or Catholic German). The cumulative increase of the Catholic-stock pool of Irish ancestry in America was thus higher than Shaughnessy demonstrates but also more complicated. The main balancing factor is that death rates amongst the Irish were unusually high, both overall and as to infant mortality, and high rates persisted well into the twentieth century, and into the next American-born generation (and their infants also). Since *nation-wide* birth and death rates amongst immigrant stocks are almost irrecoverable with any precision before 1900, one cannot propose strict corrections to the received wisdom.

These indications perhaps support those immigrant German and other European pastors who criticised Irish-American complacency. For hundreds of thousands of Irish immigrants *were* lost to the church of their origin in the century 1820-1920; adding losses among their offspring, perhaps even approaching two millions in all (in both generations). This is quite apart from the descendants of the indentured servants of the previous century (1720-1820) who, largely male and impoverished, never had the Irish wives or the resources, or encountered the clergy, to ensure their religious continuity. Much of the loss was in rural areas. While, in 1870, almost three-quarters of the Irish-born were concentrated in the minority of urban, mining and industrial counties in twenty states in the north-east and mid-west (plus California and Louisiana), there were also 460,000 of them in 944 rural counties in the same states. And their rural birth rates were even higher than their urban ones. There were also scatterings of them across hundreds of nearly 1,000 other rural counties of the south and west. Catholic Church provision for all rural settlers was very inadequate before the 1920s, especially in the latter regions, until the foundation of the Extension Society by Francis Clement Kelly in 1905, and the spread of the use of the automobile. Much of the loss implicit in our data must have stemmed from these realities.

In 1884, the American church mandated Catholic schools in every parish, an implicit confession by the regnant Irish-American bishops that the Germans amongst them were correct: that faith was better conserved by high levels of institutionalisation and Catholic education, than by the elemental provision of church seating alone. This pattern the Germans called *Vereins -*

or *Verbandskatholizismus.* Some Irish immigrant bishops had admired it in the past, notably John Purcell of Cincinnati. He saw that though they found it difficult at times, German Catholics naturally protected their subculture. The alternative was to overcome the hostility of the wider culture (as he wrote in 1837): 'if we mixed more with the mass. The only difficulty is how to mix with it & retain our religious identity.'[4] By 1883-4, however, a more chastened Irish-American bloc now moved for the adoption of at least the schooling element of such a full subculture, led by James Gibbons, archbishop of Baltimore and Michael Corrigan, coadjutor of New York, who both had experience of the German Catholic pattern. The Irish *had* been primarily committed to church building before 1880. In their relative poverty, this stemmed from a passion to put first things first, and establish both the Real Presence and its priests amongst them, a drive given edge both by past penal proscription in Ireland, and by a clear knowledge of what happened to the Irish away from churches both in colonial and early national America, as in most of America's rural counties even in the years 1830-1900. By 1870, even this provision was uneven.[5] It was best in smaller eastern industrial cities, notably in lower New England, but also in emergent yet still also manageable cities shared with Germans and French in upstate New York and the Midwest. It was weaker in those cities where immigrants had yet to find their feet, and where numbers (as in New York city) or poverty and overwork (as in Pittsburgh and Newark) were noteworthy. These patterns are consistent with current scholarship on mid-nineteenth-century Irish Catholicism: a generally Catholic population was largely but variably churched and practising at home. Where the Irish came from regions of lower practice, as Pittsburgh's Catholics came from Ulster, one might expect less commitment at mid-century, as was the case. But the general mixing of Catholics from every province, and the work of both American and Irish clergy, meant that a common model of general churchgoing was provided in cities already by 1870, if not universally availed of. Away from the cities was another matter. What proportions of the inactive were carry-overs from Ireland, and what fractions were prompted by the unavailability of parish life in most rural counties cannot be determined.

The urgency of church building abated after 1880 to allow a shift to the goal of *universal* school provision. So did the re-concentration of newer Irish immigration into eastern cities and factory towns after 1880, after a wide diffusion between 1840 and 1880. These newer Irish came with the expectation of schooling, now universal at home, but they divided on whether they regarded such schooling as functional and state-controlled, or also religious and church managed. In Ireland, where schools were both simultaneously, few parents used them for wholly Catholic, few for wholly secular reasons.[6]

In America, migrants joined Irish Americans who had grasped that the margin of advantage enjoyed by city-dwellers in America was partly one of better education. Some realised that the religious content of the public schools was already being homogenised and diluted by the legislative and judicial priorities of the nation's elites (even among overwhelmingly church-going populations, as in Iowa). The local option of simply 'Catholicising' public schools from within by the mechanism of school-board control in areas of heavy immigration was gradually made untenable. Experience of mutual past prejudice prevented their cooperation with Protestants or evangelicals to avert this. For if forced by limited income or led by personal preference to choose public schools, 'the mass of Irish Americans clearly preferred secular to Protestant schools'. Such parents quickened America's secularisation, for a general religious culture did not survive the secularisation of public schools. Ironically this pattern, to which the Irish contributed, thus intensified both pastoral and parental demands for parochial schools.[7]

Possibly the new fusion of church and school with increasing Irish geographic concentration best explains why the highest patterns of active Catholicism amongst them occurred between 1880 and 1940, but not only for obvious reasons. Voluntary schools required community mobilisation. That so many teachers were poorly paid religious created a sense of obligation amongst Catholic parents. There was now an urban Irish-American transition to the (rural) German-American pattern of parish-and-school communities, which ensured the active Catholicism of a majority of the families within the enclaves they served. This had a further effect: immigrants from Italy, France, Mexico and Iberia could benefit from this transition in cities shared with the Irish. For no group, however, was the process a universal one by any means, not least the Irish themselves.

Essential to America's national myth since the Revolution has been the notion that it embodies the changing essences of modernity: rational, democratic, knowledge-based, contract-bound, innovative, and messianically sensible. Stratified but open educational and political processes winnow straw from chaff in gauging new harvests of possibility for future progress, and in separating the talented from the also-rans to find personnel for these splendid endeavours. Irish experience in both politics and education had been considerable, but was less roseate. Quite apart from any Christian orthodox distance from liberalism, the endless hunt for ways and means on a cramped and poor island where existent interests hedged every new endeavour gave an edge of cynicism even to the most robust participation.

Education was the key to modernity in America, and its diffusion among the Irish newcomers was the benchmark of their capacities there. Yet grand theories of captivating, much less vindicating, America's original theistic rationality from within a nascent Catholic school system were thin on the ground in the era of immigration. This had much to do with the ground-level Americans whom immigrants actually encountered. For the day-to-day contrast was less startling than one might construe from any paradigm of 'peasant Irish versus urban American'. True, in the mid-twentieth century Ireland was four decades behind America's secondary education pattern (1926-1966). In 1932 nine-tenths of pupils did not proceed beyond primary school, but those with further education tended to emigrate disproportionately, and others who went acquired more education later. But before Irish independence there had been no such contrast, as few Americans received secondary education: only 2.5 per cent of 17 years olds were High School graduates in 1880, and less than 9 per cent in 1910. In Ireland in 1881 about 2.8 per cent of Catholics aged 14 to 18 were in secondary schools, and in 1911, about 9.5 per cent or 15 per cent if those taught by Irish Christian Brothers are included. Fr John Talbot Smith was accurate in his judgement at that time (1891): 'The high school is not an American institution,' in his meaning of a common or necessary one. True, in both countries, many primary schools maintained small 'higher streams' to age 14, 15 and even older, where advanced reading (including Shakespeare), computation, and algebra were often available. On the other hand, in the years 1820-1920, the numbers of Catholics receiving third-level education was skeletal in Ireland, a century in which Catholic third-level education expanded rapidly in the United States. This reflected the prestige of college education in America, its increasing secularity, and the need to balance these.

Primary schooling was thus virtually universal in both countries after 1870 (and somewhat earlier in Ireland), if in both countries standards were rather low until the 1880s. By 1910-11, the ratio of active primary pupils to total population was 1 to 6.5 in Ireland, and 1 to 5 in the US, almost identical given differences in age distributions in the two countries. In short, almost complete primary education, skeletal secondary education, and largely informal teenage education (in primary-extension and apprenticeship courses) characterised both countries. Irish commitment to education was, however, less whole-hearted than such figures suggest. In Ireland at independence in 1921 about 70 per cent of primary pupils were present on any average day. Compulsory attendance was legally required from 1927; characteristically a similar act in 1892 had exempted the rural majority from amongst whom most emigrants were drawn. In America, rural and urban work-demands by families likewise fragmented schooling. What had changed from the mid-nineteenth century was the denominational orientation of education. From the 1860s almost all schooling in Ireland was formally Catholic (or Protestant) in context and management, by contrast with the United States.

In America, Catholic schools fully developed from the 1880s, with the system only fully in place as the century of immigration ended: in 1920, 1.8 million primary and 130,000 secondary pupils, were almost all taught (unlike in Ireland) by religious, not lay, teachers.[8] In America this private system developed in competition with a state one; in Ireland the state (before 1922) underwrote a system that meant that most schools were partly denominational (their instruction being both secular and religious, with state provision and inspection of 'secular' subjects). Indeed, as late as 1950, religious made up over 80 per cent of teachers in US Catholic primary and secondary schools. Catholic practice in America between the 1880s and 1960s was thus a product of the interplay between available Irish and then Irish-American schooling patterns. That is, between *increasingly* Catholic primary education at home, (notably after the foundation of Catholic training colleges, or normal schools, in the 1880s), and, overseas, the very specific model of voluntarily supported, religiously taught, parochial schools. If true, this might suggest that the heaviest 'leakage' we have shown by criticism of Shaughnessy's work would largely have occurred before this interplay was possible. By 1900 over 90 per cent of Irish-born migrants were affiliated to Catholic parishes in New York and practice rates were very high. In turn the products of such parishes sustained remarkably high levels of sodality and confraternity life down to World War Two: levels quite unlike those after the great Famine migration, and unlike those after the 1940s. This cycle was also related to that of religious vocation. Despite Catholic growth, the need for priests from Ireland was not marked as the sons of the 1880-1920s immigration came of age. (By contrast, between 1842 and c. 1880 and again from the 1950s, demands on Ireland for priests and religious were considerable and could be partly met in the nineteenth century, but not met at all from about 1965.) Overall the commitment of the later immigrant generations was central to funding and energising the parochial school. The community efforts required thus reinforced a transatlantic pattern of active faith.

But Irish commitment to Catholic schools, whilst strikingly higher than that of Italian immigrants, was far from universal. Indeed one is embarrassed at the hauteur with which Italian attitudes to such schooling were regarded by Irish Americans between 1900 and 1950, given how recent and gradual was Irish adherence to it in America (between the 1850s and 1880s), and given how late was their grasp of the advantage of general Catholic secondary education (from c. 1910 in America, and c. 1960 in Ireland). We have noted an ambiguity in parental use of schools in Ireland, one encouraged by the joint state/church nature of the system, and made inevitable in that poverty precluded most from more wholly Catholic private schools (except those run by the Irish Christian Brothers). We have also noted the varied levels of Irish church provision to 1870 in America. Diverse approaches by Irish immigrants to both church building and parochial schooling did not cease suddenly after the 1870s. Can we relate distinct Irish populations in America any more certainly to generalisation about improvement after 1880? I believe so, and when we do, there are some interesting connections and surprises. A correlation of the US general census of 1900 with the religious census of 1906 allows us to establish a ratio between the inhabitants in major cities of Irish-born parentage and the proportion of Roman Catholic communicant members in the same cities. These ratios are, effectively, an index of the explicit vitality or activity of the Irish Catholic component (Table Two).

Table Two

Indicators of Irish American Catholic Vitality, 1906-1908[9]

City	Date of See	Catholic % of Churchgoers†	% of Inhabitants of Ir.-b. parents#	Ratio§	% Ir. Pupils Parochial*
Baltimore	1789	45	6	.146	65
Boston	1808	69	31	.457	26
Buffalo	1847	65	10	.159	—
Chicago	1843	68	13	.186	—
Cincinnati	1821	66	10	.145	—
Cleveland	1847	45	10	.219	71
Denver	1887	44	9	.194	—
Detroit	1833	66	8	.116	46
Indianapolis	1834	37	8	.207	—
Jersey City	—	74	27	.360	—
Kansas City	1880	31	8	.245	20
Louisville	1808	58	8	131	—
Milwaukee	1843	65	4	.064	43
Minneapolis	—	47	7	.144	7
New Orleans	1793	80	7	.091	31
New York	1808	77	20	.263	47
Newark	1853	62	15	.236	76
Philadelphia	1808	52	21	.398	69
Pittsburgh	1843	58	17	.300	—
Providence	1872	76	28	.365	38
St Louis	1826	69	11	.162	—
St Paul	1850	70	11	.155	—
San Francisco	1853	81	21	.255	32
Washington	1939	32	7	.223	—

†Communicant members #Those of one Irish-born parent are included. §Percentage Irish divided by percentage Catholic communicant churchgoers (before rounding). *Percentage of primary pupils with Irish-born fathers attending parochial schools, where available.

The mean or average for the relation of Catholic churchgoing and the population of Irish parentage was .219 for the twenty-four cities. The index thus ranges from around double the overall average of twenty-four such cities, in Boston and Philadelphia, to less than half the average, in Milwaukee and New Orleans. Not surprisingly, cities of continuing Irish immigration (since 1880), like Boston and Providence, have high ratios. However, New York, still the pre-eminent Irish destination in 1906, has a ratio that is only close to the average, as do surrounding cities like Newark and Jersey City; Chicago's ratio is also below the average, although it was the one midwestern city drawing heavy Irish numbers in the years 1880-1920. In larger cities, urban impersonality and the rich confusions of pluralism also drew away American-born Irish as others. Cities whose Irish immigration was more or less completed by the 1870s, such as Milwaukee, Cincinnati, Detroit, Louisville and St Louis, usually have low ratios. Does this suggest a loss of momentum in the second generation (including migrants from other cities),[10] or inadequate commitment by the immediate post-Famine immigrants? By contrast, some 'old' Irish centres, where most of the Irish were American-born, had at least average ratios or better, as in Kansas City, and Cleveland. All this suggests that the fairly recent history of each city and diocese is involved. Yet linking the findings of the early twentieth-century practice with post-Famine patterns can lead to varied results. Surprisingly, Pittsburgh and Jersey City, which show very badly in 1870 in terms of provision of church seating, have a vigorous Irish Catholic life by 1906. But New York, Newark and Philadelphia had also probably improved since 1870 (granted the indicators are not strictly comparable); perhaps a further instance of the changing Catholicism of Irish newcomers against mid-century migrants. Both in 1906-8, as earlier in 1870, the existence of a diocesan structure made a difference; but the precise difference was plainly dependent on the energy of the local ordinary and the support he received. The effect of having no local bishop (in Jersey City and in Minneapolis) was not straightforward.

In 1870, major eastern industrial cities of ethnically mixed Catholic immigration had fared poorly in church provision, without regard to whether they had Sees or not. This was true not merely, as in New York, where numbers offset much effort, but also in more manageable centres such as Pittsburgh and Jersey City, where continuing poverty met strong anti-Irish power structures. But in Massachusetts, Rhode Island and mid-Pennsylvania, the Irish alone had dominated human-scaled cities by 1870, already fully providing for themselves, despite such poverty and exclusion: new immigrant Irish joined them. By 1900, opposition had been neutralised, and an affluent middle class helped make good the deficits of the Civil War era. That New York city, despite improvement, and its skilled Irish leadership, remained only an average centre of Irish Catholic vitality, was probably due to the persistence of second-generation Irish-American poverty and its related religious irregularity, as much as to metropolitan secularity. In the west and mid-west, where the Irish had often let the Germans (or Hispanic and French-Creole stock) initiate church work at mid-century, many of their adult offspring imitated this; and such cities did not receive newcomers from Ireland. This may raise a question about the confident Americanising rhetoric of some midwestern Irish-stock bishops, pastors and editors, which can only have annoyed those, especially Germans, who knew the real score on the ground. Was it a true estimate of such things that triggered Peter Cahensly's demand for a more multiethnic episcopate in America? And paradoxically, did the same observation lead bishops like Sebastian Messmer to seek to make the Catholic vitalities of German American parishes, anglicised in language, available to the whole church in the Midwest?

The relationship of these trends to the emergence of mass Catholic schooling among Irish Americans must thus be complex. In some cities of *low or merely average* overall Irish Catholic stock vitality, such as Baltimore, Cleveland, Newark and Milwaukee, between 65 per cent and 75 per cent of the children of Irish-born fathers were in parochial schools. In these cities, a strong German tradition of parish schooling existed and was often adapted by Irish prelates like James Gibbons and John J. O'Connor. In Chicago and Cincinnati, the pattern was co-opted by Irish bishops from the start, by John Purcell, James Duggan and Patrick Feehan, anticipating the national policy of 1884. On the other hand, in some cities of *high*-level vitality and continuing immigration to factory life, such as Boston, Fall River and Providence, only between a quarter and one-half of such children attended parochial schools. Even the proportion of the children of American-born Irish going to them remained relatively static from 1880-1925. School fees, however low, may have been a deterrent. Older emphases on mere church provision thus merged with Irish working-class populations to help depress levels of parochial school provision. So paradoxically did rapid suburbanisation, in the era of cheap street-car systems.

This New England pattern of high-level church provision and low-level parochial school provision merits examination.[11] It did not stem from imported culture or traditions: for equally both illiterate and literate Irish immigrant fathers sent their children to grade schools, even in the case of labourers. In 1900 differences from native Yankee schooling patterns due to background and cultural factors had almost wholly disappeared. By then the Irish were ready to equal native-stock attainments, in school as in society. Perhaps inadequate integration between the Americanised Irish and the recently come delayed church schools. As well, Irish-American politicians were so ready to 'Hibernianise' the public schools through employment and school-board practices that they cut the demand from their Irish constituents for such schools. In its industrial towns, over a fifth of public-school teachers were daughters of Irish-born fathers, ranging from 24 per cent in Boston to 50 per cent in Worcester, a pattern unequalled in any other region. Indeed smaller factory towns in New England were a crazy-quilt of schooling patterns in 1908. In Lynn, two-thirds of Irish fathers' children were in parochial schools, in nearby Lowell, only two-fifths.

The real explanation for the pattern may lie deeper, in an anthropology of faith-transmission. To simplify boldly, a western (and outer Ulster) Irish model, identified in the 1850s with the leadership of Archbishop John MacHale of Tuam, rested assured in the church and community transmission of the faith. In the Catholic rural neighbourhood, a uniform Christian culture and moral constraints were so all pervasive that pastor and family were believed largely sufficient to the transmission of the faith (which was partly wrong, as recent scholarship has indicated!). With huge and growing Irish dominance of the Catholicism of New England towns, such patterns were trusted to perform the same task in America; the religious diversity of many New England towns (though not Boston) actually diminished between 1890-1906.[12] Elsewhere there was a more programmatic strategy of faith maintenance (in Ireland identified with Cardinal Paul Cullen, with roots going back to the mid-eighteenth century in Leinster and Munster). It grasped the national initiative from 1884 in America. But it was fully amplified twenty years later, with the movement to create Confraternities of Christian Doctrine, in large dioceses, to reach children who were not attending parochial schools. The CCD then 'took off' complementary to the flowering of Catholic schooling in the 1920s.

Of the great east-coast archdiocesan cities, Philadelphia, with a long tradition of such schools, placed most such children (over two-thirds) in parochial schools by 1908. New York, while thus placing only 47 per cent, none the less schooled 25,500 of them, the largest single such concentration in the country, and 11,000 more than in Philadelphia. 12 per cent of the children of Italian fathers were in parochial schools in New York city and in Philadelphia, with probably the best 'Irish' parochial system in the country, 36 per cent of Italian children were educated in such schools, showing the influence exercised by the Irish. In other cities, especially some in the Midwest and the West, Irish attendance at parochial school was quite low: in Kansas City, less than a fifth, in Minneapolis, less than a tenth.

All this confirms for the diaspora what historians of Irish domestic religion now stress: the variety of Irish Catholic patterns. But it also confirms that Catholic vitality can also be qualitatively assessed. Community, family, schooling, press and leadership each protected individuals and networks against uncritical absorption in the pell-mell secularities of the great society. The size and Catholic contribution of the Irish-American middle class in New York and Philadelphia, with the scope of their third-level institutions in these cities by 1900, suggests one pattern. Somewhat higher *rates* of Irish middle-class penetration in midwestern states, suggests another: there investment in churches and schools was high, but that in colleges was then lower.

From 1890, rapidly from 1910, commitment to Catholic high schooling began to expand following national trends. Catholic colleges had provided key elites in the past, and much of their course-work was, in effect, secondary education until the 1920s or after. Now high schooling was to provide more systematic advantage for greater numbers, to embody for Catholics the democratisation of knowledge-based society; this meant a shift in Irish expectations.[13] In New England, in 1880 in Providence, less than 10 per cent of the children of Irish immigrants went on to high school; by 1915, over 40 per cent did, and by 1925, almost 75 per cent. Even by the 1880s and 1890s, the young thus educated moved upwards as against their fathers' achievements, if not always from blue-collar to white-collar occupations. By the early twentieth century, this pattern was helping re-educate the Irish about schooling, even as their rising power was neutralising their old fear of 'Yankee ascendancy'. Before this further education was not greatly prized, apart from the preparation of clergy, professionals, businessmen and administrators. The special patterns of privilege in New England, favouring a Yankee upper and middle class, and confining many Irish to factory work, had perhaps reinforced such limited expectations there. In the Midwest, California and New York, where the Irish gained white-collar and skilled occupations more rapidly, the change of outlook came earlier.

A nationwide pattern emerged. Those born in 1884/5 or before to Irish fathers usually completed only primary school, if that. Those born in 1906-15 had some high-school education, even in the northeastern US. By 1915 those in Catholic high schools (even when from poorer or broken families) were more likely to finish their course than those in public high schools, whether Irish Americans or others. Thus widening social expectations could be, as it were, 'domesticated' and made familiar and successful in a Catholic school context. But the Irish also advanced in public school systems now notably less hostile to Catholics. Overall then, Irish group pressures and an episcopal change of direction joined to effect major change. An exception shows this: Archbishop George Mundelein of Chicago stopped financial aid to parish high schools in the 1920s, confident the community would now bear the full costs.[14] However, that ratios of students in Catholic high school *never* caught up with, much less surpassed, the ratio of Catholic primary pupils, to their equivalent numbers in public schools, suggests a certain ambivalence was built into the high-school enterprise.

The value of high-school education was now evident to its consumers, upwardly mobile Irish Americans. Its most successful providers, such as the Jesuits, understood the workaday horizons of most of the parents who paid for it. They also sought to upgrade the catechetical formation of primary school to a workable apologetic requisite to urban American life. But they were not in the business of creating a Catholic counterculture. The strain of providing an endorsement of the civilisation, implicit in the title of the main Jesuit journal, *America*, was all-pervasive. Their innocent claims to embody what was best in the Republic's rationality, humanity and constitutionalism were also reassuring. Any lingering social or ethnic class resentments in parents were salved by a further flattery: that working people best represented these values, and made America and its Catholicism what they were. Heretofore much Irish-American journalism had been very different. Whether as exploited outsiders, or as a marginal lower middle class, better off but unassimilated, insecure and distanced, the Irish had consumed great quantities of writing critical of America. They had updated this outlook from 1892-1916 by relating it to progressive and muckraking critiques of the power structures of the time. If they stopped short of socialist antagonism, they often fused Catholic insights and sensibility with such mistrust, at the very time that they declared their pride as citizens of America. The extraordinary turnaround whereby articulate Irish-American educators and journalists, from 1917 or so, became praise-poets of the society, was unprecedented in its scale and new lack of ambiguity. Wartime mobilisation, and the anti-foreign and anti-radical movements that accompanied it, followed by the Republican triumph (1920-32) and nativist movements of the 1920s, created an external context. As late as 1901, the American Federation of Catholic Societies emerged as a joint German- and Irish-Catholic venture in a climate of mistrust. Yet in 1919, in a climate of confidence, the bishops themselves established the National Catholic Welfare Council, to 'unify, coordinate, encourage, promote and carry on all Catholic activities in the United States …' This new outlook thus helped the upwardly bound of the period to overcome their community's past partial distrust of America. The strident accommodation preached in the 1920s also matched the new requirements of expanded Irish-American education, and explained why the new course of life was fully Catholic and American. In short, a Catholic *ralliement*. It pushed to the very limits that moderated enthusiasm for the 'great experiment' of America's republican polity and society allowed by those two letters of Leo XIII, *Testem Benevolentiae* and *Longinqua Oceani*.

There is a point at which the theory of the Jesuits, John Courtney Murray and Richard J. Regan, so influential at mid-century, is culturally, although not intellectually, rooted in these 'bromides' (as Americans call cheering but incomplete ideas).[15] The record of Robert Gannon, F. X. Talbot, Daniel Lord and Moorehouse Millar, all Jesuits prominent or emergent in the inter-war years (and all but the last Irish American), suggests this. The original idea of Tocqueville and Brownson that Catholicism was congruent with, even necessary to, American republican culture, was given early expression by Michael O'Connor, bishop of Pittsburgh 1843-60, and his contemporary, Boston editor Thomas D'Arcy Magee. A century later, the thesis had been sharpened by new demands.[16] Theistic, pluralist and patriotic, by 1960 it had won over new Irish immigrants in America, by comparison with their siblings in Ireland. This helped prepare the ground for both the naiveté and the achievements of the post-Vatican II decades in the United States, in post-immigrant communities of the suburbanising Irish. Self-criticism was often absent. For the child was father to the man, not a changeling, an interloper or a stranger. Those aged in their forties or fifties during Vatican II had been products of the parochial and Catholic high schools and colleges of the years 1925-45, everywhere schooled in the notion that American Catholics, and especially the Irish-descended among them, knew best how to uphold what was best, indeed universal, in America's polity and promise, and lead the offspring of more recent European immigrations into the light of Catholicism and America united. Arguably, this approach had been moulded by the prioritisation of philosophical over theological training. More certainly affected were those who matured during the wartime and early Cold War mobilisation of the authority of national culture.[17] One of these has himself diagnosed the process with detachment.[18] The tendency to merge the genuine perspectives of Americanisation with normative standards for the mutual adjustment of Catholicism and modernity was always strong in the American-born Irish, but was even more marked among these generations.[19] Fortunately many bishops during these years, usually robustly plebeian in origin, had often wiser minds, evident in a more balanced sense of whom to read in theology and church affairs.[20]

Catholic European visitors, even back then, had found the mixture an inspiring if jejune one. Even before the 1950s fuss about the community's intellectual attainments, Evelyn Waugh and Frank Sheed would note its shallowness or speak frankly of it.[21] They made too little allowance for this Catholic culture's recent birth, its minority status, or for its paternity in a poignant social history, that of a people caught up in Tocqueville's race for individualised and familial comfort, but haunted by the ghosts of past rural poverty; a people accompanied on their way by a chronic mix of long and hard work with costly family support, uncertain social gains, and expensive home-ownership. In the 1960s, later European visitors were blinded to this 'Only Yesterday' by the new affluence and style of Irish Americans.

This culture did not always make for good relations with Italian Catholics in America. The greatest immigration numbers between 1880-1920, the era of total Irish dominance in the church, were of course of the Italians; today they have inherited much of the urban church infrastructure built by the earlier Irish. Perhaps at first the smaller dioceses, and the more communal New England Irish parishes, may have handled things more successfully, because more personally, than did more bureaucratic Irish archdioceses like New York and Chicago, the very ones in which Italian power of numbers eased their later ascent.[22] Older scholarship emphasises the stresses between the two groups 'well into the early twentieth century'.[23] Some Irish-born editors sought immigration restriction to protect Irish-American workingmen during the depression of the 1890s, if only one was gratuitously hostile.[24] The 'depressed' Irish were largely the less-educated working-class newcomers competing directly with southern Italians, and the offspring of both remained estranged in poorer city districts a generation later.[25] Established or educated Irish Americans were more open. Some Irish Americans sought to teach each other the value of the Italians: 'there is no nationality in the Catholic religion. It is not Italian or French or English.' When the Vatican Choir came to Boston in 1919, appropriately it sang in the Irish-controlled Mechanics' Hall.[26] This better approach was prepared by a literary apologetic that defended Catholic values in context of a somewhat romanticised Latinism set against an exclusive Anglo-Saxonism. Again, many Irish understood the necessity of solidarity in face of both anti-immigration and exploitative patterns in American life, and knew that cultural and religious deficits among Italian immigrants were due to political and social oppression at home, and, some said, to papal opposition to past nationalist objectives. By 1970 Italian Americans constituted the dominant foreign stock in New York City, Philadelphia, San Francisco, Pittsburgh, Newark, Patterson (NJ), and Cleveland, and were also major elements in Boston, Providence and Buffalo. Half the country's bishops were still Irish American, however, and only 3 per cent were Italian; but then four times more priests over 55 were Irish than Italian. This took time to alter; and the Irish have always tended to confuse camaraderie with *caritas*. Today, in the rush to demythologise their religious past by a section of Irish Americans, it is sometimes Italian-American teachers and religious who ask them to reconsider.

Too much optimism can disguise real problems. To return to Shaughnessy's work, as a former teacher, he granted that 'the lack of Catholic education certainly must have caused some loss to the church'. But he did not see how great this loss was. For most American-Irish children before 1900, and a majority even thereafter, attended public schools, which were increasingly secular. Comprehensive ancillary CCD education was not nationally available until the 1930s.[27] By then the era of Irish migration was over. Already in 1900, the 'triple melting pot' had emerged. Roughly one-third of the 'Irish' second generation were of ethnically mixed parentage by then. The old notion that the faith could be passed on by kin and community alone thus lacked real foundation. Those raised in 1925-45, those maturing after 1935, naturally sought to bridge the tensions between themselves and kin and friends schooled in secular modes, or married across cultural, even religious, lines. For them, mixing inclusive Catholic theologies with the comprehensive civic nationalism of the era thus served a vital purpose. Earlier, in the decades around World War One, aware of the injustice of past criticism, and just granted fully autonomous church status in 1908, American Catholics were not ready to examine the record of painful things.

Those who owe the Catholicism of family members to American-Irish backgrounds, and have taken some measure of what any Catholic formation in modern America was up against, will always temper such insight with humility. They are conscious that many of the present global strategies in the 'war against population' may have precedent and origin in a determination, perhaps since the reports of the Dillingham Commission, and certainly since the abortive and suppressed religious census of the mid-1950s, to halter the extraordinary rise of the American Catholic Irish, both as to its subculture, and, later, even as to its robust fertility. The indications of such a tendency, among some elements in America's elites, are well known: the Oregon law compelling secular education, thrown down by the Supreme Court in 1925; the campaign against the Italo-German-Irish presidential candidate, Alfred Emmanuel Smith in 1928; the feuds over secularism and aid to Catholic schools in 1947-49; the federal laws and judicial decisions, 1947-68 constituting humanism a 'religion' and yet a special beneficiary of federal neutrality in matters of religious belief. Finally came the escalating campaign against higher Catholic fertility in the 1960s, backed by major foundations and government departments.[28]

But critics are also conscious of the common weakness affecting *all* who negotiated life in this past century in that 'one nation, under God, indivisible' to which so many millions of Irish-American children pledged allegiance each school day. In May, they did so even as they bedecked May altars with flowers to the Virgin Mary. She had been chosen, under the title of the Immaculate Conception, as patroness of the United States on the instigation of the Dublin-born Francis Kenrick, archbishop of Philadelphia, even as the Great Famine began and the new Irish flooded in.[29] Almost a century and a half later, sociologist Andrew Greeley established that among many unpractising, late twentieth century American Catholics, personal dedication to Mary as *theotokos,* the guarantee of their nation's saving theism, survived freshly and strongly when much else had gone. Francis Kenrick knew his people and he taught them well. Raised and formed before the devotional revolution either of Pius IX or of his Irish exponent Paul Cullen, this Dubliner heroically advanced the schooling and theological instruction of Irish newcomers in his care (first in Philadelphia, then Baltimore).[30] He helped establish a model pattern; had it been sooner and more widely adopted, Shaughnessy's fond dream that few Irish were ever lost to the church might have been the actuality.

Connections between religious practice, sound formation and vital Catholicity persist, and are indeed highlighted by the very problems now so widespread. As family life became contested in America from the 1970s, its solidity among Italians became clear, sustained as much by communal ties as by educational provision. Yet there was a link between their lower fertility, in the third generation, and their schooling which was more commonly secular rather than Catholic.[31] If social bonds protected some of their culture, as among the Irish in nineteenth-century New England, this too was becoming problematic. Few were convinced by those Catholic writers who sought to substitute the communal for the fuller realities of church life. We have observed Providence, today a relatively intimate city of intermarried Irish, Italian and French-Canadian stock. When the population controllers prematurely proclaimed the end of 'Catholic fertility,' more careful scholars studied its relationships in Providence to Mass attendance and frequent reception of communion; birth rates held up amidst the minority of women still regular in both.[32] Perhaps the long interplay between German, Irish and Italian experience in America suggests that not episcopal leadership, or local parish, or close family ties, or local community, or religious schools, could sustain Catholicism against America's secularity in isolation, but that each element was an inseparable support for the other. This proved especially so in a mass society that largely lacked that *campanilismo,* whereby, at its best, Christian faith became embedded in local mutuality over generations of shared history and doctrinal and moral instruction.

CHAPTER TWENTY

Church and state in modern Ireland, 1923-1970: An appraisal reappraised

Thomas Bartlett

In 1971, the late Professor John H. Whyte published his seminal work, *Church and State in Modern Ireland* in which he offered a coherent narrative of the general course of church (i.e the Roman Catholic Church) and state (i.e. 26-county Ireland) relations during the first fifty years of independence.[1] In particular, he reconstructed in great detail the Mother and Child Scheme of 1951, commonly regarded as the *cause célèbre* of church-state conflict during that period. Whyte also offered an interim assessment of the archbishop of Dublin, John Charles McQuaid (1940-72), described by him as 'probably ... the most-talked-about Irish prelate'.[2] Lastly, in his conclusion, he sought to answer a question that had been posed frequently by both hostile and friendly critics of the new state: how much influence did the Catholic Church in fact wield in post-independent Ireland? Whyte's lucid narrative, his dispassionate analysis of the issues involved, his thoughtful insights into the respective roles both of members of the hierarchy and of the various governments during the period, and his measured conclusions, won for him widespread scholarly accolades, and have earned the volume a number of reprints. Nearly thirty years after publication, his book is still an essential starting-point for any consideration of church-state relations during the first decades of independence.

The book is not, however, without its limitations. It was in the nature of things that the work could not be archivally based, and that the narrative would instead have to be pieced together through a close reading of published material (especially newspapers, magazines, lenten pastorals, papal encyclicals and such like) and that it would have to draw extensively on interviews conducted by the author with the surviving 'key players', notably the then archbishop of Dublin, John Charles McQuaid. But perhaps Professor Whyte ought to have avoided making his lack of an archival 'bottom' a positive virtue? 'People do not put everything they think onto paper,' he noted complacently. 'It is possible that some of my informants have revealed more to me in conversation ... than would ever be evident to a scholar working solely from documents in the future.'[3] In the event, the availability since the late 1980s of official Irish government documents for most of the period 1923-

60, the opening of the private papers of such politicians as Eamon de Valera, and latterly, the release of large portions of John Charles McQuaid's voluminous correspondence have enabled a dedicated group of historians to present a number of important corrections to Professor Whyte's narrative and, in general, to offer a much more nuanced and rounded picture of church-state relations than that hitherto available. Thirty years on, a reappraisal, however tentative, of Professor Whyte's pioneering appraisal might be thought timely.[4]

I

By way of introduction to his work, Professor Whyte discussed five traditions that offered insights into the special position of the Catholic Church in twentieth-century Ireland.[5] First, he noted the undoubted fact that not only was Ireland – or at least independent Ireland – a Catholic country with upwards of 90 per cent of the population *professing* Catholicism, but that it was unique in the Catholic world for the very high proportion of those Catholics who were *practising*. Second, and in some respects paradoxically, he pointed out that in the nineteenth century the very large number of practising Catholics had not in fact produced unquestioning acceptance of church teaching on issues such as agrarian crime or broader national issues. Nor would it mean automatic compliance on such matters in the future: the Irish bishops' joint pastoral of October 1922 denouncing the republican opponents of the Free State government was a dead letter; while routine phillipics against the Irish Republican Army in 1931, 1936 and on into the 1950s similarly fell on deaf ears. Irish Catholics had a tradition of compartmentalising their loyalties – and the bishops were mindful of this. Third, Professor Whyte emphasised the tradition of 'aloofness' between church and state in Ireland since the early nineteenth century. The Catholic Church had kept its distance from the British government during the nineteenth century except where vital issues – e.g. education – were concerned, and it had shown no desire to take over as the established church in Ireland after disestablishment in 1869. By and large, Professor Whyte argued that this tradition of 'aloofness' continued well into the post-1922 period. The new state had no role in the appointment of bishops. There was no demand for a concordat to lay out the respective rights of church and state. Priests could not be elected to the legislature. And there was no special recognition of canon law. In his estimation, this distance between church and state 'helps to explain the relative harmony of their relations' in the period 1923 to 1970. Fourth, and somewhat in contradiction to the previous point, Professor Whyte stressed the enormous and probably unique grip of the Catholic Church on education in Ireland. The Catholic Church in effect controlled the vast majority of primary schools, a similar proportion of secondary schools and almost all 'special' schools –

reformatories, industrial schools and indeed, orphanages. In additon, there were Catholic universities to which – unlike in other countries that also had Catholic third-level institutions – Irish Catholics were directed if they wished to pursue their studies to degree standard. In short, the Catholic church's 'aloofness' from the state stopped at the school door and, it must be admitted, the state (and successive ministers of education) were quite prepared to acquiesce in the church's control over education. This wholly unequal 'balance of power' between church and state is nicely brought out by a former Minister of Education, Pádraig Faulkner, when he recalled being told on taking up his ministerial appointment that 'the archbishop [of Dublin] never called at the Department of Education in Marlborough St. My officials explained to me that should ministers want to discuss a matter with him, they met at the archbishop's house'.[6] Lastly, Professor Whyte pointed to what he identified as 'an authoritarian strain in Irish culture': the fact that, while Ireland was indisputably a democracy, there was none the less an autocratic style of management, and a certain culture of arrogance that underpinned it, that was approved and admired everywhere – among government ministers, in civil service departments, in the universities, in the teacher-training colleges, in the schools, in the homes, at the workplace, on the farms – and in the church. Thirty years on, how valuable are these keys to understanding the course of church-state relations in twentieth-century Ireland?

The short answer is that they are inadequate *on their own* and that they need to be expanded and nuanced considerably. Whyte himself consciously avoided the question of whether widespread religious practice correlated in any meaningful way with deep religious conviction. Yet this surely must be addressed in some detail since it might be argued that the visible religiosity of the Irish merely reflected the cultural dominance of the main socio-economic class – the strong farmers – from whom the clergy were disproportionately drawn and whose values were hegemonic in Irish society. Once removed from that environment and its prevailing ethos – for example, by emigration – Irish religious practice diminished considerably. The harsh reality was that Irish society in the nineteenth and twentieth centuries was not just one which tolerated a very high rate of emigration: it was one whose very existence in fact *required* a constant haemorrhage of those people who were deemed surplus to its requirements. It was thus an emigrant society that needed a religious ideology that could reconcile huge numbers of people to permanent exile abroad or to lifelong celibacy – if they stayed at home. Hence the lay obsession with questions of sexual morality – an obsession which the clergy could not but share and give voice to; hence the near silence from both laity and clergy in the face of depopulation and resulting social anomie. Quite how these societal demands were impressed upon those seminarians pursuing their vocational training and intellectual formation in Maynooth and elsewhere is a topic which still remains unexplored.

Again, it might be argued that Whyte's treatment of the history of the Catholic Church's relations with the (British) state in the nineteenth century was altogether too perfunctory and lacking in perspective. It is not just that Whyte defined church and state in much too limited terms. There were at least four 'states' that the Irish bishops would have to deal with: the Free State (addressed by Whyte), the Northern state (largely ignored by him), the English state (ditto) and lastly the Vatican State; in this last case, the bishops were as determined as the most convinced northern Protestant that 'Home Rule' in independent Ireland would not mean 'Rome rule' over them. Some deft diplomatic footwork would be required from the hierarchy in order to resolve some of the potential for division that these issues offered.[7]

Moreover, while it is true that the Catholic Church cultivated an attitude of 'aloofness' to the (British) state during the nineteenth century, this was at no time as clear-cut as Whyte made out: Donal Kerr's work, for example, has revealed a much more involved stance on the part of the Catholic hierarchy in the 1840s.[8] What may also be suggested is that the very notion of looking to the late nineteenth century alone for the context within which the Catholic Church in the twentieth century would act, is in itself flawed. Between 1900 and 1923 the institutional Catholic Church witnessed a transition in Ireland from British rule to native rule; and this break with the past, and the violence which accompanied it, undoubtedly meant a period of profound adjustment in the years after 1923. But such a breach was not in fact unprecedented: it might be argued that the shift from the constraints of the 'Penal Era' to that of major Catholic institutional expansion – roughly 1780 to 1830 – posed as many problems for a Catholic Church which alone in Catholic Europe remained outside state control. In this respect, it is surely the career of John Thomas Troy, archbishop of Dublin, 1786-1820, rather than (as has been customary) that of Cardinal Paul Cullen, archbishop of Dublin, 1852-1878, which is the more appropriate to set beside the life, times, and achievements of the most prominent member of the hierarchy in the fifty years after independence, Archbishop McQuaid.[9]

Lastly, Whyte's attempt to set the context within which to view the conduct of the church post-1923, by and large ignores the huge impact of partition on that institution – Bishop McHugh of Derry declared that he and his fellow northern bishops would prefer another fifty years of British rule to 'a divided Ireland'.[10] Equally, the traumatic impact of the pitiless Irish Civil War on the hierarchy, at the time and later, has surely to be accorded due recognition. Who can say what effect the death of a much-loved brother, shot dead in a republican ambush in Westport, Co Mayo, had on Dr McQuaid, the future archbishop of Dublin? At the time, however, it was the ineffective episcopal lobbying in favour of clemency, largely conducted behind the scenes by Archbishop Byrne of Dublin, along with some highly public (and bitterly resented) denunciations of republicans that left the bishops and the church throughout the twenties and the thirties (and later) dangerously exposed to a lay backlash.[11]

II

Professor Whyte's discussion of the process by which 'the Catholic moral code becomes enshrined in the law of the state' in the 1920s and 1930s has retained its value.[12] He showed clearly the firm consensus that existed among all the political parties where 'moral issues' were concerned, and their determination to act decisively. Thus William Cosgrave refused to legalise divorce in the 1920s, while Eamon de Valera made it unconstitutional in his 1937 Constitution. Cosgrave's government brought in censorship of films and books, while that of de Valera regulated those notorious occasions of sin, dance-halls. And, while Cosgrave's government banned the advocacy of contraception, de Valera's prohibited the import or sale of contraceptives. Little enough of this appears to have been at the direct behest of the hierarchy, for there was in fact no need for it to make representations on any of these questions. Politicians of all hues – Cumann na nGaedheal, Fianna Fáil, or indeed Labour – vied with each other to give legislative shape to the dominant ethos of what was essentially an emigrant society. There were of course a few protests – from some Protestants and from a few literary types – but these could be ignored. On these matters, church and state were as one.

Perhaps clerical involvement was more pronounced in the drafting of the Irish Constitution of 1937? Here it would seem that Professor Whyte's claim that that Constitution 'was clearly very much Mr de Valera's own creation' could be faulted in the light of the evidence which has emerged from both the de Valera and McQuaid archives. Not surprisingly, Eamon de Valera had been unhappy from the beginning with the Constitution of the Free State, viewing it as a British imposition, possibly 'pagan', to be got rid of at the first opportunity.[13] Orthodox Catholic opinion was scarcely more favourable: the 1922 arrangement was regarded as 'forced upon us by a foreign non-Catholic power'; it was 'exotic, unnatural and quite foreign to the native tradition'.[14] In September 1936 de Valera wrote to the Jesuit social thinker, Fr Edward Cahill, seeking his assistance in drawing up 'a genuinely Christian constitution'.[15] Cahill was keen to become involved. He sent de Valera a copy of his book, *The Framework of a Christian State*, with specific pages referred to so that de Valera could devise a constitution which would mark a 'definite break with the liberal and non-Christian type of state'. Cahill, mentioned in

Whyte's book solely in connection with his hostility towards the Freemasons, was in fact to play an important role in formulating some of those general principles that underpinned the Constitution of 1937 and which were – in his words – 'merely an application of the papal teaching and of the conclusion of Catholic philosophy'.[16] For example, some responsibility for the wording of the article on the family and on that prohibiting divorce (Art 41) may be attributed to Fr Cahill.[17]

Eamon de Valera also drew on the advice of the then headmaster of Blackrock College and later archbishop, John Charles McQuaid. McQuaid was highly flattered to be invited to participate: 'Any time you want me,' he told de Valera in March 1937, 'I shall be delighted to go over [to your office]' and a month later he wrote: 'should I be able to serve, now or in the future even to a small degree, I should like to think that you will not hesitate to ask me.'[18] Accordingly, in a series of letters written to de Valera in the spring of 1937, McQuaid subjected the proposed constitution to close inspection, and especially he scrutinised the clauses in it dealing with widows and orphans, the family, and that which described the Roman Catholic Church as occupying a 'special position' in Ireland while it merely 'recognised' other Christian faiths (and the Jewish religion).[19] So far as widows and orphans were concerned, he revealingly suggested that the state should step back from total support for them: 'It is unfair,' he explained, 'to expect, as so many do, that the state will do everything.' As for the family, he heartily agreed with de Valera that 'the normal place for a woman is in the home', and while he noted that 'the feminists are getting angry and are moving into action ... they seem stung' by this, he consoled himself with the reflection that 'their thoughts are very confused'. In any case, he reckoned that the papal encyclicals, *Casti Connubii* and *Quadragesimo Anno*, would provide a complete answer to their criticisms. Referring to the proposed religious article, he told de Valera that 'I have composed very carefully the draft and attach two notes.'

In years to come, McQuaid clearly felt that his suggested emendations in these areas had been, by and large, accepted. In 1943, when he was archbishop, he wrote to de Valera acknowledging his gift of an inscribed copy of the Constitution. McQuaid took the opportunity to thank de Valera for allowing him 'the privilege of having been linked with you in the preparation of the *Bunreacht* [constitution]', and he expressed his 'gratitude to God that you have been able to put into effect as the natural law so many clauses over which we have laboured very much and into the small hours of many mornings'. (He might also have thanked de Valera for making successful representations to the Vatican in 1940 to have the youthful headmaster appointed archbishop of Dublin over the heads of the other aspirants.)[20]

In respect of the recently revealed contributions of both Fr Cahill and Dr

McQuaid, it would seem, then, that Professor Whyte's verdict that the Constitution of 1937 was de Valera's 'own creation' requires substantial modification. But is this really so? Admittedly, de Valera was a committed Catholic anxious to keep abreast of the latest Catholic social teaching, and he was undoubtedly sincere in his requests for advice; but he was also a canny political operator. It was entirely in keeping with his political style to embark on a course of action – or a formula of words – and *then* seek clerical endorsement. Moreover, where such was not forthcoming, de Valera was confident enough to press on regardless – he had after all endured clerical condemnation during the Civil War. Fr Cahill, for example, sought to enshrine various articles in the new Constitution on censorship, contraception and on the 'just wage'. He also wanted a constitutional prohibition on freemasonry in the judiciary, and he proposed a 'concordat' between church and state addressing (among other things) the question of 'Sunday opening'. Intriguingly, Cahill appears to have advocated an article dealing with those 'economic evils which even still threaten the very life of the historic Irish nation'. These he identified as 'bachelorship, depopulation of the countryside and emigration, especially of young women'. None of these saw the light of day. Cahill accepted that he could not 'outstep the limits of what you asked me to do' and he was content to accept de Valera's decisions as final. It was a similar case with Dr McQuaid; he met regularly with de Valera but there was never any doubt about who was in charge: 'I bow willingly to those who are placed above [me] and who give their decisions,' McQuaid told de Valera.

Cahill's and McQuaid's lack of influence was especially pronounced in the article dealing with the Catholic Church's 'special position'. Neither was happy with the formulation that was finally arrived at (nor indeed were other members of the Catholic hierarchy such as Cardinal MacRory). Cahill castigated the use in the Constitution of the words 'the Church of Ireland' to designate the main Protestant church, because in his view such a description implied 'approval of a piece of lying propaganda' and he expressed the 'hope that it will be changed'. For his part, McQuaid was disturbed by the inclusion of the phrase 'other Christian churches' in the Constitution. He explained that he was not sure that they were, in fact, really Christian since in his view so many denied the divinity of Christ that they could more properly be regarded as merely 'ethical'. However, in this case, as in others, McQuaid had no choice but to yield to de Valera's judgment: 'You may have already settled the question,' he noted lamely, after offering one of his increasingly futile recommendations. In other words, the conclusion seems to be that while Cahill and McQuaid undoubtedly had a major input into the wording of what became subsequently the more contentious articles of the Constitution, the document as a whole remained de Valera's responsibility. The Taoiseach accepted clerical advice where it accorded with his own viewpoint; he ignored it when it did not.[21] It may therefore be suggested that Whyte's conclusion as to the parentage of the Constitution still retains its validity, despite the opening of various archives.

III

Professor Whyte's analysis of the ill-fated Mother and Child scheme of 1951 has in general worn well, though the details and the context must now be supplemented by Ruth Barrington's work.[22] As a political scientist, Whyte could well appreciate the weaknesses of the coalition government headed by John A. Costello; and he concluded that Noel Browne, the ill-fated minister responsible for the scheme, was abandoned not because of episcopal denunciation, principally by Dr McQuaid, but because he was a threat to an already fragile government. Dr Browne himself seems to have grudgingly recognised something of this. Admittedly, in his acerbic (and moving) autobiography written many years later, he fixed on Archbishop McQuaid as his 'most powerful and uncompromising opponent', but he also maintained that he was ousted on foot of a plot orchestrated by jealous cabinet colleagues.[23] Certainly, when the storm blew up over his proposals, Dr Browne found himself very much on his own. As Alvin Jackson has commented: 'The mother-and-child affair, far from being a crisis in church-state relations, highlights the solidity of the consensus on social and religious values within the Ireland of the early 1950s.'[24] Perhaps future research into this episode will focus on the shadowy role played by the Irish Medical Association? There are some indications that that organisation, with its venomous hostility to 'socialised medicine', had great influence behind the scenes. It may yet prove to be the case that it was the scalpel, not the crozier, that brought down Browne.

Whyte's judgment, that the whole episode told us nothing about the nature of church-state relations, has, I think, stood the test of time. The *Irish Times*'s comment in 1951 that 'the Roman Catholic Church would seem to be the effective government of this country' was entirely wrongheaded; the fact that de Valera's government subsequently put through substantially similar legislation in the face of opposition from the hierarchy speaks volumes in this regard.[25] The reality is that Costello was glad to be rid of Browne: in a coalition government he was the classic 'loose cannon on a rolling deck'.[26] De Valera, having endured clerical condemnation in the Civil War, was made of sterner stuff, and besides, he controlled a united cabinet. Noel Browne later jibed that while de Valera would stand up to the bishops on the issue of a republic, he would back down where 'the lives of mothers and children in Ireland' were concerned; but this is well wide of the mark.[27] In 1953, the hierarchy was brought into line, bought off with a few concessions, and the minister of health, Dr James Ryan, put through his legislation. In the end, Fianna Fáil and de Valera won out over the hierarchy.

IV

In his discussion of the politics of Irish social policy in the 1940s and 1950s, Professor Whyte devoted much attention to the role played by Archbishop McQuaid in these matters. However, his remarks on him covered much more than his part in the Mother and Child scheme. In his wide-ranging interviews with the archbishop, Whyte provided subsequent researchers with much useful testimony on the key events in church-state relations between 1937 and 1970. McQuaid's candour on these issues was remarkable, given his well-attested reputation for reticence and his known disdain for explanation. It was clear that Whyte and McQuaid were comfortable with each other, and that Professor Whyte was eager to hear a story which the archbishop, for his part, was keen to recount. The recent opening of large portions of the McQuaid archive will undoubtedly mean that the archbishop's memory will be tested against the records of the time.

This is not the place to assess the career of Dr McQuaid in the light of the opening of his vast archive (more than 700 boxes of documents). The winter 1998 issue of *Studies* has indicated some of the directions which future research might take. As a pioneer of Catholic social services, as a diocesan administrator at a time of huge social change, as an educationalist, as a theologian, and as a builder of schools and hospitals, Dr McQuaid's career was an extraordinary one, and the quality and quantity of the papers now made available are eloquent testimony to his enormous range of interests. It is now commonplace to argue that he ought to have retired in the early 1960s. He was, and remained, a cold warrior: in 1948 he had broadcast an appeal on Irish radio for funds to help 'the Catholics of Italy in their struggle against the communists' in the general election,[28] and it was a proud moment for him when, as a gesture of solidarity with their fellow Catholics, 'the papal flag flew alone on the headquarters of the Irish Transport and General Workers Union where the Citizens' Army had flown its Plough and Five Stars in former times.'[29] He was a correspondent of John Foster Dulles, J. Edgar Hoover and various American generals. As such, he found the new liberalism of the late 1960s uncongenial. He was no ecumenist: he had opposed the Mercier Society and the Pillar of Fire Society, and he harboured an Ulster Catholic's suspicion of Irish Protestants.[30] He banned Catholics from attending, except by his permission, Trinity College Dublin, in its origins a Protestant seminary, and in the mid-1960s he was in favour of an amalgamation of TCD and University College Dublin (originally Cardinal Newman's Catholic

University) – apparently because he saw it as the end of TCD. In general, the winds of change sweeping through the church in the aftermath of Vatican II were not at all to his liking. But he was not entirely an 'Oisín after the Fianna': he played a role in the early years of the Northern Ireland conflict, controversially visiting Seán MacStiofáin, the IRA leader, when he had embarked on a hunger strike, and he helped to negotiate the first IRA ceasefire. In 1969 it was the social services agencies which he founded that were mobilised to care for the influx of refugees from Northern Ireland. Nonetheless, it remains true that the 'new era' (as Whyte calls it) in Irish society in the 1960s was not one sympathetic to the archbishop's concerns, or even to his style of leadership.

Whyte's book concludes in 1970, and in view of the enormous changes that have occurred in the relative positions of church and state in the thirty years since its publication, his choice of that particular *terminus ad quem* was surely auspicious. The period reviewed by him, 1923-1970, and its apparent obsession with sexual morality and with state power, now appears as remote from us as the early eighteenth century. Yet for all that, thirty years on, his work on church-state relations in modern Ireland retains its value. The opening of the archives will undoubtedly amplify and elaborate a good deal of what he wrote; and on occasion, new material will surely illuminate some of the murkier corners of the history of church-state relations in modern Ireland. Other bishops, for example, previously blurred, will now come into focus. But it appears unlikely that many of Whyte's conclusions will be controverted, and it may be suggested that his pioneering appraisal will remain essential.

CHAPTER TWENTY-ONE

Northern Ireland and the post-Vatican II ecumenical journey

Michael Hurley SJ

Three dates stand out in the history of official ecumenism in Ireland: 23 January 1923, 26 September 1973 and an eagerly-awaited date in the near future. On 23 January 1923 the Irish non-Roman Catholic churches met for the first time as the United Council of Christian Churches and Religious Communions in Ireland. They included the Congregationalists, the Methodists, the Moravians, the Presbyterians, the Quakers (all these non-episcopal) as well as the Anglicans of the Church of Ireland (an episcopal church). This Council was one of the first such bodies established anywhere in the world – its British counterpart was not established until 1942. Just fifty years later, on 26 September 1973, the member churches of this Irish Council of Churches – as it was called since 1966 – met together with the hierarchy and other representatives of the Roman Catholic Church at Ballymascanlon, near the border between Northern Ireland and the Republic. This was the first ever official meeting between all the Irish churches, Catholic as well as Protestant. These inter-church meetings continued subsequently and became known popularly as the Ballymascanlon Talks, officially later on as the Irish Inter-Church Meeting. The third important date in Irish ecumenical history was expected in the year 2000 but has had to be postponed. Since 1973 the Irish Council of Churches and the Irish Inter-Church Meeting have continued side by side as distinct ecumenical agencies. At a date in the not too distant future still to be decided, the Irish Inter-Church Meeting will be reconstituted. It will become the sole official agency of all the churches in Ireland as a whole and will have a new name: The Conference of Churches in Ireland (CCI). The present Irish Council of Churches will then cease to operate as an ecumenical agency.

I

What follows is an attempt to understand these three developments. First, however, I wish to highlight briefly what seems to me to be one of the most significant politico-religious facts about the island of Ireland, the fact that political partition was not followed by ecclesiastical partition in any of its churches. The Irish delight in paradoxes; one such paradox is that the island of Ireland though politically divided is not ecclesiastically divided. The primatial See for both Anglicans and Catholics is in Armagh in Northern Ireland. And there are Methodist 'districts' and Presbyterian 'presbyteries' as well as Anglican and Roman Catholic dioceses which are partly in the south, partly in the north: they straddle the political border because they predate it and have not subsequently been adjusted. It is not so surprising that Irish Catholics were unwilling to reorganise their church structures after partition. Traditionally, however, Catholic Church boundaries follow political boundaries: there is now only one Episcopal Conference in Germany whereas previously there were two; there are now four such conferences in former Yugoslavia whereas previously there was only one. However, the predominantly nationalist character of Irish Catholicism precluded any reorganisation to adjust to the new political situation. What is surprising is that Irish Protestants, being for the most part unionists, did not do so. It should be noted that the Jewish community in Ireland did reorganise itself and become 'partitioned' in 1919. An Irish Chief Rabbinate was set up in Dublin whereas Belfast and the north continued under the jurisdiction of London although maintaining traditional contacts with southern Jews.[1]

Credit for remaining unpartitioned must first go to the individual churches, especially to the Church of Ireland which had and still has its headquarters in Dublin and which retains a horror of ceasing to be 'a church of the whole country'. Credit, however, must also go to the Irish Council of Churches. It is worthy of note that 1923, the year the Council began life, was also the year the civil war ended and partition became consolidated. The institutional resistance to change, always stronger in the ecclesiastical than in the secular world, will have helped the churches to maintain the *status quo*. The Church of Ireland, despite the unionism of its members, was determined to resist any attempts to partition the church. Its prominent role in the Irish Council of Churches enabled it to influence the other members. The very existence of this Council as an all-Ireland institution was a significant factor.

But how and why did the Irish Council of Churches come into being in 1923? The answer in brief is that from the outset the 1920s was a busy and fruitful ecumenical decade. In January 1920 the Patriarchate of Constantinople advocated the establishment of a *koinonia*, a fellowship or league of churches. In August of that same year the Lambeth Conference of Anglican bishops issued a similar recommendation. The Malines Conversations between Anglican and Catholic theologians took place between 1921 and 1925 under the presidency of Cardinal Mercier. 1925 saw the beginning of the Life and Work Movement, an international, interdenominational movement emphasising the more practical aspects of Christianity.

1927 saw the beginning of the international, interdenominational Faith and Order movement emphasising the more doctrinal aspects. The Irish Protestant churches duly joined these two movements. That is part of the context in which the formation of the Irish Council of Churches in 1923 has to be understood. It must also be remembered that in the 1920s the churches were attempting to recover from the effects of the Great War, and that in Irish history the 20s are the sad, tragic decade during which a Civil War took place between advocates and opponents of the Treaty concluded with Britain. History shows that institutions, churches included, have to be weakened, to be humbled before they stretch out hands to each other.

The Catholic-Protestant body which became known as the Irish Inter-Church Meeting (IICM), began life in 1973 and since then has functioned side by side with the Irish Council of Churches. The history of the Irish Council is not a story of brilliant achievements and successes. As remembered and described by Rev Dr R. D. Eric Gallagher, Methodist minister and co-author of *Christians in Ulster 1948-1968*,[2] it had become in the late 1940s a tired, rather moribund body. When the Life and Work coalesced with the Faith and Order Movement to form the World Council of Churches (WCC) in Amsterdam in 1948, the member churches of the Irish Council became founder members of the World Council. It was only 'with some difficulty', however, that the Youth Committee persuaded the Council to hold an 'Irish Amsterdam' in 1949 and subsequently an 'Irish Evanston' in Dublin in 1956 after the World Council's second Assembly at Evanston in the USA. *Irish Amsterdam* describes the Irish Council as 'striving to move the Protestant Churches to common work for the common Lord'.[3] Its pan-Protestantism, however, was not very effective. The main ecumenical problem was neither Rome's unwillingness to cooperate with the Protestant churches nor the Protestant churches' unwillingness to cooperate with Rome, but the Protestant churches' unwillingness to cooperate with each other. There was no felt need to cooperate and there was definite disagreement about eucharistic sharing.[4] A deep-seated denominationalism, a sense of self-sufficiency comparable indeed to that of the Roman Catholic Church, enabled the Protestant churches to ignore each other. As a recent commentator writes, the Irish Protestant churches were 'long-established and numerically and financially strong ... they could afford disunity'.[5]

While in the south the Protestant minority largely acquiesced in the new political arrangements, less reluctantly because the British Crown was still recognised, the situation was quite different in the North, where the nationalist Catholic minority deeply resented and resisted the partition of the country and as far as possible withheld cooperation. Only very few, for instance, ever joined the police force, the Royal Ulster Constabulary. Indeed by equipping themselves with their own social infrastructure they can be said to have formed a kind of 'state within a state'. On the other hand, the unionist Protestant majority was characterised by a curious amalgam of superiority and insecurity. They tended, in the words of a recent history, to regard the nationalists 'as a hostile "fifth column", deserving only of second-class citizenship'.[6] To retain control they used their power unfairly, especially in the sphere of local government where only ratepayers had a vote, and so brought about the emergence in the late 1960s of the Civil Rights Association to protest against unionist injustices, e.g. discrimination in the allocation of publicly-provided housing.

Behind this discrimination there lay a deep-seated fear of Rome. In his *Religion and the Northern Ireland Problem*, John Hickey, one-time senior lecturer in sociology at the University of Ulster in Coleraine, underlined the 'deep core of fear, suspicion, and hostility' prevalent among northern unionists and concluded that 'Politics in the north is not politics exploiting religion ... It is more a question of religion inspiring politics than of politics making use of religion'.[7] Steve Bruce, formerly at the Queen's University of Belfast and subsequently professor at Aberdeen, also stresses the religious character, the anti-Catholicism of classical unionism:

> Why be a unionist? To avoid being part of a united Ireland. What is wrong with a united Ireland? It would be a Catholic country. If you do not want to be a Catholic, what are you? A Protestant. If we understand that sequence, we can understand the political success of Ian Paisley and the role of evangelicalism in the thinking of Ulster Protestants.[8]

The anti-Catholicism of Dr Paisley, the well-known evangelical, unecumenical churchman and politician, has no hesitation in unchurching the Roman Catholic Church (something which none of the sixteenth-century Reformers did) and in including in the hymnbook of his own church such provocative language as the following:

> Our Fathers knew thee, Rome of old,
> And evil is thy fame;
> Thy fond embrace, the galling chain;
> Thy kiss, the blazing flame.

> Thy sentence dread is now pronounced,
> Soon shalt thou pass away.
> O soon shall earth have rest and peace –
> Good Lord, haste Thou that day.[9]

Northern Ireland unionism, however, does not in general depend on such an extreme form of anti-Catholicism. What is more typical of Northern unionists is a fear that their civil and religious rights and liberties and their economic standard of living would be in danger under 'Rome Rule', in a state under the domination of the Roman Catholic Church as they perceive the Republic of Ireland to be. As Stanley Worrall, the distinguished English Methodist who had lived for many years in Belfast, put it:

> [The Northern Ireland Protestant] is not afraid that if he lived there [in the Republic of Ireland] he would be unable to practise his religion; but he is afraid that he would be obliged to live a great part of his life according to the pattern laid down by someone else's religion ... The philosophy of 'No Surrender', 'not an inch' is kept alive through fear [of Rome]; and I say again, it is religious fear, which only the churches can exorcise ... Unfortunately the result of such fear is not only to rule out the reunion of the country; it also produces in the popular mind a less justifiable resistance to any form of shared government in Northern Ireland.[10]

Contrary to what is often believed, this 'religious fear', the anti-Catholicism of Northern Ireland unionism, is a middle-class as well as a 'working-class' phenomenon. If this is less obvious it is only because the middle classes as everywhere are usually more sophisticated, more inhibited in expressing themselves. It may also be noted *en passant* that two new forms of unionism have now begun to emerge: a secular unionism which wants to have little or nothing to do with religion or church or such a religious political organisation as the Orange Order, and a unionism which is ecumenical in its Protestantism and studiously eschews anti-Romanism. Neither form however has – as yet – acquired much, if any, political influence.

As a result of this politico-religious estrangement, the kind of society which prevailed in Northern Ireland and to some but much lesser extent in the south, was sectarian. Instead of 'togetherness' and 'cooperation', apartheid, politico-religious segregation became the order of the day: separate churches have entailed separate schools, separate teacher-training colleges, separate hospitals, separate newspapers, separate sporting activities, separate clubs, separate neighbourhoods.

II

But how then is it possible against this unpromising background that official talks between the Catholic and Protestant churches began in 1973? From the very beginning of the ecumenical movement the official Roman Catholic attitude was negative. It found expression in the uncompromising words of the 1928 encyclical letter of Pius XI, *Mortalium Animos*:

> There is but one way in which the unity of Christians may be fostered, and that is by furthering the return to the one true church of Christ of those who are separated from it; for from that one true church they have in the past fallen away.[11]

Evidence of some softening of this negative stance can be found in a 1949 Vatican document, *Ecclesia Catholica,* and in due course during the Second Vatican Council (1962-5) the Roman Catholic Church eventually became positive in its attitude ·to ecumenism. As a result, from the early 1960s a whole variety of unofficial ecumenical initiatives were undertaken which laid the foundations for the 1973 decision by the Irish Catholic Bishops' Conference to become officially involved in inter-church, ecumenical dialogue.[12]

One example is the ecumenical conferences at Glenstal, the Benedictine abbey in the south, and at Greenhills, a Presentation convent also in the south but nearer the border. These began in June 1964. They were a Roman Catholic initiative but were conceived as interdenominational, as involving all the churches and as such they paved the way for Ballymascanlon. These conferences though unofficial were held with the knowledge and the blessing of the relevant church authorities. They involved laity as well as clergy, mostly from the south but also from the North, and addressed a variety of theological subjects and did so in a context of joint worship. A second example is the Corrymeela Centre of Reconciliation in Northern Ireland, a Presbyterian initiative which opened in October 1965 and which owes some of its inspiration to the Agape Village founded by Pastor Tullio Vinay in northern Italy some thirty miles west of Turin. Corrymeela is an Irish Taizé, interdenominational as well as international in its outreach but differs from Taizé in being a dispersed rather than a residential community, a dispersed community which originally was mostly if not entirely Protestant but became half Protestant and half Catholic. Corrymeela is significant because the suspicion of proselytism, which traditionally hung over all Irish interdenominatinal meetings, has never attached to it. It is also significant because it speaks of and works for 'reconciliation'. This is a less controversial term than 'ecumenism', which is rejected and opposed by many evangelical Protestants. A third example is the Irish School of Ecumenics inaugurated in 1970 as a centre for research and postgraduate study somewhat like the ecumenical institutes in Paderborn in Germany, Strasbourg in France and Tantur in Israel. Roman Catholic in origin, the Irish School of Ecumenics is interdenominational in its governing body. Its staff and student body are also interdenominational as well as international.

But if in 1973 the move towards Ballymascanlon and official talks had already begun by way of unofficial contacts, it took the outbreak of sectarian violence to get it under way and to gather speed. 'There can be little doubt,' the Irish Council of Churches Report for 1974 states, 'that the experience of the past few years helped to bring it [Ballymascanlon] about'.[13] It was the violence, the so-called 'Troubles' which spurred or shamed the churches into making official contact for the first time. The Troubles are generally agreed to have begun with the Civil Rights march of 5 October 1968 in Derry. The churches were caught unprepared. The ecumenical structures were not yet in place by which they could have coped more satisfactorily. Indeed the main achievement of these years was to experiment with such structures. For its part, the Roman Catholic Church in Ireland, despite the stimulus of the Second Vatican Council, was no more enthusiastic about an official relationship with the other churches than these churches themselves were. Happily, as we have seen, considerable ecumenical progress had been made at an unofficial level, so much so that when the Troubles broke out, the churches did not take sides as they had done in the Home Rule crisis at the beginning of the century and as, according to Gallagher and Worrall, they would have done a decade earlier.[14] Now however 'the churches were more ready than the political parties to stretch out hands of friendship'.[15] And in 1968 the Irish Council had appointed as its organising secretary, although only in a part-time capacity, the Rev Dr Norman Taggart of the Methodist Church in Ireland and given him a very significant brief: he was to be 'travelling advocate and interpreter of ecumenism ... monitoring the new relationships, both official and unofficial, between the Irish churches including the Roman Catholic Church'.[16]

The main ecumenical structures born out of the Troubles against the background of escalating politico-religious violence were three in number.[17] The emergence in 1968 of the four church leaders as a working group to calm fears and to promote peace is generally regarded as the first sign of official Catholic-Protestant cooperation. This was followed in May 1970 by the Joint Group 'on social and human problems' and in 1972-3 by the Ballymascanlon Talks (as the Irish Inter-Church Meeting was originally called because of its early venue). Both 'faith and order issues' and 'causes of tension in the community' were conspicuous by their absence from the agenda of the Joint Group. But a clever 'etc' at the end of its terms of reference eventually helped the churches to set up a working party on 'Violence in Ireland' which issued its challenging recommendations in 1976, recommendations however which remain unimplemented.

By contrast with the Joint Group, the Ballymascanlon initiative was quite remarkable for its inclusiveness. August 1971 brought the introduction of internment without trial but the army's dawn swoops on the morning of the 9th to arrest hundreds of suspected IRA members left twenty-two people killed (including one Catholic priest) and 7,000 homeless.[18] The early months of 1972 brought Bloody Sunday (when thirteen men were shot dead and seventeen wounded by the army in Derry), the suspension of the Northern Ireland parliament at Stormont and the imposition of direct rule from Westminster. In March 1972 at its spring meeting the executive committee of the Irish Council declared: 'We are called therefore to courageous, costly and possibly unpopular action on behalf of all including those represented by our member churches.'[19] The organising secretary of the Irish Council of Churches sent a letter to Cardinal Conway in February 1972 (no copy of which seems to have survived) about a Church of Ireland suggestion of a joint working party on mixed marriages[20] and about 'the possibilities of further dialogue on both practical and doctrinal issues'.[21] He met the Cardinal on 23 February. They had discussed, so he informed the spring meeting of the Council on 29 March,

> pastoral and other factors involved in interchurch marriages, violence, the relationship between the ICC and the Roman Catholic structures and the terms of reference of the joint group.[22]

The organising secretary had broached the possibility of setting up a working party which would discuss joint pastoral problems, including mixed marriages and violence in Ireland.[23]

What happened as a result of this intervention by the organising secretary of the Irish Council of Churches was a letter from the Catholic hierarchy. It came not from Armagh as has been previously thought but from Mullingar, not from the cardinal but from the hierarchy's secretary, the bishop of Meath, Dr McCormack. It contained an invitation to the member churches of the Irish Council to attend 'a joint meeting at which the whole field of ecumenism in Ireland might be surveyed' and on the Roman Catholic side it was to include all the members of the Episcopal Conference. According to Cardinal Daly the decision about Ballymascanlon and its scope was due 'almost entirely' to 'a recommendation from Cardinal Conway'.[24] But what or who may have led Cardinal Conway to make a recommendation so surprising in its comprehensiveness remains as yet unclear. The themes chosen for 26 September 1973 and which were to occupy the churches for the next four years were: 'Church, Scripture, Authority', 'Baptism, Eucharist, Marriage', 'Social and Community Problems', 'Christianity and Secularism'.[25] Hopes were high in September 1973. Difficulties of course lay ahead: no infrastructure was put in place and still in 1979 and 1980 complaints were being made about inadequate servicing arrangements and the lack of machinery for implementation of recommendations; and there was a reluctance to address the problem of mixed marriages and 'the problem of Northern Ireland'.[26] The motto of the venue[27] chosen for the opening session – *Festina Lente* (Hasten Slowly) – has in retrospect proved to have been only too appropriate. In the mid-80s however, after a difficult, frustrating first decade, some streamlining took place and more progress was achieved.

III

Two events which took place in Belfast during the 80s illustrate very well the sea-change which came about in Irish Inter-Church relations as a result of the Troubles; the Irish Inter-Church Meeting is one expression of that sea-change.[28] The first of these events was the installation of Bishop Cahal Daly in Belfast on 17 October 1982 as bishop of Down and Connor. In the course of his address on this occasion he stated:

> We are all called at this time to a common Christian task, to work for mutual recognition in each community of the complete legitimacy and legality, the equal dignity and rights, of the other community, with its own self-defined identity, its own sense of loyalty, its own aspirations, so long as these are peacefully held and peacefully promoted.[29]

This view of nationalism and unionism as compatible rather than mutually exclusive was quite new on the lips of an official of church or state. Only two years later it came to find expression in chapters four and five of the *Report* of the New Ireland Forum established by the Dublin government in 1983. It has since slowly gained respectability in Catholic-nationalist circles. Cardinal Cahal Daly was outstanding in encouraging the fresh political thinking and the ecumenical initiatives which reconciliation and peace in Ireland require. The contrast between his views and those of his predecessors such as Cardinal MacRory (who died in 1945) could hardly be greater.[30]

The second event was the demonstration against the Anglo-Irish Agreement which took place at the Belfast City Hall in November 1985. The Anglo-Irish Agreement, signed on 15 November of that year by the British and Irish governments, established an Inter-Governmental Conference to deal on a regular basis with political matters affecting Northern Ireland. This involvement of 'a foreign power', even if only on a consultative basis, in the administration of Northern Ireland was anathema to unionists for whom Dublin rule was 'Rome Rule'. In his fury Dr Paisley did not hesitate on the Sunday afterwards to lead his congregation at the Martyrs Memorial Church in the following prayer:

> O God, in wrath take vengeance upon this wicked, treacherous lying woman [Margaret Thatcher, British Prime Minister]; take vengeance upon her, Oh Lord, and grant that we shall see a demonstration of thy power.[31]

The protest marches which converged on the City Hall in Belfast on 23 November 1985 drew a huge crowd of over 100,000 people. It was all meant as a re-enactment of the signing of the Solemn League and Covenant against Home Rule on Ulster Day, 28 September 1912. There was, however, one immensely significant difference. The 1912 signing of the Covenant in various centres throughout the north was a religious-ecclesiastical Protestant event: it was preceded by church services, took place in church halls and was led by church ministers. In Belfast the list of signatories was headed by the two great political leaders, Sir Edward Carson and Lord Londonderry but immediately after them came the Moderator of the Presbyterian General Assembly, the Bishop of Down, Connor and Dromore, the Dean of Belfast, the General Secretary of the Presbyterian Church, the President of the Methodist Conference and the ex-Chairman of the Congregational Union.[32] In 1985, however, the Church of Ireland and the other Protestant leaders, apart of course from the presence of Dr Paisley, were conspicuous by their absence.

In May 1995 *The Irish Times* felt able to state that:

One of the profoundest changes in the political climate in the North in recent years has come from the concerted effort by the churches, among their members as well as between themselves, to further the cause of reconciliation.[33]

The occasion for this editorial was the submission of the Church of Ireland to the Forum for Peace and Reconciliation established by the Dublin government and in particular the efforts by its primate, Archbishop Robin Eames, to encourage more positive thinking among unionists and to remind all about the fears of each other that still subsist in both communities and which seriously jeopardise renewed efforts at reconciliation. Much of the 'concerted effort' noted by *The Irish Times* has been unofficial. In the 1980s many more ecumenical initiatives (encouraged by the example of the Corrymeela Community and the Irish School of Ecumenics) got under way and succeeded in exerting a very considerable influence. These new ventures included, for example, the ECONI (Evangelical Contribution on Northern Ireland) group, the Inter-Church Group on Faith and Politics, the Cornerstone Community, the Columbanus Community of Reconciliation, the Armagh Clergy Fellowship and very many others. Deserving of special mention is the fact that before the ceasefires a number of individual church people (notably the Redemptorist priest, Alex Reid, and the Presbyterian minister, Roy Magee) were outstanding in initiating and maintaining contact with paramilitary groups and acting as intermediaries between them and political and government representatives. The new interest in and appreciation of the churches' ministry of ecumenism and reconciliation is a complex phenomenon. It is not simply that the churches have become less self-sufficient and more cooperative. It is also that the events in former Yugoslavia and elsewhere have brought in their train the realisation that Northern Ireland is no monstrous anachronism, that religion everywhere and not just in Northern Ireland is indeed more potent for good and ill than much secular thinking, especially Marxist, was able previously to recognise.

Although most of the nationalists' grievances have been redressed, it has to be recognised that the violence since the 1960s has in some ways worsened the apartheid in Northern Ireland and so postponed the full achievement of present political aspirations. It set the people further apart not only psychologically but also geographically. Because of the reversal of their fortunes the unionist/Protestant community became alienated from Britain; because of the mutual killings, trust and confidence between the communities within Northern Ireland has suffered; because of the resulting fear and insecurity mixed neighbourhoods have decreased sharply in number. The city of Belfast is said to be 'more segregated than ever before with up to 80 percent of people living in segregated areas'.[34] And 'this pattern has been replicated in other towns throughout Northern Ireland, most of which now have clearly-defined areas in which the minority population – of Catholics in the east and of Protestants in the west – cluster together for mutual support and a feeling of safety.'[35]

The Ballymascanlon initiative managed to survive. Another historic event of the year 1973 was the signing of the Sunningdale Agreement.[36] This political event may indeed have been, in the words of Longman's *Chronicle of the 20th Century,* 'a dramatic moment in the history of Ireland' but at the time it proved to be a bridge too far.[37] By contrast, Ballymascanlon 1973, however historic, was hardly dramatic – it produced no other agreement except to meet again – but it survived. Pressures from without of a secular and political nature and pressures from within of a religious and Christian nature both made their contribution to this survival. But Ballymascanlon more than survived. It became the Irish Inter-Church Meeting, celebrated its silver jubilee in September 1998 and is before too long, it is hoped, to find a new future as a more mature ecumenical instrument forged and refined in the fires of the Troubles. Plans are now well advanced which will see the Irish Council of Churches cease to operate and for all practical purposes go out of existence and a reconstituted Irish Inter-Church Meeting under the new title of the Conference of Churches in Ireland become the sole ecumenical agency of the Irish churches.[38]

The survival of Ballymascanlon shows that the churches at the outbreak of the Troubles were indeed 'more ready than the political parties to stretch out hands of friendship'. It is also a reminder that the unofficial initiatives of the 1960s, such as Glenstal and Corrymeela and others, had well and truly laid the foundations for the 'courageous, costly and possibly unpopular action' taken in the early 70s. But many believers today are scandalised by the contrast they see between the statesmen of Europe and its church leaders, the former being ready to make sacrifices for the sake of political unity, the latter appearing to show no such readiness in the cause of Christian unity. The Irish churches, at the unofficial level in particular, more than played their part in encouraging and helping the politicians to produce the Good Friday Agreement of 1998.[39] But that Agreement is a challenge to the churches to go and do likewise in their own proper sphere: to show in their relationships with each other something of the politicians' magnanimity, boldness and readiness to sacrifice sectional interests for the sake of the common religious good. The projected new Conference of Churches in Ireland is a step in that direction but institutional ecumenism, like institutional religion, is a mere means to an end and far from being the only means.[40]

CHAPTER TWENTY-TWO

The troubled contemporary Irish Catholic Church

James. S. Donnelly, Jr.

When Pope John Paul II made his famous visit to Ireland in 1979, it must have looked to the outside world as if the words 'Irish' and 'Catholic' still belonged easily together, as they had for centuries. '*Semper fidelis*' was the phrase confidently pronounced by the pope just before he departed from Shannon airport.[1] As many as 2.7 million people were estimated to have turned out to greet and worship with the pope at one or another of the major venues of his visit, including the enormous throng of 1.2 or 1.3 million in the Phoenix Park in Dublin. This estimated total of 2.7 million represented more than half the people then living on the island of Ireland.[2] Appearances, however, were highly deceiving. Already in 1979, after roughly two decades of rapid economic growth, openness to the outside world, and fairly sweeping cultural change, the Catholic Church in Ireland was in serious trouble. The indications of its malaise included the steep fall in religious vocations, the worrisome decline in Mass attendance rates among adolescents and young adults, and a dramatic loss of moral credibility owing to its rigid stance on artificial contraception.[3] Indeed, the openly acknowledged purpose of the Irish hierarchy in inviting John Paul to Ireland was largely that of halting or at least slowing the damaging inroads of materialism and secularism on the attachment of Catholics to their ancient faith.[4] But apart from conferring certain limited short-term benefits, it may be doubted whether the papal visit better equipped the Catholic Church in Ireland to deal effectively with its challenges and problems.[5]

Among the more difficult challenges at the outset of this period was that of how Irish Catholics and their leaders would respond to the far-reaching alterations in liturgy, theology, church governance, and ecumenism promoted by the Second Vatican Council (1962-65). The prospects for a successful renewal of Catholic religious life in Ireland along Vatican II lines were quite unpromising, given the history of this church since 1850. At the risk of generalisation it may be said that prior to Vatican II the Irish Catholic Church was authoritarian in its governance, Manichaean in its general approach to the modern world, conversionist in its stance towards Protestants and the Protestant churches, heavily Marian in its devotional emphasis, weak in its scriptural tradition both in scholarship and popular piety, and inclined to privilege 'externalism' in religious practice over interior spirituality.[6] In all of these areas Vatican II pulled strongly in the opposite direction, urging a major role for the laity in church governance, finding much good in the modern world, encouraging respectful dialogue with other churches and common effort towards Christian unity, focusing devotion much more on Christ than on Mary, stressing the importance of interior spirituality, and grounding both theology and popular piety in the scriptures.[7] Quite a few leading Irish churchmen seemed oblivious to the whirlwind of change for which Vatican II was calling. Archbishop John Charles McQuaid, returning from one session of the Council, blithely informed his flock, 'allow me to reassure you, no change will worry the tranquillity of your Christian lives'.[8]

Against the odds, however, Irish Catholicism did accommodate itself to some of the injunctions of Vatican II, though in other areas the response was incomplete or sadly deficient. Liturgical reformers had relatively little about which to complain. Writing in 1985, the broadcaster and cultural commentator Seán Mac Réamoinn, could declare expansively, 'on the face of it, liturgical renewal has been *the* success story of Vatican II in Ireland'.[9] From the beginning, Mass in the vernaculars (English and Irish) was thoroughly accepted. Mass attendance rates remained remarkably high overall (well above 80 per cent), especially in comparison with the rest of Europe. In addition, the participation of Mass-goers in the liturgy was generally much better than in the pre-council era. As Mac Réamoinn observed, 'the days of the silent congregation are numbered, if not over, and the people's voice is heard, even – *mirabile dictu* – in song!' Common all over the country by 1985 were lay scripture readers, lay ministers of the Eucharist, and communion in the hand.[10] The use of the two vernaculars had greatly raised popular 'awareness of the importance of God's word as the essential liturgical complement of sacramental action'. As a result, remarked Mac Réamoinn, 'the Mass-going Irish know their Bible today [in 1985] as never before, even if in this at least, they still lag far behind their Protestant fellow countrymen.'[11]

If liturgical renewal inspired by Vatican II was generally a success in Ireland, change came much more slowly and hesitantly in other spheres. The lay role in church governance has certainly expanded, but more in form than in reality. Surveying this scene in 1985, Kevin O'Kelly, the RTÉ religious affairs correspondent, concluded pessimistically: 'there are many parish councils, but no evidence that any significant number have been given decisive powers in matters of importance. The national council of the laity has not been asked to make decisions of consequence. There has never been a national pastoral council, though there have been innumerable bishops' pastorals.'[12] Changes since 1985 in these respects have been unimpressive. Priests as well as laity have found it difficult to express their collective voice in effective ways, as the bishops have been reluctant to relax their control. 'The conference of priests, though officially recognised,' observed O'Kelly in 1985, 'had to work for years to achieve even the beginnings of a dialogue with the bishops' conference, and it is not clear that their encounters have produced results of significance.'[13]

The burden of the past has continued to weigh heavily not only on communication between different elements within the Irish Catholic Church but also on inter-faith relations. It has been said by the Irish theologians Gabriel Daly and Alan Falconer (Daly is an Augustinian priest, Falconer a Presbyterian minister) that in the matter of ecumenism Vatican II 'was less a reform than a revolution'.[14] No ecumenical revolution, however, has come to Ireland. Admittedly, in certain elementary respects there has been striking change since the mid-1960s. As Daly and Falconer declared in 1985, 'relations between the churches in Ireland will never again revert to a pre-conciliar situation, and an immense amount of positive worth in the restoration of relationships has been achieved in the past twenty years'.[15] The Catholic Church in Ireland has generally laid aside the conversionist mentality widely prevalent in the 1950s and earlier, though as in the Catholic world as a whole, there has been 'a hesitancy to abandon a Rome-centred juridical view of the church as a hierarchical perfect society'.[16] There has been valuable dialogue among theologians, leading to agreed statements, such as that issued by the Anglican-Roman Catholic International Commission. But in Ireland and elsewhere, observed Daly and Falconer, 'if agreed statements constitute perhaps the most encouraging achievements of the past two decades [1966-85], failure on the part of others, clerical and lay, to ponder, circulate, discuss, and respond to these documents constitutes perhaps the most disappointing parallel failure of these decades'.[17] In addition, ecumenical activity in the first twenty years after Vatican II was too often restricted to rarefied theological discussion and rarely extended to cooperation on such critical social issues as unemployment, housing and education. Nor was there much inter-faith activity at the congregational level. Though already by 1985 there were a 'large number of shared Protestant and Roman Catholic parishes in England', there were no such schemes anywhere in Ireland.[18]

Relations with the Protestant churches in Ireland should have been greatly eased by the displacement of Marianism in this period from its central place in Irish Catholicism. This major devotional change, stemming partly from Vatican II and partly from cultural developments within Ireland, began in the 1960s with what traditionalists regarded as the near-collapse of the rosary devotion, particularly the praying of the family rosary. The deep impact of television on patterns of family life received most of the blame. As the columnist John O'Brien put it in the *Irish Catholic* in October 1967, television had relegated the family rosary 'either to obscurity or to a time that suits individuals' instead of the entire family.[19] But in one important way the rosary was dealt a severe blow in the very first burst of liturgical reform dictated by Vatican II – the introduction of the vernacular in the Mass. The vernacular responses now made by the faithful in the pews increasingly extinguished the recitation of the rosary with which so many Irish Catholics had traditionally assisted at Mass.[20] In fact, the liturgical changes ushered in by the reformers went well beyond setting aside the rosary, as dramatic as that was. Other Marian devotions also went into gradual decline. Among these were the Brown Scapular and Miraculous Medal devotions, the first a Carmelite-sponsored cult associated with Our Lady of Mount Carmel, the second linked with Catherine Labouré and her famous shrine on the Rue du Bac in Paris. Strongly favoured by Lourdes and Fatima enthusiasts both before and after Vatican II, these particular devotions had once been very widespread throughout Catholic Ireland but by the late 1960s they were on the wane, along with such traditional rituals as Marian processions and household altars in the month of May.[21]

The receding of the Marian wave in Irish Catholicism was also reflected in the decline of its flagship institutions—the Legion of Mary and Our Lady's Sodality. A steep fall in membership overtook the Legion in the 1960s and continued throughout the 1970s. According to John Murray, an officer of the Legion concilium at its Brunswick Street headquarters in Dublin, membership reached an 'all-time low' at the end of the 1970s and then recovered slightly in the mid and late 1980s.[22] Though Irish legionaries continue to take pride in their overall worldwide expansion, the Irish domestic picture has long been depressing. In 1966 the organisation had some 27,000 active members in Ireland (north and south). Of this total, some 14,400 were senior or 'adult' members and about 12,600 were 'junior' or mostly adolescent members. By the end of 1995 total Legion membership in Ireland had declined to only a little more than 8,000, or less than one-third of the corresponding figure three decades earlier. The fall was much sharper in the case of junior members, reflecting the Legion's increasing difficulty in attracting young people to its ranks. The number of junior members virtually collapsed over this thirty-year period, plummeting from 12,600 in 1966 to only about 2,100 at the end of 1995. Among senior members the decline, though less steep, was still dramatically large, from 14,400 in 1966 to about 5,900 in 1995, or nearly 60 per cent.[23]

As severe as the impact of materialism, cultural openness, and Vatican II was on the Legion of Mary, the adverse consequences of rapid economic, cultural, and religious change were even worse for that other great Marian institution, the Jesuit-led Sodality of Our Lady. In 1958 there were as many as 823 local sodalities of this organisation in Ireland, with more than 250,000 members, making it second only to the Pioneer Total Abstinence Association in size among Catholic lay bodies.[24] Historically, Our Lady's Sodality was closely identified with the teaching nuns and girls in the convent schools of the country. But there were actually more sodalities in local parishes (437, or 53 per cent of the total) than there were in secondary and primary schools (329, or 40 per cent), and a third segment was located in institutions of varying types, including orphanages, seminaries, and nursing schools (57, or 7 per cent).[25] Responding to the call for religious renewal stemming from Vatican II, and as a direct result of the 1967 Rome congress of the World Federation of Marian Congregations, Irish Jesuits attempted in the late 1960s and the 1970s to transform the old-style sodalities of Our Lady into so-called Christian Life Communities (CLCs). These were to have a distinctly christological focus, with a spirituality based on retreats and grounded in the Spiritual Exercises of St Ignatius Loyola.[26] This Jesuit effort, however, was an abysmal failure. Marian sodalists overwhelmingly refused to embrace this kind of renewal and either drifted away or were demobilised. A national survey carried out early in 1975 indicated that 'there were approximately 82 sodalities in existence' – barely one-tenth of the number (823) operating in 1958. Over the next two years less than a third of these remaining old-style sodalities conformed to the CLC model, and the rest were allowed to go their own way, unrenewed.[27] Even the relatively small number of Marian sodalities that converted themselves into CLCs in the 1970s faded during the 1980s. In all of Ireland today fewer than two hundred adults belong to Christian Life Communities.[28]

Though Irish Marianism has been progressively marginalised since the 1960s, ardent Marianists have by no means disappeared or been silenced. They have identified themselves with a variety of Catholic traditionalist organisations, including the Public Rosary Movement, the Apostolate of Our Lady of Fatima, Padre Pio and Medjugorje prayer groups. Members of these primarily religious Marian organisations have also been active politically during the last three decades over the issues of contraception, abortion, divorce, and the rights of homosexuals.[29] Though politically active Marianists and other Catholic traditionalists have scored several notable victories, campaigning for a pro-life amendment to the Constitution in 1983 and for the defeat of a divorce referendum in 1986, Irish laws relating to sexual morality have been comprehensively overhauled and liberalised since the late 1970s.[30] In these political battles the Irish Catholic hierarchy and lay traditionalists (Marianists above all) have generally been aligned with one another.[31] An outspoken Irish Redemptorist priest, Fr Tony Flannery, has recently declared that the Catholic Church in Ireland 'has suffered greatly by allowing itself to be hijacked by [traditionalist] lobby groups that have grown up around the issues of abortion and divorce'.[32]

Although 'hijacked' is perhaps not the right word, there can hardly be any doubt that the Catholic Church in Ireland has lost much of its once great moral authority by its persistent mishandling of issues connected to sexual behaviour and morality. In retrospect it can fairly be said that Irish bishops and many priests seriously misjudged how they should respond to *Humanae Vitae*, Pope Paul VI's encyclical of July 1968 imposing an absolute ban on all forms of artificial contraception. On this issue the Irish bishops 'held totally to the strictest version of the Vatican line, without any deviation'.[33] Open, public dissent from priests was simply not tolerated. In a highly publicised case Bishop Cornelius Lucey of Cork and Ross banned the courageous dissenter Fr James Good from working in that diocese.[34] Unlike episcopal conferences in many other countries, the Irish bishops never issued 'pastoral guidelines on the issue that would have given priests some flexibility in their dealings with the question in confession'.[35] Gradually, understanding priests and anxious penitents worked out their own moral solutions. 'Liberal' priests would advise penitents torn between the fear of pregnancy and the fear of hell that in reaching a moral judgment on whether or not to use artificial contraceptives, they needed to take into account all of their own personal circumstances, which might well justify departing from the blanket prohibition of *Humanae Vitae*. Enough priests adopted such a pastorally sensitive approach on birth control that most married Irish Catholics, if not so inclined already, came to regard artificial contraception as morally acceptable through the exercise of the individual and informed conscience. The use of contraceptives within marriage eventually ceased to be a matter for confession.[36]

But such adjustments occurred only after much painful experience. The Redemptorist Fr Flannery ruefully recalled in 1999 how he and his clerical colleagues had 'spent endless hours in countless confession boxes listening to married people, almost invariably women, explaining their circumstances to us and asking our opinion'. As this honest priest readily conceded, that was a rather incongruous position for male celibates to be in, ill-informed as they were about married life and about women.[37] Although many priests simply avoided the birth-control issue as best they could in the confessional, others engaged in 'a great deal of moral bullying and unpardonable interference in the private lives of people'.[38] Priests thought to be unacceptably 'liberal' in this sphere risked rebuff or worse from clerics of the opposite viewpoint. In the aftermath of *Humanae Vitae* the Irish Redemptorists, despite their great popularity as missioners, were not welcome everywhere in Ireland. 'We fought many a hard battle with bishops and priests,' declared Fr Flannery, 'and we were banned from a number of dioceses for being "soft" on birth control!'[39]

Many seasoned observers of contemporary Ireland believe that rigid adherence to the Vatican line on birth control by the Irish hierarchy and numerous priests irreparably weakened the moral authority of the institutional church. Writing in the *Irish Times*, the former Taoiseach Garret FitzGerald sweepingly insisted that 'the institutional church lost virtually all moral credibility with the great majority of people ... by its insistence on elevating the issue of the possible impact of contraception on sexual mores to the level of an absolute that must take precedence over all other considerations – including the maintenance of normal relationships by many married couples, and in extreme cases the safety of a wife's life'.[40] FitzGerald pinpointed an especially potent source of the general clerical loss of credibility in all areas of moral teaching. This was the appearance of clerical hypocrisy that resulted when priests who recognised the absolute ban on artificial contraception to be morally invalid nevertheless pretended to accept the rigid rule laid down in *Humanae Vitae*.[41] Arguing against the prevalent notion in Ireland today that the scandals of the 1990s have robbed the church of its moral authority, Fr Flannery maintained in 1999 that the credibility of the institutional church was really 'lost twenty years ago on the issue of contraception'. As he sadly admitted, 'We showed ourselves to be out of touch with the reality of people's lives, rigid in our imposition of the rules, and, ultimately and most damagingly, uncaring'.[42]

To make matters worse, few lessons appear to have been learned from this distressing chapter in the recent history of the Irish Catholic Church. Early in March 1999, Archbishop Desmond Connell of Dublin elicited a furious popular reaction when he suggested that parents who planned their children were creating 'technological produce' instead of normal human beings, and that such children were fated to be resentful and unhappy, deprived as they were of a 'properly personal relationship' with their parents.[43] Archbishop Connell was mostly focusing on medically aided human fertility, particularly *in vitro* fertilisation, but his remarks were capable of extension to parental planning of births in general. Had his comments been confined to *in vitro* fertilisation, they would have been bad enough, but as extended, they unintentionally cast a slur, as the distinguished journalist Fintan O'Toole observed in the *Irish Times*, 'on a very substantial proportion – probably a majority – of Irish families'.[44] Had the Irish bishops been more willing to relax their continuing authoritarian style and to give the Catholic laity a more meaningful role in church governance, perhaps they would have been able to avoid the costly errors repeatedly committed in handling issues of sexual morality.

Even if the contention is accepted that the Irish Catholic Church as an institution had already forfeited most of its moral authority long before its standing was depressed even further by the scandals of the 1990s, no honest account of the contemporary church could pass over these scandals in silence. The decade just closed has exposed the church and its religious personnel to an avalanche of scandals, and though defenders of the church are certainly correct in pointing out that only a small fraction of Irish priests, brothers, and nuns have been guilty of crimes or serious misconduct, the significance and impact of the scandals cannot be gauged by numbers alone. Other issues, especially betrayal of trust, absence of accountability, and the exercise of deception in various forms, have come to dominate the way in which the media have presented these scandals and ordinary people have understood them. Though the scandals have been of different kinds, sex has been the common thread running through virtually all of them. Though unrepresentative and in most respects the least troubling, the 1992 sex scandal centring on Bishop Eamonn Casey of Galway riveted the country. The *Irish Times* disclosed that almost two decades earlier, when he was bishop of Kerry, Casey had fathered a son by Annie Murphy, an American woman seeking refuge in Ireland from a broken marriage, and that he had used diocesan funds to make payments to her. In human terms Casey came off badly as the scandal unfolded, not so much because of his repeated violations of his priestly vow of celibacy but because of other deeds or omissions: his indecent pressure on Annie Murphy to give up the child for adoption; his failure to develop any significant relationship with the son whom he had fathered, and the deceptions which he had practised to keep what had happened from disclosure, including the diversion of diocesan funds.[45] Bishop Casey's fall from grace was all the more painful and damaging to the institutional church because he had seemed to embody the most modern and attractive features of its multivalent modern face. He had built his considerable national reputation as an effective proponent of welfare centres for the emigrant Irish in Britain, as an outspoken leader of Trócaire, the agency of the Irish episcopal conference for Third World development, and as an activist bishop with a strong interest in expanding social services for all age groups.[46] What's more, he was media savvy and 'could sing on chat shows'. As Fintan O'Toole has perceptively remarked, Casey had in effect been 'appointed as the friendly face who could win through media charm the authority which the church had previously maintained by haughty power'.[47] Now, ironically, the media brusquely toppled the populist pedestal on which he stood. Resigning quickly as bishop of Galway, he did reasonable penance for his sins through lowly service in the Latin American missions. This scandal underscored for Irish Catholics how difficult was the priestly vow of celibacy, and it was a lot harder in 1992 than when Casey broke it in the early 1970s.[48]

Hypocrisy, a deadly cardinal sin in the court of public opinion, was a relatively minor note in the Bishop Casey affair, but it was the dominant feature of the scandal of 1994-95 surrounding the name of Fr Michael Cleary. About a year after his death in December 1993, it was revealed that Cleary had long had a common-law wife, his 'housekeeper' Phyllis Hamilton, and that with her he had fathered two children. What gave this sordid revelation its potency and capacity for much wider damage was Fr Cleary's status as 'Ireland's most famous Catholic priest' – a media personality and a notorious defender of Catholic traditional values, especially in the sexual realm. Long in the public eye, he had held a string of media positions, writing a regular column in the *Sunday Independent* for five years, followed by another column in the *Star*, and serving as the compere of a phone-in radio show on 98FM that ran for an hour five nights a week over a period of four years.[49] Though Cleary delighted traditionalists with his vehement advocacy of 'the official line on contraception and on Catholic church teaching on sexuality generally', he infuriated 'liberals' and non-believers as much by his tone and style as by his message. Referring specifically to his column in the *Sunday Independent*, the Redemptorist Fr Flannery declared, 'I was constantly irritated by the way he insistently churned out a hard, unbending line on all moral issues and seemed to make no effort to reach out to people who were struggling in their own lives.'[50] Also exasperated by Fr Cleary's conduct as a journalist and broadcaster was Fintan O'Toole, who held him 'as responsible as anyone else for the coarsening of public discourse to the point where we now have a dead man's [i.e. Cleary's] Valentine cards reproduced in full colour in a national newspaper'.[51]

O'Toole was particularly incensed at Fr Cleary's role in the 1983 campaign to add a pro-life amendment to the Constitution. In this campaign even the Irish Catholic hierarchy conceded 'the right of each person to vote according to conscience'. In Cleary's view, however, this was namby-pambyism. In his *Sunday Independent* column he urged priests to 'start this Sunday by telling your people about life and its origins ... Tell them to vote "yes" and make no apology for it.' In the afterglow of victory Cleary could not restrain himself from crowing that the architects of this dramatic success were 'individual priests like myself', not the bishops, whom he denigrated as 'very soft'. As Fintan O'Toole acidly commented, 'the sheer vulgarity of such an approach to political debate, flattening out even the subtleties and complexities of his own church's position, did a great deal to coarsen public life in Ireland'.[52] But it was the hypocrisy that most people found so galling. Among Cleary's traditionalist utterances was this declaration: 'the church can alter certain regulations and laws that it makes itself, but it can't change the laws of God. We give the maker's instructions and we can't bend them – they're not ours to bend.'[53] But bending the rules was the very essence of Cleary's secret life, as virtually every Irish adult and adolescent learned some six months after his death.

In between the Casey and Cleary scandals the case of Fr Brendan Smyth, a Norbertine priest, hit the headlines in the autumn of 1994 after he was convicted in a Belfast court of sexually abusing children. A television documentary entitled 'Suffer Little Children' (aired in October 1994) disclosed that Fr Smyth had an appalling record of paedophilia in the United States, Britain, and Ireland stretching back to the 1950s.[54] His grievous misconduct was known to his order and to diocesan authorities: 'each time he was sent to a parish, whispers of scandal would begin to emerge. Each time he would be sent back to Ireland and then posted off to another parish.'[55] In this case, and in the many other cases of clerical paedophilia which sprang into the harsh light of day earlier and later, critics declared that the church authorities had habitually shielded the perpetrators or covered up their heinous misdeeds. What usually happened, however, was reflected in the official ecclesiastical response to the Brendan Smyth case. As Fintan O'Toole described it, 'over four decades the church authorities treated his behaviour as an internal affair to be dealt with by admonition or attempts at medical treatment, not as a criminal matter in which the law of the state should have any remit'.[56] In those many instances in which admonitions or medical treatment did not work, or work permanently, paedophile priests and brothers were not restrained from resuming contact with children. In the days of its haughty power such responses were accepted without public complaint, but by the 1980s and 1990s those days were long gone. The moral credibility of the church now suffered again when this and other paedophilia cases demonstrated that most people considered its traditional approach intolerable because it did not ensure the accountability either of the perpetrators of sexual abuse or of the responsible officials. As scores of victims of sexual abuse, often years after the events, came forward to press charges, the Irish hierarchy, in consultation with priests and professional psychiatrists and psychologists, belatedly (in 1995) developed a series of pastoral guidelines to ensure that suspected criminal activity would be reported to the police for investigation, and that church officials would be accountable in the way that the public has come to expect.[57] But because the bishops were slow to take decisive action, the church has paid a heavy price for its dilatory response. As recently as March 1999, in the notorious case of the paedophile priest Fr Seán Fortune, who committed suicide as a trial approached on twenty-nine charges relating to the alleged abuse of eight boys, serious questions were raised as to whether Bishop Brendan Comiskey of Ferns had acted responsibly some years earlier when serious complaints were lodged against Fr Fortune.[58]

Among the scandals which badly tarnished the church in the 1980s and

especially the 1990s, none have been more deeply distressing than those arising from the disclosure of the sexual and physical abuse of children and adolescents in residential institutions run by religious orders, male and female.
The worst abuses occurred in the years before 1970, but there have been others
of a serious nature which have taken place since then.[59] Though it may well
be unfair to hold the religious orders responsible today for the offences of a
small minority of their members committed three or more decades earlier,
neither the surviving victims, nor the media, nor the general Irish public have
been inclined towards leniency in relation to the distant or the more recent
faults of the institutional church.[60] Even before victims began to tell their stories and the media started to focus on the issue, many people knew at least
indistinctly that something was wrong. 'At the level of raw experience,'
Fintan O'Toole has observed, 'hundreds of thousands of people in Ireland
have known for most of their lives that there is a problem of paedophilia
within the church. Ask anyone who attended a boys' school in Ireland and
they will tell you that while most of the teachers were decent and professional, there was always one brother or priest who was regarded as a bit of a
menace.'[61] But a considerable body of firsthand testimony has accumulated
in recent years and revealed that both sexual and physical abuse were much
more widespread and deep-seated than had previously been thought. This
became indisputable with the publication in 1983, 1988, and 1991 of three
books detailing abuses in three different industrial schools: Mannix Flynn's
Nothing to Say (about Letterfrack in Co Galway), Paddy Doyle's *The God
Squad*, and Patrick Touher's *Fear of the Collar* (about Artane in Dublin).[62]

A far greater impact, however, was made by Mary Raftery's television documentary series *States of Fear*, which RTÉ broadcast in late April and early
May 1999.[63] For their thoroughly researched set of programmes the editors of
this powerful series mined the files of the Department of Education, which
exercised supervisory authority in this sphere after 1921, and interviewed
more than a hundred people who had come through the industrial school
system, which at its peak embraced fifty-two such schools with almost 7,000
inmates.[64] Although the system was abolished in the 1970s following the
publication in 1971 of the damning Kennedy report, Mary Raftery estimated
in April 1999 that there were as many as 40,000 people still alive who had
been inmates of the system at one time or another.[65] Sexual abuse occurred
all across the system. 'Virtually no industrial school where there were boys
over ten,' declared Raftery, 'has not had or is not having a Garda investigation into sexual abuse, and this includes the schools for the blind, the deaf,
[and] the mildly handicapped.' In absolute terms the offenders among the
religious teachers and custodians were numerous. Referring to the now
notorious Sister Xavieria of Goldenbridge in Dublin, Raftery insisted: 'every

place had one, two, or three Xavierias. The brothers had hundreds [altogether].'[66] And besides the sexual abuse there was usually serious physical deprivation and often outrageous corporal punishment. (The physical deprivation owed much to the scantiness of the state financial provision, which was only a fraction of that furnished by the government in Northern Ireland, England and Scotland.) Magnifying the impact of Raftery's documentary series was the fact that *States of Fear* was 'splashed on news and features pages, spoken about on radio, [and] heavily promoted on television'.[67] Although *States of Fear* was about the past, even the rather distant past, the Catholic Church of the late 1990s could not escape all blame or responsibility, and the general public was again reminded that the church in Ireland had been irresponsibly slow to deal with paedophilia within its own ranks and among the lay staff who helped to administer its educational and social welfare institutions.[68]

The haemorrhaging of the church over this issue is likely to persist for many months, if not years. So far-reaching was the impact of *States of Fear* that even before the last instalment of the series was broadcast on 11 May 1999, the government announced a package of measures to deal with the sexual abuse of children. Included in the package was the establishment of a commission to hear testimony from victims. As the political reporter Maol Muire Tynan put it in her front-page story in the *Irish Times* on 12 May of that year, 'the possibility now exists that hundreds, if not thousands, of victims may avail of the opportunity to explain "in a healing forum" the abuses they suffered under the care of religious orders or state institutions, including primary and secondary schools, from at least 1940 to the present day'. In addition, the government announced its intention to introduce legislation removing existing restrictions under the statute-of-limitations laws on the bringing of cases by victims of childhood sexual abuse. At present such a plaintiff must take legal action within three years of reaching the age of eighteen. The proposed changes would mean that even adults in middle age would not be debarred from instituting suits for damages.[69] For victims of sexual abuse this is good news. But for the Irish Catholic Church the commission and the changes in the statute-of-limitations laws will continue to cast a pall over its sunken reputation and to embarrass and dispirit its rapidly dwindling personnel.

There is some reason, however, for guarding against exaggeration in assessing the consequences of all this for the institutional church. Deeply worried that the scandals might be inflicting heavy damage on the church, the Irish episcopal conference authorised the conduct of an independent survey of religious beliefs and practices among Catholics in July 1997. This survey, carried out by the firm Irish Marketing Surveys, involved 1,400 adults in the Republic of Ireland drawn from 'a controlled, representative cross-section of the population in terms of age, sex, geographic distribution, and social class'.[70] Most of the findings of the survey were reassuring, or at least were presented as such. In what was termed 'something of a pleasant surprise', 72 per cent of respondents asserted that their religious beliefs and practices had been 'completely unaffected by various revelations which have become public since the beginning of the decade'. By wide majorities respondents indicated that their confidence in the priests of their parish and in the bishop of their diocese had remained unimpaired. As many as 63 per cent of respondents maintained that the scandals had not adversely affected their confidence in their local priests, and exactly the same per centage made an equivalent declaration about the diocesan ordinary. These findings were hailed as 'surely good news, suggesting that the vast majority of Irish Catholics have the maturity of vision to differentiate between the unacceptable actions of a tiny minority and the work of the church as a whole'.

On the other hand, the pollsters conceded that some of their other findings gave grounds for serious concern. Slightly more than half the respondents (51 per cent) 'felt that the church in Ireland had been permanently damaged by the recent scandals involving clergy and religious' – a proportion that might well be higher still if the same question were asked today in the wake of *States of Fear*. In addition, as many as 'four in ten respondents did not believe the bishops had taken appropriate action to deal with the issue of child sex abuse by priests and religious, and only 25 per cent thought the media had dealt unfairly with the issue'. Even so, suggested the pollsters, the worst was over: 'it would appear that the initial trauma which was felt when the first revelations came to light has been considered, worked through, and dealt with by a great many Catholics, and we are now in a situation of dealing with the aftershocks'. But as we have seen, the atmosphere of scandal has persisted remorselessly and the end is not yet in sight.

Alarmingly, the survey also confirmed earlier evidence that Mass attendance rates began to sag badly in the 1990s, though whether or not the scandals had much to do with this development is debatable.[71] Throughout the 1970s and 1980s, in spite of the uninterrupted advance of materialism and secularism into most corners of Irish society, the general Mass attendance rate remained impressively high, especially by international standards. Even as late as 1990, according to the European Value Systems Survey of that year, 85 per cent of the Irish adult population attended church at least weekly. In a country where rapid economic and cultural change had become almost an automatic rule of life since the 1960s, the population seemed to be clinging to regular attendance at Sunday Mass as the one fixed element of stability and security in an insecure world. This at least was the most common explanation of sociologists and social commentators for what otherwise appeared to be a cultural aberration. But a national survey carried out by Adelaide Market Research in 1992 indicated that for the first time since such data began to be collected, weekly Mass attendance had fallen below 80 per cent (78 per cent, to be exact). Three subsequent polls, all conducted by Irish Marketing Surveys, showed that the slippage had worsened considerably, though around a new plateau, with approximately two-thirds of Irish Catholics eighteen or older still faithfully attending Mass every Sunday. Mass attendance rates (weekly or more often) of 64, 67, and 65 per cent were recorded in 1995 and in July and September 1997 respectively. Though these figures could still be regarded as remarkably high by any other than recent Irish standards, the decline of twenty per centage points since 1990 alone (85 to 65 per cent) sounded the alarm bells among the bishops.

More worrisome still were the disaggregated statistics on Mass attendance by age and region. According to the 1997 survey results, attendance at Sunday Mass was no longer treated as an obligation by a majority of urban adolescents and young adults. Among those aged between 15 and 24 living in urban areas, only 39 per cent of males and 32 per cent of females attended Mass weekly. For those aged 25 to 34 in urban areas the figures were quite similar, though with the gender ranking reversed: 31 per cent of males and 37 per cent of females went to Mass at least once a week. As the pollsters observed, these statistics meant that 'the majority of the urban young have turned their backs on a part of Irish life which was almost universal less than a generation ago'. Even among urban dwellers of all age groups in 1997, the weekly Mass attendance rate was a rather anaemic 54 per cent and contrasted sharply with the much more robust average rate of 83 per cent in rural areas. Eagerly searching for some sunlight amid this gloom, the pollsters called attention to the strong correlation between advancing age and higher rates of weekly Mass attendance. These rates rose from 69 per cent among those aged 35 to 49, to 81 per cent among those aged 50 to 64, and to 88 per cent among those aged 65 or older. This pattern prompted the pollsters to point out optimistically that 'the young man or woman of today who feels that the practice of their religion has little to offer them may not always feel thus'. These analysts therefore suggested the obvious – that the church and its personnel begin 'honing the skills needed to bring back into the fold those who have strayed in the years of early adulthood'. But the experience of other countries in western Europe that underwent thoroughgoing industrialisation and urbanisation much earlier than Ireland does not suggest that the inroads of secularisation can be reversed in this fashion.

If the thinning of the pews was generally delayed until the 1990s, the same can hardly be said of depletion in the ranks of the clergy and religious. The impact of secularisation and modern sexuality was evident in the downward spiral in the number of priests, brothers, and nuns in Ireland from the late 1960s. Since 1967 the total number of priests, brothers, and nuns in Ireland has plunged from almost 34,000 to slightly less than 20,000, or by 41 per cent.[72] The decline has so far been quite modest for the diocesan clergy, whose numbers have fallen from just under 4,000 in 1967 to about 3,500 in 1998, or by only 11 per cent. But very much larger declines have been registered over the same period in the number of brothers (67.4 per cent), religious-order priests (45.8 per cent), and sisters (41.5 per cent). The pace of these decreases in church personnel has been fairly steady over the past thirty years in the cases of regular priests and nuns, with no great variation from decade to decade. But different patterns are evident for brothers and diocesan priests. Since 1985 alone, following almost twenty years of remorseless decline, the number of brothers has fallen by another 43 per cent, and in the years 1990-98 all of the orders of brothers in Ireland together managed to recruit merely thirty new entrants.[73] Obviously, at this rate the brothers' orders in Ireland are rapidly headed for extinction, and the average age of surviving brothers has escalated dramatically.[74]

But far more worrisome to the institutional church has been the plunge in vocations to the priesthood since 1990, a plunge that has affected the diocesan clergy almost as much as the clerical religious orders. Here the scandals of the past decade may have played a major role, with the widespread perception of a crisis in the priestly ministry contributing to the continuing downturn in vocations. From a peak of 412 in 1965, the annual number of ordinations to the priesthood fell to 259 in 1970 and 150 in 1980. It was still 129 in 1990, but it was only 44 in 1998. Between 1990 and 1998 ordinations plummeted by 66 per cent, and the decline for the diocesan clergy alone was as much as 63 per cent over that same period.[75] In 1998 deaths (172) and departures (38) from the religious life among Irish priests, diocesan and regular, outnumbered ordinations (44) by a factor of almost five to one. Even if ordinations do not decrease any further or departures rise any higher, the situation overall will inevitably worsen owing simply to increased mortality as the Irish Catholic clerical population, starved of new recruits, continues to age radically.[76] Indeed, across the entire spectrum of its personnel the Irish Catholic Church is in dire straits. The present is bleak and the future is even darker. No statistics illustrate this better than those which record entrants into religious life. In 1966, when vocations reached a peak before turning down sharply, some 1,400 people in Ireland began formal preparation for the priesthood or the religious life. The corresponding figures in 1970 and 1990 were 750 and 254. In 1998 fewer than 100 people (92, to be exact) were registered as beginning their preparation to become that ever-scarcer trio of figures in Ireland – a priest, a nun, or (rarest of all) a brother.

The radical contraction in personnel has largely disabled the institutional church from continuing to staff schools, hospitals and other public services – a set of functions which constituted a major part of its power and influence prior to the 1970s. With the disappearance of ever greater numbers of its front-line troops, the church has been compelled to retreat into the management of schools and hospitals and to depend increasingly on lay women and men, who are no longer easily amenable to clerical control. Thus the last three decades have seen the institutional church transformed to the point that its political influence, its moral authority, and its practical role in Irish society have never been less in the one hundred and fifty years since the Great Famine or perhaps in the two hundred years since the Act of Union. It is of course possible that the institutional church will recover a substantial portion of this lost ground in the new millennium. The Irish Catholic Church may be passing through the institutional equivalent of the dark night of the soul, with a future in which a purified church becomes a more faithful witness to the gospel. Certainly, there are some signs of hope, some achievements on which to build – the training of significant numbers of Irish lay people in pastoral and catechetical work as well as in theology, the addressing of major social problems such as substance abuse, inner-city poverty, and the plight of Travellers by self-sacrificing Irish priests and nuns, and the work of the Conference of Religious of Ireland in sensitising politicians and the public in general to the needs of the poor at home and indeed all over the world. It is also a healthy sign that some Irish bishops are deliberately shedding the trappings of wealth and power which long distinguished the episcopate, and are embracing a more modest lifestyle in an effort to reduce social distance between themselves and the people of their dioceses.[77] Indeed, a thoroughgoing repudiation of clericalism in its various non-spiritual dimensions would seem to be a necessary requirement for an effective repositioning of the institutional Catholic Church in Ireland at the beginning of the new millennium.

CHAPTER TWENTY-THREE

Religion in Ireland: Its state and prospects

Noel Barber SJ

The 1990s were traumatic for the church in Ireland as scandals afflicted it to the horror of its friends and to the delight of its enemies. Yet to assess the position of the church in Ireland or to speculate about its future, one would do well to attend to underlying social and religious trends rather than to concentrate on specific issues that arose in recent years. The impact of the revelations of clerical child sexual abuse or of salacious clerical conduct should not be minimised. However in the long term, cultural and social changes are more likely to affect the church than the incidents, however serious, that have received such publicity. One might expect that as Ireland modernised, became more prosperous and was more integrated into Europe, it would become more secularised and so, independently of specific Irish conditions, there would have been an underlying trend in Irish society away from a religious and towards a secular culture. Moreover, one suspects that this trend has been apparent for some time. The recent incidents might have simply made a bad situation worse.

In 1976 an American, Bruce Francis Biever, published a survey of religious and moral attitudes of Dublin Catholics that was carried out in the 1960s.[1] 87 per cent of the respondents *disagreed* with the statement that if there is a conflict between the church and the state, the state should prevail. 84 per cent *agreed* that 'if I had a son, I would surely wish him to be a priest, above and beyond everything else in the world'. 88 per cent *agreed* that the church can and does do more for the welfare of society than any other institution. 69 per cent *disagreed* that what a person does in his heart is more important than going to Mass on a Sunday. 82 per cent *disagreed* that the church views on sex are out of date. 73 per cent *disagreed* that the pleasurable sensations connected with sex are good. 88 per cent *disagreed* with the proposition: 'I can't see how a celibate clergy can ever give any worthwhile advice on the problems of marriage.' 51 per cent *agreed* that the church has a right to dictate behaviour in all areas, not just those of religion and morals. 61 per cent *agreed* that whatever the church tells me to do I would do it whether it makes sense or not. Finally, 88 per cent *disagreed* that the doctrine of sin is too harsh for modern times. These results show an extraordinary reverence for the church, an exceptional regard for its authority and an amazing esteem for its ministers. The modernisation of Ireland, the cultural changes of the 60s and the impact of the Second Vatican Council were soon to change the Irish cultural and religious landscape.

In 1983 Liam Ryan reviewed a number of surveys of Irish religious beliefs, attitudes and practice.[2] The picture that emerged from the surveys was of a society uniquely religious by European standards:

> By any standards Ireland is still a pre-eminently religious country. A weekly Mass attendance of 90 percent, a 95 per cent belief in God's existence, a 95 per cent belief in Christ and his church, a 90 per cent belief that Christ is present in the Eucharist, is something very exceptional, if not unique, in the late twentieth century.[3]

The surveys, however, brought to light strands of unorthodoxy:

> Though nearly all believe in God, nearly a quarter are not sure what sort of God this might be; some 35% either reject or are not sure of a life after death; nearly half do not believe in hell or the devil; over a third of those surveyed had some difficulty with some aspect of church teaching; when one looks at young people separately the proportion having difficulty with church teaching has risen to almost half.[4]

One particularly significant finding was that one-third of those surveyed stated that religious principles seldom if ever guided their behaviour; an increasing number questioned the authority of the church over their private lives. In short, from the surveys a picture emerged of a 'new' Catholic whose practice of religion had increasingly little impact either on behaviour in the public sphere or on many areas of private life. When one focused on the young it was clear that they had vaguer beliefs, poorer religious practice and a more critical attitude towards the church. Those whose beliefs were weakest and practice poorest came predominantly from the young, urban skilled workers, a group that was increasing numerically within the population.

The findings of the surveys indicated trends that were not favourable to the church or the religious culture of Irish society. One would wonder if the high level of practice could be maintained given the drift away from acceptance of the church's teaching on personal moral issues. One might then wonder to what extent was the practice fruitful if a sizable proportion of the population did not base their decisions on religious principles. Also, the emergence of a young, urban group with far weaker religious attachment and practice was a danger sign. Finally, it was also clear that the rural population, the great strength of the church in Ireland, was in decline at the same time as a young urban cohort was on the increase.

Ryan concluded his review by noting that it was not at all inevitable that Ireland would become secularised and suggested that the impressive number who continued to attend weekly Sunday Mass should ensure the continuance of Ireland's traditional culture. He did, nevertheless, make a further observation:

> It may be that the problems facing the church are due to general cultural and structural forces, and that the urban young are simply the most vulnerable group who are first affected by what later becomes a more widespread phenomenon.[5]

Are there now signs that these forces have in fact eroded further the role of religion and the place of the church in Irish society?

The European Values Survey (EVS) of 1990 set out to measure religious, moral, political, economic and familial values in ten western European countries including Ireland and Northern Ireland. This it did by questioning a representative sample of 1,000 adults. *Values and Social Change in Ireland* reported the results relevant to Ireland.[6] A similar survey had been carried out in 1981 and so the 1990 survey enables one to examine the extent of changes in the religious and moral values of the Irish during the 1980s.

During the 1980s the percentage of the population belonging to a church fell from 98 to 96 per cent. The corresponding figure for Europe was 42 per cent in 1990. The proportion attending weekly Mass fell also slightly from 87 to 85 per cent. There is, however, considerable variation within the overall figures. Firstly, weekly Mass attendance increased significantly with age: 76 per cent of those aged 18-26 attended Mass every week, whereas 93 per cent of those over 71 did so. There were some surprising variations in the results. While weekly Mass attendance of the cohort aged 18-26 in 1981 decreased, the EVS survey of 1990 shows that the cohort then aged 27-44 (i.e. including the 1981 cohort of 18-26) increased their attendance at Mass as they aged. What an analysis of the figures revealed was a falling off in the practice of weekly Mass-going on the part of the youngest cohort over the 1980s. Nevertheless the practice of this group remained far above the European average. Women were more likely to attend weekly Mass than were men, the discrepancy being greatest in urban areas (80 to 65 per cent). However, women in fulltime employment were quite similar to men in their weekly attendance (78 to 75 per cent). The proportion taking comfort from prayer, while lower than the proportion attending Mass weekly, increased from 80 per cent to 82 per cent between 1981 and 1990. It is clear that as people grow older they take increasing comfort from prayer. So 69 per cent of the cohort aged between 27 and 35 in 1981 found prayer comforting, but as many as 82 percent of that same group in 1990, by then aged between 36 and 44, did so.

Domicile has a major impact on religious practice. Overall, 89 per cent of those living in rural areas attended weekly Mass, while 73 per cent did so in urban areas. Domicile had a particularly strong impact on the younger groups. While 82 per cent of rural people aged between 18 and 26 attended weekly Mass, only 62 per cent did so in urban areas. In the 27-35 cohort the difference was 82 per cent (rural) to 56 per cent (urban) and in the 36-44 cohort the difference was 90 per cent (rural) to 70 per cent (urban). The impact of class and education was significant and especially so when age was taken into account. 94 per cent of those who had non-manual employment attended church every week, whereas 84 per cent of manual workers did so. This picture was reversed for those under 40; amongst this group 64 per cent of non-manual workers attended church every week; 78 per cent of manual workers did so. Education, too, influenced religious practice. While the level of education made little impact on those over 40, it was very different in the case of the under 40s. 71 per cent of those who had a Primary Certificate or less attended church every week; only 57 per cent of those with third-level education did so. There is, therefore, a strong possibility that social class and level of education will in time have a negative impact on religious practice.

The survey discerned little change in moral and religious values. On items such as belief in God, life after death, the soul, heaven, hell, sin and the devil, there was no marked overall change in beliefs. There was however a slight decline in confidence in the church. There was a considerable increase in permissiveness shown by the fact that the 1990 respondents were significantly less likely than those in 1981 to hold that there were no circumstances under which divorce and abortion could be justified. Nevertheless, Irish respondents remained far less willing than other Europeans to permit divorce and abortion. The survey looked at the respondents' understanding of God. It reported that between 1981 and 1990 the percentage believing in a personal God fell from 77 to 67 per cent. While among the older age groups the belief in a personal God was strongest, overall the belief itself weakened among all age groups. So while 76 per cent of those aged 18-26 attended Mass weekly, only 56 per cent of that group believed in a personal God – and so practised regularly while not subscribing to a core belief of Christianity. The percentage of respondents considering themselves 'religious' increased from 67 per cent to 72 per cent over the ten years. This ranged from 63 per cent for those under twenty five to 85 per cent for those of seventy and over.

The conclusion from this survey was that that a notable cultural shift had occurred among those born since 1950. The impact that youth, education, sex and domicile (urban/rural) have on church attendance, and on religious and moral values tends to be negative and could well have long-term consequences.

A survey by the International Social Survey Programme (ISSP) was carried out in 1998. The results of this survey can be compared to the results of the ISSP survey of 1991 and thus, like the EVS, cast light on the change and development in religious attitudes and behaviour.

Religious attitudes and behaviour as indicated by belief in life after death, in God, in heaven, and in miracles, did not change significantly between 1991 and 1998. There was no significant change in the percentage attending Mass, in the percentage feeling very religious or in the percentage participating in religious organisations.[7] There was, however, a significant increase in the number who described themselves as having no religion. Confidence in the church plummeted; disapproval of the power of the church increased significantly. The number accepting the official church teaching on premarital sex, extramarital sex and same-sex relations decreased substantially. Compared to 1991, a significantly larger number believed that abortion was not always wrong. When one looks at the age groups, although 85 per cent of the group aged between 18 and 28 believe in God, this belief is significantly weaker in this age group than in others. Similarly a significantly smaller percentage of this group attended weekly Mass. One fascinating finding was that while only 7 per cent of those born after 1970 expressed a high level of confidence in the church, this group had great confidence in the local priest. In fact, young women born after 1970 had the highest level of confidence in the local priest and young men of the same age had the same level of confidence with men born before 1929.

The youngest age group selected out five essential aspects of Catholic identity: the presence of God in the sacraments, charitable efforts on behalf of the poor, the real presence of Christ in the Eucharist, devotion to Mary, Mother of God, and the Pope. The group aged between 18 and 28 actually scored higher on this test than all the other groups. In so far as the youngest group saw these as essential components of the Irish Catholic heritage, one might argue that they were even more orthodox than the older groups who score less well on this scale.[8] Two points need to be made. Firstly, the identity of Jesus is the core belief of Christianity and it does not even figure in the questionnaire. Secondly, it is not clear from the survey if the respondents are simply describing attitudes that they observe in 'good' Catholics in Ireland and so the answers given may not refer to their own beliefs or values but to those of people they observe. It would be quite possible for a person to accept these as essential traits of Catholics but think little of them themselves, perhaps not believing in the presence of God in the sacraments or in the presence of Christ in the Eucharist. Finally, this youngest age group was more likely to say that it feels close or very close to the church. This is indeed strange given its low esteem for the church and its low level of religious practice. These results call for further and deeper examination.

There was a sharp move towards imaging God as mother and spouse. Between 1991 and 1998 the percentage that imagined God as a mother (*versus* father) increased from 32 to 39 per cent and the percentage that imagined

God as a spouse rather than a master had increased from 33 to 42 per cent. The percentage that imagined God as a lover increased from 46 per cent to 49 per cent and the percentage that imagined God as a friend rather than a king remained more or less stable at 79 per cent. This would seem to represent a move away from a stern and forbidding God to a gracious and loving one. However, one notes that people were not given the opportunity of opting for an impersonal God or of stating that they had no image of God. So all one can conclude from this question is that when forced to select in this way, this is how the Irish opted. One would like to know how those without belief in God and those who did not believe in a personal God 'voted'.

The survey suggests that education and age do not affect attitudes to church leadership or to sexual behaviour. However, the survey did show that age had a marked impact on practice and religious affiliation. As we saw, the younger the person, the less likely he/she was to practise and the more likely he/she was not to be affiliated to a church. The survey did not raise the impact of education on the practice of religion among the younger groups. Had it done so it might well have discovered, as the European Values Survey did, that the younger educated group was less likely to practise than the older educated group, a finding that has important implications.

What can we say about the trends in Irish religious belief and practice and their future projection? The youngest cohort, those aged 18-28, is largely unchurched but not completely secularised. It retains many core religious beliefs but is distant from the church. The survey did not test its knowledge of the faith nor did it explore its understanding of its religious beliefs and practices.

In the European Value Survey of 1999, 93 per cent of respondents described themselves as Christian, down from 95 percent in 1990, and 88 per cent described themselves as Catholic, down from 97 per cent in 1990.[9] Those not affiliated to a church (secularists) increased from 5 per cent to 9 per cent. Weekly Mass attendance fell from 81 to 65 per cent. Monthly attendance increased from 7 to 11 per cent and irregular attendance (less than once a month) grew from 9 to 19 per cent. Age continued to exercise a significant impact on practice. Over the past 10 years Mass attendance amongst all ages fell, and it fell most sharply among the youngest. Just under 24 per cent of the group aged between 18 and 24 went to Mass every week as against 75 per cent in 1990, while in the 25 to 34 group the fall-off in attendance has been from 38 to 68 per cent. While generally women attended Mass more regularly than men, the percentage decrease in women's attendance is stark. In the last 10 years the percentage of men and women in the 18-24 age group who attended Mass less than once a month increased by 31 per cent. For those between 27 and 44, the increase was over 20 per cent in the case of both men and women with the men on 25 per cent.

In the 1990 survey, the respondents were asked about taking comfort from prayer. This time, the question concerned taking comfort from religion. 76 per cent said that they took comfort from religion, higher than the proportion attending weekly religious service. The older the respondents the more likely were they to find religion comforting. Of the oldest age group 96 per cent did so, whereas of the youngest age group 51 per cent did so. There was a continuing decline in confidence in the church. 31 per cent said that they had little or no confidence in the church compared to 22 per cent in 1990. However, 69 percent had a great deal or quite a lot of confidence in the church, this despite the scandals that beset it over the 1990s. Domicile increased its impact on religious practice. Overall 82 per cent (down from 89) of those living in rural areas attended weekly Mass, 48 per cent (down from 73) did so in urban areas. Domicile had a particularly strong impact on the younger groups. The impact of class allied with age softened; the classes tended to converge at a much lower level of weekly practice. The weekly attendance of manual workers under 45 fell to 41 per cent and that of non-manual workers fell to 42 per cent. Similarly amongst people over 45 the difference was no longer very significant.

This survey, like that of the ISSP, reports little change in moral and religious values between 1990 and 1999. On items such as belief in God, life after death, the soul, heaven, hell, and sin there was no overall change in beliefs. In so far as there was a change in the youngest age group, it frequently was towards more orthodox beliefs. 94 per cent of 18-24 year olds expressed belief in God as against 92 per cent in 1990. 69 per cent of this group believed in life after death, the same proportion as in 1990. 43 per cent of the group believed in hell; 39 per cent did so 10 years earlier. The proportion of this group believing in sin increased from 79 to 83 per cent. While the percentage believing in a personal God did not change significantly since 1990, belief in a personal God has declined by about 20 per cent over twenty years. The survey confirmed an increase in permissiveness since 1990. On abortion the percentage saying that it was never justified fell from 83 in 1981 to 66 in 1990, to 60 percent (66 per cent of Catholics and 60 per cent of Protestants) in 1999. On homosexuality, the percentage saying that it is never justified fell from 62 per cent in 1981, to 56 per cent in 1990, to 38 per cent (41 per cent of Catholics and 52 per cent of Protestants) in 1999. The percentage saying that divorce was never justified fell from 52 per cent in 1981, to 35 per cent in 1981, to 29 per cent (30 per cent of Catholics and 22 per cent of Protestants) in 1999. The older the respondents the more conservative were their attitudes. However, there is a general, though not universal, tendency for the older groups to hold more 'liberal' views in the later surveys.

Education, too, had affected these attitudes: there was a wide gulf between those who had not completed secondary education and those who had third level education. Age reinforced this gap. For instance, 36 per cent of those under 45 and 74 per cent of those over 45 with third-level education accepted that abortion was never justified; of those who had not completed secondary education 60 per cent of the under 45s and 82 per cent of the over 45s did so.

Attachment to the church affected attitudes significantly. Those who are not affiliated to a church think differently about these issues than those who are. Of those who attended weekly Mass 48 per cent believed that homosexuality was never justified, 74 per cent that abortion was never justified and 36 per cent that divorce was never justified. Amongst those who never or rarely attend Mass the percentages were 28, 49 and 18. The differences among practising and non-practising Protestants are similar but not as great.

To assess the extent of secularisation in Ireland it is helpful to look at the European situation. The level of Irish weekly church attendance is exceeded only by Malta and equalled by Poland. In fact the attendance of the 18-42 age group, the worst in Ireland (22 per cent), exceeds the *average* weekly church attendance in all but a handful of European countries. In Europe, belief in God, in sin, in life after death all receive the support of a majority of those surveyed. However, indicators of attachment to churches show a strong secularisation tendency, with a marked difference between the more religious Catholic countries of southern Europe and the less religious northern Protestant countries. In Ireland, however, belief in God, in a life after death, in the devil, in sin, in heaven is much stronger than in the vast majority of European countries.

The Irish attitude towards divorce is more negative than that of any country in western Europe with the exception of Malta and much more negative than in the northern Protestant countries. On divorce the pattern is the same as regards western Europe. In eastern Europe there are some countries that are less accepting of divorce than is Ireland. On the acceptance of homosexuality Ireland is near the mean. The western Europeans are more accepting (Malta and Portugal are exceptions). The eastern European countries with a few exceptions are inclined to judge that homosexuality is never justified. So while Ireland stands out as quite different to the rest of Europe on many indices of religious belief and practice, the surveys show that there has been a substantial shift towards the liberal positions common in other countries.

How secular is Ireland? The answer depends to an extent on what one means by secularisation. If lack of religious affiliation is a sign of secularisation, then Ireland with a mere 9 per cent 'unaffiliated' is not secularised. If one takes the abandonment of religious belief as a more appropriate indication, then, again, Ireland shows no sign of being or of becoming secularised since belief in God, in life after death, in heaven and in sin command such a high level of acceptance. If, however, one defines secularisation as non-attendance at church, non-acceptance of church teaching, a lack of trust in the church as an organisation and lack of confidence in its leadership, one can say that there are signs of secularisation. However, the tendency to detach oneself from the church in Ireland and not to accept its teaching on a range of issues has not been accompanied by the abandonment of core religious beliefs. It might, therefore, be better to say that there is a move towards Ireland becoming 'unchurched' rather than secularised. However, distance from the practice of religion leads inevitably to an ignorance of the basic understandings of Christianity and that is not reassuring. In this situation, how will religious beliefs be passed on from generation to generation?

It is frequently asserted that modernisation necessarily leads to a decline of religion, both in society and in the minds of individuals. On that basis it is only a matter of time before Ireland becomes completely secularised. Many, however, dispute this fact, arguing that it is simply false to say that we live in a secularised world; there is not the empirical evidence to support the thesis that modernisation leads to secularisation.[10] While there is a strong secularisation trend in modern societies, there is also a strong counter-secularisation current. Even in a society as thoroughly secularised as Sweden, there remains a core of strongly religious people. Furthermore, the secularisation thesis comes to grief completely in the USA which is, by any standards, a most religious society. Looking around the world it is hard to see much evidence that religion is fading away. We have witnessed in our own lifetime a resurgence of Islam, as well as an evangelical revival in the USA, Latin America, the Philippines, South Korea and in sub-Saharan Africa.

The Irish sociologist, Tony Fahey, writing in the Irish quarterly review *Studies*, sums up the anti-secularisation thesis:

This approach rejects the dominant social scientific view of religion as an irrational hangover from tradition that somehow survives in a few atypical modern societies. Instead it regards religiosity, in one form or another, as an essential and enduring part of the human condition. Religion, in this view, is here to stay: it may change in form and fluctuate in social significance but there is no reason to believe that it is set on a long-term course of decline.[11]

This approach shifts the attention from social trends to those who 'provide' religion, namely, the churches. He argues that the explanation for the varying fortunes of organised religion is to be found in the ability or otherwise of the churches to respond appropriately to the demand that is there for religion. The organisations will thrive in so far as they are properly responsive to the religious needs of the people. He concludes:

There is no inevitability about either the decline or revival. The Catholic

Church in Ireland could go the way of its counterpart in France – which is towards extreme contraction, or of the many Protestant denominations in the United States – which is towards continuing vitality within a more pluralist system. Which of these paths it follows may depend in part on the receptiveness of Irish people in the future to religious experience and ideals. But it may also depend on the adaptability of the church itself, that is, on its ability to remain rooted in Christian tradition while at the same time feeling out and responding to the evolving spiritual demands of the age.[12]

This conclusion is similar to that of Liam Ryan (1983) discussed above:

It would be wrong to give the impression that social and cultural trends are going to continue irrespective of what people do about them. Organised religions have the ability to fashion their own future, and that future is in the hands of those now living.[13]

Is there any indication that the Irish church will be able to reinvigorate itself and adopt a strategy that will respond to the demands of the age? If it has not done so in the past twenty years, what is the possibility that it will do so over the next twenty? What shape would that strategy take? Where could the Irish church look for an example of 'best practice', a strategy that has been successful in Europe in stemming the secularist trend? One would have great difficulty finding such a strategy. If one looked to France, where the church has been in the vanguard of liturgical, theological and scriptural reform, one would find little encouragement. If one looked to the Protestant churches that have implemented liberal policies with regard to the ordination of women, declericalisation and democratisation, one would receive cold comfort. In the areas most affected by the Reformation the process of secularisation is most advanced. There is no evidence that the liberal road would be fruitful. As sociologists of religion point out, it is the conservative/orthodox/traditionalist movements that are on the rise throughout the world. Those churches that had most strenuously adapted to secular culture are almost everywhere in decline. Witness the fate of the mainline Protestant churches in the USA.[14] It would appear that European society has succumbed to secular cultural trends and that the churches have been unable to devise a way of withstanding those trends. As a result, over the past twenty years 'church religion' has declined throughout Europe. Given the awareness for twenty years of the need 'to do something' to halt the decline and revitalise the church and the failure of strategies to do so, one would have to presume that 'church religion' will continue to decline both in Europe and in Ireland. A dispassionate analysis of religious and social trends in Ireland and Europe would have to conclude that unless there is an enormous external upheaval that shakes the cultural foundations of Europe, organised religion will attract an increasingly small number of adherents. There is no doubt that there will be a committed small core that will work to revitalise the churches and attempt to devise strategies to evangelise that mainstream secular culture. The possibility of such strategies succeeding continues to look bleak.

What if the church in Ireland and in the rest of Europe became a small remnant? Would the church be less the People of God? Did Israel become increasingly less God's people as it moved from being a powerful kingdom under David and Solomon to becoming a divided kingdom, then to being a single small kingdom that the Babylonians smashed, then to becoming a vassal state and finally to being scattered and persecuted for the best part of 2000 years? Does the fact that the cradle of Christianity, modern Turkey, has only vestigial remains of Christianity, break our faith in God?

I think that we Catholics in Ireland as well as in the rest of Europe could profitably reflect on the Old Testament story, apply it to ourselves and accept that in failure and humiliation the Lord is with us, perhaps more so than when we were powerful and successful. The church throughout the western world is going through its 'Israelite' experience, moving from being great and powerful to being peripheral and insignificant. This indeed may be no bad thing. When powerful the church has always faced the temptation, into which it frequently fell, of acting as if it was a secular power with secular goals and was indistinguishable from other secular organisations. The humiliation of decline and the experience of powerlessness may well so change the focus and character of the church as to lead to an inner transformation. It is only when it is purified and transformed that the church will be able to devise a strategy to respond to the spiritual needs of the age.

Donal Kerr

Kevin B. Nowlan

On 8 September 2000, I was delighted to be associated with the launch of Donal Kerr's study of the life of Jean-Claude Colin, the founder of the Marist congregation, of which Donal was a member. The book is not just a normal filial tribute but a major contribution to modern church history. Since the publication of the book Donal Kerr died, on 10 May 2001. He is a great loss not merely to his confrères and family but to the world of history.

Donal Kerr was a latecomer to full-time academic teaching and publication. He had been a civil servant before he joined the Marists and in the congregation he was to fill a number of important positions. He was in his fifties when he was granted his D. Phil. from Oxford University. Earlier he had studied in University College Dublin and read theology in Rome. In 1978 he became professor of ecclesiastical history in St Patrick's College Maynooth. He suited well the academic character of the place but what really established him as a major historian of the nineteenth century was the publication by the Clarendon Press, Oxford of his book *Peel, Priests and Politics*. The book appeared in 1992 with the subtitle *Sir Robert Peel's Administration and the Roman Catholic Church in Ireland 1841-1846,* which hardly does full justice to the contents of the book. His control of the material and his sense of the drama in the relationship between Rome, London and Ireland give a special value to the work. It was the age of Daniel O'Connell's Repeal movement, a time when Robert Peel was making a determined effort to win over support in Ireland among the Catholic population. Peel was to fail in his major objective but his Irish policies ensured a better financial situation for St Patrick's College Maynooth in terms of government financial support and he also improved the administrative arrangements for Catholic charities. Sadly, he did not find a solution to the pressing problems of the Irish land system in the years leading up to the Great Famine of the mid-nineteenth century.

With *Peel, Priests and Politics* Donal Kerr showed how source material from a wide range of archives could be combined in a fashion seldom seen in the writing of modern Irish history. In the use of source material, especially from Rome, he made a unique contribution to historical studies. The Peel book was followed in 1994 by his second major publication on Irish history, again published by the Clarendon Press. Its title was challenging: *A Nation of Beggars? Priests, People, and Politics in Famine Ireland 1846-1852*. Again, one is impressed by his well-integrated text and by his assessment of the policies of Lord John Russell, who as a successor of Peel attempted to deal with the Famine situation in Ireland, the O'Connellite movement and relations with Rome, all of this against a background of revolution in Europe and eventually in Ireland. The limitations of Russell's policies during the Famine are well known but what is interesting is to see how he sought closer relations with Rome at a time when Rome was under political pressure but was normally suspicious of London's intentions. This theme of diplomatic exchanges is very fully considered in Donal's book. He also writes with great understanding of the social and political happenings of the Famine period. On a political level the ecclesiastical titles bill disputes of the early 1850s brought to an end any hope of an easy settlement between London and Rome. Neither politically nor socially was the scene in Ireland a happy one at the end of the 1840s with the Famine still running its course and the involvement of religious bodies in Famine relief was a major issue. The attitude of the Catholic Church to the problems led Donal to write yet another book, *The Catholic Church in the Great Famine in Ireland* (Dublin 1998), in which he examines the difficulties of organising Famine relief and also pays tribute to the many priests and others who gave their lives in the attempt to alleviate the plight of their neighbours.

When Donal told me he had embarked on a new project which would take him away from nineteenth-century Irish history and into the field of biography, the life of the founder of his congregation, I was a little unhappy as so much work still needed to be done on the second half of the nineteenth century. However, I now realise that with his study of the early career of Jean-Claude Colin he has made a significant contribution not merely to the history of the Marists but also to the great Catholic revival in Europe in the wake of the French Revolution. This is something that should be emphasised. As in his Irish publications he again drew on a wide range of source material. He gives us a picture of Colin and his associates which is well rounded and as a good historian he makes no attempt to avoid the difficulties and controversies of those early years of the congregation. It remains, however, a story of determination and of how a small group of clerics in the south-east of France could create an organisation which was to be of great significance in the missionary work of the Catholic Church. The book was published in 2000 by Columba Press under the title *Jean-Claude Colin Marist. A founder in an era of revolution and restoration: the early years 1790-1836.*

In addition to his other commitments, Donal Kerr worked with the European Science Foundation, Strasbourg, from 1985 onwards. The Foundation had sponsored a major comparative study of governments and non-dominant ethnic groups in Europe between 1850 and 1940, a rather roundabout way of saying the relations between the state and minorities. Donal was to be the chairman and principal editor of the section on religious affairs. This international action resulted in the publication by the Foundation of eight volumes in 1992. Donal was the editor of the second volume under the title *Religion, State and Ethnic Groups*. In addition to the introductory overview of the contributions, he also wrote one of the essays 'Government and Catholicism in Ireland 1850-1940'. The final words of his essay have a lasting significance in terms of any analysis of Anglo-Irish relations. He emphasised the extent of British government disengagement from Northern Ireland after 1922 as a factor in the continuation of major problems in Anglo-Irish relations, a situation which in no way eased the problems of church-state relations. The problems were to survive, as we know, even after World War II.

With his books, articles and lectures and through his religious life Donal Kerr gave of his best, with a dedication to the truth in history. He was a good man and a fine friend. To end may I quote a few lines from Sheridan Gilley's obituary of Donal in the *Tablet*: 'He was the sort of perfectly balanced author who can be always quoted as an abiding authority.'

A Chronology of Irish History *

c. 5th-12th CENTURIES CE: EARLY CHRISTIAN IRELAND

5th century: 431: The earliest documentary reference to Christianity in Ireland occurs in the form of an entry in a Roman chronology stating that Pope Celestine sent one Palladius as bishop to 'the Irish who believe in Christ', indicating that Christianity had begun to penetrate Ireland sometime earlier. **432:** The mission of St Patrick, revered as 'the apostle of Ireland' – though his activities seem to have been confined to the north – is generally dated by historians to 432-461/492, though a fourth-century dating is also supported. Remarkably for such an early period, two authentic writings of Patrick survive, his *Confession*, testifying to the working of God's providence in his life, and his *Letter to Coroticus*, protesting against attacks upon defenceless Christians – both reflect a warm, humble personality, fired by Christian faith and charity.

The O'Neills of Tyrone and their confederates extended control over most of Ulster and then more widely through the northern half of Ireland; the Dal Riada of north-east Ulster migrated to the adjacent north-west of Scotland, possibly under pressure from the expanding O'Neills, thus in time providing the name of North Britain i.e. Scotland (*Scoti* = Gaelic/Irish).

6th-7th centuries: The episcopal-diocesan structure of the Patrician church assumed a monastic character more congenial to the Irish tribal system. The 'golden age' of Celtic Christianity was based upon a burgeoning monastic culture, especially as cultivated in a number of major monastic centres, renowned for sanctity and learning, and hallowed by association with an especially venerated founder, e.g. Kildare, St Brigid; Clonfert, St Brendan; Clonmacnoise, St Finnian. The characteristic marks of Celtic Christian culture included a severely ascetical spirituality and morality (cf. the Rule and Penitential of St Columbanus) softened by a joyous celebration of nature, high artistic achievement which succeeded in exploiting pagan Celtic forms and motifs to construct a distinctively Christian iconography (high crosses, bee-hive cells, chalices, reliquaries, illuminated manuscripts), a multifaceted literature in Latin and in the vernacular (hagiography, hymnody, lyric poetry, history, mythology), and a vigorous missionary outreach (the *perigrinatio pro*

---

*This chronology was originally devised by Carlo Maria Pelizzi, translated from Italian by Seán Fagan SM, and revised for this edition by Brendan Bradshaw SM.

Christo), extending to north Britain (Colmcille, 521-97) and Europe (Columbanus, 543-615, Virgilius, c. 700-84). The Easter controversy arose when the Celtic church sought to retain its traditional method of computing the date of Easter in preference to the Roman system adopted by the Anglo-Saxon church at the synod of Whitby (664). The Irish church relented in the second half of the seventh century, led by Armagh which now began to claim primatial status as the See of Patrick. **664-6:** Plague devastated the population. **697:** The law of Adomnán – successor to Colmcille as abbot of Iona and his biographer – forbade the killing of women and children or their involvement in battle. The secularisation of Irish monasticism began with the imposition of laymen, scions of local ruling septs, as hereditary abbots.

8th century: 734: Armagh, asserting its primacy, claimed the right to receive tithes throughout Ireland and promulgated the 'law of Patrick' forbidding the killing of clerics. The *Céli Dé*, seeking to recall Gaelic monasticism to its original austerity and spirituality, spread in the second half of the eighth century, partly as separate monastic communities and partly as individuals within larger communities.

795-1014: The Viking Era: 795: A raid on Rathlin Island provides the first evidence of Viking activities in Ireland. Viking raids occurred with increasing frequency through the ninth century, particularly on monasteries which were vulnerable and offered the prospect of rich booty. **804:** Iona, the mother house of Columban monasticism off the west coast of Scotland, was abandoned and the jurisdictional centre of the Columban federation transferred to Kells, thus subordinating it to the church of Armagh. **840-:** Viking settlements were established as trading posts along the coast (Dublin, Wexford, Waterford) or at the head of navigable rivers (Limerick), and the settlers began to convert to Christianity as intercourse with the native population increased through trade and political or marriage alliances. **9th century:** The Dal Cais of Thomond, (north Munster), exploiting the weakness of older ruling kindreds through conflict with the Vikings, expanded their suzerainty in Munster and eventually wrested the provincial kingship from its traditional holders, the Eoganacht of Cashel. **976-1014:** Brian Bóraimhe (Boru), the most powerful of the Dal Cais kings and the eponymous founder of the O'Brien dynasty, established himself as high king (1002) and sought to develop his position as such from that of a *primus inter pares* among provincial kings to that of a national monarch exercising sovereign power in line with developments then taking place elsewhere in western Europe. The church of Armagh supported Brian's aspiration and he reciprocally supported Armagh's claim to ecclesiastical primacy – thus a scribal entry in the *Book of Armagh* recording his visit to Armagh (1005) accords him the title of *imperator Scottorum.* **1014:** At the battle of Clontarf Brian and his Gaelic allies defeated a far-flung Viking alliance supplemented by the Gaelic lords of Leinster, and though Brian lost his life in the battle his victory is regarded as breaking Viking power in Ireland.

1014-1169: 'Kings in opposition': The century and a half between the death of Brian Bóraimhe and the coming of the Normans (1169) was marked by an ongoing power-struggle for the high-kingship between powerful provincial royal dynasties, the O'Briens (Munster), the O'Neills (Ulster), the O'Connors (Connacht) from which the O'Connors had emerged triumphant by the 1160s in the person of Rory O'Connor.

c 1060-: The Gregorian reform gained ground in the Irish church in the late eleventh century, initially through the influence of two reforming archbishops of Canterbury, Lanfranc (1070-89) and Anselm (1093-1109), exercised through the bishops of the Viking cities who gave allegiance to Canterbury. Patrick, bishop of Dublin, and Gilbert, bishop of Limerick played a prominent part at this stage. Native reformers assumed a leading role from the early twelfth century – Ceallach of Armagh (1105-29), his renowned successor, St Malachy (fl. 1095-1148), and St Laurence O'Toole of Dublin (fl. 1128-80) were key figures. Political support was provided by the powerful O'Briens (Turlough, 1063-86, Muirchertach, 1086-1119) and later notably by Donnchadh Ua Cerbaill of Oirghialla (Louth) among others. A reform agenda was established by means of a series of episcopal synods – Cashel (1101), Rathbreasail (1111), Kells (1152) – which legislated against hereditary succession to ecclesiastical office, and abuses connected with sexual morality (e.g. clerical concubinage), sought to uphold sanctuary, asserted the freedom of the clergy from lay taxation and prosecution in the secular courts, and finally established a diocesan episcopate, divided into four metropolitan districts, to replace the existing monastic system of church organisation. The reform of the monastic system was also put in train with the introduction by St Malachy of the continental reformed orders of the Cistercians – Mellifont, 1142 – and the Augustinian canons who had established 70 Irish foundations by 1170.

THE ANGLO-NORMAN CONQUEST, 1169-1315

1155: The bull *Laudabiliter*, issued by the English pope, Adrian IV, conferred the title of *Dominus Hiberniae* on Henry II, king of England, deputing him thereby to undertake the reform of the church in Ireland. **1169:** (May) A force of Anglo-Norman feudatories led by Robert Le Clare (Strongbow) landed at Waterford on the invitation of Diarmaid Mac Murchada to assist him in securing his position as king of Leinster. **1171:** (October) Henry II came to Ireland with an army to assert his lordship and ensure the loyalty of his feudatories. **1172:** The Irish bishops at the synod of Cashel acknowledged

Henry II's title, anticipating his support in the reform of the church, and most of the Irish dynastic lords made their submission including eventually the high-king, Ruadhrí Ua Concobair (O'Connor). **1175-1315:** The Anglo-Normans colonised most of Ireland, establishing the feudal system and building castles to protect their territories from marauding natives. Craftsmen, peasants and merchants from England settled and new cities and towns were established – Drogheda, Dundalk, Sligo, Galway, Kilkenny. Gaelic natives living in the colonised territories were denied the 'liberties and privileges' of English subjects, including the protection of the law but Gaelic law and custom continued to operate in the Gaelic lordships. The new mendicant orders (friars and sisterhoods) spread to Ireland and expanded rapidly: Dominicans, 1224, Franciscans, c. 1230, Augustinians, c. 1280, Carmelites, c. 1270. **1202-c. 1227:** The Mellifont Conspiracy, reflecting the tension between natives and newcomers, concerned the attempt of native Cistercians to resist the intrusion of English monks into their communities and the 'meddling' of Visitors sent from the mother-house, Cîteaux. **1291:** the Franciscan provincial chapter at Cork occasioned racial violence and loss of life. **14th century:** The Irish church became divided between the *ecclesia inter anglicos* (the colonised territory) and the *ecclesia inter hibernicos* (the native lordships).

THE GAELIC RESURGENCE: c 1315-1530

1315-18: The Bruce rebellion erupted with the arrival at Larne (1315) of Edward Bruce, brother of Robert, king of Scotland, to lead a native confederation against English domination. **1316:** Bruce was inaugurated as (the last) high-king of Ireland. **1317:** The Remonstrance of Dónal O'Neill defended the Bruce rebellion against the pope's condemnation of it and of O'Neill's cession of the title of high-king to Edward. **1318:** At the battle of Faughart Bruce's forces were routed and the most serious challenge to English lordship in Ireland in the medieval period collapsed, leaving both the Irish and English territories devastated.

1348: The Black Death reached Ireland, ravaging the towns and the most densely populated areas of the colony but leaving the sparsely populated Gaelic territories relatively unscathed. It served to escalate the migration of peasants from the colony to England, causing depopulation and facilitating the settlement of native Irish in the colony.

1366: The Statutes of Kilkenny attempted to stem the cultural erosion of the English colony (Gaelicisation) by codifying earlier statutes against the colonists' use of Irish customs, dress and speech, and by curbing growing tension between the colonists (English 'by blood') and the metropoles (English 'by birth') by banning provocative name-calling between them, e.g. 'English hobbe', 'Irish churl'. The statutes applied explicitly to the colonial territory alone, highlighting the tacit partition that had developed between the English and the native territories.

1394-9: Richard II visited Ireland, 1394-5 – the only medieval English monarch to do so apart from John – with the largest army (5,000 troops) deployed in Ireland in the medieval period. Having secured the submission of most of the Gaelic lords – O'Donnell was a prominent exception – he returned to England (summer, 1395). Richard returned to Ireland, 1399, to quell further Gaelic restiveness but was strongly resisted on this occasion, notably by Art Mac Murrough Kavanagh in Leinster, and was recalled, with little accomplished, by a political crisis in England where he lost his throne to his Lancastrian rivals.

c. 1440-: The Observant reform, aiming to recall the mendicants to their primitive rules and spirit, reached Ireland from the Continent in the early 1440s and spread steadily through the Gaelic territories, penetrating the colony from 1500 onwards; here it continued to spread until arrested by the introduction of the English Reformation (1534) and the dissolution of the religious orders (1537-9). By 1534 Observant foundations in Ireland numbered 40 Franciscan and 8 each of Dominicans and Augustinians. Many Observants were also dispersed among conventual communities. The Carmelites seem to have been little affected by the movement. Evangelistic in spirit, the Observants played a significant part in resisting the Reformation in Ireland.

c. 1450-: The (English) Pale describes the area in the hinterland of Dublin to which, along with the towns in the east and south, the direct, regular, jurisdiction of the Crown had now receded. The Anglo-Norman earldoms, Kildare (Fitzgerald), Ormond (Butler), Desmond (Fitzgerald), enjoyed virtual self-government while acknowledging the Crown's overlordship – Desmond remained aloof following the judicial murder of the 7th earl (1468), while Anglo-Norman lordships further afield became integrated within the native territory and were almost completely Gaelicised, e.g. the de Burgos of Connacht.

1460-1534: Colonial 'home-rule': **1460:** The Irish (colonial) parliament proclaimed by statute that the Lordship of Ireland was 'corporate of itself', governed by its own laws and parliament under the Crown but independently of the English parliament. **1462:** Gerald Fitzgerald, 7th earl of Desmond was appointed lord deputy and, following his judicial murder (1468) during the brief intermission of the English lord deputy, Sir John Tiptoft (1467-70), the office was filled successively by the 7th and 8th earls of Kildare – though with occasional brief intermissions – as an economic means of securing the government of the colony. **1494:** Poynings' Law curbed the independence of the Irish parliament by enacting that bills could not be introduced there without first being approved under the royal seal in England.

THE ENGLISH CONQUEST, REFORMATION AND PLANTATION, 1534-1691

Henry VIII (1507-46) and Ireland: 1534-5: The Kildare rebellion, led by Silken Thomas, heir to the 8th earl, erupted when a false rumour reached Dublin of his execution while under detention in the Tower of London where he had been detained following his dismissal as lord deputy in 1533. The rebels appealed unsuccessfully for assistance from the kings of France and Spain by representing themselves as defenders of the pope against the heretic Henry VIII. The rebellion was ruthlessly suppressed by an army sent from England under Sir William Skeffington, the new lord deputy – the entire garrison at the Fitzgerald stronghold of Maynooth was put to the sword despite surrendering on promise of a pardon (hence 'the pardon of Maynooth' to denote English treachery), and Silken Thomas and his five uncles were executed in London (1537) also despite surrendering on promise of a pardon.

1536-: The Tudor reform of government: Thomas Cromwell, first minister of Henry VIII, reformed the Crown's system of government in Ireland by installing an English lord deputy in place of the customary colonial magnate, by appointing English officials to key posts in the administration in place of the magnate's clients, by substituting an English garrison for the magnate's retinue as a security force, and by ensuring close supervision of Irish government by the English privy council. These arrangements provided the basis for the government of Ireland down to the establishment of the Free State in the 1920s. **1541:** The act 'for the kingly title' proclaimed the king of England to be *ipso facto* king of Ireland, thereby incidentally elevating the status of the Lordship to that of a kingdom and strengthening the claim of the Irish parliament to sovereignty under the Crown – a case that was to be argued incessantly by patriots thenceforward. **1541-4:** 'Surrender and regrant', promoted by the conciliatory lord deputy, Sir Anthony St Leger, was designed to bring the Gaelic lordships within the Crown's jurisdiction by offering the ruling dynasties secure legal title in return for acknowledging the overlordship of the English Crown. The process had been completed in only a small number of cases when it was abandoned – O'Neill had been created earl of Tyrone and O'Brien earl of Thomond and a number of lesser lords had received noble titles *pro rata.*

1534-47: The Henrician Reformation: 1534: Thomas Cromwell, Henry VIII's first minister, directed the Dublin government to resist the 'bishop of Rome's pretended jurisdiction'. **1536-7:** The Irish Reformation Parliament enacted a series of statutes in line with those already enacted in England, declaring Henry VIII to be 'supreme head' of the church in Ireland and the pope to be a usurper of royal authority, appropriating papal revenues, dissolving the religious orders and confiscating their properties. **1537-9:** The religious orders were disbanded within the colony by royal 'visitors' though they continued to flourish in the Gaelic territories. Shrines were closed, e.g. Our Lady of Trim, and their precious ornaments confiscated, relics were destroyed, e.g. the *bacalus Jesu*. The oath of supremacy was administered by George Browne in many towns throughout the colony in the course of a preaching campaign to gain popular support for the Reformation, and he reported general acquiescence apart from the lower clergy, many of whom agitated against it in secret. The Observants and the lay lawyers were singled out as especially active opponents of the Reformation.

1547-53: The reign of Edward VI: The Edwardian Reformation substituted a Protestant Communion Service in English for the Latin Mass-sacrifice but the Dublin government forbore to introduce the change generally in Ireland, anticipating popular resistance. Bishop John Bale's attempt to introduce Protestantism in his diocese of Waterford provoked much hostility and he was forced to flee overseas on the accession of the Catholic Queen Mary. Fortresses were established along the borders of the colony and in strategic locations on the coast in response to increasing restiveness in the Gaelic lordships and attempts to persuade the French and Scottish kings to send an invading force to Ireland.

1553-8: The reign of Queen Mary: 1553: Catholic worship was spontaneously restored in anticipation of official authority throughout the colony. **1556-7:** The plantations of Laois and Offaly, the first of the Tudor plantations, was undertaken by Lord Deputy Sussex to create a buffer zone between the Pale and the Irish territory, but the expulsion of the O'Mores and the O'Carrolls from their patrimonies to make way for the plantation increased the restiveness of the 'Irishry' by raising the prospect of a 'general conquest'. **1557:** The Reformation legislation was repealed by the parliament of the colony but the property of the religious orders was allowed to remain in the hands of the laity who had purchased it.

1559-1603: The reign of Elizabeth I: 1560-: The Elizabethan Reformation restored the Royal Ecclesiastical Supremacy and reintroduced a *Book of Common Prayer* which provided a Communion Service in place of the Mass. The *Book of Common Prayer* was imposed in all churches in which reformers – usually from England – officiated, but leading reformers such as Archbishop Loftus of Dublin and Bishop Lyon of Cork reported that the people were failing to attend the services or to receive the sacraments as prescribed in the Prayer Book and that local officials were leading the way in opposition, evading the oath of supremacy, and neglecting to apply the penalties imposed by law on those who refused to conform. The religious houses in the Irish territory were dissolved as the Crown extended its control but the friars remained active with the connivance of the local lords and campaigned vigorously on behalf of Roman Catholicism. **1571:** A Reformation catechism in Irish was published – sponsored by the Dublin alderman, William Ussher – but Irish versions of the *Book of Common Prayer* and the New Testament did not appear until the seventeenth century, thus confirming the view of the Reformation among the Irish as an alien (*Gallda*) heretical innovation. **1592:** Trinity College Dublin was established to train a native Reformation clergy, but even when it succeeded in attracting students from the Gaelic districts these tended to remain in the colony after ordination instead of returning to serve cures among the 'Irishry'. **c. 1570-:** The Counter-Reformation took root in Ireland as Catholic priests, trained in Counter-Reformation colleges on the continent, returned to serve on the Irish mission. 'Massing houses' were established with the assistance of the local elites, where Mass was celebrated and the sacraments administered as an alternative to the Prayer Book liturgy provided in the churches. The Franciscans were especially prominent in the native territories – St Anthony's, Leuven was established in the opening decade of the seventeenth century with Flaithrí Ó Maolchonaire (Florence Conry) as Guardian, to provide devotional, catechetical and polemical literature in Irish for the mission. The Jesuit mission became active in the colonial territory, especially in the towns, from the 1580s. **1584:** Archbishop Dermot O'Hurley of Cashel was hanged, the most celebrated of the Catholic martyrs in the sixteenth century.

1569-1603: The Elizabethan Conquest and Plantation: The conquest was conducted piecemeal as the military establishment increased exponentially to overcome rebellions provoked by the plantations and the intrusion of royal government into the lordships of the Irishry. **1569-70:** The rebellion of James Fitzmaurice Fitzgerald was the first to espouse an ideology of 'faith and fatherland', though local politics were also involved. Exemplary terror was used by Sir Humphrey Gilbert and Sir John Perrot to suppress it and James Fitzmaurice fled to the continent. **1579-83:** the Desmond rebellion was triggered by the return of James Fitzmaurice from exile with a small papal expeditionary force, accompanied by Nicholas Sanders, an English Counter-Reformation priest, as chaplain. The earl of Desmond reluctantly assumed leadership of the rebellion when James was killed in a local skirmish shortly after his return. Terror was deployed to suppress it as before – a 500 strong papal invading force was massacred at Dún an Óir (Smerwick) – as well as a scorched-earth policy which resulted in an horrendous famine, graphically described by the poet-colonist, Edmund Spenser. The fugitive earl of Desmond was tracked down and assassinated in 1583. **1580:** a chain of rebellions in Leinster led by the Counter-Reformation militants, Viscount Baltinglass and Sir William Nugent and the turbulent Gaelic lord, Fiach Mac Aodha Ó Broin (Fiach McHugh O'Byrne), were suppressed with relative ease, despite Fiach Mac Aodha's spectacular victory over the forces of the Crown at Glenmalure in the Wicklow mountains. Baltinglass and Nugent took refuge on the continent and Fiach Mac Aodha was eventually captured and hanged. **1584-8:** The Munster Plantation, the first of the major plantation schemes, allocated some 600,000 acres of land in the south-west, confiscated from the earl of Desmond and 163 other rebels, to English colonists but it enjoyed only limited success in its aim of establishing an English settlement since many of the purchasers did not take up residence, leasing back the land instead to its original owners, and many of the settlers retained the existing native tenantry who were willing to pay higher rents than English tenants. Nevertheless the plantation effected a transfer of ownership on a vast scale from (Catholic) Gaelic and Old English to (Protestant) New English.

1594-1603: The Nine Years War developed from a rebellion (1594) by the Ulster lords, Red Hugh O'Donnell of Tyrconnell and Hugh Maguire of Fermanagh, against the increasing intrusion of Crown government (administrative and military) into the hitherto impenetrable north. **1595:** Hugh O'Neill, the highly-astute and politically-experienced earl of Tyrone, joined the rebellion and, responding to the promptings of influential clerics, highlighted the religious grievances of the rebels as he sought the support of all the disaffected elements in Ireland and the intervention of the Spanish monarchy. **1596-7:** The uprising assumed the dimensions of a national war of liberation – the first of the modern period – as the disaffected lords of Leinster and Connacht, and finally of Munster, rallied to the cause of 'faith and fatherland', though the Catholic Old English of the Pale remained loyal to the crown. **1598:** At the battle of the Yellow Ford in Armagh, Hugh O'Neill, with the assistance of O'Donnell and Maguire, inflicted a spectacular defeat on a 4,000 strong invasionary force led by his old enemy Sir Henry Bagenal. **1600:** Pope Clement VIII, through the persuasion of the influential theologian and antiquarian, Peter Lombard, issued a letter indicating his support for the rebellion and granting a plenary indulgence to all who participated, but failed to accede to Hugh O'Neill's request to excommunicate those who refused to join. **1601:** At Kinsale the Irish suffered a decisive setback when their combined forces were routed by an English army under the new lord deputy, Mountjoy, as they attempted to relieve a Spanish expeditionary force under siege in the port. **1602:** Red Hugh O'Donnell died in Spain while attempting to secure further military assistance. **1603:** The Treaty of Mellifont brought the war to a close with O'Neill's submission to Lord Deputy Mountjoy on generous terms. Ironically, Queen Elizabeth died just before O'Neill's submission.

1603-47: Ireland under the early Stuarts: 1603: James VI of Scotland succeeded to the Crown of England as James I, to general rejoicing in Ireland where James was expected, as the son of the Catholic Mary, to be favourably disposed towards Catholicism. Public celebration of the Mass was resumed in the towns of the south where the Catholic clergy repossessed the churches, but Lord Deputy Mountjoy marched south with an army to suppress the Mass and extrude the Catholic clergy. Catholic priests were outlawed, fines were imposed for sheltering them and rewards were offered for informing on them. Religious persecution resulted in adding further names to the list of Catholic martyrs – *inter alia* Conor O'Devany, the aged Franciscan bishop of Down and Connor (1612) and Francis Taylor, a Dublin alderman who died after seven years in prison for recusancy (1621). **1607: The 'flight of the earls':** Hugh O'Neill, Rory O'Donnell, successor to Red Hugh, Maguire and other Ulster lords set sail from Lough Swilly to seek refuge in Counter-Reformation Europe as their position in Ulster became increasingly threatened. The lamentations of the poets reflect the sense of desolation their departure caused in Gaelic Ireland.

1609-: The Jacobean plantations: The Ulster Plantation (1609-22) in its final radical form was the brainchild of James I. It transferred the land of six Ulster counties – Armagh, Derry, Fermanagh, Tyrone, Donegal and Cavan – from native to British (mainly Scottish) ownership though it did not succeed in its aim of establishing a fully British settler community in the historically rebellious north. 'Deserving natives' received small holdings in the less fertile areas while elsewhere settlers leased land to natives and employed them as labourers and artisans. Down and Antrim, historically an area of Scottish migration, experienced a fresh wave of Scottish settlers with James's encouragement. New towns – Dungannon (1612), Coleraine, Londonderry, Belfast (1613) – were established to serve the planted areas. Plantation projects on a smaller scale took place in Leitrim, Laois and Offaly, and Wexford. The dispossession entailed in the planted areas caused bitter resentment, and the challenging of long-standing leases on the ground of 'defective title' generated tension among the Old English as well as the Gaelic population.

1628: The 'Graces', negotiated between Charles I, the successor of James I (d 1625) and representatives of the Irish Catholic community, offered a series of concessions by 'grace and favour' of the king including security of tenure for property titles of more than sixty years standing, and freedom of worship with some limitations in return for a substantial subsidy. Despite payment of the subsidy, Charles I failed to implement the Graces, continuing to use them as a carrot with which to secure further payments.

c. 1635: Geoffrey Keating (Seathrún Céitinn), c. 1570-1644, an Old English priest, scholar and poet, wrote *Foras Feasa ar Éirinn,* a history of early Ireland which reflects the changing Old English sense of identity, celebrates the Old English and the Gaelic Irish as together constituting the Irish nation (*Éireannaigh*) in virtue of their common devotion to the Catholic faith and to Ireland as their *patria*. The same sense of Irishness is found in the poetry of other Old English *literati* – the Franciscan, Pádraigín Haicéad and the Kerry landlord, Piaras Firtéar, for example.

1641-9: The war of the Catholic Confederation: 22-3/10/1641: An uprising by disaffected natives erupted in Ulster, led by the remnants of its old Gaelic nobility (*inter alia* Sir Phelim O'Neill, Rory Maguire, and Rory O'More) who feared the consequences for Irish Catholics of a victory for the Scottish Covenanters in alliance with the English Puritan parliament in their power struggle with Charles I. A peasant fury ensued in which the exploited natives – many of them casualties of the Ulster Plantation – extruded the planters from their lands, subjected them to humiliating forms of ritualistic torture (e.g. stripping them naked) and massacred many, though the number of victims was grossly inflated for propaganda purposes in England. The uprising spread to Leinster and the Pale (late November 1641) where the Old English made common cause with the Ulster Gaelic on the basis of their common loyalty to the Catholic faith, to the king and to the Irish *patria*. **1642:** The Catholics of Connacht and of Munster, including the Old English towns, joined with the insurgents. The 'Confederation of Kilkenny' (a nineteenth-century coinage) was instituted (May 1642) on the initiative of the Catholic bishops to coordinate the Catholic war effort and to govern the areas under the control of the insurgents, adopting the motto '*pro fide, pro rege, pro patria unanimis*'. Owen Roe O'Neill, nephew of the now legendary Hugh, returned from Spanish service and took command in Ulster. Thomas Preston, O'Neill's old rival and brother of Lord Gormanstown, was given charge of the Leinster forces. A Scottish army led by General Robert Monro landed in Carrickfergus to defend the Scottish planters, incidentally facilitating the establishment (1642) of a Presbyterian Church separate from the Protestant Church of Ireland. **1645:** Cardinal Rinuccini was sent to Ireland as papal nuncio but his uncompromising defence of the rights of the church alienated the Confederate moderates, mainly Old English, while identifying him with the radicals, mainly Old Irish, including Owen Roe. **1646:** At Benburb, Owen Roe inflicted a crushing defeat on the Scottish army but the advantage was lost as moderates and radicals debated the terms of an alliance with the king proposed by his lord lieutenant, the Duke of Ormond. **1649:** Charles I, who had fallen into the hands of the parliamentary army in 1647, was tried by parliament and executed (January). The moderates of the Confederation concluded an alliance with Ormond, now acting on behalf of the new king, Charles II, and dissolved the Confederation, though Owen Roe continued to hold out in the north.

1649-59: Cromwellian Ireland; 1649-50: The Cromwellian conquest:

Oliver Cromwell, having led the New Model Army to victory on behalf of parliament in England and Scotland, landed in Dublin with an army (August 1649) to subdue Ireland also. The indiscriminate massacre of civilians and military defenders at Drogheda (September 1649) and Wexford (October 1649) ensured the speedy capitulation of other towns as Cromwell progressed south as far as Cork, Kinsale and Bandon. The death of Owen Roe (November 1649) obviated the possibility of an Irish rally. **1650:** The submission of Limerick and Galway to Henry Ireton, after Cromwell returned to England (mid-May), completed the conquest. Catholic worship was everywhere suppressed, and priests were rounded-up, transported overseas or executed. Many others fled to the continent, and those who remained ministered in secret, constituting an 'underground church'. **1652-6:** The Cromwellian Plantation was devised both to recompense the soldiers of Cromwell's Irish army and to secure the conquest by depriving the Catholic elite of their lands – a minority of so-called 'innocents' were allotted reduced holdings in the infertile region west of the Shannon. Catholic-owned land was now reduced from 59% (1641) to 22% (1660). The major beneficiaries were the 'old' (pre-Cromwellian) planters who availed of an over-supplied land market to increase their holdings at little cost. An emerging Irish national identity was incidentally advanced since Cromwell rejected the distinction between Old English (English 'by blood') and Gaelic Irish, treating them indiscriminately as 'Irish Catholics'.

1660-91: Restoration Ireland: 1660-85: The reign of Charles II: The restoration of Charles II to fill the power vacuum created by the death of Cromwell (1658) did little to relieve the plight of Irish Catholics despite their loyalty to the Stuarts, since Charles depended on the support of the 'Protestant interest' to maintain his position. **1661:** the (Anglican) Church of Ireland was restored as the 'church by law established' and penalties were reimposed for nonconformity, though generally they were laxly applied. **1662:** Acts 'of settlement' and of 'explanation' in effect underwrote the Cromwellian plantation – the clause in the act 'of settlement' that provided for the restoration of the lands of 'innocent' Catholics was allowed to lie dormant with only a tiny fraction of claims examined. **1666:** The Remonstrance of the Franciscan, Peter Walsh, upholding the 'divine right' of monarchs irrespective of creed, was denounced by Rome and rejected by the great majority of the Irish clergy, but a less radical proclamation denying the pope's 'deposing power' was generally supported with a view to reassuring the government of Catholic loyalty. **1672:** A 'declaration of indulgence' by Charles II suspended the penal laws of religion. **1678:** Titus Oates alleged a 'popish plot' to murder the king, causing panic among Protestants in Ireland – mindful of the 1641 massacres – and led to the suppression of 'massing houses' and the banishment of bishops and the religious clergy. **1681:** Oliver Plunkett, archbishop of Armagh, was found guilty in London on a trumped-up charge of conspiring to procure a French invasion and was executed – he was subsequently canonised as a martyr.

1685-91: The reign of James II: The accession of James II, brother of Charles II and a convert to Catholicism, transformed the position of Catholics in Ireland. **1685:** Richard Talbot, earl of Tyrconnell, an Old English Catholic, was given charge of the army in Ireland in line with James II's policy of reversing the discrimination practised against Catholics and dissenters. Tyrconnell set about the extensive recruitment of Catholics. **1687:** Tyrconnell, appointed lord deputy – the first (and only) Catholic to fill the post after the Reformation – extended the recruitment of Catholics to the judiciary and the civil administration. **1689:** James II, ousted in the 'Glorious Revolution' (1688) by the Protestant William of Orange, husband of his daughter, Mary, landed in Kinsale with 3,000 French troops in a bid to recover his throne. The Patriot Parliament, overwhelmingly Catholic in membership, assembled in Dublin and repealed the acts 'of settlement' and 'of explanation' – James II consented with reluctance, fearing to alienate the 'Protestant interest'. The siege of Derry, one of the last centres of opposition to James, was lifted after an epic defence when two supply-ships from England succeeded in crossing the boom built by French engineers on the Foyle. **1690:** William of Orange led a large army to Ireland against James. At the battle of the Boyne (1 July) William gained a celebrated victory over James, who fled into exile (4 July). **1691:** At Aughrim the Catholic forces suffered a devastating defeat (12 July). The Treaty of Limerick, concluded after a celebrated defence of the city by the Catholic forces led by the dashing Patrick Sarsfield, brought the 'war of the two kings' to a close, allowing the Jacobite forces safe passage to France, guaranteeing the property titles of a wide range of Catholics, and freedom of worship as enjoyed under Charles II.

c. 1692-1829: THE PENAL ERA
AND THE PROTESTANT ASCENDANCY

On the departure of the Jacobite army to France, following the victory of William of Orange over James II in the 'war of the two kings,' the 'Protestant interest' set about undermining the concessions made to Catholics under the terms of the Treaty of Limerick, and consolidating their own position by means of a series of 'penal laws', set in place piecemeal in the 1690s and the opening decades of the eighteenth century, which aimed to reduce Catholics to a state of landlessness, and therefore of powerlessness. **1695:** Catholics were forbidden by law to bear arms, to own a horse of more than £5 in value, to attend colleges on the continent, or to conduct schools in Ireland. **1697:** Catholic bishops and regular clergy were banished. Protestant heiresses on marriage to Catholics lost title in favour of their nearest male Protestant relative. Protestant men, on marriage to Catholics, were deemed to have converted and became subject to the Penal Laws. **1703:** The property of Catholics was subjected to divisible inheritance (gavelkind) ensuring the fragmentation of Catholic estates, and they were forbidden to acquire land by purchase or on long lease. **1728:** Catholics were excluded from the franchise in local elections – the property qualification (40-shilling freehold) excluded most from the parliamentary franchise. **1703-76:** The effect of the Penal Laws was to reduce the share of Catholic-owned land from 14% to 5% and to secure a considerable number of conversions to Protestantism by Catholic landowners concerned to maintain family estates intact – the 'convert rolls' record 5,870 conversions over the period.

1692-: The 'Hidden Ireland', a term coined by the literary scholar, Daniel Corkery (1924), refers to the rich popular culture of the Catholic, Irish-speaking, underclass of the eighteenth century, best exemplified by the *amhránaíocht* (stressed-metre poetry) of the period, most notably in the *genre* of *Aisling* (vision poetry) and of *aor* (satire), practiced *inter alia* by Aodhgán Ó Rathaille (1670-1726), Eoghan Ruadh Ó Súilleabháin (1748-84), and Seán Clárach Mac Domhnaill (1691-1754). The mindset reflected in the poetry reveals a strong Jacobite current, associated in the *Aisling* with a millennial expectation of deliverance on the return of the Stuart pretender, and, when that dream faded, of an apocalyptic revolution secured with French assistance. The poetry also reflects a deeply sectarian mentality: Catholicism is identified with patriotism over against Protestantism, the religion of the foreign oppressor (*na tíoránaigh Ghallda*).

1698-1798: The Protestant Nation: The planters in time developed a sense of common identity as a colonial community, set apart from the English metropoles on the one side and the Catholic natives on the other. As in the case of their Old English predecessors, this colonial collective identity became suffused with patriotic sentiment focused upon the Irish parliament whose sovereignty they upheld against claims to an overriding jurisdiction by the Westminster assembly. **1698:** William Molyneux's *Case of Ireland ... Stated* reformulated, by reference to legal precedent, the case for Irish legislative independence made earlier (1640s) by the Old English lawyer Patrick Darcy, who in turn stood within a tradition that stretched back to the fifteenth century. **1720:** The Declaratory Act (6° George I) passed by the Westminster parliament asserted that the Irish kingdom was a dependent of the English one and accordingly that the Irish parliament was subordinate to parliament in England. The assertion was strenuously rejected in Jonathan Swift's *Drapier's Letters* (1724), as it was also implicitly by the grandeur of the House of Parliament erected (1729) on College Green in Dublin. **1763:** The *Freeman's Journal* was founded by Charles Lucas as the mouthpiece of patriots and parliamentary reformers. **1768:** The 'octennial act', an early measure of reform, provided for elections to parliament on an eight-yearly basis rather than on the death of the monarch, thus conducing to greater responsiveness on the part of MPs to public opinion and to a gathering groundswell of patriotic sentiment. **1782:** The Declaratory Act was repealed and Poynings' Law was substantially modified in response to pressure from patriotically-minded MPs led by Henry Flood (1732-91) and Henry Grattan (1746-1820). **1783:** An 'act of renunciation', passed by the Westminster parliament, further consolidated Irish parliamentary independence by acknowledging that legislation on Irish affairs was the proper prerogative of parliament in Ireland and that it constituted the final court of appeal for Irish lawsuits. The Irish Volunteers, founded as a citizens' militia in 1778 to defend Ireland against French invasion, at a national convention in Dublin's Rotunda, pressed for further parliamentary reform including some Catholic representation, but the measure, introduced by Henry Flood in Volunteer uniform, was decisively defeated. **1785:** The Royal Irish Academy was founded to cater for a growing Ascendancy interest in Irish antiquities and in Ireland's literary and cultural heritage. **1795:** Full Catholic emancipation was proposed in a bill sponsored by the liberal lord lieutenant, Fitzwilliam, and introduced by Henry Grattan but the measure was heavily defeated in parliament, indicating the limitations of the toleration towards Catholics that had gained ground in Ascendancy circles with the subsidence of the Stuart threat following the defeat of the Stuart pretender ('Bonnie Prince Charlie') in 1745.

1791-8: The United Irishmen: 1791: Theobald Wolfe Tone (1763-98), a young, radical, Protestant lawyer, imbued with the spirit of the Enlightenment and the French Revolution, in *An Argument on Behalf of the Catholics of Ireland* urged the right of Catholics to membership of parliament and advocated an alliance between Catholics and Protestants to secure legislative reform. The Society of United Irishmen was established in Belfast (October) by a group of radical Presbyterians to advance parliamentary reform by uniting people of all religious persuasions. A similar club was established in Dublin a month later. **1795:** The United Irishmen, despairing of constitutional methods, reorganised itself as an oath-bound secret society aiming 'to break the English connection' – Tone's phrase – and to establish an Irish republic with French assistance. On the exposure of the plan for armed insurrection, Tone fled to America and on to France where he secured assistance for an invasion of Ireland. The Orange Order was founded in Armagh to unite Protestants of all denominations and social classes in defence of the 'Protestant interest' in response to the 'uniting business' of the radicals. **1796:** Clubs of United Irishmen were established throughout Ireland, frequently absorbing groups of Defenders – a militant, Catholic secret society – and of Freemasons. A hard-line 'insurrection act' was passed and a yeomanry corps established to assist in maintaining law and order in an increasingly menacing political climate. A French invading force of 15,000, accompanied by Wolfe Tone, attempted to land in Bantry Bay but was foiled by bad weather and returned to France. **1797:** A ruthless campaign of repression conducted by the military in Ulster under General Lake successfully pre-empted rebellion there; in 1798 a United Irish assault on Antrim, led by Henry Joy McCracken, and an attempted uprising in Co Down under Henry Munro were quickly defeated. **1798:** United Irish rebellion erupted in Leinster (May 23-4). Insurgents were defeated at Tara Hill, Co Meath (May 26). Rebel victory at the Battle of Oulart Hill (May 27) gave impetus to Wexford United Irishmen who went on to capture the county and occupied Wexford town (May 30-June 21). Insurgent defeat at New Ross was followed by the massacre of 200 Protestants, burned alive in a barn at nearby Scullaboge (June 7). Wexford insurgents were defeated at Vinegar Hill, Co Wexford (June 21). A French force of 1,000 men under General Humbert landed at Killala (August 22) but after an initial runaway success (the 'Castlebar Races') it was suppressed by government troops. Wolfe Tone was captured accompanying a French expedition intercepted on Lough Swilly and condemned to death. He died of wounds self-inflicted in an attempted suicide on being refused a soldier's death by firing squad (November 19). The rebellion claimed an estimated 30,000 casualties, mostly non-combatants, as against 512 military losses, but the aspiration of Tone and the United Irishmen to unite Catholic, Protestant and Dissenter owning a common national identity in a sovereign Irish republic was to inspire successive generations of militant Irish nationalists. **1803: The rebellion of Robert Emmet (1778-1803):** one of the new group of republican leaders to emerge after 1798, Emmet conspired with United Irish veterans including Thomas Russell and Miles Byrne to stage a second insurrection. He planned to seize Dublin Castle and other strategic buildings as a prelude to a widespread rising. The rebellion, which commenced prematurely (July 23), was put down within hours. Fifty people were killed in street battles in Dublin, including the Chief Justice Lord Kilwarden who was piked to death in his carriage. Despite the rapid defeat Emmet gained an enduring place in the nationalist pantheon, partly as a result of an eloquent speech from the dock on the eve of his execution (September 20) with its ringing conclusion: 'when my country takes its place among the nations of the earth, then, and not till then, let my epitaph be written'.

1798-1801: The Union of Ireland with Great Britain was determined upon by Prime Minister William Pitt, convinced of the inability of the colonial government to ensure the security of the kingdom as demonstrated by the rebellion of the United Irishmen, and also as a means of enfranchising Catholics without jeopardy to the Protestant Ascendancy. **1801:** (January) The act of Union was carried after substantial opposition had been overcome by a year of intensive lobbying and the lavish distribution of patronage. The Irish parliament thus dissolved itself after some 500 years of existence but Catholics would have to wait until 1829 for their promised emancipation.

1778-1829: Catholic Emancipation: 1778: The first measure of relief from the Penal Laws, reflecting growing tolerance under the influence of the Enlightenment, the withering away of the Stuart threat, and Britain's military needs, allowed full property rights to Catholics on condition of an oath of allegiance only. **1793:** A further 'Catholic relief' act granted the vote to Catholics in both local and parliamentary elections, as well as the right to bear arms and to fill all but the most senior civil and military posts, but they remained excluded from membership of parliament. **1795:** St Patrick's College, Maynooth (the Royal College) was endowed by the Crown as a national seminary and granted an annual subsidy in order to provide aspirants to the priesthood with an alternative to training on the Continent where they were liable to imbibe radical ideas. **1790-:** Testifying to a general Catholic revival, a spate of church building was set in train, e.g. cathedrals at Waterford (1793), Cork (1799), Dublin (1815), Killala and Tuam (1827), Carlow (1828). A network of Catholic schools was established, both private and parochial, and new religious brotherhoods and sisterhoods were founded, dedicated to the practical service of the community through teaching, care of the sick, and the alleviation of poverty, e.g. the Presentation Sisters/Irish Christian Brothers (Edmund Rice, 1802), the Loreto Sisters (Frances Ball, 1821), the Irish Sisters of Charity (Mary Aikenhead, 1826), the Sisters of Mercy (Catherine McAuley, 1828). **1823-9: Daniel O'Connell and Catholic Emancipation: 1823:** Daniel O'Connell (1775-1847), a highly successful Catholic barrister, prominent liberal Catholic and patriot, head of one of the few surviving landed Catholic families (Derrynane, Co Kerry), founded a Catholic Association to secure emancipation by constitutional but aggressive political agitation. **1824:** O'Connell mobilised the Catholic masses for his cause by means of the 'Catholic rent', i.e. a penny a month subscription levied *in lieu* of the guinea fee for full membership of the Catholic Association, and by utilising the clergy as local organisers – thereby creating the first democratic mass movement in European politics. **1826:** At the general elections, liberal Protestant candidates, sympathetic to emancipation, scored notable successes with the assistance of Catholic voters emboldened to vote in defiance of the interests of their landlords by membership of the

Catholic Association. **1828:** O'Connell won the Clare by-election, ousting the sitting MP and local landlord, Edward Vesey Fitzgerald, and becoming the first Catholic MP since the seventeenth century. **1829:** A bill granting Catholic Emancipation was steered through parliament by Prime Minister Robert Peel, persuaded of the need to ameliorate Catholic discontent in the light of O'Connell's election victory, but the property qualification for the right to vote was raised from 40 shillings to £10, reducing the number of eligible Catholics from 216,000 to 37,000.

1829-1922: THE STRUGGLE FOR INDEPENDENCE

1830-47: O'Connell and Repeal: O'Connell's commitment to an independent Irish parliament was publicly manifested in his opposition to the Act of Union (1801) and reiterated at intervals down to the achievement of Catholic Emancipation (1829). **1830-:** In the aftermath of his emancipation victory, O'Connell sought to achieve redress of outstanding Catholic grievances by organising Catholic MPs as a ginger-group within the Westminster parliament. **1835:** In the Lichfield House Compact, O'Connell entered into an alliance with the Whigs which enabled them to form a government in return for a measure of influence on his part over Irish affairs. The Compact secured a number of limited concessions – a tithe reform act (1839) converted the tithe into a money payment levied on local property-owners, a municipal reform act (1840) ended Protestant control of the municipalities and enabled O'Connell to become the first Catholic lord mayor of Dublin since the seventeenth century (1841). **1841:** The foundation of the Loyal National Repeal Association reflected O'Connell's dissatisfaction with the Lichfield House Compact and his conviction that justice for Catholics would only be obtained by the restoration of an Irish parliament. **1842:** O'Connell organised the Repeal campaign on the pattern of the campaign for emancipation with a 'Repeal rent' of a penny a month to secure popular participation and the utilisation of the Catholic clergy to organise Repeal clubs in their local areas. **1843**, projected as the 'year of Repeal' by O'Connell, was marked by a series of 'monster meetings' at historic locations – the Tara gathering was estimated at a million by the *London Times* – but the limitations of constitutional agitation were revealed when the government called out the military to enforce its ban on the final rally scheduled for Clontarf (8 October) and O'Connell, true to his non-violent principles, called off the meeting rather than risk bloodshed. **1844:** O'Connell was sentenced to a year in prison on a charge of sedition and, though he secured release after four months, the Repeal campaign never regained momentum and finally petered out with the onset of the Great Famine (1845-9). **1847:** O'Connell died (May 15) at Genoa on pilgrimage to Rome. Despite the failure of the Repeal campaign it had served to place the issue of legislative independence at the centre of the Irish political agenda where it was to remain down to the establishment of the Free State (1922). More generally, O'Connell's achievement lay in securing full Catholic emancipation, in politicising the Catholic masses and in demonstrating their potential as an organised political force. Negatively, the thrust of his campaigns and the rhetoric he deployed in advancing them, served to perpetuate a confessional perception of Irish nationality – Catholicism was perceived as a condition of Irishness – and thereby to ensure the persistence of Catholic sectarianism despite his own disavowal of such attitudes in line with his liberal principles.

1842-8: Young Ireland: 1842: A group of nationalist intellectuals – Catholic and Protestant – styling themselves Young Ireland, came to public attention when they launched a weekly paper, *The Nation*, to promote a conception of national identity deeply influenced by the European romantic movement, grounded in a distinctive cultural heritage irrespective of religious affiliation. *The Nation* quickly gained a wide readership under the editorship of Charles Gavan Duffy, with Thomas Davis, the acknowledged if unappointed leader of the movement, as an indefatigable and highly popular contributor. **1843-5:** Dissension developed between Young Ireland and O'Connell over the issues of non-denominational education and physical force as an instrument of nationalist politics – O'Connell joined with the Catholic bishops in denouncing the non-denominational university colleges proposed by the government as 'godless'. Thomas Davis died suddenly at the age of thirty (16/9/1845) but despite O'Connell's genuine distress the rift between him and Young Ireland never mended. **1848:** The Young Ireland rebellion, coinciding with a series of uprisings by liberal nationalists across Europe, failed to evoke a response from a people ravaged by Famine and was derided thereafter as the 'cabbage-patch rebellion'. Its leaders, William Smith O'Brien and Francis Meagher, were deported – John Mitchel *(Jail Journal)* had already been banished – and the movement was eclipsed, but its ideal of an 'Irish Ireland', especially as conveyed in the essays and popular verse of Thomas Davis, added a highly influential cultural dimension to the ideology of Irish nationalism.

c. 1800-c. 1850: The Evangelical Revival and the Second Reformation: The so-called Second Reformation in Ireland was driven by an evangelical revival in the opening decades of the nineteenth century that affected all mainline Protestant churches – Anglican, Presbyterian, Methodist and Baptist – in Britain as well as Ireland. Reflecting this evangelical ethos, a new proselytising zeal towards the Catholic community characterised the movement. Societies were established for the propagation of the Bible, and the publication of pamphlets promoting a biblically-focused, fundamentalist form of Protestantism, enthusiastically promoted by the northern Presbyterian, the Rev Henry Cooke (1788-1865). It gave rise to a new awareness of the common bond uniting all Protestants in face of the politicisation of the Catholic masses by O'Connell, an awareness that found outlet in the Orange Order in which Protestants of all denominations secured a common meeting ground. The result was a heightening of Protestant confessional awareness and the recharging of the sectarianism that had marked community relations in Ireland since the Reformation, at a time when such attitudes were diminishing elsewhere under the influence of the Enlightenment and the French Revolution. In consequence, the non-denominational national school system established by the government in 1831 was transformed in practice into a network of religiously-affiliated schools.

1845-9: The Great Famine: A potato blight spread to Ireland from northern Europe in 1845, destroying a third of what was the staple and, for most of the year, almost the sole diet of the Irish masses. The blight recurred more virulently in 1846, 1848 and 1849, resulting in the greatest demographic disaster in recorded Irish history – deaths from hunger are estimated at a million, but more ruinously the Famine greatly accelerated the pace of emigration, causing a steady decline in population which continued into the second half of the twentieth century. In 1841 the census recorded a population of 8,100,000 which had dwindled to 4,500,000 by 1901. Politically the Famine served to intensify bitterness and resentment against the British government which was blamed for ineptitude at best, and at worst for attempted genocide. The generous assistance provided by Protestant bodies was tainted by its association with proselytism in some cases – thus 'souperism' entered the stock of Catholic sectarian pejoratives.

1850-78: The 'Devotional Revolution': More centralised control of the Irish Catholic Church, immediately by bishops in their dioceses but ultimately by the papal curia, resulted in a transformation of its religious culture whereby traditional religious practices, e.g. pilgrimages to holy wells and shrines, 'patterns' (the celebration of the feast of the patron saint of the parish), 'stations' (house-Masses in outlying areas and attendant feasting), 'wakes' (vigils beside a corpse accompanied by keening and merry-making), were replaced by 'Latin', church-centred devotions, e.g. benediction and adoration of the Blessed Sacrament, processions, parish missions, novenas, the veneration of Latin rather than local saints. A more austere (Jansenistic) moral code was also a feature. This 'devotional revolution' (a controversial term coined in 1972 by Emmet Larkin) is usually associated with the return of Paul Cullen from the Irish college in Rome, first as archbishop of Armagh (1849-52) and then of Dublin (1852-78). He was also the first (1866) of what was to be a continuing succession of Irish cardinals. Important landmarks in the history of the revolution were the first episcopal synod since the twelfth century at Thurles (1850); the founding of a Catholic university in Dublin (1854) with John Henry Newman, the distinguished English convert and theologian, as its first president, though the latter project foundered amidst wrangling between Newman and Cullen. The disestablishment of the Protestant Church of Ireland (1869) may also be seen as facilitating the emergence of the Roman Catholic Church as virtually the established Church in Ireland:

1858-67: The Irish Republican Brotherhood (popularly called the Fenians) was formed in 1858 as an oath-bound secret society pledged to establishing an Irish republic by means of armed insurrection. Fenian 'circles' spread rapidly in response to energetic promotion by James Stephens, attracting support mainly from the artisan-shopkeeper and small-farmer class, and from the Irish emigrant communities in Britain and America. A Fenian rebellion was attempted in 1867 but proved largely abortive, the government having gained ample advance warning in consequence of the loose observance of secrecy by the rebels. The 'cause' was redeemed when it acquired three martyrs, Allen, Larkin and O'Brien, who were executed for accidentally shooting a policeman while attempting to rescue two of their leaders from a police van in Manchester. Despite its denunciation (and the excommunication of members) by churchmen as a secret, oath-bound society espousing violence, the Brotherhood survived, reformed as a small, highly secret organisation, lending tacit support to groups who shared the aspiration for the establishment of a sovereign Irish state:

1875-91: Parnell and Home Rule: 1875: Charles Stewart Parnell (1846-91), an Anglo-Irish, Protestant landlord – of a debt-burdened estate in Co Wicklow (Avondale) – was elected Irish Parliamentary Party MP for Meath and became prominent among the group of 'obstructionists' within the party. **1879:** Parnell's growing political stature was reflected in the invitation to him to become the first president of the Land League, founded that year by Michael Davitt, a returned emigrant from Co Mayo, for the purpose of securing fairer treatment for tenants by a variety of means including the 'Boycott' – the ostracisation of the rack-renting landlord and/or his agent. In the 'New Departure', Parnell secured the support of the IRB and its American ancillary, Clann na Gael, for the IPP by combining Home Rule with the land agitation as a means of creating a militant, political mass movement, ultimately aiming to secure an independent Ireland. **1880:** Parnell was elected leader of the Irish Parliamentary Party at the age of 34. **1881:** A land act, the product of the constructive approach of the Liberal prime minister, W. E. Gladstone, to land reform in Ireland, initiated a process that was ultimately to transfer the bulk of Irish land from the landlords to tenant proprietors, but as a *quid pro quo* Parnell was imprisoned on a charge of inciting sedition. The political momentum was maintained during Parnell's imprisonment by the Ladies' Land League under his sister, Anna; he was released in 1882. **1885:** the IPP, reorganised under Parnell as a centralised, tightly-disciplined, (modern) party machine, secured 85 seats at the general election with the support of the church, and Gladstone was persuaded of the need to concede Home Rule. **1886:** A Home Rule bill sponsored by Gladstone was heavily defeated in the Commons and resulted in the rout of his party in the ensuing general election – the Liberals were to remain out of office for the next 20 years apart from a brief intermission in 1892-3. **1889:** A series of letters implicating Parnell in the notorious murder by the Invincibles of the Irish chief secretary, Lord Cavendish, and his under-secretary, T. H. Burke, were exposed as forgeries by a commission of enquiry. **1890:** Parnell was cited as co-respondent in a divorce suit brought by Captain W. H. O'Shea against his wife, Kitty, but despite the urging of Gladstone and of the Catholic Church in Ireland, Parnell refused to bow to pressure from within his own party to stand down as leader, resulting in a split with only a third of the party members remaining loyal to him. **1891:** Parnell died (6 October), exhausted by a campaign to rally support. The split persisted thereafter, seriously impairing the effectiveness of the Home Rule movement until unity was restored with John Redmond as leader in 1900.

c. 1880-c. 1937: Irish Ireland: Renewed enthusiasm for Ireland's Celtic heritage – cultural, literary, archaeological and historical – marked the decades spanning the turn of the nineteenth century, mirroring the vogue for Celticism on the European continent – the popularising writings of S. H. O'Grady (1846-1928) on historical and mythical themes provide an early example. **1884:** The Gaelic Athletic Association was founded by Michael Cusack with Archbishop Croke of Cashel as its first patron, to promote native games, in particular hurling, football and handball. **1892:** Dubhglas de hÍde (Douglas Hyde, 1860-1947) called for the cultural de-Anglicisation of Ireland and in **1893** founded the Gaelic League (Conradh na Gaedhilge) in association with Eugene O'Growney, professor of Irish at Maynooth, to revive the Irish language as a national vernacular. **1898:** The Irish Literary Theatre, forerunner of the Abbey, was founded by W. B. Yeats and Lady Gregory, seeking to create a distinctively Irish theatre. **1900:** D. P. Moran established *The Leader*, a weekly journal in which he advocated 'thorough' nationalism, political, cultural and economic, delivered scathing attacks on the Anglo-Irish literary revival and pronounced the Irish nation to be *de facto* a Catholic nation. **1907:** J. M. Synge's *Playboy of the Western World* resulted in rioting at the Abbey Theatre by audiences shocked by the attempt at a realistic portrayal of Irish peasant life. **1915:** Dubhglas de hÍde resigned as president of the Gaelic League in protest against the politicisation of the organisation, which had become infiltrated by the IRB who now aspired, in the phrase of P. H. Pearse, to an Ireland 'not only free but Gaelic as well, not only Gaelic but free as well'. **1922:** With the achievement of independence, the resources of the state were directed to the reinstatement of Irish as the national vernacular. **1937:** de Valera's new Constitution declared Irish to be the state's first language.

1910-22: Nationalism versus Unionism: 1910: Home Rule was restored to the British political agenda when the IPP under John Redmond secured 84 seats at the general election and its support became crucial to the Liberals to maintain power. **1912:** The Liberal prime minister, Asquith, introduced a Home Rule bill which passed the Commons but was defeated by the Conservatives in the Lords, thereby delaying its implementation for two years and allowing the Tory leader, Bonar Law, to mount a campaign against it. Edward Carson, a Dublin lawyer, and James Craig, a highly successful Belfast stockbroker and Orange Order Grand Master, led the campaign of resistance to Home Rule in the north of Ireland and secured almost 250,000 signatures to a Solemn League and Covenant through which signatories pledged to use 'all means' to defeat it. **1913:** the Ulster Volunteer Force (UVF) was founded to defend the Union. The socialist James ('Big Jim') Larkin organised a general strike in Dublin to secure better pay and conditions for workers, but it was defeated by an employers' lockout organised by William Martin Murphy, prominent Catholic and Home Ruler, founder of the *Irish Catholic* and *Irish Independent* newspapers. The Catholic clergy agitated against Larkin's project to send the children of strikers to families in England, fearing proselytism. **1914:** The Irish Volunteers were founded by nationalists in response to the UVF, with Cumann na mBan as a women's ancillary. The UVF's well-stocked arsenal was further augmented by the much publicised Larne gun-running. A similar landing of arms for the Irish Volunteers at Howth was harassed by the military and resulted in 4 civilian casualties. The outbreak of World War I led the British government to suspend the home rule bill for the duration of the war and John Redmond urged Volunteers to join the British army to secure 'the freedom of small nations'. A minority of Volunteer dissenters formed an alternative force with Eoin MacNeill, the professor of Irish History at UCD, as commander in chief. **1916:** The IRB, who had heavily infiltrated MacNeill's Volunteers, secretly planned an insurrection for Easter. MacNeill, learning of the plan in the preceding week, countermanded the order for general manoeuvres on Easter Sunday but the Military Council persisted, re-scheduling the manoeuvres for Easter Monday. Because of the confusion that resulted from the countermanding order, the Rising was confined almost entirely to Dublin where P. H. Pearse, as 'president of the Irish Republic', read a proclamation from the steps of the GPO, the main centre of the Rising, which declared the Republic to be 'virtually established'.

Pearse surrendered after 5 days (24-9 April) to avoid further civilian casualties – an estimated 300 had lost their lives. 15 of the rebels were executed under martial law and Sir Roger Casement, world-renowned humanitarian, was hanged in London for attempting to smuggle a consignment of German arms to the rebels. The reaction of the public, initially hostile, turned to sympathy as the executions proceeded and Bishop O'Dwyer of Limerick gave public expression to the outrage of the clergy. **1917:** Sinn Féin, an obscure political party founded by Arthur Griffith in 1905, became identified with the rebels and won a series of by-elections, signalling growing disenchantment with the IPP. Eamon de Valera, the sole surviving commander of the rebels, won the Clare by-election (July) and was elected president of Sinn Féin (October), Griffith having stood aside. **1918:** A military service act threatened conscription in Ireland and aroused widespread opposition, including from the IPP and the Catholic Church, but Sinn Féin was the main beneficiary, securing 73 of the 79 seats won by nationalists at the general election (December). **1919:** Sinn Féin, adhering to the policy of abstention advocated by Griffith from the beginning, convened the first Dáil (parliament) in Dublin (January) and set up an alternative government and civil service with de Valera as *príomh-aire* (prime minister). The Irish Republican Army (IRA) – the reconstituted Irish Volunteers – ambushed a consignment of explosives at Soloheadbeg, Co Tipperary (21 January), killing two police guards, and launching a guerilla war masterminded by Michael Collins, a survivor of 1916 and now Sinn Féin's minister for finance and chief of the IRA's highly effective intelligence system. **1920:** The 'Black and Tans' and the 'Auxiliaries' were formed as militarised special-service units to supplement the RIC in coping with a deteriorating security situation, and they soon gained notoriety for their ruthless, extra-legal methods. They shot Tomás Mac Curtain, lord mayor of Cork, and mayors O'Callaghan and Clancy of Limerick in their own homes. 14 spectators and 1 player died when they fired indiscriminately at a crowd attending a hurling match in Croke Park on 'Bloody Sunday' (21 November) in retaliation for the assassination of 14 suspected spies by Michael Collins's 'Gang' (assassination squad) earlier that morning. The Government of Ireland Act (23 December), envisaged as a settlement of the 'Irish question', provided for separate parliaments and administrations in a 26-county, nationalist, southern territory and a six-county, unionist one in the north-east, with a council of Ireland comprised of parliamentary representatives from each, while the United Kingdom government retained ultimate jurisdiction. The act was implemented in the case of the unionist 'sub-dominion' (22 June 1921) but was discarded for the south as unacceptable to the ascendant Sinn Féin. **1921:** Peace talks between de Valera and Lloyd George having failed (July), de Valera deputed Arthur Griffith and Michael

Collins to head a five-man team of plenipotentiaries at fresh talks in October. After prolonged negotiations (11 October-5 December), the Irish delegation, under the stress of an ultimatum from Lloyd George, reluctantly agreed to a treaty involving a substantially modified oath of loyalty to the Crown and a Boundary Commission to review the partition arrangement. **1922:** After an intense debate in the Dáil, the terms of the Treaty were endorsed by 64 votes to 57 (7 January), upon which the anti-Treaty faction, led by de Valera, withdrew. The Irish Free State was inaugurated when the British viceroy formally transferred power to Michael Collins as chairman of the provisional government (16 January). A general election (16 June) showed strong public support for the Treaty – the anti-Treatyites led by de Valera secured only 36 out of a total of 128 seats, while the pro-Treatyites, headed by Griffith and Collins, secured 58. The remainder went to an amalgam of smaller parties including Labour, who also supported the Treaty. Civil war ensued (28 June) when the Free State army, on the insistence of the British government, shelled the Four Courts which had been occupied by the anti-Treaty IRA and forced their withdrawal after a two-day siege in which the national archives housed there were destroyed. The anti-Treaty forces were dislodged from a number of urban centres over the summer but continued to conduct a guerilla war in the countryside, marred by brutal atrocities on both sides – the government summarily executed 77 anti-Treatyite prisoners through the autumn and spring in reprisal for casualties suffered by their own forces. Arthur Griffith died suddenly (12 August) from a cerebral haemorrhage induced by stress, and Michael Collins was shot in an ambush at Béal na Bláth, Co Cork (22 August). The Catholic bishops condemned the guerilla campaign in a joint pastoral and excluded the guerillas from the sacraments, though some priests ignored the ban. **1923:** De Valera, convinced of the futility of the military campaign, ordered the guerillas to 'dump' their arms and brought the civil war to a close, though the bitterness it engendered continued to bedevil the politics of the Free State so long as its protagonists remained politically active.

1922-2000: PARTITIONED IRELAND

1922-32: Cumann na nGaedheal and the shaping of the Free State: Pro-Treaty Sinn Féin (Cumann na nGaedheal from 1923), led by W. T. Cosgrove in succession to Michael Collins, assumed the government of the Free State and sought to establish the institutions of an inclusivist parliamentary democracy despite the antagonisms engendered by the civil war and sporadic outbursts of IRA violence thereafter. A secular constitution was provided, enshrining liberal values, establishing a bicameral parliament with special provision for minority representation in the upper house (*An Seanad*) and election by proportional representation in the lower house (*An Dáil*). An unarmed police force (*An Gárda Síochána*) was formed (1922) and the army was scaled down after the civil war and firmly subordinated to the civil power when the 'army mutiny' was defeated in 1924. The resources of the state were brought to bear on preserving the Irish language and reviving it as the national vernacular by means of special grants, by making Irish a compulsory examination subject on the school curriculum and a necessary condition for employment in the civil service. A disappointment for the Free State government, the Boundary Commission (1924-5) in effect confirmed the existing partition arrangement, but the government exploited the state's dominion status to maximise its independence, gaining admission to the League of Nations (1923), equality with the United Kingdom within the British Commonwealth (the Balfour Declaration, 1926), and legislative autonomy in relation to the United Kingdom parliament (the statute of Westminster, 1931). On the negative side, the approach to social and economic problems was conservative, unadventurous and penny-pinching, pandering to the grazier interest while neglecting the need to stimulate growth in more labour-intensive tillage and in industry – the old-age pension was cut by 10% and the salaries of civil servants pruned. Some positive initiatives were taken, e.g. the hydroelectric scheme on the Shannon near Limerick (1925), the establishment of the Electricity Supply Board (1927), the Agricultural Credit Act (1927). Culturally important was the establishment of Radio Éireann, the state broadcasting service (1926).

1916-37: The Church Triumphant: Reflecting the fervently Catholic ethos of nationalist Ireland, five new missionary societies were established between 1916 and 1937 – St Columban's Foreign Mission Society (the Maynooth Mission to China), 1916; the Missionary Sisters of St Columban, 1922; the Missionary Sisters of the Holy Rosary, 1924; St Patrick's Foreign Missionary Society (the Kiltegan Fathers), 1932; the Medical Missionaries of Mary, 1937 – as well as a rapidly expanding lay movement, the Legion of Mary (1921), devoted to self-sanctification and the sanctification of others through house-to-house visitation, street contact, and 'rescue work'. *Maria Duce*, a right-wing Catholic action group, was formed in the 1940s. The celebration of the international Eucharistic Congress in Dublin in 1932 provided a spectacular affirmation of nationalist Ireland's devotion to 'faith and fatherland'. Politicians were profuse in their expressions of loyalty to the church and to its moral teaching, borne out by legislation against birth control and divorce (1925), and by the introduction of a strict censorship of films (1923) and of periodicals and books (1929), most of all perhaps by de Valera's Constitution of 1937 which was strongly influenced by the Catholic social teaching of the period and acknowledged the 'special position' of the Catholic Church in Ireland as the 'guardian of the faith of the majority of Irish citizens'. Despite special legislation guaranteeing Protestants religious and educational freedom, the decade of the 1920s saw a substantial exodus to Britain and the British colonies, reducing the Protestant population by 3% to 7.4%, partly in reaction to the burgeoning Catholic climate, partly through fear of sectarian 'reprisals' – e.g. the burning of 'Big Houses' – while the effects of the papal decree *Ne temere* (1908), requiring the partners in a mixed marriage to undertake to bring the children up as Catholics, ensured that the Protestant population continued to dwindle.

1921-: Unionist Ulster: Fearing its substantial nationalist minority and led by a grand master of the Orange Order, James Craig (1921-40), the government of unionist Ulster created a blatantly sectarian statelet. Electoral constituencies were 'gerrymandered' to ensure the return of unionist candidates in nationalist areas, and proportional representation was abandoned (1929). The police force, the Royal Ulster Constabulary (1921), was armed and was almost entirely Protestant in composition. Its paramilitary adjunct, the B Specials, were recruited mainly from the Orange Order and constantly harassed the Catholic population, being suspected of a number of sectarian murders. Nationalist celebrations – e.g. of 1916 – were suppressed by means of a repressive Special Powers Act (1922) while the commemoration of William of Orange's victory at the Boyne was celebrated as a public holiday (12 July). Catholics were passed over in favour of Protestants in the allocation of scarce public housing and for employment in a tight job market as Northern heavy industry entered a terminal decline – unemployment stood at 27% in Northern Ireland in the period 1931-9, a period of gradual recovery in Britain. Sectarian rioting was frequent and fatalities not uncommon – rioting on the occasion of the celebration of George V's silver jubilee (1935) claimed 8 Protestant lives and those of 5 Catholics and resulted in the expulsion of 430 Catholic and 64 Protestant families from their homes.

1932-48: The de Valera Era: De Valera succeeded in bringing the great majority of anti-Treatyite republicans into constitutional politics by founding Fianna Fáil, the Republican Party, in 1926 and his party entered the Dáil the following year when it won 57 seats at the general election. The successful candidates signed the book subscribing to the oath of allegiance as 'an empty political formula'. **1932:** Fianna Fáil won 72 seats to Cumann na nGaedheal's 57 at the general election, sufficient to enable de Valera to form a government with the support of Labour deputies. De Valera as head of government set about removing the remaining vestiges of the British connection – the oath of allegiance was abolished by statute and the role of Governor General was first marginalised and then allowed to fall into abeyance. The land annuities, payable to the British government in respect of loans to tenants to buy out their holdings under the land acts were repudiated, resulting in a debilitating economic war when the British government responded by placing an embargo on Irish imports. **1933:** Eoin O'Duffy, dismissed by de Valera from his post as Commissioner of the Gárda Siochána, assumed leadership of the Army Comrades Association (Blueshirt movement), a mildly fascist organisation, and was elected first president of Fine Gael, a new political party formed from a coalition of Cumann na nGaedheal and two small parties led by James Dillon and O'Duffy himself. **1936:** The Blue Shirt movement was wound up, having been disowned by Fine Gael and having lost the support of right wing (Catholic) intellectuals because of its association with violence. O'Duffy led a bedraggled remnant of 700 renamed the Irish Brigade to conduct a brief and inglorious campaign in support of Franco in the Spanish civil war. **1937:** De Valera devised a new Irish constitution enshrining his conception of Ireland as a sovereign, culturally Gaelic, nation – it claimed the whole island as the national territory (art. 2), and defined Irish as the state's 'first language'. The Catholic Church was accorded a 'special position' as the religious communion of the majority (art. 44), though de Valera resisted clerical pressure to declare Ireland a Catholic state and extended constitutional recognition also to the other main Christian communions as well as to the state's two small Jewish communities. On social values the Constitution reflected contemporary Catholic teaching, emphasising the centrality of the family and the role of motherhood while precluding divorce. **1938:** Dubhglas de hÍde, a Protestant, was elected unopposed as Ireland's first President (*Uachtarán*) under the new constitution. The Anglo-Irish Agreement, regarded by de Valera as his greatest political achievement, brought the economic war to a close. The British waived payment of the annuities for a modest lump-sum payment (£10m) and agreed also to evacuate the 'Treaty ports' (Berehaven, Cobh and Lough Swilly), thus facilitating the Free State's neutral stance in World War II.

1939-45: World War II: Appealing to partition in justification, de Valera steered the Free State through the war as a neutral power, though in practice there was much tacit cooperation with the allies. Despite the North's lacklustre war effort – recruitment to the armed forces was below the UK average and the productivity of the workforce was low – the Free State's neutrality further emphasised the growing divergence between the two partitioned areas. The British and American governments deeply resented Irish neutrality which deprived them of access to strategically important sea and air ports. A reproof from Prime Minister Winston Churchill in the flush of victory drew a dignified response from de Valera which won widespread approval in Ireland. Neutrality led to the blocking of the Free State's entry to the United Nations by means of a Soviet veto until 1955. In the aftermath of war the Free State contributed generously from meagre resources to alleviate the plight of Germany and other war-ravaged countries.

1946: A National Teachers' strike brought Archbishop John Charles McQuaid into confrontation with his erstwhile ally de Valera in support of the teachers' claim. Fianna Fáil lost further support from its republican constituency because of the continuing detention of IRA internees after the war – the death of Seán MacCaughey, a leading internee, on hunger strike (11/5/46) provoked a public outcry. Seán MacBride, son of an executed 1916 leader and a distinguished barrister, founded Clann na Poblachta as a radical republican alternative. **1948:** De Valera called a general election (16 February) a year early in a bid to pre-empt growing dissatisfaction as unemployment increased, emigration remained unacceptably high (30,000 p.a.), and pay rises fell far behind spiralling prices. But Fianna Fáil lost 8 seats, enabling Fine Gael's John A. Costello to form a rainbow coalition and end Fianna Fáil's 16-year tenure:

1948-53, Church and State: 1948: Outdoing Fianna Fáil in professions of loyalty, the new coalition government telegraphed Pope Pius XII, following its first cabinet meeting, expressing devotion to his 'august person and to the teaching of Christ'. **1950:** A special commemorative stamp was issued to mark the Holy Year, the traditional jubilee celebration of the Roman primacy; · Noel Browne (Clann na Poblachta), the coalition's dynamic minister for health, proposed a free 'mother and child' scheme in line with British maternity welfare care, but the Catholic hierarchy opposed it in alliance with the conservative Irish Medical Association as an intrusion upon the rights of parents. **1951:** In face of the hierarchy's opposition, the coalition cabinet withdrew Browne's measure and forced his resignation (April), but Fianna Fáil was returned to power in the general election that followed shortly after (May), the coalition having lost credibility through a series of 'jobbery' scandals as well as through its handling of the 'mother and child' scheme. **1953:** Fianna Fáil enacted a revised mother and child scheme, having wrongfooted critics by establishing through a highly-placed contact in Rome that the Irish hierarchy did not accurately express the church's teaching in this area.

1948-56: North and South: 1949: The coalition government, outdoing Fianna Fáil also in its nationalism, declared the Free State a Republic (Easter Monday), thus cutting the state's tenuous links with the United Kingdom and further alienating unionists. The Ireland Act, enacted by the UK's Labour administration in response to the declaration of the Republic (2 June), guaranteed the North's status as part of the UK unless the Stormont parliament decreed otherwise, and conferred automatic British citizenship on Irish residents of the UK. **1955:** The Republic gained membership of the UN as part of a package deal through which the Soviet Union agreed to waive its veto. Ireland adopted a non-aligned position in the General

Assembly and contributed contingents regularly to UN peace-keeping forces around the world. **1956:** The IRA launched a fresh offensive in the North which resulted in the death of 12 volunteers and 6 policemen and reinforced the prejudices of unionists. The census showed the population of the Republic at an all-time low despite the high birth rate, highlighting the twin problems of a severe economic slump and massive emigration:

1957-66: The Lemass Years: 1957: Fianna Fáil was returned to power in the general election and Seán Lemass was appointed Tánaiste (second minister). **1958:** T. K. Whitaker, the young (41) secretary of the Department of Finance, published *Economic Development,* plotting a new way forward for the Republic's economy based on export-driven development financed by foreign investment instead of traditional protectionism. **1959:** De Valera retired as Taoiseach bringing the era of Treaty politics to a close, though he continued to occupy high public office as President until 1973. Lemass succeeded to the office of Taoiseach and, adapting Whitaker's ideas in two five-year plans, produced an unprecedented 4.5% growth in the economy, resulting in the arrest of emigration and population growth for the first time since the Great Famine. **1961:** Telefís Éireann, the national television service, was established and contributed substantially to cultural liberalisation – BBC television had been available via Belfast since 1953. **1963:** The establishment of the first comprehensive schools, combining academic and technical training, inaugurated a process of educational reform. **1965:** An exchange of visits between Lemass and Terence O'Neill, the Prime Minister of Northern Ireland, to discuss cross-border cooperation signalled a new approach to the problem of partition. **1966:** Educational reform was further advanced by the provision of free secondary education. The relaxation of the censorship laws marked another step towards cultural liberalisation.

1962-73: The modernisation of Irish Catholicism: 1962-5: In response to the directives of the Second Vatican Council, the language of the liturgy was changed from Latin to the vernacular (English or Irish) and Mass was celebrated *coram populo* (facing the people). The church's religious code (regarding fasting etc) was relaxed, and a more open ecumenical stance was adopted, though traces of the old triumphalism lingered. **1970:** The hierarchy removed the ban on Catholics attending Trinity College Dublin. **1972:** The Constitution of the Republic was amended by referendum to delete the reference to the 'special position' of the Catholic Church (art. 44).

1963-8: Modernisation in Northern Ireland: 1963: The election of Terence O'Neill as prime minister of Northern Ireland in succession to the 75 year old Lord Brookeborough inaugurated a new approach to the North's ailing economy and its attendant social problems. **1964:** Tom Wilson, a distinguished Ulster-born economist commissioned by O'Neill, published a Whitaker-like report on economic development in Northern Ireland. **1965-8:** In a promising political initiative, Lemass and O'Neill exchanged formal visits for the purpose of discussing cross-border cooperation but its effect was undermined ironically by the apparently biased manner in which the North's programme for socio-economic development was implemented – capital investment was concentrated in the Protestant east to the neglect of the Catholic west, blatant bias continued to be exercised in the allocation of newly-developed public housing, the new university was located in sparsely-populated but Protestant Coleraine despite the claims of Catholic Derry's Magee teacher-training college.

1968-73: The Northern 'Troubles': 1968: A series of marches organised by the Northern Ireland Civil Rights Association, founded (9/4/1967) on the model of Martin Luther King's movement in the United States, encountered aggressive counter-demonstrations by loyalists and violence from the RUC and B Specials in the name of enforcing law and order. Their cause was brought to international attention when a march in Derry (5 October) was set upon by police and B Specials and the resultant carnage was relayed on television. **1969:** The turbulence continued – spectacularly in the confrontation between Civil Rights marchers and loyalist protesters at Burntollet Bridge near Derry (4 January) – and the northern Prime Minister, James Chichester-Clark, was forced to call in the British army when nationalists barricaded themselves into their own areas to protect themselves from the RUC and B Specials following riots triggered by the Apprentice Boys march in Derry (12 August). The British government forced a series of moderate reforms on the Stormont administration – the RUC were disarmed, the B Specials were replaced by the Ulster Defence Regiment and the voting system at local elections was democratised. But nationalists remained dissatisfied and were now being subjected to constant harassment by the army. The IRA split between Provisionals, concerned with defending the nationalist community in the North, and Officials pursuing a socialist agenda – the corresponding political parties, Provisional and Official Sinn Féin emerged the following year. **1970:** Two members of the Fianna Fáil government – Charles J. (Charlie) Haughey and Neil Blaney – were allegedly implicated in a gun-running plot on behalf of the IRA and, although the charge was not proved (May), the Taoiseach, Jack Lynch, forced them from office, while a third member of the government, Kevin Boland, resigned in protest. The Social Democratic and Labour Party (SDLP) was formed (August), to represent mainstream nationalist opinion in the North with Gerry Fitt, a veteran socialist and nationalist politician as chairman, and John Hume, a prominent Civil Rights activist as vice-chairman. **1971:** Internment without trial was introduced (9 August) when 346 IRA suspects were detained. Applied initially only against republicans it deepened the resentment of the nationalist community. The Ulster Defence Association was formed (September) combining a number of existing loyalist paramilitary organisations. The Democratic Unionist Party was founded (5 October) by the Rev Ian Paisley, a Presbyterian fundamentalist, representing Protestant populism. **1972:** 13 unarmed Civil Rights marchers died when the Parachute Regiment opened fire on a banned march in Derry ('Bloody Sunday', 30 January). Following disagreement between Edward Heath, Conservative British Prime Minister and Brian Faulkner, the unionist Prime Minister, direct rule was imposed on Northern Ireland (24 March). IRA bombs killed 11 civilians in Belfast ('Bloody Friday', 21 July).

1973-2000: TOWARDS A NEW IRELAND

1973: The Republic was granted formal membership of the European Economic Community (1 January) following a referendum indicating overwhelming support for entry. Negotiations involving Northern Ireland's main political parties and the governments of the UK and Republic resulted in the Sunningdale Agreeement (December), providing for the restoration of devolved government in Northern Ireland but with power-sharing and an Irish dimension in the form of a North-South Council of Ireland, while the Irish government conceded that the status of Northern Ireland within the UK was to remain unchanged unless a majority of its people voted otherwise. The first inter-church meeting was held at Ballymascanlon Hotel, Co Louth. **1974:** The British Prime Minister, Harold Wilson, withdrew support for the Sunningdale Agreement (May) when an Ulster Workers' strike in protest, prominently supported by Ian Paisley and the loyalist paramilitaries, brought Northern Ireland to a standstill. UVF bombs in Dublin and Monaghan resulted in 31 deaths and 100 serious injuries in the worst day of carnage in the history of the Troubles. IRA explosions in Birmingham (November) killed 21 people – the conviction finding the 'Birmingham Six' guilty of the offence was overturned in 1991. **1977:** In conformity with a European Union directive (1975) the Republic's Employment Equality Act secured equal pay for women and equality of opportunity. **1979:** A visit by Pope John Paul II to Ireland elicited wild enthusiasm – an estimated 1¼ million attended Mass celebrated by him in the Phoenix Park in Dublin – testifying to the country's continuing Catholic ethos. Yet legislation the same year legalised the import and sale of contraceptives, pointing to the growing secularism of Irish society. The Republic's participation in the European Monetary System broke Ireland's historic link with sterling.

1981: A hunger strike by republican prisoners in Long Kesh internment camp, in protest against their treatment as criminals rather than as political prisoners, resulted in 10 deaths, causing an intensification of nationalist resentment against an uncompromising British government led by Margaret Thatcher (Conservative) and boosted recruitment to the Provisionals and support for Sinn Féin. **1983:** Gerry Adams, president of Sinn Féin, was elected MP for West Belfast. **1985:** In the Anglo-Irish Agreement (November) the government of the Republic repeated its acceptance of Northern Ireland's status within the United Kingdom so long as this accorded with the will of the majority, the UK government accepted that the question of a united Ireland was to be decided by the people of Ireland themselves, and a system of government was devised for the North involving power-sharing and a British-Irish Council. Loyalist protests at the Irish dimension of the new system of government failed to achieve the momentum of the earlier Sunningdale protest (1974) and petered out inconclusively in 1988.

1992: A judgment of the Supreme Court in Dublin legalised abortion in exceptional circumstances. Eamonn Casey resigned as bishop of Galway following disclosure that he had fathered a son two decades earlier. **1993:** A peace initiative by John Hume (SDLP) and Gerry Adams (Sinn Féin) brought Sinn Féin within the political process and reactivated Anglo-Irish negotiations, leading to the Downing Street Declaration (December) in which Albert Reynolds (Fianna Fáil) as Taoiseach reiterated the Republic's acceptance of the right of the majority in Northern Ireland to determine its position as part of the United Kingdom, and also undertook to review features of Irish law found offensive by unionists or to be in conflict with the notion of a pluralistic society, while the British Prime Minister, John Major (Conservative), agreed to pursue 'inclusivist' peace talks involving all parties who permanently rejected violence, as well as renouncing 'any selfish or economic interest' by Britain in the North. **1994:** The Provisionals announced a 'complete cessation of hostilities' (31 August) to enable Sinn Féin to participate in peace negotiations. The Republic experienced spectacular economic growth from the mid 1990s (the 'Celtic Tiger') as it reaped the benefit of wisely-used EU subventions (£14 bn, 1973-91) and of its attractiveness to investors as a means of access to the European market. A feature of economic growth was greater diversification of Ireland's export market, breaking its traditional dependence on the UK. The Fr Brendan Smyth affair – a child abuse scandal – precipitated the fall of Albert Reynolds's Fianna Fáil led government. **1995:** A divorce referendum was passed by a narrow majority, and the Catholic hierarchy published pastoral guidelines, *Child Sexual Abuse: framework for a church response*. **1996:** The publication of the George Mitchell report outlined principles committing participants in all-party talks on Northern Ireland to non-violence. The Provisionals terminated their ceasefire with a devastating bombing raid on the Canary Wharf in London, indicating their dissatisfaction with the prevarication, as they perceived it, by

John Major and the unionists, on the issue of peace talks. **1997:** The IRA ceasefire was restored in the more hopeful climate created by the landslide victory of Tony Blair's Labour Party – ending the dependence of John Major's Conservative government on unionist support – and the succession of the more acceptable Albert Reynolds (Fianna Fáil) to John Bruton (Fine Gael) in the Republic. The continuing pressure of the ever-helpful Bill Clinton, US president, also helped enormously. **1998:** The Good Friday Agreement (10 April), signed by all the North's main political parties with the exception of Ian Paisley's DUP, and by the governments of the UK and the Republic, repeated the undertaking given earlier by both governments, established a British-Irish Council to explore the possibility of cooperation on a range of matters of mutual interest, while the pragmatic UUP leader, David Trimble, bound unionists to accept power-sharing, cross-border institutions, demilitarisation, the phased release of political prisoners, and a sweeping review of human rights issues. In Omagh a bomb, planted by dissident republicans, killed 29 people and injured many others seriously in one of the bloodiest atrocities of the 30-year-long Troubles (15 August) but the Real IRA declared a ceasefire in the midst of a general wave of revulsion and the peace process remained intact. The provisions of the Good Friday Agreement were approved by substantial majorities in referendums in the Republic and in Northern Ireland. **1999:** The European single currency, Euro, was launched. A devolved government took office in Northern Ireland with David Trimble (UUP) as First Minister and Seamus Mallon (SDLP) as his deputy. The IRA appointed an intermediary to enter discussions with the decommissioning body. The broadcast by RTÉ of the *States of Fear* documentary provoked widespread outcry and prompted Taoiseach Bertie Ahern to appoint the Laffoy Commission to examine allegations of child abuse in institutions, largely administered by religious orders. **2000:** IRA stated a commitment to put arms beyond use 'completely and verifiably' in the context of a complete implementation of the Good Friday Agreement (May 6).

Notes

CHAPTER ONE

Further reading:

Bieler, L., *The life and legend of St Patrick: problems of modern scholarship* (Dublin, 1949)

—, *Libri Epistolarum S. Patricii Episcopi,* 2 vols, (Dublin, 1952)

—, *The Works of St Patrick* (London, 1953)

—, *Ireland: Harbinger of the Middle Ages* (Oxford, 1966)

—, *Four Latin lives of St Patrick* in *Scriptores Latini Hiberniae,* viii (Dublin, 1971)

Binchy, D.A., 'Patrick and his biographers: ancient and modern', *Studia Hibernica,* ii (1962), pp. 7-173

Bury, J.B., *The Life of St Patrick and his place in history* (London, 1905)

Carney, J., *The problem of St Patrick* (Dublin, 1961)

Esposito, M., 'Notes on the Latin Writings of St Patrick', *Journal of Theological Studies,* xix (1918), pp. 342-6

Gwynn, J. (ed.), *Liber Ardamachanus: the Book of Armagh* (Dublin, 1913)

Hanson, R. P. C., *St Patrick: a British missionary bishop* (Nottingham, 1965)

—, *Saint Patrick: his origins and career* (Oxford, 1968)

Hood, A. B. E. (ed.), *Saint Patrick: his writings and Muirchú's life* (London and Manchester, 1978)

MacNeill, E., *St Patrick: Apostle of Ireland* (Dublin, 1934)

Mohrmann, C., *The Latin of St Patrick* (Dublin, 1961)

O'Rahilly, T. F., *The Two Patricks* (Dublin, 1942)

—, *Early Irish History and Mythology* (Dublin, 1946)

Shaw, F., 'Post-mortem on the second Patrick', *Studies,* li (1952), pp. 237-67

—, 'The myth of the second Patrick', *Studies,* l (1961), pp. 5-27

Stokes, W. (ed.), *The tripartite life of Patrick,* 2 vols (London: Rolls Series w. 89, 1887)

Thompson, E.A., *Who was Saint Patrick?* (Woodbridge, 1985)

Todd, J. H., *St Patrick: Apostle of Ireland* (Dublin, 1864)

Walker, G. S. M. (ed.), *S. Columbanus: Opera in Scriptores Latini Hiberniae,* ii (Dublin, 1957)

CHAPTER TWO

1. J. Ryan, *Irish monasticism, origins and early development* (Dublin, 1931[reprinted Dublin, 1993]).
2. A.O. Anderson and M.O. Anderson (eds*), Adomnán's Life of Columba* (Edinburgh, 1961).
3. J-M. Picard, '*Princeps* and *Principatus* in the Early Irish Church: a reassessment', in A.P. Smyth(ed.), *Seanchas: Studies in medieval Irish archaeology, literature and history presented to Francis J. Byrne* (Dublin, 1999), pp. 149-51.
4. M. Herbert, *Iona, Kells, and Derry: the History and Hagiography of the Monastic Familia of Columba* (Oxford, 1988), pp. 91, 99, 103.

Further reading:

Anderson, A. O. and Anderson M. O. (eds), *Adomnán's life of Columba* [text, translation and notes] (Edinburgh, 1961)

Byrne, F. J., *Irish kings and high-kings* (London, 1973)

Gwynn, A., *The Irish Church in the eleventh and twelfth centuries* (Dublin, 1992)

Herbert, M., *Iona, Kells, and Derry: the history and hagiography of the monastic* familia *of Columba* (Oxford, 1988)

Hughes, K., *The Church in Early Irish Society* (London, 1966)

Hughes, K., *Early Christian Ireland: Introduction to the Sources* (London, 1972)

Kenney, J. F., *The Sources for the Early History of Ireland: Ecclesiastical* (New York, 1929 [reprint Dublin 1979])

Ó Cróinín, D., *Early Medieval Ireland, 400-1200* (London, 1995)

Ryan, J., *Irish Monasticism: its origins and early development* (Dublin, 1931 [reprint Dublin, 1993])

Smyth, A. P., *Celtic Leinster: towards an historical geography of Early Irish Civilization* (Dublin, 1982)

Smyth, A. P, *Warlords and Holy Men: Scotland A.D. 80-1000* (Edinburgh reprint, 1989)

Smyth, A. P., 'The effect of Scandinavian raiders on the English and Irish Churches: a preliminary reassessment', in B. Smith(ed.), *Britain and Ireland 900-1300: Insular Responses to Medieval European Change* (Cambridge, 1999), pp. 1-38

CHAPTER THREE

1. *Qui sunt pene extremi et, ut ita dicam, mentagrae orbis terrarum*: M. Walsh and D. Ó Cróinín, *Cummian's letter 'de controversia paschali 'and the 'de ratione conputandi'* (Toronto, 1988), p. 72.

2. Cf. St Patrick in his *Confessio*, § 1 *ad ultimum terrae*; § 34 *usque ubi nemo ultra est*; § 38 *usque ad extremum terrae*; § 51 *usque ad exteras partes ubi nemo ultra erat*; § 58 *in ultimis terrae*; tract on the crimes of Coroticus, §6: *usque ad extremum terrae*; §9 *in ultimis terrae* in D. Conneely, *The letters of Saint Patrick* (Dublin, 1993), pp. 25, 41, 42, 47, 48, 52.

3. Cf. *Sancti Columbani opera*, p. 36, line 29. Cf. Patrick, *peregrinus propter nomen suum*: *Confessio*, §26 in Conneely, *Letters of Saint Patrick*, p. 38.

4. J. Duft, 'Iromanie-Irophobie: Fragen um die frühmittelalterliche Irenmission exemplfiiziert an St Gallen und Alemannien' in *Zeitschrift für schweizerische Geschichte*, 50 (1956), pp. 241-63.

5. E. Coccia, 'La cultura irlandese precarolingia: miracolo o mito' in *Studi medievali*, ser. 3, 8 (1967), pp. 257-420. A more recent though more narrowly focused discussion is that of M.W. Herren, 'Classical and secular learning among the Irish before the Carolingian renaissance' in *Florilegium*, 3 (1981), pp. 118-57, reprinted in M.W. Herren, *Latin letters in early Christian Ireland*, (Aldershot, 1996), chapter 1. A modern manifestation of Hiberno-mania is Thomas Cahill, *How the Irish saved civilization: the untold story of Ireland's heroic role from the fall of Rome to the rise of medieval Europe* (New York, 1995).

6. For a general survey cf. Herren, *Latin letters in early Christian Ireland*, chapters 1, 4.

7. Seminal are the series of conferences and published papers under the auspices of the Europa-Zentrum, Tübingen, namely H. Löwe (ed.), *Die Iren und Europa im früheren Mittelalter*, 2 vols (Stuttgart, 1982); P. Ní Chatháin and M. Richter (eds), *Irland und Europa: die Kirche im Frühmittelalter / Ireland and Europe: the early church* (Stuttgart, 1984); P. Ní Chatháin and M. Richter (eds), *Irland und die Christenheit: Bibelstudien und Mission / Ireland and Christendom: the Bible and the missions* (Stuttgart, 1987); P. Ní Chatháin and M. Richter (eds), *Irland und Europa im früheren Mittelalter: Bildung und Literatur / Ireland and Europe in the early middle ages: learning and literature* (Stuttgart, 1996).

8. Patrick's tract on the crimes of Coroticus, §1 in Conneely, *Letters of Saint Patrick*, p. 50.

9. See the illuminating remarks in T. M. Charles-Edwards, 'The context and uses of literacy in early Christian Ireland' in H. Pryce (ed.), *Literacy in Celtic societies* (Cambridge, 1998), pp. 62-79.

10. Texts conveniently listed in M. Lapidge and R. Sharpe, *A Bibliography of Celtic-Latin literature, 400-1200* (Dublin, 1985).

11. *Qui sapientiam desiderat, non orreat artem grammaticam, sine qua nemo eruditus et sapiens esse potest*. Anonymus ad Cuimnanum: expositio Latinitatis; B. Bischoff and B. Löfstedt (eds), *Corpus Christianorum, series latina*, cxxxiiiD (Turnhout, 1992), p. 17; translated in M. Richter, *Ireland and her neighbours in the seventh century* (Dublin, 1999), p. 164.

12. L. Holtz, 'Irish grammarians and the continent in the seventh century' in H.B. Clarke and M. Brennan (eds), *Columbanus and Merovingian monasticism*, BAR International Series, 113 (Oxford, 1981), pp. 135-52; Herren, *Latin letters in early Christian Ireland*, especially chapter 2. For a more sceptical assessment of Hiberno-Latin grammarians see V. Law, *Grammar and grammarians in the early middle ages* (London, 1997), especially chapter 2; also her *The insular Latin grammarians* (Woodbridge, 1982).

13. See M. W. Herren, 'Some new light on the life of Virgilius Maro Grammaticus' reprinted in his *Latin letters in early Christian Ireland*, chapter 7; V. Law, *Wisdom, authority and grammar in the seventh century: decoding Virgilius Maro Grammaticus* (1995); *Grammar and grammarians in the early middle ages* (1997), pp 224-45; M. W. Herren, 'Virgil the

grammarian: a Spanish Jew in Ireland?' in *Peritia: journal of the Medieval Academy of Ireland*, 9 (1995), pp. 51-71 and the literature cited there including the important work of Dáibhí Ó Cróinín.

14. B. Löfstedt, *Der Hiberno-Lateinischer Grammatiker Malsachanus* (Uppsala, 1965); V. Law, 'Malsachanus reconsidered: a fresh look at a Hiberno-Latin grammarian' in *Cambridge Medieval Celtic Studies*, 1 (1981), pp. 83-93.

15. M. B. Parkes, 'The contribution of insular scribes of the seventh and eighth centuries to the "grammar of legibility"' in *Graffia e Interpuzione del Latino nel medioevo: seminario internazionale Roma, 27-29 settembre 1984* Lessico intellettuale Europeao, xli (Rome, 1987), pp. 15-31; P. Saenger, 'Word separation and its implications for manuscript production' in *Rationalisierung der Buchherstellung im Mittelalter und in der frühen Neuzeit: Ergebnisse eines buchgeschichtlichen Seminars, Wolfenbüttel 12-14 November 1990* (Marburg an der Lahn, 1994), pp. 41-50 especially at p. 45.

16. Milan, Biblioteca Ambrosiana, MS C.5 inf.; edited by F.E. Warren, *The Antiphonary of Bangor*, 2 vols, Henry Bradshaw Society, (London, 1893-5); for commentary on the text see M.E. Curran, *The antiphonary of Bangor and the early Irish monastic liturgy* (Dublin, 1984).

17. Law, *Grammar and grammarians*, p. 251.

18. R. Sharpe, 'An Irish textual critic and the *Carmen paschale* of Sedulius: Colmán's letter to Feradach' in *Journal of Medieval Latin*, 2 (1992), pp. 44-54.

19. B. Bischoff, 'Wendepunkte in der Geschichte der lateinischen Exegese im Frühmittelalter' in *Sacris Erudiri* 6 (1954), pp 189-279 translated into English in M. McNamara (ed.), *Biblical Studies: the medieval Irish contribution* (Dublin, 1976), pp. 74-160.

20. J. F. Kelly, 'A catalogue of early medieval Hiberno-Latin biblical commentaries' in *Traditio*, 44 (1989), pp. 435-7, 45 (1990), pp. 393-434.

21. C. Stancliffe, 'Early "Irish" biblical exegesis' in *Studia patristica*, 12 (1975), pp. 361-70; M. Cahill, 'Is the first commentary on Mark an Irish work? Some new considerations' in *Peritia*, 8 (1994), pp. 35-45.

22. T. M. Charles-Edwards, 'The social background to Irish *peregrinatio*' in *Celtica*, xi (1976), pp. 43-59.

23. *Confessio*, §§ 23, 26, 36, 37, 43, 46; Tract on the crimes of Coroticus, §§ 1, 10, 16 in Conneely, *Letters of Saint Patrick*, pp. 36, 38, 41, 44, 45, 50, 53, 55.

24. N. McLeod, *Early Irish contract law* [Sydney nd], p. 22.

25. *Vita S. Columbani*, Bk I, c. 3; B. Krusch (ed.), *Ionae vitae sanctorum Columbani, Vedastis, Iohannis*, Monumenta Germaniae Historica, Scriptores in usum scholarum (Hanover, 1905), p. 156.

26. See J.N. Hillgarth, 'Modes of evangelization of Western Europe in the seventh century' in *Irland und die Christenheit*, pp. 311-31.

27. J. M. Wallace-Hadrill, *The Frankish church* (Oxford, 1983) and specifically on Columbanus, pp. 63-70.

28. Hillgarth, 'Modes of evangelization', p. 322.

29. P. Riché, *Education and culture in the Barbarian West* (Columbia, 1976), pp. 180, 324-36.

30. Cited in D. Bethell, 'The originality of the early Irish church' in *Journal of the Royal Society of Antiquaries of Ireland*, cxi (1981), pp. 36-49 at p. 45.

31. See P. Rousseau, *Ascetics, authority and the church in the age of Jerome and Cassian* (Oxford, 1978).

32. See F. Prinz, 'Columbanus, the Frankish nobility and the territories east of the Rhine' in Clarke and Brennan (eds), *Columbanus and Merovingian monasticism*, pp. 73-87.

33. For details of editions of the penitentials attributed to Columbanus and discussion of the texts see T.M. Charles-Edwards, 'The penitential of Columbanus' in M. Lapidge (ed.),

Columbanus: studies on the Latin writings (Woodbridge, 1997), pp. 217-39; P. Riché, 'Columbanus, his followers and the Merovingian church' in Clarke and Brennan (eds), *Columbanus and Merovingian monasticism*, pp. 59-72.

34. *Sancti Columbani opera*, pp. 36-7.

35. The identification of Columbanus's *opera omnia* has generated a great deal of scholarly debate. Crucial is the collection of essays in Lapidge (ed.), *Columbanus: studies on the Latin writings*, as above note 33.

36. *Sancti Columbani opera*, pp 140-1. It has been suggested, however, that this may be a later elaboration to Columbanus's original rule: Columbanus, *Le Opere*, I. Biffi and A. Granata (eds), (Milano, 2001), p. xlii, 312, n. 138.

37. E. John '"Secularium prioratus" and the rule of St Benedict' in *Revue Bénédictine*, 75 (1965), pp. 212-39. Ian Wood suggested that Columbanus may have had access to a copy of Benedict's rule: I. Wood, 'The *vita Columbani* and Merovingian hagiography' in *Peritia*, 1 (1982), pp. 63-80 at 74.

38. M. Dunn, *The emergence of monasticism: from the Desert Fathers to the early middle ages*, (Oxford, 2001), pp. 169-75, 182-5, 191-3.

39. On crossing the Alps as a radical form of *peregrinatio* in a continental context see A. Angenendt, 'Die irische *peregrinatio* und ihre Auswirkungen auf dem Kontinent vor dem Jahre 800' in *Die Iren und Europa im früheren Mittelalter*, i, pp. 52-79.

40. See J. C. King and Werner Vogler (eds), *The culture of the abbey of St Gall: an overview* (Stuttgart, Zürich, 1991), especially pp. 119-28.

41. See J. F. Kenney, *Sources for the early history of Ireland* (New York, 1929), pp. 500-7; Richter, *Ireland and her neighbours*, pp. 126-33.

42. Kenney, *Sources*, p. 515-6; but see Richter, *Ireland and her neighbours*, p. 182, where a case is made for Bobbio as 'the most prolific centre of Irish continental manuscript production in the seventh century'.

43. Kenney, *Sources*, pp. 184-6, 619; J. Hennig, 'Cathaldus Rachau: a study in the early history of diocesan episcopacy in Ireland' in *Medieval studies*, viii (1946), pp. 217-32; 'A note on the traditions of St Frediano and St Silao of Lucca' in *Medieval studies*, xiii (1951), pp. 234-42; A. M. Tommasini, *Irish saints in Italy*, translated with some additional notes by J. F. Scanlan (London, 1937), pp. 360-82, 401-32.

44. See K. Hughes, 'The changing theory and practice of Irish pilgrimage', *Church and society in Ireland, AD 400-1200* (1987), chapter 14.

45. See most recently M. Garrison, 'The English and the Irish at the court of Charlemagne' in P. Butzer, M. Kerner and W. Oberschelp (eds), *Karl der Grosse und sein Nachwirken: 1200 Jahre Kultur und Wissenschaften in Europa / Charlemagne and his heritage: 1200 years of civilization and science in Europe* (Turnhout, 1997), pp. 97-123.

46. J. J. O'Meara, *Eriugena* (Oxford 1988); D. Moran, *The philosophy of John Scottus Eriugena: a study of idealism* (Cambridge, 1989).

47. J. J. Contreni, *The cathedral school of Laon from 850 to 930: its manuscripts and masters* (München, 1978); 'John Scottus, Martin *Hiberniensis*, the liberal arts, and teaching' in M. W. Herren (ed.), *Insular Latin studies: Latin texts and manuscripts of the British Isles, 550-1066* (Toronto, 1981), pp 23-44; Lapidge and Sharpe, *Bibliography of Celtic-Latin literature*, pp. 181-2.

48. R. E. Reynolds, 'Unity and diversity in Carolingian canon law collections: the case of the *collectio Hibernensis* and its derivatives' reprinted in his *Law and liturgy in the Latin church, 5th-12th centuries* (Aldershot 1994), chapter 4; Richter, *Ireland and her neighbours*, pp 216-25; T. M. Charles-Edwards, 'The construction of the *Hibernensis*' in *Peritia*, 12 (1998), pp. 209-37.

49. Vatican. Bibliotheca Apostolica, lat. 378, f. 72v; A. Wilmart, 'La Trinité des Scots à Rome

et les notes du *Vat. Lat.* 378' in *Revue Bénédictine*, 41 (1929), pp. 218-30; 'Finian parmi les moines romains de la Trinité des Scots' in *Revue Bénédictine*, 44 (1932), pp. 359-61; cf. Tommasini, *Irish saints in Italy*, pp 94-9. Independent testimony from an Irish source is afforded by the death notice in the Annals of Inisfallen, 1095, of Eógan, *cend manach na Gaedel hi Roim*, 'head of the monks of the Irish in Rome': Seán Mac Airt (ed.), *Annals of Inisfallen* (Dublin, 1951), 1095.13.

50. Kenney, *Sources*, no. 440.

51. Kenney, *Sources*, nos 443-5.

52. P. A. Breatnach, 'The origins of the Irish monastic tradition at Ratisbon' in *Celtica*, 13 (1980), pp. 58-77.

53. M. P. Sheehy, *Pontificia hibernica: medieval papal chancery documents, 640-1261*, 2 vols (Dublin, 1962-5), ii, no. 307.

54. See A. Gwynn, *The Irish church in the 11th and 12th centuries* (Dublin, 1992).

55. D. Ó Corráin, 'Foreign connections and domestic politics: Killaloe and the Uí Briain in twelfth-century hagiography' in D. Whitelock, R. McKitterick, D. Dumville (eds), *Ireland in early medieval Europe* (1982), pp. 213-31; D. Ó Riain-Raedel, 'German influence on Munster church and kings in the twelfth century' in A.P. Smyth (ed.), *Seanchas: studies in early medieval Irish archaeology, history and literature in honour of Francis J. Byrne* (Dublin, 2000), pp. 323-30.

56. 'The Irish today promise great things of their knowledge of language and grammar, but the truth is that they are less than safe guides to the formation of Latin words and the proper speaking of Latin': William of Malmesbury's Life of Saint Dunstan in W. Stubbs (ed.), *Memorials of St Dunstan*, Rolls Series (London, 1874), p. 25.

57. J. Leclercq, C. H. Talbot and H. M. Rochais (eds.), *Sancti Bernardi opera*, 8 vols (Rome, 1957-77), iii, pp. 295-378; English translation in R. Meyer (ed.), *The life and death of St Malachy the Irishman* (Kalamazoo, 1978).

58. Still valuable on the medieval usage of the term *insula sanctorum* is L. Gougaud, 'The isle of saints' in *Studies*, 13 (1924), pp. 363-80.

59. Richter, *Ireland and her neighbours*, p. 15.

CHAPTER FOUR

Select Bibliography

Asplin, P. W., 'Bibliography', in A. Cosgrove (ed.), *A New History of Ireland*, II, *Medieval Ireland 1169-1534* (Oxford, 1987), pp. 859-66 (Ecclesiastical Records), pp. 891-96 (Ecclesiastical History)

Cosgrove, A., 'The medieval period' in R. Ó Muirí (ed.), *Irish Church History Today* (Armagh, 1990)

General Histories of Medieval Ireland

Nicholls, K., *Gaelic and Gaelicised Ireland in the Middle Ages* (Dublin, 1972)

Otway-Ruthven, A.J., *A History of Medieval Ireland* (2nd ed, London and New York, 1980)

Frame, R., *Colonial Ireland 1169-1369* (Dublin, 1981)

Cosgrove, A. (ed.), *A New History of Ireland, II, Medieval Ireland 1169-1534* (Oxford, 1987)

Duffy, S., *Ireland in the Middle Ages* (Dublin, 1997)

European Background and Context

Bartlett, R., *The Making of Europe. Conquest, Colonization and Cultural Change, 950-1350* (Penguin Books, 1994)

Translated Sources

Meyer, R.T., (ed.), *Bernard of Clairvaux. The Life and Death of Saint Malachy the Irishman* (Cistercian Fathers Series 10, Kalamazoo, 1978)

Scott, A. B. and Martin, F. X. (eds), *Expugnatio Hibernica. The Conquest of Ireland by Giraldus Cambrensis* (Dublin, 1978)

General Ecclesiastical History

Hughes, K., *The Church in Early Irish Society* (London, 1966)

Gwynn, A., *The Irish Church in the Eleventh and Twelfth Centuries*, ed. G. O'Brien (Dublin, 1992)

Corish, P. J. (ed.), *A History of Irish Catholicism*, vol. 2 (1968), fasc. 1A. Gwynn, 'The twelfth century reform'; Fasc. 3, G.J. Hand, 'The Church in the English lordship, 1216-1307'; Fasc. 4, A. Gwynn, 'Anglo-Irish Church life: fourteenth and fifteenth centuries'; Fasc. 5, C Mooney, 'The Church in Gaelic Ireland: thirteenth to fifteenth centuries'.

Watt, J. A., *The Church and the Two Nations in Medieval Ireland* (Cambridge, 1970)

—, *The Church in Medieval Ireland* (2nd ed, Dublin, 1998)

Corish, P. J., *The Irish Catholic Experience. A Historical Survey* (Dublin, 1985)

History of the Religious Orders

Conway, C., *The Story of Mellifont* (Dublin, 1958)

Gwynn, A. and Hadcock, R. N., *Medieval Religious Houses: Ireland* (London, 1970)

Martin, F. X., 'The Irish Augustinian reform movement in the fifteenth century' in J. A. Watt, J. B. Morrall and F. X. Martin (eds), *Medieval Studies Presented to A. Gwynn SJ* (Dublin, 1961), pp. 230-64

Empey, A., 'The sacred and the secular: the Augustinian priory of Kells in Ossory 1193-1541', *Irish Historical Studies*, 24 (1984-5), pp. 131-51

Stalley, R., *The Cistercian Monasteries of Ireland*, (Yale, 1987)

Episcopate

Gwynn, A., and Gleeson, D. F., *A History of the Diocese of Killaloe*, vol. 1 (Dublin, 1962)

Walsh, K., *A Fourteenth-Century Scholar and Primate. Richard FitzRalph in Oxford, Avignon and Armagh* (Oxford, 1981)

Watt, J. A., 'John Colton, justiciar of Ireland (1382) and archbishop of Armagh (1383-1404)' in J. Lydon (ed.), *England and Ireland in the Later Middle Ages. Essays in Honour of Jocelyn Otway-Ruthven* (Dublin, 1981), pp. 196-213

—, 'Ecclesia inter Anglicos et inter Hibernicos: confrontation and coexistence in the medieval diocese and province of Armagh' in J. Lydon (ed.), *The English in Medieval Ireland* (Dublin, 1984)

—, 'The Church and the two nations in late medieval Armagh', *Studies in Church History* 25, (1989), pp. 37-54

Lynch, A., 'The administration of John Bole, archbishop of Armagh, 1457-71' *Seanchas Ard Mhacha*, 14 (1991), pp. 39-108

Flanagan, M. T., 'Henry II, the council of Cashel and the Irish bishops', *Peritia,* 10 (1996), pp. 184-211

Parochial Clergy

Nicholls, K., 'Rectory, vicarage and parish in the western Irish dioceses', *Royal Society of Antiquaries of Ireland Journal,* 101 (1971), pp. 53-84

Simms, K., 'Frontiers in the Irish Church – regional and cultural', in T. Barry, R. Frame and K. Simms (eds), *Colony and Frontier in Medieval Ireland. Essays Presented to J. F. Lydon* (Dublin, 1995), pp. 177-200

CHAPTER FIVE

1. See Anthony Lynch, 'Religion in late medieval Ireland' in *Archivium Hibernicum*, xxxvi (1981), pp. 3-15; John Bossy, *Christianity in the West, 1400-1700* (Oxford, 1985); R. Whiting, *The Blind Devotion of the People: Popular Religion and the English Reformation* (Cambridge, 1989); Euan Cameron, *The European Reformation* (Oxford, 1992), Peter O'Dwyer, *Towards a History of Irish Spirituality* (Dublin, 1995).

2. Margaret R. Sommerville, *Sex and Subjection: Attitudes to Women in Early Modern Society* (London, 1995), pp. 42-3.

3. *Ibid.*, p. 43; Malcolm Underwood, 'Politics and piety in the household of Lady Margaret Beaufort' in *Journal of Ecclesiastical History*, xxxviii, no. 1 (Jan. 1987), p. 39.

4. See Katherine Simms, 'Women in Norman Ireland' in Margaret MacCurtain and Donncha Ó Corráin (eds.), *Women in Irish society – The Historical Dimension* (Dublin, 1978), p. 21.

5. See *Annála Connacht: The Annals of Connacht, AD 1224-1544*, ed. A.M. Freeman (Dublin, 1983) (hereinafter *AC*); *Annála Rioghachta Éireann: Annals of the Kingdom of Ireland by the Four Masters from the Earliest Period to the Year 1616*, ed. and trans. John O'Donovan (6 vols, Dublin, 1854; repr., New York, 1966), iv-v (hereinafter *AFM*); *Annála Uladh, Annals of Ulster: A Chronicle of Irish Affairs, 431-1131, 1155-1541*, ed. W. M. Hennessy and Bartholomew MacCarthy (4 vols, Dublin, 1887-1901), iii (hereinafter *AU*).

6. Marty Newman Williams and Anne Echols, *Between Pit and Pedestal: Women in the Middle Ages* (Princeton New Jersey, 1994), p. 111.

7. Colm Lennon, *Richard Stanihurst the Dubliner 1547-1618* (Dublin, 1981), p. 156.

8. See John A.F. Thomson, *The Early Tudor Church and Society, 1485-1529* (London & New York, 1993), pp. 334, 336.

9. Bossy, *Christianity in the West 1400-1700*, p. 144.

10. See *AC*; *AFM*, iv, v; *AU*, iii.

11. *AC*, p. 621.

12. *AC*, pp. 664-7.

13. John A.F. Thomson, 'Piety and charity in late medieval London' in *Journal of Ecclesiastical History*, xvi, no. 2 (Oct. 1965), p. 194.

14. *AFM*, v, p. 1373; *AU*, iii, p. 555.

15. Elizabeth McKenna, 'Women as patrons of the arts in medieval Ireland' in Christine Meek (ed.), *Women in Renaissance and Early Modern Europe* (Dublin, 2000), p. 91.

16. *Ibid.*, p. 91.

17. A. Gwynn and & R.N. Hadcock, *Medieval Religious Houses in Ireland* (Dublin, 1988 repr.), p. 258.

18. *Ibid.*, p. 300. Gwynn & Hadcock state that Margaret was assisted in this project by her husband; McKenna, 'Women as patrons of the arts', p. 88.

19. *AFM*, v, pp 1300-01; *AC*, p. 621; *AU*, iii, p. 501; Gwynn & Hadcock, *Medieval Religious Houses in Ireland*, p. 248.

20. McKenna, 'Women as patrons of the arts', pp. 90-91.

21. Gwynn & Hadcock, *Medieval Religious Houses in Ireland*, pp. 247, 231.

22. *AC*, p. 667; *AFM*, v, p. 1393.

23. McKenna, 'Women as patrons of the arts', p. 91.

24. Thomson, 'Piety and charity in late medieval London', p. 194.

25. See *AC*; *AFM*, iv, v; *AU*, iii.

26. David Postles, 'Monastic burials of non-patronal lay benefactors' in *Journal of Ecclesiastical History*, xlvii, no. 4 (Oct. 1996), pp. 622, 634-5; Jens Röhrkasten, 'Londoners and London mendicants in the late middle ages' in *Journal of Ecclesiastical History*, xlvii, no. 3 (July 1996), pp. 462, 465, 466.

27. *AFM*, v, p. 1393. See Postles, 'Monastic burials', p. 635.

28. 'The annals of Ireland from the year 1443 to 1468', trans. Dudley Firbisse, ed. John O'Donovan in *The miscellany of the Irish Archaeological Society*, vol. 1 (Dublin, 1846), p. 218 (hereinafter 'Annals').

29. *AC*, p. 667.

30. *AFM*, v, pp. 1379, 1423; *AC*, p. 657; *AC*, p. 687 where she is referred to as Siobhan.

31. Thomson, 'Piety and charity in late medieval London', p. 190.

32. *AU*, iii, p. 431.

33. *AC*, p. 479.

34. *AFM*, iv, pp. 953-5, 1202-3; 'Annals', p. 217.

35. *AU*, iii, p. 263; *AFM*, iv, p. 1103; Gwynn & Hadcock, *Medieval Religious Houses in Ireland*, p. 185.

36. *Leabhar Chlainne Suibhne: An Account of the MacSweeney Families in Ireland, with Pedigrees*, ed. Paul Walsh (Dublin, 1920), pp. 68-9.

37. See John Hunt, *Irish Medieval Figure Sculpture, 1200-1600: A Study of Irish Tombs with Notes on Costume and Armour* (2 vols, Dublin, 1974), i, pp. 166-7, 175-6.

38. Postles, 'Monastic burials', p. 632.

39. Hunt, *Irish Medieval Figure Sculpture*, i, pp. 121-26.

40. See *Dictionary of National Biography*, xli (London, 1895), p. 350 (*D.N.B.*); Roger Stalley, 'Sailing to Santiago: medieval pilgrimage to Santiago de Compostela and its artistic influence in Ireland' in John Bradley (ed.), *Settlement and Society in Medieval Ireland: Studies Presented to F. X. Martin* (Kilkenny, 1988), p. 404.

41. *AFM*, iv, p. 972; *AC*, p. 493.

42. Williams and Echols, *Between Pit and Pedestal*, pp. 108-09.

43. *AFM*, iv, p. 972; *AC*, p. 493. For examples of other women's attention to the material upkeep of churches see *Register of Wills and Inventories of the Diocese of Dublin in the Time of Archbishops Tregury and Walton 1457-1483*, ed. H. F. Berry (Dublin, 1898) (hereinafter *Register of wills*) and Clive Burgess, '"For the increase of divine service": chantries in the parish in late medieval Bristol' in *Journal of Ecclesiastical History*, xxxvi, no. 1 (Jan. 1985), pp. 62-4.

44. *AFM*, iv, p. 972; *AC*, p. 493; *D.N.B.*, p. 350.

45. *Leabhar Chlainne Suibhne*, pp. 66-9; Gywnn & Hadcock, *Medieval Religious Houses in Ireland*, p. 291. Eight years before, their son, Ruaidhrí, had been buried in Rathmullen church. His was the first body to be laid to rest there and for this reason, the couple resolved to have a monastery erected on the site.

46. *Leabhar Chlainne Suibhne*, pp. 68-9.

47. *Ibid.*, pp. 66-7.

48. *Ibid.*, pp. xliv-lxiii.

49. *Holinshed's Irish chronicle*, p. 286 quoted in Elizabeth McKenna, 'A political role for women in medieval Ireland' in Christine Meek and Katharine Simms (eds.), *'The Fragility of Her Sex'?: Medieval Irishwomen in their European Context* (Dublin, 1996), p. 171.

50. See *AC*, pp. 620-21, 664-7, 676-7; *AFM*, iv, pp. 972-3, v, pp. 1372-3; *AU*, iii, pp. 554-5.

51. Gwynn & Hadcock, *Medieval Religious Houses in Ireland*, p. 297.

52. Johanna was the daughter of James, earl of Desmond. See Gwynn & Hadcock, *Medieval Religious Houses in Ireland*, p. 242.

53. John Bradley, 'The chantry college, Ardee' in *Journal of the County Louth Archaeological Society*, xxii, no. 1 (1989), p. 18.

54. *Irish Monastic and Episcopal Deeds, AD 1200-1600*, ed. Newport B. White (Dublin, 1936), p. 236.

55. *Calendar of the Patent & Close rolls of Ireland, of the Reigns of Henry VIII, Edward VI, Mary*

I and Elizabeth, ed. James Morrin (Dublin, 1861), pp. 2, 56; *Calendar of Entries in the Papal Registers Relating to Great Britain and Ireland, Papal Letters 1471-1484*, xiii, pt. ii, ed. J. A. Twemlow (London, 1955), p. 636.

56. H.F. Berry, 'History of the religious guild of St Anne in St Audoen's church, Dublin, 1430-1740, taken from its records in the Haliday Collection, R.I.A.' in *Proceedings of the Royal Irish Academy*, xxv, sect. C (1904-5), p. 23; *Irish Monastic and Episcopal Deeds*, ed. White, pp. 235, 237, 239; *The Registers of Christ Church Cathedral, Dublin*, ed. Raymond Refaussé and Colm Lennon (Dublin, 1998), p. 20 (hereinafter *Registers of Christ Church*); Colm Lennon, 'The chantries in the Irish Reformation: the case of St Anne's Guild, Dublin, 1550-1630' in R.V. Comerford, Mary Cullen, Jacqueline Hill and Colm Lennon (eds), *Religion, Conflict and Coexistence in Ireland: Essays Presented to Monsignor Patrick J. Corish* (Dublin, 1990), pp. 6-25; *Directory of Historic Dublin Guilds*, ed. Mary Clark and Raymond Refaussé (Dublin, 1993), pp. 32-40; Colm Lennon, 'The foundation charter of St Sythe's guild, Dublin, 1476' in *Archivium Hibernicum*, xlviii (1994), pp. 3-12.

57. C.W. Fitzgerald, *The Earls of Kildare and their Ancestors from 1057 to 1773* (Dublin, 1857), pp. 75-6.

58. *Crown Surveys of Lands 1540-41 with the Kildare Rental begun in 1518*, ed. Gearóid MacNiocaill (Dublin, 1992), pp. 312-14; Mary Ann Lyons, 'Sidelights on the Kildare ascendancy: a survey of Geraldine involvement in the Church, c.1470-c.1520' in *Archivium Hibernicum*, xlviii (1994), p. 82; Hunt, *Irish Medieval Figure Sculpture*, i, pp. 138, 203.

59. Eamon Duffy, *The Stripping of the Altars: Traditional Religion in England 1400-1580* (New Haven & London, 1992), p. 156.

60. See Hunt, *Irish Medieval Figure Sculpture*, i, pp. 144-7, 158-9, 186-8, 210-13, 225-6; Colm Lennon, 'The Reformation in the Pale', p. 4 (unpublished paper).

61. Raymond Gillespie, 'Irish funeral monuments and social change 1500-1700: perceptions of death' in Raymond Gillespie and Brian P. Kennedy (eds), *Ireland: Art into History* (Dublin & Colorado, 1994), pp. 155-68.

62. Hunt, *Irish Medieval Figure Sculpture*, i, pp. 124, 143, 145, 159, 186, 187, 191, 195, 204, 205, 212, 226, 230.

63. *Ibid.*, i, p. 191.

64. See *Register of Wills*, pp. 53, 56, 81.

65. See Robert Dinn, 'Monuments answerable to men's worth: burial patterns, social status and gender in late medieval Bury St Edmunds' in *Journal of Ecclesiastical History*, xlvi, no. 2 (Apr. 1995), p. 241.

66. Lord Walter Fitzgerald, 'Miscellanea: the Kerdiffs of Kerdiffstown, County Kildare' in *Journal of the Kildare Archaeological Society*, vii (1912-14), pp. 182-86; *Register of Wills*, p. 126.

67. *Registers of Christ Church*, pp. 48, 62, 72, 76, 84-6. However, not all gifts were motivated entirely by self-interest: the memorials of Adare Manor, Co Limerick record that 'the wife of Fitzgibbon, added ten feet to the length of the chancel, in order that the priests might have ampler space about the great altar'. See Caroline, countess of Dunraven, *Memorials of Adare Manor* (Oxford, 1865), p. 76.

68. For an analysis of surviving medieval wills in general from Dublin archdiocese, see Margaret Murphy, 'The high cost of dying; an analysis of *pro anima* bequests in medieval Dublin' in W.J. Sheils and Diana Wood (eds), *The Church and Wealth* (Oxford, 1987), pp. 111-22.

69. *Register of Wills*, pp. 12, 48.

70. Murphy, 'The high cost of dying', p. 115.

71. See *Register of Wills*.

72. Gwynn & Hadcock, *Medieval religious houses in Ireland*, pp. 246, 251-2; Hunt, *Irish Medieval Figure Sculpture*, i, pp. 158-9, 194-6, 225-6.

73. Hunt, *Irish Medieval Figure Sculpture*, i, pp. 146-7.

74. P. Ariès, *Western Attitudes towards Death: From the Middle Ages to the Present* (Baltimore, 1974) and idem, *The Hour of Our Death* (London, 1981); David Postles, 'Monastic burials', pp. 620-21.

75. See *Register of Wills*.

76. Clive Burgess, '"By quick and by dead": wills and pious provision in late medieval Bristol' in *English Historical Review*, cccci (Oct. 1987), p. 841.

77. *Register of Wills*, pp 56, 134; Hunt, *Irish Medieval Figure Sculpture*, i, pp. 144, 210, 207, 211, 225, 204.

78. *Register of Wills*, p. 159; Hunt, *Irish Medieval Figure Sculpture*, i, pp. 158-9.

79. *Register of Wills*, p. 2; Postles, 'Monastic burials', p. 634; Dinn, 'Monuments answerable to men's worth', p. 255.

80. See Hunt, *Irish Medieval Figure Sculpture,*, i and *Register of Wills*.

81. See *Register of Wills*; *The Register of John Swayne Archbishop of Armagh and Primate of Ireland 1418-1439*, ed. D.A. Chart (Belfast, 1935), p. 202; *Calendar of Ormond Deeds*, ed. Edmund Curtis (6 vols, Dublin, 1932-43), ii, pp. 346, 364, iii, p. 301; Hunt, *Irish Medieval Figure Sculpture*, i, pp. 146, 159, 158, 121, 166.

82. *Registers of Christ Church*, p. 18.

83. *Register of Wills*, pp 12, 53; *Registers of Christ Church*, pp. 25, 89.

84. Hunt, *Irish Medieval Figure Sculpture*, i, p. 186.

85. *Ibid.*, i, p. 208.

86. See *Registers of Christ Church*, pp. 20-21, 39-83.

87. Cameron, *The European Reformation*, p. 13.

88. Gwynn & Hadcock, *Medieval Religious Houses in Ireland*, p. 360.

89. *Ibid.*, pp. 359, 361; Bradley, 'The chantry college, Ardee', p. 18.

90. F.E. Ball, *Howth and its Owners* (Dublin, 1995 edn.), p. 47; Gwynn & Hadcock, *Medieval Religious Houses in Ireland*, p. 360; Lennon, 'The Reformation in the Pale', p. 4.

91. See David Postles, 'Monastic burials', p. 621.

92. *The Register of John Swayne*, p. 202.

93. H.F. Berry, 'Some ancient deeds of the parish of St Werburgh, Dublin, 1243-1676' in *Journal of the Royal Society of Antiquaries of Ireland*, xlv, pt. 1 (1915), p. 34. For similar arrangements in the context of late medieval Bristol see Burgess, "By quick and by dead", p. 849.

94. *Calendar of Inquisitions formerly in the Office of the Chief Remembrancer of the Exchequer*, ed. Margaret C. Griffith (Dublin, 1991), p. 3.

95. *Christ Church Deeds*, ed. M. J. McEnery and Raymond Refaussé (Dublin, 2001), p. 221.

96. *Register of Wills*, pp. 56, 64; Berry, 'Some ancient deeds of the parish of St Werburgh', p. 43; Burgess, "By quick and by dead", pp. 842-3.

97. *Register of Wills*, pp. 104, 134-5; Berry, 'Some ancient deeds of the parish of St Werburgh', p. 43.

98. *Calendar of Ormond Deeds*, ed. Curtis, iii, p. 301.

99. *Register of Wills*, p. 12.

100. See *Register of Wills*; Thomson, 'Piety and charity in late medieval London', p. 183.

101. *Register of Wills*, p. 161; Thomson, 'Piety and charity in late medieval London', pp. 184-5.

102. *Register of Wills*, pp. 124-5.

103. See Berry, 'History of the religious guild of St Anne', pp. 47-8.

104. See *Register of Wills*; Thomson, 'Piety and charity in late medieval London', p. 187.

105. Lynch, 'Religion in late medieval Ireland', p. 13.

106. Robert Dinn, 'Burial patterns in Bury St Edmunds', p. 255.
107. Burgess, 'By quick and by dead', p. 856.
108. *Ibid.*, p. 857.

CHAPTER SIX

Select Bibliography

Original Documents
Brady, W. M. (ed), *State Papers Concerning the Irish Church* (London, 1868)
Shirley, E. P. (ed), *Original Letters and Papers of the Church in Ireland* (London, 1851)

Secondary Works
Bradshaw, B., *The Dissolution of the Religious Orders in Ireland Under Henry VIII* (Cambridge, 1974)
— and J. Morrill (eds), *The British Problem* (London, 1996)
— and P. Roberts (eds), *British Consciousness and Identity* (Cambridge, 1998)
Bettig-Haimer, 'Revisionism and the Irish Reformation', *Journal of Ecclesiastical History*, 51, 3, (2000), pp. 581-6
Brady, C. and H Gillespie (eds), *Natives and Newcomers* (Dublin, 1986)
Caball, M., *Poets and Politics, 1558-1625* (Cork, 1998)
Canny, N., *From Reformation to Restoration: Ireland 1534-1660* (Dublin, 1987)
Corish, P., (ed), *A history of Irish Catholicism,* iii (Dublin, 1967)
—, *The Irish Catholic Experience* (Dublin, 1985)
Ellis, S.G., *Ireland in the age of the Tudors, 1447-1603* (London, 1998)
Ford, A. M., McGuire, J. and Milne, K. (eds.), *As by Law Established: The Church of Ireland since the Reformation* (Dublin 1989)
Lennon, C., *The Lords of Dublin in the Age of the Reformation* (Dublin, 1989)
—, *Sixteenth Century Ireland* (Dublin, 1994)

CHAPTER SEVEN

Bibliography

Bradshaw, B., 'Geoffrey Keating: apologist of Irish Ireland' in B. Bradshaw, A. Hadfield and W. Maley (eds), *Representing Ireland: Literature and the Origins of Conflict, 1534-1660* (Cambridge, 1993)

Cause for the Beatification of Dermot O'Hurley and Companions, i (Rome, 1988)

Corish, P. J., 'The origins of Catholic nationalism' in P. J. Corish (ed.), *Irish Catholicism*, iii, 8 (Dublin, 1968)

—, 'The rising of 1641 and the breakdown of Catholic confederacy, 1641-5' in T. W. Moody, F. X. Martin and F. J. Byrne (eds), *A New History of Ireland: III, Early Modern Ireland, 1534-1691* (Oxford, 1976)

—, 'Ormond, Rinuccini and the Confederates, 1645-9' in T. W. Moody *et al* (eds), *A New History of Ireland: III, Early Modern Ireland, 1534-1691* (Oxford, 1976)

—, 'The Cromwellian conquest, 1649-53' in T. W. Moody *et al* (eds), *A New History of Ireland: III, Early Modern Ireland, 1534-1691* (Oxford, 1976)

—, *The Catholic Community in the Seventeenth and Eighteenth Centuries* (Dublin, 1981)

Cunningham, B., 'The culture and ideology of Irish Franciscan historians at Louvain, 1607-1650' in C. Brady (ed.), *Ideology and the Historians* (Dublin, 1991)

—, *The World of Geoffrey Keating: History, Myth and Religion in seventeenth-century Ireland* (Dublin, 2000)

Ford, A., *The Protestant Reformation in Ireland, 1590-1640* (Dublin, 1996)

—, 'James Ussher and the creation of an Irish Protestant identity' in B. Bradshaw and P. Roberts (eds), *British Consciousness and Identity: The Making of Britain, 1533-1707* (Cambridge, 1998)

Forrestal, A., *Catholic Synods in Ireland, 1600-1690* (Dublin, 1998)

Jones, F. M., 'The Counter-Reformation' in P. J. Corish (ed.), *A History of Irish Catholicism*, iii, 3 (Dublin, 1967)

Lennon, C., *An Irish Prisoner of Conscience of the Tudor Era: Archbishop Richard Creagh of Armagh, 1523-1586* (Dublin, 1999)

—, 'Political thought of Irish Catholic churchmen: the testimony of the writings of Bishop David Rothe' in H. Morgan (ed.), *Political Ideology in Ireland, 1541-1641* (Dublin, 1999)

Morgan, H., 'Hugh O'Neill and the Nine Years War in Tudor Ireland' in *Historical Journal*, xxxvi (1993)

Ó Buachalla, B., '"James our true king": the ideology of Irish royalism in the seventeenth century' in D. George Boyce, R. Eccleshall and V. Geoghegan (eds), *Political Thought in Ireland since the Seventeenth Century* (London, 1993)

Ó Siochrú, Mícheál, *Confederate Ireland 1642-1649: A Constitutional and Political Analysis* (Dublin, 1999)

O'Sullivan, W., 'Correspondence of David Rothe and James Ussher, 1619-23' in *Collectanea Hibernica*, 36-7 (1993)

Ronan, M. V., *The Reformation in Ireland under Elizabeth, 1558-80* (London, 1930)

Silke, J. J., 'Later relations between Primate Peter Lombard and Hugh O'Neill' in *Irish Theological Quarterly*, xxii (1955)

CHAPTER EIGHT

1. J. Bossy, 'The Counter Reformation and the people of Catholic Ireland, 1596-1641,' in *Historical Studies*, VIII, (1971); N. Canny, 'Why the Reformation failed in Ireland: *Une Question Mal Posée*,' in *Journal of Ecclesiastical History*, XXX, (1979); B. Bradshaw, 'Sword, word and strategy in the Reformation in Ireland,' in *Historical Journal*, XXI, (1978); *Idem.*, 'The Edwardian Reformation in Ireland,' in *Archivium Hibernicum*, XXVI, (1976-1977); *Idem.*, 'The Reformation in the cities: Cork, Limerick and Galway,1534-1603,' in J. Bradley (ed.), *Settlement and Society in Medieval Ireland. Studies Presented to F. X. Martin, OSA* (Kilkenny, 1988); B. Millett, 'Survival and Reorganisation 1650-'95', in P. J. Corish (ed.), *A History of Irish Catholicism* , vol. III, pts. VII & VIII, (Dublin, 1968), pt. VII, pp. 1-63; J. Brady & P.J. Corish, ' The Church under the Penal Code', in P. J. Corish (ed.), *A History of Irish Catholicism,* vol. IV, pts. II & III, (Dublin, 1971), pt. II, pp. 1-8.

2. A good overview is provided in C. Giblin, 'Irish Exiles in Catholic Europe', in P.J. Corish (ed), *A History of Irish Catholicism,* vol. IV, pts. II & III, (Dublin, 1971), pt. III, pp. 1-65; J. Brady, 'The Irish Colleges in Europe and the Counter Reformation', *Proceedings of the Irish Catholic Historical Committee* (1957).

3. D. M. Downey, 'Culture and Diplomacy. The Spanish Habsburg Dimension in the Irish Counter Reformation Movement, c.1529-c.1629' (Cambridge, Ph.D. thesis unpublished, 1994), pp. 137-190.

4. F. M. Jones, 'Canonical faculties on the Irish Mission in the reign of Queen Elizabeth,' in *Irish Theological Quarterly*, XX, (1953) pp. 152-171; D.F. Cregan, 'The Social and Cultural Background of a Counter Reformation Episcopate, 1618-1660,' in A. Cosgrove and D. MacCartney (eds.), *Studies in Irish History presented to R. Dudley-Edwards* (Dublin, 1979), pp. 85-117 ; P. J. Corish, *The Catholic Community in the Seventeenth and Eighteenth Centuries* (Dublin, 1981), pp. 18-42; *Idem. The Irish Catholic Experience, A Historical Survey* (Dublin, 1985), pp. 63-122.

5. D. M. Downey, 'Culture and Diplomacy', pp. 137-90.

6. B. Bradshaw, *Dissolution of the Religious Orders in Ireland,* (Cambridge, 1974), pp. 8-16; A. Gwynn and N. Hadcock, *Medieval Religious Houses: Ireland* (London, 1970), pp. 224-226; F. X. Martin, 'The Irish Augustinian reform movement of the fifteenth century,' in J. A. Watt, J. B. Morrall and F. X. Martin (eds.), *Medieval Studies presented to Aubrey Gwynn, SJ* (Dublin, 1961), pp. 230-264; F. X. Martin, 'The Irish Friars and the Observant Movement in the fifteenth century,' in *Proceedings of the Irish Catholic Historical Commission* (1960).

7. B. Bradshaw, 'The Reformation in the Cities', pp. 447-52.

8   D. M. Downey, 'Cult. and Diplomacy', pp. 138-40; T. O'Neill, *Merchants and Mariners in Medieval Ireland* (Blackrock, 1987), pp. 44-57; R. Hitchcock, 'Dingle in the Sixteenth Century', in *Journal of the Royal Society of Antiquaries of Ireland*, II, (1852-'53), pp. 133-134; R. Hayes, 'Ireland's links with Compostella', in *Studies*, XXXVII, (1948), pp. 326-332; T. O'Neill, 'A Fifteenth Century Entrepreneur, Germyn Lynch, fl.1441-1483', in J. Bradley (ed), *Settlement and Society,* p. 425; A. Chambers, *Granuaile: The Life and Times of Grace O'Malley, c.1530-1603* (Dublin, 1983), pp. 20-25.

9. *Ibid.*

10. P. Conlan, *Franciscan Ireland* (Mullingar, 1988), pp. 21-25; C. Mooney, *Devotional Writings of the Irish Franciscans*, 1224-1950 (Killiney, 1952).

11. P .J. Corish, *Catholic Experience*, pp. 57, 74-75; B. Bradshaw, *Dissolution*, pp. 8-16; F. X. Martin, 'Augustinian Reform', pp. 230-64.

12. H. Hammerstein, 'Aspects of the Continental Education of Irish Students in the reign of Elizabeth I', in *Historical Studies*, VIII, (1971), 141.

13. D. M. Downey, 'Cult. and Diplomacy', pp. 140-41; Also see P. J. Corish, *Catholic Experience,*

pp. 75-6 for the example of Thady O'Sullivan OFM who had studied in Spain and died in 1597. R. Stalley, 'Sailing to Santiago: Medieval Pilgrimage to Santiago de Compostella and its artistic influence in Ireland', in *Settlement and Society*, pp. 397-420.

14. P. Conlan, *Franciscan Ireland*, pp. 23-25.

15. J. Lynch, *Spain under the Habsburgs*, I, 1516-1598, (Oxford, 2nd ed, 1981), pp. 64-68, 273-74 ; D. M. Downey, 'Cult. and Diplomacy' (1994), pp. 137-90.

16. Lynch, pp. 257-72.

17. Lynch, pp. 273-86 and by same author, 'Philip II and the Papacy', in *Transactions of the Royal Historical Society*, 5th series, II, (1961), pp. 23-42.

18. D. M. Downey, 'Cult. and Diplomacy', pp. 1-58; Of all the Catholic martyrs in Ireland, 1559-1591, about one third were Franciscan friars. See J. Brady, 'Canonisation of the Irish Martyrs', in *Irish Ecclesiastical Record*, XI, (1918), pp. 313-4.

19. *Cal. S. P. Spain*, vii, 164; C. Hayes-McCoy (ed), 'Unpublished letters of King James V of Scotland relating to Ireland', in *Analecta Hibernica*, no.12, (June, 1943), p. 179.

20. *Supra* notes (18) and (19).

21. S. G. Ellis, *Tudor Ireland*, pp. 278-82; J. Silke, *Kinsale*, 21; D. M. Downey, 'Cult. and Diplomacy', pp. 59-88.

22. J. Silke, 'Hugh O'Neill, The Catholic Question and the Papacy', in *Irish Ecclesiastical Record*, series 5, CIV, (1965), pp. 65-79; D. M. Downey, 'Cult. and Diplomacy', pp. 89-136.

23. E. Hogan, 'Irish worthies of the sixteenth century', in *The Month*, LXVIII, (1890), pp. 352-3.

24. In 1625 the Irish Franciscan College of St Isidore was founded in Rome. In 1627 the Irish Pastoral College of St Patrick was founded in Rome. The Pastoral College was entrusted to Jesuit supervision.

25. B. Bradshaw, 'Fr Wolfe's description of Limerick, 1574', in *North Munster Antiquarian Journal*, XVII, (1976/77), pp. 83-99; J. Begley, *The Diocese of Limerick in the sixteenth and seventeenth centuries* (Dublin, 1927), pp. 494-515.

26. B. Bradshaw, 'The Reform in the Cities', pp. 462, 470.

27. *Ibid.* p. 469; One example worth noting is that of Thomas FitzJohn Arthur, bailiff of Limerick in 1547 and 1568 and mayor in 1565, 1573 and 1577, who on 7 July 1575, petitioned Pope Gregory XIII for absolution from censure for his arrest of Edmund Daniel, SJ (minor orders), who 'broke the Queen's law'; copy of petition in *Archivio Segreto Vaticano, Suppl. Lateranen*, vol. 33, no.3355, fo.99. Daniel was the first Jesuit to be executed in Europe, see J.Begley, *Limerick*, p. 176.

28. For Woulfe see E. Hogan (ed), *Ibernia Ignatiana*, pp. 10, 14-15, and *idem*, 'Irish Worthies', pp. 352-369; D. M. Downey, 'Cult and Diplomacy', pp. 143-45.

29. J. Brady, 'The Irish Colleges', pp. 2, 4; B. Jennings, 'Irish Students in the University of Louvain', in S. O'Brien, (ed.) *Measgra i gcuimhne Mhichíl Uí Chléirigh* (Dublin, 1944), pp. 74-97.

30. E. J. M. van Eijl, *Facultas S. Theologiae Lovanensis* (Leuven,1977), pp. 69-70; J. Visser, *Rovenius und Seine Werke*, (Assen, 1965), pp. 9-10.

31. J. Lynch, *Spain under the Habsburgs*, I, pp. 263-5; A.F. Bell, *Luis de Léon. A Study of the Spanish Renaissance* (Oxford, 1926).

32. P. Guilday, *The English Catholic Refugees on the Continent, 1558-1795* (London, 1914); J. Brady, 'The Irish Colleges', pp. 2-4; From 1548 onwards Anglo-Irish names appear with increasing frequency on the registers of Leuven University.

33. Quoted in J. Brodrick, *Robert Bellarmine* (2 vols., London, 1950), I, p. 94.

34. The Count Caracena, Governor of Galicia, to Philip III, August 1602, *A.H.N.* B. 1217.

35. On the concept of 'Old Ordered Society' and educational institutions see R. L. Kagan, *Students and Society in Early Modern Spain* (Baltimore and London, 1974); R. Trevor-

Davies, *The Golden Century of Spain, 1507-1621* (London, 1967), pp. 280 ff.; and for Irish professional-aristocratic structures see L. Bieler, 'The Island of Scholars', in *Revue du Moyen Age Latin*, VIII, No.3, (1952), 213; K. Nicholls, *Gaelic and Gaelicised Ireland, passim*.

36. D. M. Downey, 'Cult. and Diplomacy', pp. 14-32; J.MacErlean, 'Ireland and World Contact', in *Studies*, VIII, iii, Pt.i, (1919), pp. 307-09; A.J. Loomie, 'Religion and Elizabethan Commerce with Spain', in *Catholic History Review*, LX, (1964), pp. 46-48.

37. J. Brady, 'Irish Colleges in Europe', p. 3.

38. See J. Brady, 'Father Christopher Cusack and the Irish College of Douai, 1594-1623', in S. O'Brien (ed.), *Measgra i gcuimhne Mhíchil Uí Chléirigh*, pp. 98-117. For Valladolid and Thomas White see E. Hogan, *Ibernia Ignatiana*, p. 31; See also T. Corcoran, 'Early Irish Jesuit Educators', in *Studies*, XXIX, (1940), pp. 545 ff.

39. T. Corcoran, *op. cit.* 546; and J. Corboy, 'The Irish College at Salamanca', in *I. E. R.*, LXIII, (1944), pp. 248-49.

40. For the foundation at Alcalá see J. J. Silke, 'The Irish Abroad, 1534-1691', in T. W. Moody, F. X. Martin & F. J. Byrne (eds), *A New History of Ireland*, vol. III (Oxford Clarendon Press, 1976), p. 627; For the foundation at Seville, see *Salamanca Papers at St Patrick's College Maynooth*, legajo 40, no.1, f. 1n., and f. 7n.u.; theological chairs at the Irish College in Lisbon were endowed by Count Antonio Fernando Ximénez, see *Ir. Jesuit Arch., MacErlean Transcripts, Rectores Coll. Hib. Hispaensis; B.L.* Landsdowne Ms. vol.71, no.49, and P.F. Moran, *Spicil.Ossor.*, I, 82. J. Couselo Bouzas, 'El Seminario de Irlandeses en Santiago', in *Boletin de la Real Academia Gallega*, 16, (1926-27). Santiago and Salamanca were foremost among the Spanish cities to offer shelter and education to Irish students.

41. B. Jennings, *The Irish Franciscan College of St Anthony at Louvain* (Dublin, 1925).

42. C. Mooney, 'The Irish Sword and the Franciscan Cowl', in *Irish Sword*, I, (1949), p. 82; J. Casway, *Owen Roe O'Neill: A Study of Gaelic Ireland's Struggle for Survival in the Seventeenth Century*, (Philadelphia University Press, 1984), pp. 132, 139-140; P. J. Corish, *Catholic Experience*, pp. 42, 54-55, 97-98; G. Henry, *The Irish Military Community in Spanish Flanders, 1586-1621* (Dublin, 1992), pp. 98-108.

43. Robert Persons SJ to Philip III, May 1605, A.G.S. Estado 843/12; see also A.J. Loomie, 'Spain and the Jacobean Catholics, 1603-1612', in *Catholic Record Society*, LXIV, (London, 1960), pp. 66-67.

44. For government donations to Irish students at Douai, the Scots seminary at Douai, English and Irish Benedictine nuns at Brussels see *A.G.R., E.G.C.*, reg.177/167. In 1596, money allocated to the Irish infantry in Flanders included a grant to the forty-three Irish students at Douai, see A.G.S., negoc. de Flandes, Estado 612/125-126.

45. The Council of State to Philip III, 8 June 1600, A.G.S., Secretaria de Estado, 840, f. 288.

46. '[I] cannot think such as serve with the Archduke to be truly hearted and affected to the King [James I], and his government; the difference in religion being such and other hatreds to this country [England], so naked,' Sir Arthur Chichester, Irish Viceroy, to Lord Salisbury, 29 October 1605, *Cal. S .P. Ireland, 1603-1606*, pp 340.

47. J. Lynch, *Spain under the Habsburgs*, I, pp. 269-72.

48. Aquaviva to Acosta, 31 August 1592, *Ir. Jesuit Arch.*, MacErlean Transcripts, Arch. Roman. Soc. Jesu, Castellana, 6, f. 129.

49. A more detailed account of this episode is available in D. M. Downey, 'Cult. and Diplomacy', pp. 152-53.

50. *Ibid*, pp. 110, 127-28.

51. J. Corboy, 'The Irish College at Salamanca', pp. 247-53.

52. J. J. Silke, 'The Irish Abroad', p. 624.

53. M. Browne, (Bishop of Galway), 'The Irish College at Salamanca: Last Days', in *The Furrow*, (November 1971), p. 697.

54. E. Hogan, *Ibernia Ignatiana*, pp. 141-2.

55. C. M. Voorvelt, *De Amor Poenitens van Johannes van Neercassel (1626-1686), Onstaansgeschiedenis en Lotqevallen van een Verhandeling over de Strenge Biechtpraktijk*, (Kerkebosch BV-Zeist, 1984), pp. 28-9.

56. D. M, Downey, 'Cult. and Diplomacy, pp. 154-6; R. Clark, *Strangers and Sojourners at Port Royal* (Cambridge, 1932), pp. 1-9; L. Ceyssens, 'Florence Conry, Hugh de Burgo, Luke Wadding and Jansenism', in *Father Luke Wadding Commemorative Volume* (Dublin, 1957), *passim*.

57. On their profession in the province of Santiago and its association with the 'reformador' Cardinal Ximénez de Cisneros see: M.R. Pazas, 'Religiosos irlandeses de la Provincia de Santiago', in *El Eco Franciscano*, 62, (Santiago, 1945), pp. 168-211; M. Castro, 'San Francisco de Santiago de Compostela', in *Archivo Ibero-Americano*, 14, (1964), 60; Luke Wadding always considered himself a son of the Province of Santiago cf. M. de Castro, 'Wadding and the Iberian Peninsula', in. *Wadding Comm.*, pp. 120-1.

58. *'Florentium Conrium, doctrina in Augustini operibus ultra omnes quos noverim versatissimum'*, L. Wadding, *Annales Minorum seu trium ordinum a S. Francisco institutorum continuati a P. Aniceto Chiappini*, (ed.) A. Chiappini, (Quaracchi, 1948-1951), III, 409; For Conry's diplomatic career in the Spanish service see M. Kerney-Walsh, *"Destruction by Peace": Hugh O'Neill after Kinsale*, (Cumann Seanchais Ard Mhaca, Monaghan, 1986).

59. C. Giblin, 'Hugh MacCaghwell OFM, and Scotism at St Anthony's College, Louvain', in *De Doctrina Ioannis Duns Scoti*, iv (Rome, 1968), pp. 375-397.

60. M. de Castro, 'Wadding and the Iber. Penin.', pp. 140 ff., and C. Balic, 'Wadding the Scotist', in. *Wadding Comm.*, pp. 463 ff.

61. B. Jennings, *The Ir. Francisc. Coll. St. Anth. Louvain*, *passim*; V. de Buck, 'L'Arch. irl. couv. St. Antoine', 400 ff.

62. C. Mooney, *Irish Franciscan relations with France, 1224-1850* (Killiney, 1951).

63. D. F. Cregan, 'Social and Cultural Background', pp. 110-11.

64. Jacques Janson to Secretary Charles de la Faille, 15 April 1624, in B. Jennings (ed.), 'Miscellaneous Documents, I, 1588-1624', in *Archivium Hibernicum*, XII (1946), pp. 103-104; See the 'Attestation of the University of Louvain concerning Edmund Dungan', July 1622-1624, in B. Jennings (ed), *Wadding Papers* (Dublin, 1953), pp. 76-7.

65. A. Bellesheim, *Geschichte der Katholischen Kirche in Irland* (2 vols., Mainz,1890), II, *passim*.

66. See Fr Thomas White SJ to Fray Gaspar de Cordoba OP, 7 February 1606, in which he mentions Lombard's complaint to the pope about Jesuit control of the Irish colleges in the Iberian peninsula, *Archiv. Gen. Ord. Praed., Santa Sabina, Rome*, sect. XIV, Ms. 165.

67. On Dungan's academic and episcopal career see D.F. Cregan, 'Social and Cultural background', pp. 110-11.

68. On Rovenius' friendship with Conry see L. Ceyssens, 'Conry, De Burgo, Wadding and Jansenism', p. 309; also B. Jennings, *Wadding Papers*, pp. 28-9.

69. L. Ceyssens, 'Conry, De Burgo, Wadding and Jansenism', p. 331.

70. L. Ceyssens, 'Conry, De Burgo, Wadding and Jansenism', pp. 309-10; R. Clark, *Strangers and Sojourners*, pp. 1-3.

71. L. Ceyssens, 'Autour de la publication de la bulle In Eminenti', in *Revue d'Histoire Ecclésiastique*, 49, (1954), pp. 109-110, 818-826.

72. D. M. Downey, 'Cult. and Diplomacy', pp. 158-60.

73. See L. Wadding, *Annales*, III, 409; A. Bellesheim, *Gesch. Kath. Kirche*, II, pp. 326 327; *'Bei der Jansenisten standen die schriften Conrys in hohen ansehen'*.

74. C. M. Voorvelt, *De Amor Poeniten*, pp. 28-9; L. Ceyssens, 'Conry, De Burgo, Wadding and Jansenism', pp. 313-4.

75. *Ibid*, (L. Ceyssens), pp. 328-30.

76. *Ibid*, pp. 310-23.

77. Jansen to St Cyran, 4 November 1621 in J. Orcibal (ed), *Les Origines du Jansénisme. La Correspondence de Jansénius*, (Louvain & Paris, 1947), p. 67. See L. Ceyssens, 'Conry, De Burgo, Wadding and Jansenism', pp. 313-4.

78. R. Clark, *Strangers and Sojourners*, p. 3.

79. Jansen to St. Cyran, 29 April 1622 in J. Orcibal, *Corresp. de Jansénius*, p. 133.

80. *Ibid*, p. 198, Jansen to St. Cyran, 10 February 1623; See also L. Ceyssens, 'Conry, De Burgo, Wadding and Jansenism', pp. 320-3.

81. *Ibid*, (J. Orcibal), pp. 190-92, Jansen to St Cyran, 1 December 1622; see L. Ceyssens, *op. cit.* (1957), pp. 319-21.

82. D. M. Downey, 'Cult. and Diplomacy', pp. 160-2.

83. Jansen to St. Cyran mentions this in letters of 24 June 1622 and 1 July 1622, printed in J. Orcibal, *Corresp. de Jansénius*, pp. 158-9, 163.

84. R. Clark, *Strangers and Sojourners*, pp. 4-6.

85. L. Ceyssens, 'Conry, De Burgo, Wadding and Jansenism', pp. 308-9.

86. D. M. Downey, 'Cult. and Diplomacy', pp. 162-3.

87. See J.M. Pou y Monti, 'Embajadas de Felipe III a Roma pidiendo la definición de la Inmaculada Concepcion de Maria', in *Archivo Ibero Americano*, 34 (1931), pp. 371-417, 508-35 (1932), pp. 72-88, 424-434, 482-525; 36 (1933), pp. 5-48.

88. *Ibid*.

89. *De Linguae Hebraïcae origine praestantia et utilitate*, (Rome,1621); See M. de Castro, 'Wadding and the Iber. Penin', pp. 134-162; and L. Wadding, *Scriptores Ordinis Minorum* (new edit., Rome,1906), p. 161.

90. D. M. Downey, 'Cult. and Diplomacy', pp. 163-5; L. Ceyssens, 'Conry, De Burgo, Wadding and Jansenism', p. 328.

91. *Ibid*. (Ceyssens), p. 329.

92. *Ibid*.

93. G. Cleary, *Fr. Luke Wadding and St. Isidore's College, Rome* (Rome,1925), pp. 185-194; also for the spread of Scotism in Europe see: B. Millett, 'The Irish Franciscans, 1651-1655', *Analecta Gregoriana*, 129, (Rome,1964), pp. 129-30, 365-466, 472-6, 478-80, on Scotism in Prague pp. 154.

94. B. Jennings, 'The Irish Franciscans in Prague', in *Studies*, (1939), pp. 210-22. On Magennis' defence of MacCaghwell's writings see D.F. Cregan, 'Social and Cultural background', p. 109.

95. L. Wadding, *Annales*, XXVIII, pp. 34 ff.

96. C. Giblin, ' Bonaventure O'Connor Kerry: A Seventeenth-Century Franciscan Abroad', in *Kerry Archaeological and Historical Society Journal, XVII, (1984)*, pp. 37-60.

97. *Ibid*. p. 37; Ioannes Poncius, 'Scotus Hiberniae Restitutus', in *Comentarii Theologici,* vol. I, pt. i, (Paris, 1661), 23

CHAPTER NINE

1. For a good bibliography of work on the Church of Ireland see 'The Church of Ireland: a critical bibliography, 1536-1922' in *Irish Historical Studies*, xxviii (1993), pp. 345-84.

2. National Archives, Dublin, RC10/2, pp. 389-90.

3. C. Lennon, *Archbishop Richard Creagh of Armagh, 1523-86* (Dublin, 2000), p. 29.

4. R. Gillespie, 'The coming of Reform' in K. Milne (ed.), *Christ Church Cathedral, Dublin: A History* (Dublin, 2000) discusses this and the relics of the church.

5. For this phase B. Bradshaw, 'The Edwardian Reformation in Ireland, 1546-53' in *Archivium Hibernicum*, xxxiv (1976-7), pp. 83-99.

6. A. J. Fletcher, 'The civic pageantry of Corpus Christi in fifteenth- and sixteenth-century Dublin' in *Irish Social and Economic History*, xxiii (1996), pp. 92-6; P. Happe and J.N. King (eds), *The vocacyon of Johan Bale* (New York, 1990) p. 57.

7. For this episode, Henry Jefferies, 'The Irish parliament of 1560: the anglican reforms authorised' in *Irish Historical Studies*, xxvi (1998), pp. 128-41.

8. A. Clarke, 'Varieties of uniformity: the first century of the Church of Ireland' in W.J. Shiels and D. Wood (eds), *The Churches, Ireland and the Irish: Studies in Church History xxv* (Oxford, 1989), pp. 105-22.

9. The theology of the Church of Ireland is dealt with in chapter 8 of A. Ford, *The Protestant Reformation in Ireland, 1590-1641* (2nd ed, Dublin, 1998).

10. A. Ford, 'James Ussher and the creation of an Irish Protestant identity' in B. Bradshaw and P. Roberts (eds), *British Consciousness and Identity: The Making of Britain, 1533-1707* (Cambridge, 1998), pp. 185-212.

11. P. Kilroy, 'Sermon and pamphlet literature in the Irish reformed church, 1613-34' in *Archivium Hibernicum*, xxxiii (1975), pp. 110-21.

12. For the activities of one such bishop, J. McCafferty, 'John Bramhall and the Church of Ireland in the 1630s' in A. Ford *et al* (eds), *As by Law Established: The Church of Ireland since the Reformation* (Dublin, 1995), pp. 100-111.

13. The best study remains, St John D. Seymour, *The Puritans in Ireland, 1647-1661* (Oxford, 1912).

14. P. Kilroy, *Protestant Dissent and Controversy in Ireland, 1660-1714* (Cork, 1994) and J. C. Beckett, *Protestant Dissent in Ireland, 1687-1780* (London, 1948).

15. R. Gillespie, 'Dissenters and nonconformists, 1661-1700' in K. Herlihy (ed), *The Irish Dissenting Tradition, 1650-1750* (Dublin, 1995), pp. 11-28.

16. R. Gillespie, *Devoted People: Belief and Religion in Early Modern Ireland* (Manchester, 1997), pp. 97-8.

17. S. J. Connolly, *Religion, Law and Power: The Making of Protestant Ireland, 1660-1750* (Oxford, 1992), pp. 171-190. For a general history A. Acheson, *A History of the Church of Ireland, 1691-1996* (Dublin, 1997), parts 2 and 3.

18. J. Kelly, 'The genesis of "Protestant Ascendancy": the Rightboy disturbances of the 1780s and their impact upon Protestant opinion' in G. O'Brien (ed), *Parliament, Politics and People: Essays in Eighteenth-century Irish History* (Dublin, 1989), pp. 93-127.

19. Trinity College, Dublin, MS 826, f. 244.

20. Trinity College, Dublin, MS 826, f. 299.

21. J. Rogers, *Ohel or Beth Shemesh* (London, 1653), p. 413. A Church of Ireland equivalent may be Henry Blaney of Monaghan who told rebels in 1641: 'I am of the true church as so assured of my salvation. That though you would spare my life yet I will not alter my faith.' Trinity College, Dublin, MS 834, f. 143.

22. Armagh Public Library, Dopping MSS, no. 50

23. A. Day and P. McWilliams (eds), *Ordnance Survey Memoirs of Ireland: Parishes of County Antrim 1* (Belfast, 1990), p. 12.

24. [Tristram Whetcombe], *The Truest Intelligence from the Province of Munster* (London, 1642), p. 5.

25. J. Boyse, *Remarks on a late discourse of William, lord bishop of Derry, concerning the inventions of men in the worship of God* (Dublin, 1694), pp. 93, 98 145; Union Theological College, Belfast, Robert Chambers, MS 'Explanation of the Shorter Catechism', p. 28; Raymond Gillespie, 'Reading the Bible in seventeenth-century Ireland' in Bernadette Cunningham and Máire Kennedy (eds), *The Experience of Reading: Irish Historical Perspectives* (Dublin, 1999), pp. 10-39.

26. Boyse, *Remarks*, p. 85; Thomas Hall, *A Plain and Easy Explication of the Assembly's Shorter Catechism* (Edinburgh, 1692), sig A2v.

27. Presbyterian Historical Society, Belfast, Larne session book, 1701.

28. Boyse, *Remarks*, p. 86.

29. *An Agreement and Resolutions of the Ministers of Christ associated with the City of Dublin and the Province of Leinster* (Dublin, 1659), p. 6.

30. I. Green, '"The necessary knowledge of the precepts of religion"', in Ford *et al*, *As by Law Established*, pp. 85-6.

31. Presbyterian Historical Society, Belfast, Diary of John Cook, 1698.

32. Union Theological College, Belfast, Robert Chambers, MS 'Explanation of the Shorter Catechism' sig B2.

33. Hall, *A Plain and Easy Explication*, sig A2v. The same is true of Thomas Lye, *A Plain and Familiar Method of Instructing the Younger Sort* (Dublin, 1683); p. 6 explains the rationale for the typography, the most important words being those in blackest print.

34. Union Theological College, Belfast, Burt Session book; Bodleian Library, Oxford, Carte MS 45, f. 437

35. Boyse, *Remarks*, p. 93; Bodleian Library, Oxford, Carte MS 45, f. 437. It was claimed that the Church of Ireland offered two sermons every week, each an hour long, E. Wetenhall, *The Gifts and Offices in the Public Worship of God* (Dublin, 1678), p. 681.

36. Wetenhall, *The Gifts and Offices in the Public Worship of God*, p. 578.

37. Presbyterian Historical Society, Belfast, Larne Session Book, 30 April, 1701; Armagh Public Library, Dopping correspondence, no. 36.

38. J. Dunton, *The Dublin Scuffle* (Dublin, 1699), pp. 331, 337, 354.

39. For example, *Calendar of State Papers, Ireland, 1660-2*, pp. 41-3, 115-6.

40. C. McNeill (ed.), *Tanner Letters* (Dublin, 1943), pp. 452-3.

41. Union Theological College, Belfast, Robert Chambers, MS 'Explanation of the shorter catechism', sig A2.

42. Edward Wetenhall, *Collyrium: a sermon of destructive ignorance and saving knowledge preached in Christ Church, Dublin, August 4, 1672* (London, 1672), pp. 14-5, 22. The importance of gesture is also highlighted in one satirical account of the highwayman Redmond O'Hanlon who, it was claimed, was recruited by Presbyterians in Armagh because of his ability to make 'wry faces' and to imitate the ministers 'pulpit postures', *Life and death of the incomparable and indefatigable Tory, Redmond O Hanlyn, commonly called Count Hanlyn in a letter to Mr R.A. in Dublin* (Dublin, 1682), pp. 7-8.

43. W. Sheridan, *St Paul's confession of faith or a brief account of his religion in a sermon preached at St Warboroughs church, Dublin, March 22 1684/5* (Dublin, 1685), p. 11. For similar comments by Dudley Loftus, Marsh's Library, Dublin, MS Z4.5.14, p. 105.

44. E. Wetenhall, *A Practical and Plain Discourse of the Form of Godliness Visible in the Present Age* (Dublin, 1683), pp. 111-2.

45. J. Boyse, *A Vindication of the Remarks of the Bishop of Derry's Discourse* (Dublin, 1695), p. 2; William King, *An Admonition to the Dissenting Inhabitants of the Diocese of Derry* (Dublin, 1694), pp. 5-6.

46. This is argued in Gillespie, *Devoted People*, passim.

47. Gillespie, *Devoted People*, pp. 120-1.

CHAPTER TEN

Reading list:

Roger Blaney, *Presbyterians and the Irish Language* (Belfast, 1986)

Peter Brooke, *Ulster Presbyterianism* (Dublin, 1987)

John Dunlop, *A Precarious Belonging: Presbyterians and Conflict in Ireland* (Belfast, 1995)

Finlay Holmes, *The Presbyterian Church in Ireland: A Popular History* (Dublin, 2000)

Finlay Holmes, *Our Presbyterian Heritage* (Belfast, 1985 and 1992)

David Livingstone and Ronald Wells, *Ulster-American Religion: Episodes in the History of a Cultural Connection* (Notre Dame, 1999).

Phil Kilroy, *Protestant Dissent and Controversy in Ireland, 1660-1714* (Cork, 1994)

Marilyn Westerkamp, *The Triumph of the Laity: Scots-Irish Piety and the General Awakening* (Oxford, 1988)

CHAPTER ELEVEN

1. This long process has recently been studied, though largely from a political point of view, by T. Bartlett, *The Fall and Rise of the Irish Nation: The Catholic Question, 1690-1830* (Dublin, 1992).

2. C. Chevenix Trench, *Grace's Card: Irish Catholic Landlords, 1690-1800* (Dublin, 1997).

3. P. Fagan, *Catholics in a Protestant Country: The Papist Constituency in Eighteenth-century Dublin* (Dublin, 1998), pp. 69-73.

4. H. Fenning, 'The three kingdoms: England, Ireland and Scotland', in J. Metzler (ed), *Sacrae Congregationis de Propaganda Fide Memoria Rerum,* vol. 2, (Rome, 1973), pp. 604-15.

5. The various factors which prevented the bishops from organising their dioceses properly before 1750 have been analysed by E. O'Flaherty, 'Clerical indiscipline and ecclesiastical authority in Ireland, 1690-1750', in *Studia Hibernica,* no. 26, (1991-92), pp. 7-29.

6. H. Fenning, 'John Kent's Report on the State of the Irish Mission, 1742', in *Archivium Hibernicum,* vol. 28 (1966), pp. 76-98.

7. H. Fenning, *The Undoing of the Friars of Ireland: A Study of the Novitiate Question in the Eighteenth Century* (Louvain, 1972).

8. C. Giblin, 'The Stuart nomination of Irish bishops, 1687-1765', in *Irish Ecclesiastical Record,* no. 1177 (Jan. 1966), pp. 35-47.

9. P. Fagan, *Dublin's Turbulent Priest: Cornelius Nary 1658-1738* (Dublin, 1991), especially pp. 113-42.

10. P. Fagan, in *Divided Loyalties: The Question of an Oath for Irish Catholics in the Eighteenth Century* (Dublin, 1997).

11. R.E. Ward *et al* (eds), *Letters of Charles O'Conor of Belanagare: A Catholic Voice in Eighteenth-century Ireland* (Washington, 1988).

12. Quoted in H. Fenning, *The Undoing of the Friars of Ireland,* p. 33.

13. The political role of some bishops in the passing of these acts is explained by E. O'Flaherty, 'Ecclesiastical politics and the dismantling of the penal laws in Ireland, 1774-82', in *Irish Historical Studies,* vol. 26, (May 1988), pp. 33-50.

14. P. Fagan, *Divided Loyalties: The Question of an Oath for Irish Catholics in the Eighteenth Century* (Dublin, 1997), pp. 168-74.

15. J. Brady and P .J. Corish, 'The church under the penal code', in P .J. Corish (ed.), *A History of Irish Catholicism,* vol. 4, part 2, (Dublin, 1971). The rest of this text is largely based on this excellent survey. The visitation-book of Cashel has since been edited by C. O'Dwyer, 'Archbishop Butler's visitation book', in *Archivium Hibernicum,* vol. 33 (1975), 1-90.

16. Published by A. Cogan, *The Diocese of Meath* (Dublin 1867, 1870), vols. 2 and 3.

17. S. Ó Súilleabháin, *Irish Wake Amusements* (Cork, 1967).

18. P. Logan, *The Holy Wells of Ireland,* (Gerrards Cross, 1980).

19. In 1794, Bishop Anthony Coyle had fourteen students, of whom nine were already ordained, lodging in his own house in Letterkenny. The bishop claimed that this was the first seminary in Ulster. H. Fenning, *The Undoing of the Friars,* p. 43, note.

20. The impact of the penal laws and the rate of recovery from them varied from place to place, as also from time to time, making generalisations rather difficult. Patrick Corish has partly overcome this difficulty by considering each province in turn, with a wealth of local detail. P. Corish, *The Catholic Community in the Seventeenth and Eighteenth Centuries* (Dublin, 1981), pp. 73-139.

CHAPTER THIRTEEN

1. S. J. Connolly, *Religion, Law and Power: The Making of Protestant Ireland 1660-1760* (Oxford, 1992), pp. 263-314.

2. See T. Power and K. Whelan (eds), *Endurance and Emergence; the Catholic Community in Eighteenth-century Ireland* (Dublin, 1990).

3. H. Fenning, 'Catholics in 'A purely Protestant town'; a catalogue of Cork imprints from 1723 to 1830' in *Cork Arch. Jn.*, 100 (1995), pp. 129-148.

4. Troy Correspondence, Dublin Diocesan Archives.

5. R. D. Edwards (ed), 'The minute book of the Catholic Association, 1791-93' in *Arch. Hib.*, XL (1942), p. 157. See D. Keogh, 'Archbishop Troy, the Catholic Church and Irish Radicalism, 1791-3' in D. Dickson, D. Keogh and K. Whelan (eds) *The United Irishmen; Republicanism, Radicalism and Rebellion* (Dublin, 1993) pp. 124-34.

6. Troy to Brancadero, 18 May 1792, Dublin Diocesan Archives.

7. J. Keogh to T. Hussey, 29 March 1792, P.R.O. H.O. 100/38/243.

8. C. D. A. Leighton, *Catholicism in a Protestant State: A Study of the Irish Ancien Régime* (Dublin, 1994) p. 65.

9. J. W. to — 24 July 1796, Nat. Arch. Reb. Papers, 620/36/227.

10. F. H. to — 26 February 1798, Nat. Arch. Reb. Papers, 620/18/14.

11. T. Roche to E. Cooke, 12 May 1798, Nat. Arch. Reb. Papers, 620/37/61.

12. J. Little, Diary, in *Anal. Hib.*, 11, p. 67.

13. Mrs Brownrigg to E. Cooke, 27 August 1797, Nat. Arch. Reb. Papers, 620/32/77.

14. J. McCary, *The Sure Way to Heaven* (Belfast, 1797).

15. Circular letter of Dr Dillon of Tuam, 27 March 1799, DDA.

16. *Morning Post*, 8 December 1796; *The Times*, 12 April 1797, cited in J. Smyth, *The Men of No Property* (Dublin, 1992) p. 155.

17. *Northern Star*, reported in the *Morning Post*, 8 December 1796.

18. D. Keogh, *A Patriot Priest; The Life of Rev James Coigly, 1761-98* (Cork, 1998).

19. See D. Keogh, '"The most dangerous villain in society": Fr John Martin's mission to the United Irishmen of Wicklow in 1798' in *Eighteenth Century Ireland* (1992) pp. 115-35; J. Gray, 'A loyal sermon of 1798' in *Linen Hall Review*, 1990.

20. P. J. Corish, *Maynooth College, 1795-1995* (Dublin, 1995), pp. 1-19.

21. *Dublin Evening Post*, 24 June 1797; Andrew Newton to — 1 February 1798, Nat. Arch. Reb. Papers 620/35/102. For a recent study of radical politics in Ulster, see L. M. Cullen, 'The United Irishmen: problems and issues of the 1790s' in *Ulster Local Studies*, vol. 18, no. 2, (Spring, 1997), pp. 7-27.

22. See D. Keogh, *The French Disease : the Catholic Church and Radicalism in Ireland 1790-1800* (Dublin, 1993) pp. 258-61.

23. Address of the Catholics of Cappoquin, *Dublin Evening Post*, 17 March 1798.

24. Downshire, __ 14 January 1798, Nat. Arch. Reb. Papers, 620/35/34.

25. *Press*, 21 December 1797; 8 February 1798.

26. *Dublin Journal*, 22 May 1798.

27. R. McHugh (ed), *Carlow in '98*, p. 227.

28. Duignan cited in J. D'Alton, *The Memoirs of the Archbishops of Dublin* (Dublin, 1888), p. 486; Camden to Portland, April 1798, H. O. 100/76/91-4.

29. *The Press*, 26 December 1797.

30. R. Musgrave, *Memoirs of the Different Rebellions in Ireland* (Dublin, 1800) p. 67; M. Byrne, *Memoirs*, l, p. 54.

31. D. Kelliher, 'Republicanism ...' in *Irish Times*, 2 September 1998.

32. Troy to Castlereagh, 15 December 1795, Public Records Office of Northern Ireland, D3030/412.

33. See D. Keogh and K. Whelan (eds), *Acts of Union: Context, Causes and Consequences of the Act of Union* (Dublin, 2001).
34. Troy to L. Concanen, Spring 1800, DDA.
35. Bartlett, *Fall and Rise of the Irish Nation; the Catholic Question in Ireland 1691-1830* (Dublin, 1992).

CHAPTER FOURTEEN

Bibliography:

Cannon, S., *Irish Episcopal Meetings, 1788-1882; A Juridico-Historical Study* (Rome, 1981)

Connolly, S. SJ, *Priests and People in pre-Famine Ireland: 1780-1845* (Dublin, 1982).

—,*Religion and Society in Nineteenth-century Ireland* (Dundalk, 1985)

Corish, P. J., *The Irish Catholic Experience; A Historical Survey* (Dublin, 1985)

Crossman, V., *Politics, Law and Order in Nineteenth-century Ireland* (Dublin, 1996)

Enright, S., 'Women and Catholic Life in Dublin, 1766-1852', in J. Kelly and D. Keogh (eds), *History of the Catholic Diocese of Dublin* (Dublin, 2000), pp. 268-293

Gallogly, D., *The Diocese of Kilmore, 1800-1950* (Cavan, 1999), pp. 31-60

Grogan, G., *The Noblest Agitator:Daniel O'Connell and the German Catholic Movement, 1830-50* (Dublin, 1991)

Jackson, A., *Ireland 1798-1998* (Oxford, 1999).

Keenan, D., *The Catholic Church in Nineteenth-century Ireland: A Sociological Study* (Dublin, 1983)

Kerr, D. A. *Peel, Priests, and Politics: Sir Robert Peel's Administration and the Roman Catholic Church in Ireland, 1841-1846* (Oxford 1982)

—, *'A Nation of Beggars'? Priests, People, and Politics in Famine Ireland 1846-1852* (Oxford, 1994)

—, *The Catholic Church and the Famine* (Dublin, 1996)

—,'Dublin's forgotten archbishop: Daniel Murray, 1768-1852', J. Kelly and D. Keogh (eds), *History of the Catholic Diocese of Dublin* (Dublin, 1999), pp. 355-65

Kerrigan, C., *Father Mathew and the Irish Temperance Movement, 1838-1849* (Cork, 1992)

MacDonagh, O., *The Hereditary Bondsman: Daniel O'Connell, 1775-1829* (London, 1988)

—, *The Emancipist: Daniel O'Connell, 1830-1847* (London, 1989)

McGrath, T., *Religious Renewal and Reform in the Pastoral Ministry of Bishop James Doyle of Kildare and Leighlin, 1786-1834* (Dublin 1999)

—, *Politics, Interdenominational Relations and Education in the Public Ministry of Bishop James Doyle of Kildare and Leighlin, 1786-1834* (Dublin, 1999)

Millar, D. W., 'Irish Catholicism and the Great Famine', *Journal of Social History,* ix (1975-76), pp. 81-98

Montalembert, Charles de, *Journal Intime Inédit,* ed. L. Le Guillou and N. Roger-Taillade (Paris, 1990)

Murphy, I., *The Diocese of Killaloe 1800-1850* (Dublin, 1992)

O'Connell, M. R. (ed), *Daniel O'Connell: Political Pioneer* (Dublin, 1991)

O'Ferrall, F., *Catholic Emancipation: Daniel O'Connell and the birth of Irish Democracy* (Dublin, 1985)

Vaughan, W. E., (ed), *New History of Ireland* (Oxford, 1989)

Notes

1. Charles de Montalembert, *Avenir,* 18 Jan. 1831.
2. Gustave de Beaumont, *L'Irlande Sociale, Politique et Religieuse* , ii 7th ed. 1863, vol. 2, p. 38.
3. J. G. Kohl, *Travels in Ireland* (London, 1844), p.107.
4. D. Ó Laoghaire, *Ár bPaidreacha Dúchais* (Dublin, 1975).
   P. Ó Fiannachta (ed.), *Léachtaí Cholm Cille VII: Ár nDúchas Creidimh* (Dublin, 1970).
5. S. J. Connolly, *Priests and People in pre-Famine Ireland: 1780-1845* (Dublin, 1982), pp. 135-74.
6. *Histoire Générale de l'Église….traduit de l'Anglois de Mgr Pastorini,* Hovius, St Malo, 1790, vol. 3, p. 23.
7. *First Report of the Commissioners of Public Instruction, Ireland, PP 1835, xxxiii.* D.W.

Miller, 'Mass Attendance in Ireland in 1834' in S.J. Brown and D.W. Miller (eds), *Piety and Power in Ireland 1760-1960: Essays in Honour of Emmet Larkin* (Notre Dame, 2000), pp. 158-179.

8. Miller, 'Mass Attendance', pp. 161-71.

9. P. J. Corish, *The Irish Catholic Experience; a historical survey* (Dublin, 1985), p. 233.

10. Diary of Reverend Thomas O'Carroll, 7,8, 9, 12, 14, 15 Jan; 8, 9, 10, 11, 12, 13 Mar. 1846, Cashel Diocesan Archives. Thomas O'Carroll (1810-65) professor at Thurles College (1838-42); curate at Clonoulty (1842-52); parish priest at Clonoulty (1855-65).

11. A. de Tocqueville, *Journey in Ireland, July-August 1835*, ed E. Larkin, 1990, p. 64.

12. T. McGrath, *Religious Renewal and Reform in the Pastoral Ministry of Bishop James Doyle of Kildare and Leighlin, 1786-1834* and *Politics, Interdenominational Relations and Education in the Public Ministry of Bishop James Doyle of Kildare and Leighlin, 1786-1834* (Dublin, 1999).

13. D. Kerr, 'Dublin's forgotten archbishop: Daniel Murray, 1768-1852', in J. Kelly and D Keogh (eds), *History of the Catholic Diocese of Dublin* (Dublin, 1999), pp. 355-65.
    S. Enright, 'Women and Catholic Life in Dublin, 1766-1852', *ibid.* p. 278.

14. Connolly, *Priests and People,* pp. 82-3.

15. W. Meagher, *Notice on the Life and Character of His Grace Most Rev Daniel Murray…* (Dublin 1853), pp. 102-7.

16. V. Conzemius, 'Les foyers internationaux du Catholicisme Libéral hors de France au XIXe siècle: esquisse d'une géographie historique', in ed. J. Gadille, *Les Catholiques Libéraux au XIXe Siècle,* pp. 18-20.

17. Maginnis to MacNally, 22 July 1836, MacNally Papers, Clogher Diocesan Archives.

18. Pamphlet on the affairs in Kilmore in 1817, Franciscan Library, Killiney, Dublin. Consulted on microfilm.

19. McNally to James Duffy, 12 Sept. 1838, McNally Papers, Clogher Diocesan Archives.

20. Browne to Cullen, 14 Mar. 1839, Cullen Papers, Irish College Rome; T. Cunningham and D. Gallogly, *St Patrick's College and the Earlier Kilmore Academy: A Centenary History* (1974), p. 5.

21. L. Bailly, *Theologia Dogmatica et Moralis ad usum Seminariorum*, 8 vols (Lyons, 1810, 3rd ed).

22. Among the many excellent works on O'Connell it suffices to mention O. MacDonagh, *The Hereditary Bondsman: Daniel O'Connell, 1775-1829* (London 1988); *The Emancipist: Daniel O'Connell, 1830-1847* (London, 1989).

23. D. Gallogly, *The Diocese of Kilmore, 1800-1950* (Cavan, 1999), pp. 31-60.

24. D. A. Kerr, *Peel, Priests, and Politics: Sir Robert Peel's Administration and the Roman Catholic Church in Ireland, 1841-1846* (Oxford, 1982), p. 58.

25. S. J. Brown, 'The New Reformation in the Church of Ireland', in S. J. Brown and D. W. Miller (eds), *Piety and Power in Ireland 1760-1960: Essays in Honour of Emmet Larkin* (Notre Dame, 2000), pp. 180-208.

26. Enright, 'Women and Catholic Life', p. 283.

27. William Makepeace Thackeray, *Irish Sketch Book of 1842* (London, 1843), pp. 40-1.

28. Kohl, *Travels*, pp. 110, 125.

29. Corish, *Irish Catholic Experience*, p. 208.

30. Greville, *Past and Present Policy* (London, 1845), p. 305.

31. Enright, 'Women and Catholic Life', p. 278.

32. Kerr, *Peel, Priests, and Politics,* pp. 155-164, 204-209.

33. This voluntary Society although not founded by Pauline Jaricot is usually associated with her because of the major role she played in it. It was quite distinct from the Congregation of Propaganda in Rome.

34. *The Nation,* 22 July 1846.

35. *The Tablet,* 8 Aug 1846.
36. C. Kerrigan, *Father Mathew and the Irish Temperance Movement, 1838-1849* (Cork, 1992).
37. Kohl, *Ireland,* p. 54.
38. McGrath, *Politics in the Ministry of Bishop Doyle,* p. 76.
39. *L'Avenir,* 18 Oct. 1830, cited in C. de Montalembert, *Journal Intime Inédit,* ed. L. Le Guillou and N. Roger-Taillade, Paris, 1990 vol. 2, p. 110.
40. *Ibid.,* p. 357.
41. McNally to Cullen, 3 Jan. 1846, McNally Papers, Clogher Diocesan Archives.
42. *Minutes of Evidence, Select Committee on Disturbances, PP 1825,* vii. 357
43. Diary of John O'Sullivan, parish priest of Kenmare (1839-74), Kerry Diocesan Archives.
44. Connolly, *Priests,* pp. 186-91.
45. D. Kerr, *The Catholic Church and the Famine* (Dublin, 1996), p. 40.

CHAPTER FIFTEEN

Select Bibliography

Bane, L., 'John MacHale and John MacEvilly: conflict in the nineteenth-century Catholic hierarchy' in *Archivium Hibernicum*, xxxix (1984)

Biscelgia, L.R., 'The Fenian funeral of Terence Bellew MacManus' in *Eire-Ireland*, xiv (Autumn, 1979)

Cannon, S., 'Irish Episcopal meetings, 1788-1882: a juridico-historical study' in *Annuarium Historiae Conciliorum*, xiii (1981), 2

Comerford, R.V., *The Fenians in Context: Irish Politics and Society, 1848-1882* (Dublin and New Jersey, 1988)

Connolly, S.J., *Priests and People in Pre-Famine Ireland, 1780-1845* (Dublin, 1982)

Corish, P.J., 'Political Problems, 1860-78' in P.J. Corish (ed.), *A History of Irish Catholicism, V* (Dublin, 1967)

Gilley, S., 'The Catholic Church and revolution in Ireland' in Y. Alexander and A. O'Day (eds), *Terrorism in Ireland* (London, 1984); *Irish Catholic Directory and Almanac*

Keenan, D., *The Catholic Church in the Nineteenth Century: A Sociological Survey* (Dublin, 1983)

Kerr, D. A., *'A Nation of Beggars?': Priests, People and Politics in Famine Ireland, 1846-1852* (Oxford, 1994)

Larkin, E., *The Consolidation of the Roman Catholic Church in Ireland, 1860-70* (Chapel Hill, 1987)

—, *The Making of the Roman Catholic Church in Ireland, 1850-60* (Chapel Hill, 1980)

—, *The Roman Catholic Church and the Home Rule Movement, 1870-74* (Chapel Hill, 1990)

MacSuibhne, P., *Paul Cullen and his Contemporaries*, 5 vols. (Naas, 1961-74)

Moran, G., *A Radical Priest in Mayo: Fr Patrick Lavelle, The Rise and Fall of an Irish Nationalist, 1825-1886* (Dublin, 1994)

—, (ed), *Radical Irish Priests* (Dublin, 1998)

—, 'John Miley and the crisis at the Irish College, Paris in the 1850's' in *Archivium Hibernicum*, l (1996)

—, 'Near Famine: The Crisis in the West of Ireland, 1879-82' in *Irish Studies Review*, no. 18 (Spring, 1997)

—, '"From Connaught to North America": State-aided emigration from Galway to North America in the 1880s' in G. Moran and R. Gillespie (eds), *Galway: History and Society* (Dublin, 1996)

Norman, E.R., *The Catholic Church and Ireland in the Age of Rebellion, 1859-1873* (London, 1965)

Ó Fiaich, T., 'The clergy and Fenianism, 1860-1870' in *The Irish Ecclesiastical Record*, civ (Feb 1968)

Rafferty, O., *The Church, the State and the Fenian Threat, 1861-1875* (London, 1999)

CHAPTER SIXTEEN

1. Cullen Papers, Irish College, Rome.
2. T. Murphy, 'Life of Father Dowley and Life of Father Lydon', p. 89. Archives of the Congregation of the Mission, St. Peter's, Phibsboro, Dublin.
3. Archives of the Congregation of the Mission, Dublin.
4. *Ibid.*
5. *Ibid.*, Thomas McNamara, 'Memoirs of the Congregation of the Mission in Ireland England and Scotland,' p. 325.
6. E. Larkin, 'The Rise and Fall of Stations in Ireland, 1750-1850,' *Chocs et Ruptures en Histoire Religieuse, Fin XVIIIe-XIXe Siècles* (Rennes, 1998), p. 22.
7. *Ibid.*
8. McNamara, p. 127.
9. Kirby Papers, Irish College, Rome.
10. *Ibid.*, Cullen to Kirby, 24 December, 1853.
11. *Missions in Ireland: Especially with Reference to the Prostelytizing Movement; Showing the Marvellous Devotedness of the Irish to the Faith of Their Fathers* (Dublin, 1855). By One of the Missioners [Angelo Maria Rinolfi]; Kevin A. Laheen, *The Jesuits in Killaloe, 1850-1900* (Limerick, 1998).
12. McNamara, *op. cit.,* Chapter X, 'The Missions in Ireland,' pp. 84-127.
13. Laheen, *op. cit.,* pp. 43-53.
14. J. Prost, *A Redemptorist Missionary in Ireland, 1851-1853* (Cork, 1998). Edited and translated by Emmet Larkin and Herman Freudenberger, pp. 77-78.
15. McNamara, *op. cit.,* pp. 106-107.
16. *Ibid.,* p. 116.
17. *Ibid.,* pp. 116-117.
18. D. W. Miller, 'Irish Catholicism and the Great Famine,' *Journal of Social History,* September, 1975.
19. J. Blanchard, *The Church in Contemporary Ireland* (Dublin, 1963), pp. 29-31.
20. The figures for 1847 are estimated from the *Census of Ireland, 1841* and the *Census of Ireland, 1851* and the *Irish Catholic Directory* (1847). The figures for 1880 are taken from the Census of Ireland, 1881.
21. *Royal Commission of Inquiry into Primary Education* (Ireland), Vol. 4: Minutes of Evidence Taken Before the Commissioners, from November 24, 1868 to May 29, 1869 (C 6-III), H. C. 1870, 28, pt. 3. Cullen, February 25, 1869, pp. 1252-1253.
22. E. Larkin, 'The Devotional Revolution in Ireland, 1850-1875,' *The American Historical Review,* 77 (1972): 625-52.

CHAPTER SEVENTEEN

1. J. F. Hogan, 'The *Irish Ecclesiastical Record* and the *Tablet*', *Irish Ecclesiastical Record*, VIII, 4th series, December 1900, pp 529-30. The correspondence in question followed a strongly worded article in the *Record* on French education. The author, C.M. O'Brien, was severely criticised in the *Tablet* for his rather extreme views.
2. F. Callanan, *T.M. Healy* (Cork, 1996), pp 227-8.
3. E. Larkin, *The Historical Dimensions of Irish Catholicism* (Dublin, 1997), pp 112-3.
4. D. W. Miller, 'The Roman Catholic Church in Ireland, 1898-1918' in A. O'Day (ed.), *Reactions to Irish Nationalism* (London, 1987), p. 173.
5. S. Paseta, *Before the Revolution: Nationalism, Social Change and Ireland's Catholic Elite, 1879-1922* (Cork, 1999), chapter 2.
6. P. O'Leary, *The Prose Literature of the Gaelic Revival: Ideology and Innovation* (Pennsylvania, 1994), p. 23.
7. *Ibid*, p. 23-4.
8. *Ibid*, pp 15-6.
9. J. Hutchinson, *The Dynamics of Cultural Nationalism: the Gaelic revival and the creation of the Irish Nation State* (London, 1987), p. 9.
10. D. Ferriter, *A Nation of Extremes: The Pioneers in Twentieth-century Ireland* (Dublin, 1997), p. 97.
11. M. Ward, *Unmanageable Revolutionaries: Women and Irish Nationalism* (London, 1983), p. 41.
12. O'Leary, *The Prose Literature of the Gaelic Revival*, pp. 141, 429.
13. D. Ó Súilleabháin, *Cath na Gaeilge sa Chóras Oideachais 1893-1911* (Dublin, 1988), p. 52.
14. T. J. Morrissey, *Towards a National University: William Delany, S.J. 1835-1924* (Dublin, 1983), ch. 18.
15. J. MacMahon, 'The Catholic Clergy and the Social Question in Ireland, 1891-1916', *Studies* 70/280 (Winter 1981) p. 279.
16. Ferriter, *A Nation of Extremes,* ch. 1.
17. L. McKenna, 'The relations of Catholics to Protestants in Social Work', *The Irish Monthly* 45 (July 1917), p. 451.
18. MacMahon, 'The Catholic Clergy', p. 275.
19. E. Larkin, *James Larkin: Irish Labour Leader 1876-1947* (London, 1989), pp. 138-40.
20. For McKenna's career see Morrissey's introduction to McKenna, Lambert, *The Social Teachings of James Connolly with Commentary and Introduction by Thomas J. Morrissey SJ* (Dublin, 1991).
21. M. Harris, *The Catholic Church and the Foundation of the Northern Irish State* (Cork, 1993), p. 46.
22. D. W. Miller, *Church, State and Nation in Ireland, 1898-1921* (Dublin, 1973), pp. 287 ff.
23. B. Mac Giolla Choille, *Dublin Castle Intelligence Notes 1913-16* (Dublin, 1966), pp. 166-174.
24. F. X. Martin, 'Extracts from the Papers of the late Dr Patrick McCartan, part 2', *Clogher Record* 5:2 (1965), p. 187.
25. F. X. Martin, 'The McCartan documents 1916', *Clogher Record* 6:1 (1966), pp 32-33.
26. T. Ó Fiaich, *Má Nuad* (Maynooth, 1972), p. 68.
27. J. Newsinger, '"I Bring not Peace but a Sword": The Religious Motif in the Irish War of Independence', *Journal of Contemporary History* 13 (1978), p. 615.
28. E.P. O'Callaghan, 'Correspondence between Bishop O'Dwyer and Bishop Foley on the Dublin Rising 1916-7', *Collectanea Hibernica* 18-19 (1976-7), pp. 184-212 and Harris, *The Catholic Church* p. 50.

29. T. Ó Fiaich, 'The Irish Bishops and the Conscription Issue 1918', *Capuchin Annual* 35 (1968) pp. 351-368.
30. Harris, *The Catholic Church* p. 67.
31. *Ibid*, p. 91.
32. T. Ó Fiaich, 'The Catholic Clergy and the Independence Movement', *Capuchin Annual* 37 (1970) pp. 480-502.
33. J. Newsinger,' "I Bring not Peace but a Sword", p. 623.
34. D. Keogh, *The Vatican, the Bishops and Irish Politics* (Cambridge, 1986), pp. 39-42.
35. The text of this statement is reprinted in *Irish Catholic Directory*, 1923, pp. 608 ff.
36. P. Murray, *Oracles of God: The Roman Catholic Church and Irish Politics, 1922-37* (Dublin, 2000), ch. 4.
37. Murray, *Oracles of God*, pp. 222 ff.
38. Keogh, *The Vatican, the Bishops and Irish Politics*, p. 105.
39. D. Keogh, *Ireland and the Vatican: the Politics and Diplomacy of Church-State Relations, 1922-1960* (Cork, 1995).
40. D. Keogh, 'The Role of the Catholic Church in the Republic of Ireland', in Forum for Peace and Reconciliation, *Building Trust in Ireland* (Belfast, 1995), p. 94.
41. *Ibid*, p. 107.
42. Harris, *The Catholic Church*, p.17.
43. D.W. Miller, *Church, State and Nation in Ireland 1898-1921* (Dublin, 1973), p. 337.
44. *Derry Journal*, 6 June 1916.
45. *Irish Independent* 18 February, 1920)
46. Harris, *The Catholic Church*, p. 134.
47. C. O'Halloran, *Partition and the Limits of Irish Nationalism: An Ideology under Stress* (Dublin, 1987), p. 60 and Harris, *The Catholic Church*, p. 171-2.
48. E. Phoenix, *Northern Nationalism: Nationalist Politics, Partition and the Catholic Minority in Northern Ireland 1890-1940* (Belfast, 1994), p. 358 ff.
49. Harris, 'Catholicism Nationalism and the Labour Question in Belfast, 1925-38, *Bullán: An Irish Studies Journal*, 3/1 (1997) pp. 15-32.
50. Harris, *The Catholic Church*, p. 265.
51. Harris, *The Catholic Church*, p. 84.
52. B. Rolston, *Drawing Support: Murals in the North of Ireland* (Belfast, 1992), pp. 28, 30, 33.
53. P. Harbinson, *No Surrender* (London, 1960).

CHAPTER EIGHTEEN

1. G. Seaver, *John Allen Fitzgerald Gregg, Archbishop* (Dublin, 1963), p. 119.
2. *Church of Ireland Gazette*, 6 Jan. 1922.
3. F.S.L. Lyons, 'The minority problem in the 26 counties', in F. MacManus (ed.), *The Years of the Great Test 1926-39* (Cork, 1967), p. 94.
4. D. McCartney, 'MacNeill and Irish-Ireland', in F.X. Martin and F.J. Byrne (eds), *The Scholar Revolutionary: Eoin MacNeill, 1867-1945, and the Making of the New Ireland* (Shannon, 1973), p. 91.
5. J. J. Lee, *Ireland 1912-1985: Politics and Society* (Cambridge, 1989), p. 158.
6. D. Keogh, *Ireland and the Vatican: The Politics and Diplomacy of Church and State Relations, 1922-1960* (Cork, 1995), p. 38.
7. Quoted in J. Lydon, *The Making of Modern Ireland from Ancient Times to the Present* (London, 1998), p. 393.
8. Richard Dunphy, *The Making of Fianna Fáil: Power in Ireland 1923-1948* (Oxford, 1995), p. 209.
9. F. S. L. Lyons, *Ireland since the Famine* (revised ed., 1973), p. 683n.
10. J. J. Lee, *Ireland 1912-1985*, p. 317.
11. W. B. Stanford, *A Recognised Church: The Church of Ireland in Éire* (Dublin, 1944), e.g. p.28.
12. T. Keane, 'Demographic trends', in M. Hurley (ed.), *Irish Anglicanism 1869-1969* (Dublin, 1970), pp168-78.
13. *Senate debates*, v, 434-443 (11 June 1925).
14. T. Brown, 'The Church of Ireland: some literary perspectives', in *Search*, iii, no 2 (Winter 1980), pp 5-19.
15. *Ibid.*, pp. 6-7. See also F.S.L Lyons, *Culture and Anarchy in Ireland 1890-1939* (Oxford, 1979).
16. Compiled from figures in W. E. Vaughan and A. J. Fitzpatrick (eds), *Irish Historical Statistics: Population: Population 1821-1971* (Dublin, 1978), pp 69-73. Church of Ireland members comprised 22.0% of the population of Northern Ireland in 1971, and 17.7% in 1991. In fact all the Protestant Churches sustained a decreased percentage of population over that period; the Roman Catholic Church alone recorded an increase, from 31.8% to 38.4%. ('The 1991 census and the Church of Ireland' by J. L. B. Deane and R. E. Turner, in *Search*, xix, no. 1 (Spring, 1996), p.41.)
17. R. B. McDowell, *The Church of Ireland 1869-1969* (London, 1975), p.104; R. F. Foster, *Modern Ireland 1600-1972* (1988), pp. 466-7 n.v.
18. *The Irish Times*, 20 May 1999, p.6.
19. See, for example, 'Standing one's ground: religion, polemic and Irish history since the Reformation', by Alan Ford, in A. Ford, J. McGuire and K. Milne (eds) *As by Law Established* (Dublin, 1995), pp 1-14.
20. 'Report of the subcommittee on sectarianism', in *General Synod Reports* (1999).

CHAPTER NINETEEN

1. Basic sources with a focus on the church: Jay Dolan, *The American Catholic Experience* (Garden City, NY, 1985); James Hennesy, *American Catholics* (New York, 1981); Thomas McAvoy, *History of the Catholic Church in the United States* (Notre Dame, 1969); Michael Glazier and T. J. Shelley, (eds.), *The Encyclopedia of American Catholic History* (Collegeville, MN, 1997).
    Basic sources with a focus on the Irish: D.N. Doyle, 'The Irish in North America, 1776-1845', and 'The Re-Making of Irish America, 1845-1880,' in W. E. Vaughan (ed.), *A New History of Ireland*, v. 5, *Ireland Under the Union 1 (1801-1870)* (Oxford, 1989), pp. 682-725, and v. 6, *Ireland Under the Union II (1870-1921)*, pp. 725-763; M.A. Glazier, *Encyclopedia of the Irish in America*, 2 vols. (Notre Dame, IND, 1999); L.J. McCaffrey, *The Irish Catholic Diaspora in America* (Washington, DC, 1997); K. A. Miller, *Emigrants and Exiles* (Oxford and New York, 1985).

2. G. Shaughnessy, *Has the Immigrant Kept the Faith?* (New York, 1925, reprinted 1969); Philip Gage, S.M., 'Shaughnessy, Gerald (1887-1950)' in Glazier and Shelley, *Encyclopedia*, p. 1282; Rev John McGlynn, Gortahork, Co Donegal to the author, 6 Oct 1998; Fr. McGlynn was an assistant at St James Cathedral, Seattle, in 1949. Of Massachusetts Irish background, Shaughnessy was a late vocation to the Marist order, and a theologian and spiritual writer.

3. 'Cohort depletion' is the technical term involved: I have calculated the populations aged 15-24 at each census against those of 25-34 a decade later, from W. E. Vaughan and A. J. Fitzpatrick, *Irish Historical Statistics: Population, 1821-1971* (Dublin, 1978), tables 24 and 25, pp. 24-25, 78-81. As Irish migration was disproportionately from that cohort, its depletion is an indicator (*not* a measure) of defective emigration data. For critical study of migration figures, see e.g., R.P. Swierenga, 'Dutch International Migration Statistics, 1820-1880,' *International Migration Review*, 15(1981), 445-68. For a modern study compounding Shaughnessy's misreading if with greater demographic skills and for Irish Americans overall, see M. Hunt and J.R. Goldstein 'How 4.5 Million Irish Immigrants Became 40 million Irish Americans,' *American Sociological Review*, 59 (1994), pp. 64-82.

4. A. H. Deye, 'Archbishop John Baptist Purcell of Cincinnati: the pre-Civil War Years,' (unpublished Ph.D. Univ. of Notre Dame, 1959), p. 191.

5   D. N. Doyle, 'The Irish in Australia and the United States: Some Comparisons, 1800-1939,' *Irish Economic and Social History*, 16 (1989), table 2, pp. 88-89.

6. D. H. Akenson, 'Pre-university Education, 1782-1870,' and his 'Pre-university Education, 1870-1921,' in W. E. Vaughan, (ed.), *Ireland Under the Union 1, (1801-1870)*, pp. 533-36, and in *ibid.*, II, *(1870-1921)*, pp. 532-37; M. Daly and D. Dickson, (eds.), *The Origins of Popular Literacy in Ireland 1720-1900* (Dublin, 1990).

7. H. R. Weisz, *Irish-American and Italian-American Educational Views and Activities, 1870-1900: A Comparison* (New York, 1976), pp. 161-62; R. L. Moore, 'What Children Did Not Learn in School,' *Church History*, 68(1999), pp. 57-61; W. K. Dunn, *What Happened to Religious Education...in the Public Elementary Schools, 1776-1861* (Baltimore, 1958); W. A. Nord, *Religion and American Education* (Chapel Hill, NC, 1995).

8. *Statistical History of the United States*, ser. H 535-544, p. 377; H. Buetow, *Of Singular Benefit* (New York, 1970); T. Walch, *Parish School: A History* (New York, 1995); J. W. Sanders, 'Catholics And the Schools Question in Boston: the Cardinal O'Connell Years,' in R. E. Sullivan and J. M. O'Toole, *Catholic Boston...1870-1970* (Boston, 1985); For a summary, F. M. Perko, 'Catholic Education, Parochial,' in Glazier and Shelley (eds.), *Encyclopedia*, pp. 255-259.

9. Sources: Calculated from US Bureau of the Census, *Twelfth Census, Population* [1900], vol.1, pp. 430, 434, 796, 875, 877, 883, 885, 891 and 893; *idem, Special Reports, Religious*

Bodies, 1906. 2 vols. (Washington, 1910), vol. 1, pp. 80-81; Weisz, *Irish-American and Italian-American Educational Views,* table 2, p. 96.

10. Second generation is used in the European sense, i.e., the America-born offspring of the first, or immigrant, generation.

11. What follows departs from accounts in T.H. O'Connor, *Boston's Catholics* (Boston, 1998); *idem., Fitzpatrick of Boston, 1846-1866* (Boston, 1984); D. Merwick, *Boston's Priests, 1848-1920* (Cambridge Mass., 1973); R. E. Sullivan and J.M. O'Toole, *Catholic Boston, 1870-1970* (Boston, 1985); R.W. Hayman, *Catholicism in Rhode Island...1780-1886* (Providence, 1982); *idem., Catholicism in Rhode Island...1887-1921*(Providence, 1995); for a new departure, T.J. Meagher, 'The Grand Privilege of Our Public Schools': Parochial Education among Irish Catholics in Worcester,' *Historical Journal of Massachusetts,* 12(1984), pp. 44-59.

12. K. J. Christiano, *Religious Diversity and Social Change*, pp. 178-79, 181-84. For early 20th c. memoirs of New England by west of Ireland immigrants, Barbara Mullen, *Life is my Adventure* (London, 1937); Pat Mullen, *Man of Aran* (London, 1934), pp. 33-43, and John Healy, *Nineteen Acres* (Galway, 1978; Achill, 1987).

13. P. J. Coleman, 'A Roman Catholic High School,' *Donahoe's Magazine,* 34 (Feb. 1895), pp. 181-189; P. Gleason, *Contending with Modernity: Catholic Higher Education in the Twentieth Century* (New York, 1995).

14. E. R. Kantowicz, *Corporation Sole: Cardinal Mundelein and Chicago Catholicism* (Notre Dame, 1983), pp. 87-89; J. Perlmann. *Ethnic Differences: Schooling and Social Structure among the Irish, Italians, Jews and Blacks in an American City, 1880-1935* (New York, 1988), table 2.6, p. 60 and table 2.15, p. 78.

15. J. Courtney Murray, SJ, *We Hold These Truths: Catholic Reflections on the American Proposition* (New York, 1960); *idem, Religious Liberty,* (ed.), J.L. Hooper (Louisville, 1993); R.J. Regan, *American Pluralism and Catholic Conscience* (New York, 1963). See (on Murray) J. L. Hooper, *The Ethics of Discourse* (Washington D.C., 1987); R. McElroy, *The Search for an American Public Theology ...* (New York, 1989).

16. P. Gleason, 'Pluralism, Democracy and Catholicism in the Era of World War II,' *Review of Politics,* 49 (1987), pp. 208-230.

17. e.g., Daniel Berrigan (b. 1921, BA 1946); Daniel Callahan (b.1930, BA, 1948); Charles Curran (b. 1934, BA, 1955); Andrew Greeley (b. 1928, BA, 1950)), E. Michael Harrington (b. 1928, BA 1947); Eugene Kennedy (b. 1928, BA 1950), Gabriel Moran (b 1935, BA, 1958). See relevant *Contemporary Authors* entries. Callahan, Kennedy and Moran were reported as having 'greatly' influenced their thinking by respectively 4%, 41% and 26% of younger American priests (born 1935-1944) in 1970: A. Greely, *The Catholic Priest in the United States: Sociological Investigations* (Washington, 1972), table 9.17, p. 190. For wartime and post-war culture, R. Polenberg, *War and Society* (Philadelphia, 1972); S. Hartmann, *The Homefront and Beyond* (Boston, 1982); G. L. Sittser, *A Cautious Patriotism: American Churches and the Second Word War* (Chapel Hill, NC, 1997).

18. P. Gleason, 'World War II and the Shaping of American Identity,' *Review of Politics ,* 43(1981), pp. 483-518 and 'World War II and the Development of American Studies,' *American Quarterly,* 26 (1984), pp. 343-358; its resonance in Catholic society and education can be seen in J. Hennesey, *American Catholics* (New York, 1981), c.20, 'Cross and Flag', pp. 280-296; D.F. Crosby, *God, Church and Flag ...1950-1957* (Chapel Hill, 1978); William Au, *The Cross. the Flag and the Bomb: American Catholics Debate War and Peace, 1960-1983* (Westport, CT., 1985).

19. e.g. J. Courtney Murray, *We Hold These Truths*, pp. 65-72, 174-78. American systems, first positively assessed, are then turned into normative realities, and a prescriptive 'modernity' is identified with America.

20. J. D. Donovan 'The American Catholic Hierarchy: A Social Profile,' *American Catholic Sociological Review,* 19(1958), pp 98-112; Greeley, *The Catholic Priest in the United States: Sociological Investigations,* tables 2.4, 9.16, 10.3, 10.5, pp. 27, 187-88, 203, 206.

21. E. Waugh, 'The American Epoch in the Catholic Church,' [1949], in D. Gallagher (ed.), *The Essays, Articles and Reviews of Evelyn Waugh* (London, 1983), pp. 377-88; *The Letters of Evelyn Waugh* (ed.), Mark Amory (London, 1980), pp. 289-93; F. Sheed, *The Church and I* (Garden City, New York, 1974).

22. For one study, D. Tricarico, 'Influence of the Irish on Italian Communal Adaption in Greenwich Village,' *Journal of Ethnic Studies,* 13, n.4 (1986), pp. 127-37. Studies of intra-church relations between Irish, Irish-American and Italian Catholics in the era 1880-1940 are listed in Hennesy, *American Catholics,* p. 353, n.9; and in Glazier and Shelley, *Encyclopedia,* p. 711; add R.M. Linkh, *American Catholicism and European Immigrants* (New York, 1975); D. Liptak, *The European Immigrant and the Catholic Church in Connecticut, 1870-1920* (Staten Island, 1987); J. M. O'Toole, 'The Newer Catholic Races': Ethnic Catholicism in Boston, 1900-1940,' *New England Quarterly,* 65(1992), pp. 117-34.

23. L. J. Iorizzo and S. Mondello, *The Italian Americans* (New York, 1971), p. 35.

24. *Irish World* [New York], 21 March 1891; *New World,* [Chicago], 29 Aug. 1896, 26 Dec. 1896; *Michigan Catholic* [Detroit], 11 and 18 Jan., 20 Sept. 1894, 25 July 1895. By contrast, *The Irish-American,* 2 May 1891, cited by Iorizzo and Mondello, p. 73, was an organ of the Democratic Party of New York; for the party's views, see T. Henderson, *Tammany Hall and the New Immigrants* (New York, 1976).

25. Iorizzo and Mondello, pp. 34-35, 60-61, 81; Henderson, *Tammany Hall,* pp. 83-84, 150-154; R. H. Bayor and T. J. Meagher, *The New York Irish* (Baltimore 1996), tables A.9 to A.11, pp. 561-62; R. H. Bayor, *Neighbors in Conflict...New York City, 1929-1941* (Baltimore, 1978). J.F. Stack, *International Conflict in an American City, Boston's Irish, Italians and Jews* (Westport, CT, 1979).

26. e.g., *The Pilot* [Boston], 26 May, 7 Dec. 1895, 14 March 1897; *Irish World* , 25 Oct., 1890, 21 March 1891, 8 August 1891; Joseph Gavan, 'Washington Letter,' Cincinnati *Catholic Telegraph,* 9 April 1891; *ibid.,* 6 Oct. 1892, 12 July 1894, 6 and 20 Sept. 1894 (quotation); *New World* 7 Jan. and 18 Mar. 1899; [Milkwaukee] *Catholic Citizen,* 6 and 13 Feb. 1897; Mechanics Hall programme, Sunday, Nov. 30, 1919.

27. (Except notably in Philadelphia, Chicago, Cleveland and Newark).

28. J. Kasun, *The War Against Population* (San Francisco, 1988); D. J. Bogue, 'How Demography was Born,' *Demography,* 30(1993), pp. 519-21; D. Hodgson, 'Ideological Origins of the PAA,' *Population and Development Review,* 17(1991), pp. 1-34 (on the Population Association of America); J. R. Wilmot and P. B. Ball, 'The Population Debate in American Popular Magazines, 1946-1990,' *ibid.,* 18 (1992), pp. 631-68; J. Hitchcock, 'The American Press and Birth Control: Preparing the Ground for Dissent,' *Homilectic and Pastoral Review* , 80(1980), pp. 10-26.

29. J. Hennesey, 'Prelude to Vatican I: American Bishops and the Definition of the Immaculate Conception,' *Theological Studies,* 25 (1964), pp. 409-19.

30. D. Light, 'The Reformation of Philadelphia Catholicism, 1830-1860,' *Pennsylvania Magazine of History and Biography,* 112 (1988), pp. 375-405; Hugh Nolan, in J.F. Connolly (ed.), *The History of the Archdiocese of Philadelphia* (Philadelphia, 1976), pp. 113-208; T.W. Spalding, *The Premier See...Baltimore, 1789-1989* (Baltimore, 1989), pp. 154-78,

31. H. M. Bahr, B. Chadwick and J. Strauss, *American Ethnicity* (Lexington, Mass., 1979), pp. 114, 117; A. F. Rolle, *The American Italians* (Belmont CAL, 1972), pp. 104-05; Greeley, *The Catholic Priest in the United States: Sociological Investigations, pp.* 28, 30; S. Levitan,

R. S. Belous and F. Gallo (eds.), *What's Happening to the American Family*, rev. ed. (Baltimore, 1988); T. K. Burch, 'The Fertility of North American Catholics,' *Demography*, 3 (1966), pp. 180, 181; F. Femminella, 'The Italian-American Family,' in M. Barash and A. Scourby (eds.), *Marriage and the Family* (New York, 1970), c. 6.

32. L. Williams and B. Zimmer, 'The Changing Influence of Religion on US Fertility: Evidence from Rhode Island,' *Demography*, 27 (1990), pp. 475-81; cf. W. D. Mosher and others, 'Religion and Fertility in the United States: New Patterns', *ibid.*, 29 (1992), table 5, p. 209; contrast C. Westoff and L. Bumpass. 'The Revolution in Birth Control Practices of US Roman Catholics,' *Science*, 179 (1972), pp. 41-44; C. Westoff and E. Jones, 'The End of 'Catholic' Fertility,' *Demography*, 16 (1979), pp. 209-18.

CHAPTER TWENTY

1. Dublin, 1971; reprint 1974.
2. Whyte, *Church and State,* p. 76.
3. *Ibid.* p. ix.
4. The de Valera papers are currently housed in the Department of Archives at University College Dublin where they are being catalogued: a substantial portion of these papers, largely relating to the period pre-1940 are available for inspection. The McQuaid papers are in the Dublin Diocesan Archives and large amounts of them are open to researchers. I have to thank Seamus Helferty and Helen Hewson at UCD Archives department for their assistance with the de Valera papers; thanks also to David Sheehy, Dublin Diocesan Archives, for allowing me access to the voluminous papers of Archbishop McQuaid.
5. Whyte, *Church and State,* pp. 3-21.
6. Pádraig Faulkner, 'A Friend of Education' in *Studies,* vol. 87, no. 348 (Winter 1998), pp. 379-80. This entire issue of *Studies* is devoted to an assessment of Dr McQuaid.
7. See Dermot Keogh, *The Vatican, the Bishops and Irish Politics, 1919-39* (Cambridge, 1986).
8. Donal Kerr, *Peel, Priests and Politics: Sir Robert Peel's Administration and the Roman Catholic Church in Ireland* (Oxford, 1982).
9. On Troy see the assessment by Daire Keogh in J. Kelly and D. Keogh (eds), *A History of the Dublin Diocese* (Dublin, 2000).
10. Bishop McHugh of Derry, in a letter published in the press, 19 June 1916 (UCD archives, de Valera papers, no. 274).
11. Archbishop Byrne to W. T. Cosgrave, 18, 19 March 1923 and the latter's reply, de Valera papers, no. 1319.
12. *Church and State,* Chapter 2, *passim.*
13. Republicans in 1922 denounced the new constitution as 'pagan' and criticised the Catholic hierarchy for supporting such an arrangement: de Valera papers, 'Republican appeal to Rome, 1923'.
14. Fr Cahill to de Valera, 4 September 1936: de Valera papers, no. 1095.
15. *Ibid.*
16. *Ibid.*
17. For an assessment of Cahill's role see Finola Kennedy, 'Two priests, the family and the Irish constitution', in *Studies,* vol. 87, no. 348 (Winter 1998), pp. 353-64.
18. McQuaid-de Valera correspondence, March-April 1937, de Valera papers, no. 1091.
19. Given the conventional wisdom that the 1937 Constitution was a conservative, if not reactionary, document, this article according recognition to the Jewish faith has not received the recognition it deserves. At a time when the most culturally advanced and sophisticated nation in Europe, Germany, was promulgating the Nuremberg laws and contemplating with equanimity the extermination of the Jews, de Valera's gesture was startlingly progressive.
20. Whyte did not believe that de Valera intervened on McQuaid's behalf when the archbishopric of Dublin fell vacant in 1940; archival research has established that representations were in fact made to Rome. Whyte, *Church and State,* p. 76; Deirdre MacMahon, 'The Politician [John Charles McQuaid]: a re-assessment' in *Studies,* vol.87, no. 348 (Winter 1998), p. 346.
21. For a more detailed argument along these lines see Finola Kennedy, 'Two priests, the family and the Irish constitution', in *Studies,* vol.87, no. 348 (Winter 1998), pp. 353-64.
22. Ruth Barrington, *Health, Medicine and Politics in Ireland* (Dublin, 1987).
23. Noel Browne, *Against the Tide* (Dublin, 1986), p. 143.
24. Alvin Jackson, *Ireland 1798-1998: Politics and War* (Oxford, 1999), p. 312.

25. Quoted in Whyte, *Church and State*, p. 231.
26. To pursue the late eighteenth-century analogy noted above: it may be suggested that Browne was essentially a Fitzwilliam, a well-meaning man but an inept politician, sacrificed to serve the needs of a flimsy coalition government.
27. Quoted in Whyte, *Church and State*, p. 295.
28. J. C. McQuaid to J. B. Montini, 12 April 1948: J.P. Walshe file, McQuaid papers, Dublin Diocesan Archives.
29. *Ibid*, 2 May 1949.
30. Michael O'Carroll, 'Inspired educationalist and ecumenist of sorts' in *Studies*, vol. 87, no. 348 (Winter 1998), pp. 365-71, These organisations had promoted inter-faith dialogue between Protestants and Catholics and between Christians and Jews respectively.

CHAPTER TWENTY-ONE

1. I owe this information to Ms Marilyn Taylor who very kindly obtained it for me from Mr Asher Benson, Archivist of the Irish Jewish Museum. cf D. Keogh, *Jews in Twentieth-Century Ireland* (Cork, 1998), pp. 76ff.

2. In lectures (of which tapes exist) to the students of the Certificate course of the Irish School of Ecumenics at Magee College, Derry. *Christians in Ulster 1968-1980* (Oxford, 1982). Dr Gallagher's co-author was Dr Stanley Worrall.

3. *Irish Amsterdam* (Dublin, n.d.), p.31.

4. *Irish Amsterdam*, p. 7. 'Some of the Commission feel that common participation in the Lord's Supper would hasten unity. Others of us believe that such participation must be the culminating act and reward of unity rather than a means to that end.' cf *Irish Evanston*, p. 8.

5. I. Ellis, *Vision and Reality, A Survey of Twentieth-century Irish Inter-Church Relations* (Belfast, 1992) p. 93.

6. E. Phoenix, *Northern Nationalism* (Belfast 1994), p. 399. Cf O. P. Rafferty, *Catholicism in Ulster 1603-1983* (Dublin, 1994), p. 221.

7. (Dublin, 1984), pp. 122, 167.

8. *The Edge of the Union* (Oxford, 1994), p. 29.

9. Quoted by D. Cooke *Persecuting Zeal: A Portrait of Ian Paisley* (Dingle, 1996), p. 42.

10. S. Worrall, *Conference on the Role of the Churches in British-Irish Relationships Dublin 26-27 November 1985* (Dublin, 1986), pp. 36-7.

11. Quoted by O. Stratford Tomkins, 'The Roman Catholic Church and the Ecumenical Movement 1910-1948', in R. Rouse and S. Charles Neill (eds.), *A History of the Ecumenical Movement 1517-1948*, (London, 1954), p. 683.

12. Cf M. Hurley,.SJ, 'The Preparatory Years', *The Irish Inter-Church Meeting; Background and Development* (Belfast 1998), pp. 7-13.

13. *Journal of General Synod [of Church of Ireland] 1974*, p. 209.

14. Gallagher & Worrall, *op.cit.,* p. 38.

15. *Ibid,* p. 130.

16. 'ICC Annual Report 1968', *Journal of General Synod [of Church of Ireland] 1968*, p. 160. In 1970 ICC agreed that the appointment of a full-time executive secretary was desirable. The Rev. Ralph Baxter was appointed to the post in July 1972: J. M. Barkley *The Irish Council of Churches 1923-1983*, (Belfast, 1983), pp. 13-4).

17. Michael Hurley, SJ, *art.cit.,* pp. 18-28.

18. Bew and Gillespie, *Northern Ireland: A Chronology of the Troubles 1968-1993* (Dublin, 1993), pp. 36-7.

19. *Irish Council of Churches, Fiftieth Annual Report 1972*, p. 2.

20. Made in the Autumn of 1971; cf 'Church Unity Committee Report' *Journal of General Synod 1973*, p. 184.

21. 'Church Unity Committee Report', *Journal of General Synod 1973*, p. 184. No copy of this letter is extant in the ICC archives or in Dr Taggart's private papers. An extract, not the letter itself, is on file in the archives of the Secretary to the Irish Episcopal Conference. The extract is quoted in my 'The Preparatory Years', *op. cit.,* p. 36, note 87.

22. *Church of Ireland Gazette,* 21 April 1972.

23. *Irish Times,* 14 April 1972; *Church of Ireland Gazette,* 21 April 1972, reporting Spring meeting of ICC.

24. In a conversation on 1 June 1998.

25. C. Daly & S. Worrall, *Ballymascanlon* (Belfast-Dublin, 1978).

26. Cf I. Ellis,'The Period since 1973', *The Irish Inter-Church Meeting*, pp. 40-64.

27. Ballymascanlon House Hotel, Dundalk, near the border between North and South.
28. Cf M. Hurley, SJ, 'Reconciliation and the Churches in Northern Ireland', *Christian Unity: An Ecumenical Second Spring?* (Dublin, 1998), pp. 220-235; G. Baum & H. Wells (eds.), *The Reconciliation of Peoples: Challenge to the Churches* (Geneva & New York, 1997), pp. 118-28.
29. C. B. Daly, *Steps on my Pilgrim Journey* (Dublin, 1998), p. 321.
30. Cf J. J. Murphy, *The People's Primate. A Memoir of Joseph Cardinal MacRory* (Dublin, 1945), pp. 35-41; O. P. Rafferty, *Catholicism in Ulster 1603-1983* (Dublin, 1994) *passim.*
31. Quoted by Bew and Gillespie, *op. cit.,* p. 189; cf Dennis Cooke, op. cit., pp. 1, 97-8.
32. G. Lucy (ed.), *The Ulster Covenant, A Pictorial History of the 1912 Home Rule Crisis* (Banbridge, 1989), p. 29.
33. 16 May 1995.
34. According to the (Methodist) Superintendent of the Belfast Central Mission, *The Irish News,* 24 March 1995.
35. K. Boyle & T. Hadden, *Northern Ireland: The Choice* (Penguin, 1994), p. 7.
36. Involving a power-sharing executive between unionists and nationalists and a Council of Ireland; a strike by the Ulster Workers' Council led in May 1974 to the resignation of Mr Brian Faulkner, Chief Executive Minister and of the unionist members of the executive and thus to the collapse of the whole venture.
37. p. 1073.
38. The new Conference will have no doctrinal basis and will not, it is stipulated, 'be a forum for church union negotiations'.
39. This is the agreement reached in multiparty talks at Stormont, Belfast, signed on 10 April 1998 and subsequently approved by significant majorities in referendums held on the same day in both South and North. It involved new institutional and constitutional arrangements: an Assembly and Executive in Northern Ireland, a North/South Ministerial Council, a British/Irish Council and a British-Irish Intergovernmental Conference and amendments to British Acts of Parliament and the Constitution of Ireland.
40. M. Hurley, SJ, 'Christian Unity by 2000?' *Christian Unity: An Ecumenical Second Spring?,* pp. 21-53.

CHAPTER TWENTY-TWO

1. *Irish Times* (hereafter cited as *IT*), 2 Oct. 1979.
2. *Ibid.*
3. For a discussion of the loss of moral credibility by the institutional church owing to its rigid stance against artificial contraception, see below, pp. 276f. For a discussion of the steep decline in vocations to the priesthood and religious life in Ireland since the late 1960s, see below, p. 278.
4. *Irish Catholic* (hereafter cited as *IC*), 26 July 1979.
5. *IC*, 22 Nov. 1979.
6. See F. O'Toole's essay 'Mixed Blessings: The End of the Irish Church' in O'Toole, *The Lie of the Land: Irish Identities* (London and New York, 1997), pp. 65-75.
7. See A. Falconer, E. McDonagh, and S. Mac Réamoinn (eds.), *Freedom to Hope? The Catholic Church in Ireland Twenty Years after Vatican II* (Dublin, 1985). Though brief, this is an extremely valuable collection of essays.
8. Quoted in O'Toole, *Lie of the Land*, p. 74.
9. S. Mac Réamoinn, 'Renewal or Revision?' in Falconer et al., *Freedom to Hope*, p. 5.
10. Mac Réamoinn, 'Renewal or Revision?', p. 5.
11. Mac Réamoinn, 'Renewal or Revision?, p. 6.
12. K. O'Kelly, 'Communication in the Church', *ibid.*, p. 22.
13. O'Kelly, 'Communication in the Church', pp. 21-22.
14. G. Daly and A. Falconer, 'To Be One', *ibid.*, p. 28.
15. Daly and Falconer, 'To Be One', p. 38.
16. Daly and Falconer, 'To Be One', p. 35.
17. Daly and Falconer, 'To Be One', pp. 30-31.
18. Daly and Falconer, 'To Be One', p. 37.
19. *IC*, 5 Oct. 1967. See also *IC*, 6, 13, 27 Feb. 1969.
20. *Knock Shrine Annual* (1966), p. 10. The introduction of evening Mass on Sundays and certain other days of the week also dealt a blow to evening devotions centred on or including the rosary. Such evening Masses also stemmed from the Christological emphasis of Vatican II. I owe this point to Monsignor Ambrose Macaulay, PP, St Brigid's parish, Belfast.
21. *IC*, 13 Feb. 1969, 14 April 1977, 9 May 1985.
22. *IC*, 5 Jan. 1989.
23. For his generous assistance in securing statistical data about Legion membership I am extremely grateful to Dr Kieran A. Kennedy, former director of the Economic and Social Research Institute in Dublin and a Legion member himself for many years. I also wish to thank Edna Dunleavy and Rosaleen Brogan for providing statistical data used above.
24. *IC*, 6 May 1943, 8 May 1958.
25. *IC*, 8 May 1958.
26. See *Irish [Jesuit] Province News* XIII/1 (Jan. 1968), pp. 7-10; *ibid.*, XIV/8 (Oct. 1972), p. 291; F. K. Drolet, SJ, *Christian Life Communities from Sodalities of Our Lady* (Irish Messenger Publications, Dublin, 1978), pp. 6-8, 14-25. See also M. Erraught, SJ, *Promises to Keep: Commentary on the General Principles and Statutes of the Christian Life Communities (Sodalities of Our Lady)*, (Irish Messenger Office, Dublin, 1971).
27. Drolet, *Christian Life Communities*, pp. 25-31. For the results of the national survey, see *ibid.*, p. 30.
28. This information was supplied by Father Dermot Murray, SJ, rector of Clongowes Wood College, Co Kildare, and spiritual director of the Christian Life Communities in Ireland.
29. For an important work of investigative journalism uncovering the secretive leadership and hard-hitting tactics of traditionalist Irish Catholics operating in the political sphere, see Emily O'Reilly, *Masterminds of the Right*, (Attic Press, Dublin, 1992).

30. On this whole subject, see C. Hug, *The Politics of Sexual Morality in Ireland* (New York, 1999).

31. See the chapter entitled 'The Contested Decline of Marianism in Ireland, 1965-90' in my forthcoming book *Knock, Marianism, and Modern Irish Catholicism*.

32. T. Flannery, *From the Inside: A Priest's View of the Catholic Church* (Cork, 1999), p. 135.

33. Flannery, *From The Inside*, p. 120.

34. Flannery, *From The Inside*, pp. 109-10.

35. Flannery, *From The Inside*, p. 121.

36. Flannery, *From The Inside*, pp. 110-18, 120.

37. Flannery, *From The Inside*, pp. 111-12.

38. Flannery, *From The Inside*, pp. 114-15.

39. Flannery, *From The Inside*, p. 111.

40. Quoted in Flannery, *From The Inside*, p. 118.

41. Flannery, *From The Inside*, p. 119.

42. Flannery, *From The Inside*, pp. 119-20.

43. For this address by Archbishop Connell and the angry reaction which it prompted, see *IT*, 3-6, 8-13 March 1999. Hardly was this damaging controversy beginning to fade than the suicide of the paedophile priest Fr Seán Fortune and the revelations arising from it inflicted serious new wounds on the church. See *IT*, 15-21 March 1999.

44. *IT*, 5 March 1999. In the course of his address Archbishop Connell made the customary theological distinction between 'artificial' and 'natural' contraception, rejecting the first as immoral but accepting the second as perfectly moral. The former Taoiseach Garret FitzGerald used his *Irish Times* column to declare in reply, 'It is the failure of the Roman Catholic church authorities to understand how unconvincing such minute theological distinctions appear to ordinary people that has lost it the confidence of so many of its members' (*IT*, 13 March 1999). It did not help to heal the wounds caused by Archbishop Connell's address when less than two weeks later, Fr John Dardis, director of the Dublin Diocesan Communications Office, issued a statement to the *Irish Times* maintaining that a study recently published in the *British Journal of Medical Psychology* had 'found that women whose children were unplanned stood a better chance of strengthening relationships with their families, friends, and partners than those who had planned pregnancies' (*IT*, 15 March 1999).

45. See F. O'Toole, 'Annie and the Bishop, Ireland and America' in O'Toole, *Lie of the Land*, pp. 76-82; Annie Murphy (with Peter de Rosa), *Forbidden Fruit: The True Story of My Secret Love for Eamonn Casey, the Bishop of Galway* (London, 1993), *passim*.

46. Fr B. J. Canning, *Bishops of Ireland, 1870-1987* (Donegal, 1987), pp. 270-71.

47. O'Toole, *Lie of the Land*, p. 74. Bishop Casey's media charm may have been something of a mask. Fr Tony Flannery, who served as a Redemptorist missioner in Casey's Galway cathedral, found the bishop 'to be an old-style authoritarian whose tendency was to lay down the law without feeling the need to listen to anyone. This was in sharp contrast to his public image.' See Flannery, *From the Inside*, p. 178.

48. In its May 1995 issue the Redemptorist magazine *Reality* reported that as many as 63 per cent of its readers ('most of whom are committed Catholics aged over 50') who responded to a survey indicated a preference for ending mandatory celibacy for priests. See O'Toole, *Lie of the Land*, p. 120.

49. See F. O'Toole, 'Scenes from the Birth of a New Morality' in *Lie of the Land*, pp. 117-18.

50. Flannery, *From the Inside*, p. 181.

51. O'Toole, *Lie of the Land*, p. 119.

52. O'Toole, *Lie of the Land*, pp. 119-20.

53. O'Toole, *Lie of the Land*, p. 120.

54. Chris Moore, the television journalist who made this documentary for UTV in Belfast, has chronicled the whole sad story in *Betrayal of Trust: The Father Brendan Smyth Affair and the Catholic Church* (Dublin, 1995). In his foreward to this book Fr Kevin Hegarty, former editor of the Catholic-church magazine *Intercom*, noted that he had 'incurred severe episcopal disapproval' when he published 'a temperate article on clerical child abuse six months before the Brendan Smyth affair surfaced' (*ibid.*, p. 10). Indeed, the incident appears to have played a major role in Fr Hegarty's subsequent removal as editor of *Intercom*.

55. O'Toole, *Lie of the Land*, p. 111. See also *ibid.*, pp. 104-12.

56. O'Toole, *Lie of the Land*, p. 111.

57. See the report of the Irish Catholic Bishops' Advisory Committee on Child Sexual Abuse by Priests and Religious. This report was published as *Child Sexual Abuse: Framework for a Church Response* (Dublin, 1996).

58. *IT*, 15 March 1999. Paul Molloy, one of the victims of Fr Fortune's sexual abuse, told the journalist Alison O'Connor of the *Irish Times*: 'I feel that the bishop put the welfare of the priest and the image of the Catholic church way ahead of his parishioners. I reported this in 1988, but they seemed to do nothing serious about it' (*ibid.*).

59. The state began to close the industrial schools in the 1970s after the Kennedy report of 1971 recommended their abolition. But in two cases which have recently been the focus of controversy, one involving St Joseph's home for children in Kilkenny city in 1977, the other relating to Madonna House in Dublin in the 1990s, the Sisters of Charity who ran both institutions failed to act quickly to stop child sexual abuse after it was initially reported. See Fintan O'Toole's discussion of these cases in *IT*, 22 May 1999.

60. Extreme – and extremely unfair – diatribes are now not uncommon, such as the statement heard on 'Chris Barry's Phone Show' on 98FM radio one day in late April 1999: the Christian Brothers 'were all monsters and demons, every one of them. If they weren't abusing children, they knew about it and did nothing. They should all be shot.' See *IT*, 1 May 1999. There is indeed much truth in the charge often heard from the side of the clergy and religious that the media, or sections of the media, have been hypercritical of the church, to the point of demonstrating anti-clericalism. Why do media personnel, it is insistently asked, so often neglect the great good done by priests and religious, now and in the past, and concentrate only on the failings of the institutional church and a small minority of those who have served it? For an important exploration of the church-media relationship, with both sides represented, see Frs Eamonn Conway and Colm Kilcoyne, *Twin Pulpits: Papers of the Conference on Church and Media in Modern Ireland, All Hallows College, July 1997* (Dublin, 1997).

61. O'Toole, *Lie of the Land*, p. 105.

62. O'Toole, *Lie of the Land*, pp. 105-6. Another deeply disturbing book about child abuse in residential institutions managed by religious orders is the work of Mavis Arnold and Heather Laskey, *Children of the Poor Clares: The Story of an Irish Orphanage* (Belfast, 1985).

63. The first programme in this series was broadcast on 27 April, the last on 11 May 1999. See *IT*, 27 April, 12 May 1999.

64. *IT*, 27 April, 1 May 1999.

65. *IT*, 27 April, 22 May 1999.

66. *IT*, 27 April 1999.

67. *IT*, 1 May 1999.

68. *States of Fear* refocused attention on the so-called Madonna House report concerning child sex abuse earlier in the 1990s in this Dublin institution run by the Sisters of Charity. The report, which the government has refused to publish for legal reasons, is thought to detail delays in taking the actions necessary to stop the sexual abuse of children in the care of religious there (*IT*, 12 May 1999).

69. *ibid.* The Commission to Inquire into Child Abuse, also known as the Laffoy commission, after its head, High Court Judge Mary Laffoy, did not hold its first public sitting until the end of June 2000. During its full proceedings, which are now estimated to continue for two years, there will be two kinds of hearings over which the commission will preside. The first will be confidential and will permit the surviving victims of abuse to tell their stories; the findings eventually reached by the commission on the basis of these hearings will be general. The second set of hearings will be investigative, with the commission having the power to compel witnesses to attend and to give evidence under oath; its findings from these investigative hearings will extend to the naming of institutions and individuals judged to have been guilty of child abuse, sexual or physical. Evidence developed in these investigative hearings, however, may not be used by victims in future criminal or civil actions. Their cases will need to be based on evidence that is independent of incriminating statements made before the commission. Many victims are reportedly unhappy with some of the rules and procedures under which the commission will operate, but the legal and other difficulties surrounding its work are formidable. For an admirably clear and careful report, see Susan McKay's article in *Sunday Tribune*, 2 July 2000.

70. See 'Religious Confidence Survey', presented in December 1997 by Ann Hanley of Irish Marketing Surveys to the Council for Research and Development, St Patrick's College, Maynooth, Co. Kildare. This document is the source for the quotations and for the statistics relating to 1997 in this and the next three paragraphs. The Council for Research and Development is the research arm of the Irish Catholic Episcopal Conference. I wish to express my gratitude to Ms Teresa Ward, the secretary to the council, for her exceedingly helpful and prompt response to my requests for information.

71. Collected from various surveys undertaken since 1973, the data on mass attendance in this paragraph and the next have been provided by the Council for Research and Development.

72. Unless otherwise stated, the statistics presented in this concluding section of the essay are based on data compiled and provided by the Council for Research and Development.

73. During the four years 1995-9 a total of only five persons have entered the brothers' orders.

74. By 1990 over 68 per cent of all religious brothers in Ireland were 50 years of age or older. Nearly 47 per cent were over 60. See *Irish Catholic Directory and Diary, 1992* (Dublin, 1992), p. 230. The age structure of female religious, however, was skewed even more heavily towards the oldest groups. In 1990 more than 77 per cent of all Irish nuns were over 50 years old, and 57 per cent were over 60 (*ibid.*).

75. Insofar as the Catholic Church in Ireland is concerned, the statistics on ordinations contain an upward bias because they include priests ordained for dioceses abroad. In 1965 about 30 per cent of all priests ordained (123 out of 412) were intended for dioceses abroad. But this number was much smaller by 1986, when the corresponding figure was about 9 per cent (11 out of 125). For the 1986 data, see *Irish Catholic Directory, 1987* (Dublin, 1987), p. 337. Only two of the twenty-seven secular priests ordained in 1998 were intended for dioceses abroad.

76 In 1998 almost three-fifths (59 per cent) of all Irish diocesan priests were at least 50 years of age, and nearly two-fifths (38 per cent) were 60 or older.

77 See the special articles on the Catholic bishops by Ronnie Bellew and Eugene Masterson in *Ireland on Sunday*, 13 June 1999. I owe this reference to the kindness of Dr Nollaig Ó Muraíle of the Celtic Department in Queen's University, Belfast. At several other points as well, this essay has benefited from his deep knowledge and helpful advice. He bears no responsibility, however, for the views expressed here.

CHAPTER TWENTY-THREE

1. Biever, B. F., *Religion, Culture and Values. A Cross-National Analysis of Motivational Factors in Native Irish and American-Irish Catholicism* (Arno Press, 1976).
2. Ryan, L, 'Faith Under Survey' in *The Furrow,* vol. 34, no.1 (1983).
3. *op. cit.,* p. 14.
4. *op. cit.,* p. 5.
5. *op. cit.,* p. 15.
6. Christopher T. Whelan (ed.), *Values and Social Change in Ireland* (Dublin, 1994).
7. It would appear from this that the decrease from the exceptionally high percentage attending Mass every Sunday occurred before 1991 This however is contrary to the findings of the EVS and other surveys carried out in the 1980s.
8. see Andrew Greeley and Conor Ward, 'How Secular Is the Ireland We live In? – A report on a Survey', in *Doctrine and Life,* December 2000.
9. At the time of writing the report of this survey of values, carried out in thirty countries of Europe, had not been published. However thanks to the kindness of Tony Fahey of the Economic and Social Institute I have been given a 'sneak preview' of the EVS survey in Ireland. The ESRI under Dr Fahey's direction carried out the survey in Ireland.
10. See P. Berger (ed.) *The Desecularisation of the World – Resurgent Religion and World Politics,* (Grand Rapids: Ethics and Policy Centre and Wm. B. Eerdmans Publishing Company, 1999).
11. Fahey, T., 'Religion and Prosperity', in *Studies,* Spring 2001, vol. 90, no. 357, p. 43.
12. *op. cit.,* p. 45.
13. Ryan, L., (1983), op. cit. p. 15.
14. See Berger, P. (1999) 'A Dessecularization of the World: A Global Overview', in Berger, P. (ed.), *op. cit.*

Index

The Contributors

Noel Barber SJ, Milltown Park, Dublin.

Thomas Bartlett, University College, Dublin.

Brendan Bradshaw SM, Queens' College, Cambridge.

Dudley Levistone Cooney, President, Wesley Historical Society (Irish branch).

James S. Donnelly, Jr., University of Wisconsin, Madison.

David N. Doyle, University College, Dublin.

Declan. M. Downey, University College, Dublin.

Hugh Fenning OP, St Mary's Priory Tallaght, Dublin.

Marie Therese Flanagan, Queen's University, Belfast.

Raymond Gillespie, National University of Ireland, Maynooth.

Mary N. Harris, National University of Ireland, Galway.

Finlay Holmes, Queen's University, Belfast.

Michael Hurley SJ, Irish School of Ecumenics, Dublin.

Dáire Keogh, St Patrick's College, Drumcondra.

Donal Kerr SM, St Patrick's College, Maynooth.

Emmet Larkin, University of Chicago.

Colm Lennon, National University of Ireland, Maynooth.

Mary Ann Lyons, St Patrick's College, Drumcondra.

Kevin B. Nowlan, University College, Dublin.

Kenneth Milne, Historiographer for the Church of Ireland.

Gerard Moran, European School, Culham, Oxford.

Alfred P. Smyth, Canterbury Christ Church University College.

John A. Watt, University of Newcastle upon Tyne.